2

GANGSTA:CURSED.
MARCO ADRIANO

Story by KOHSKE

Art by SYUHEI KAMO

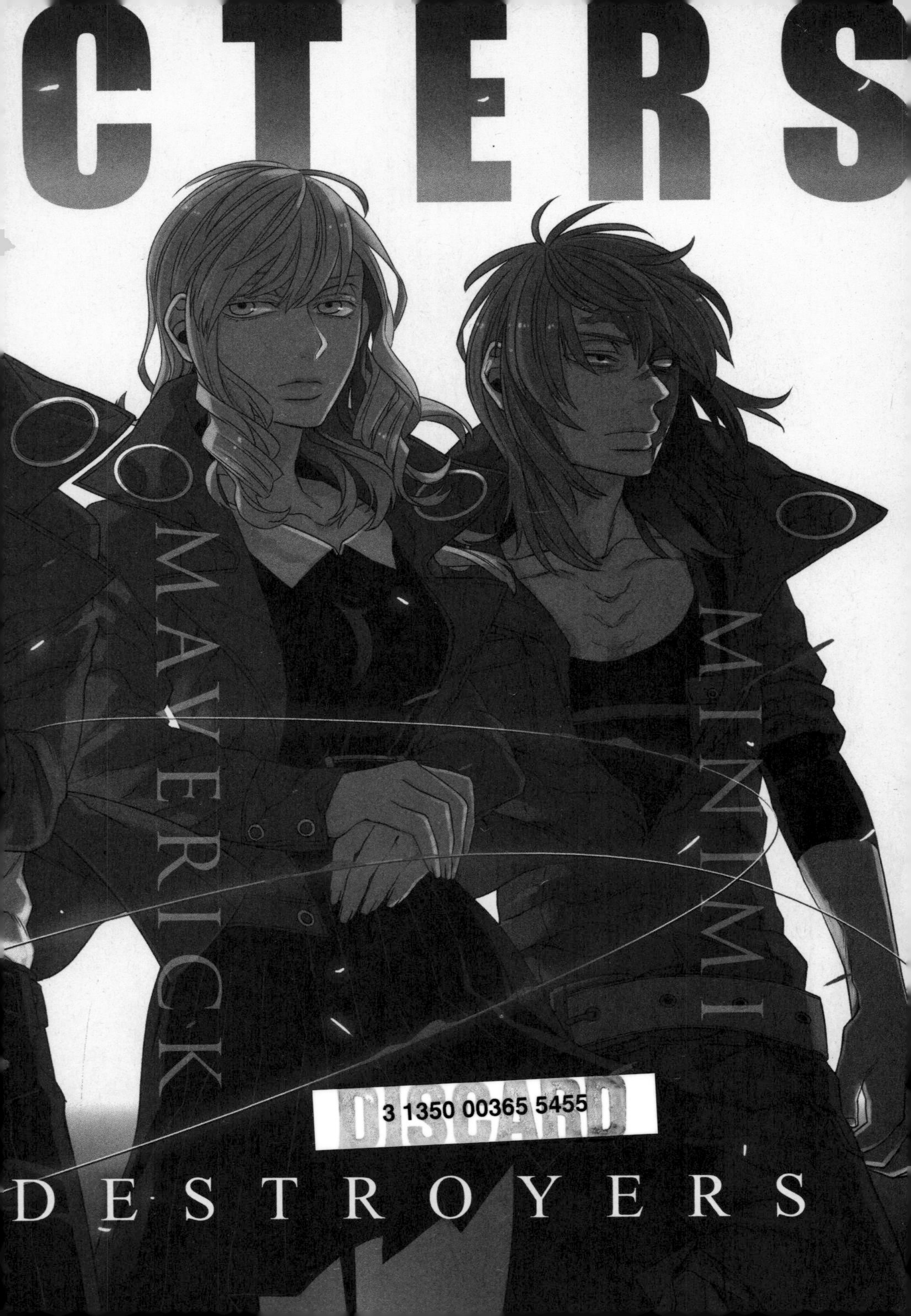
CTERS
MAVERICK
MINIMI
DESTROYERS

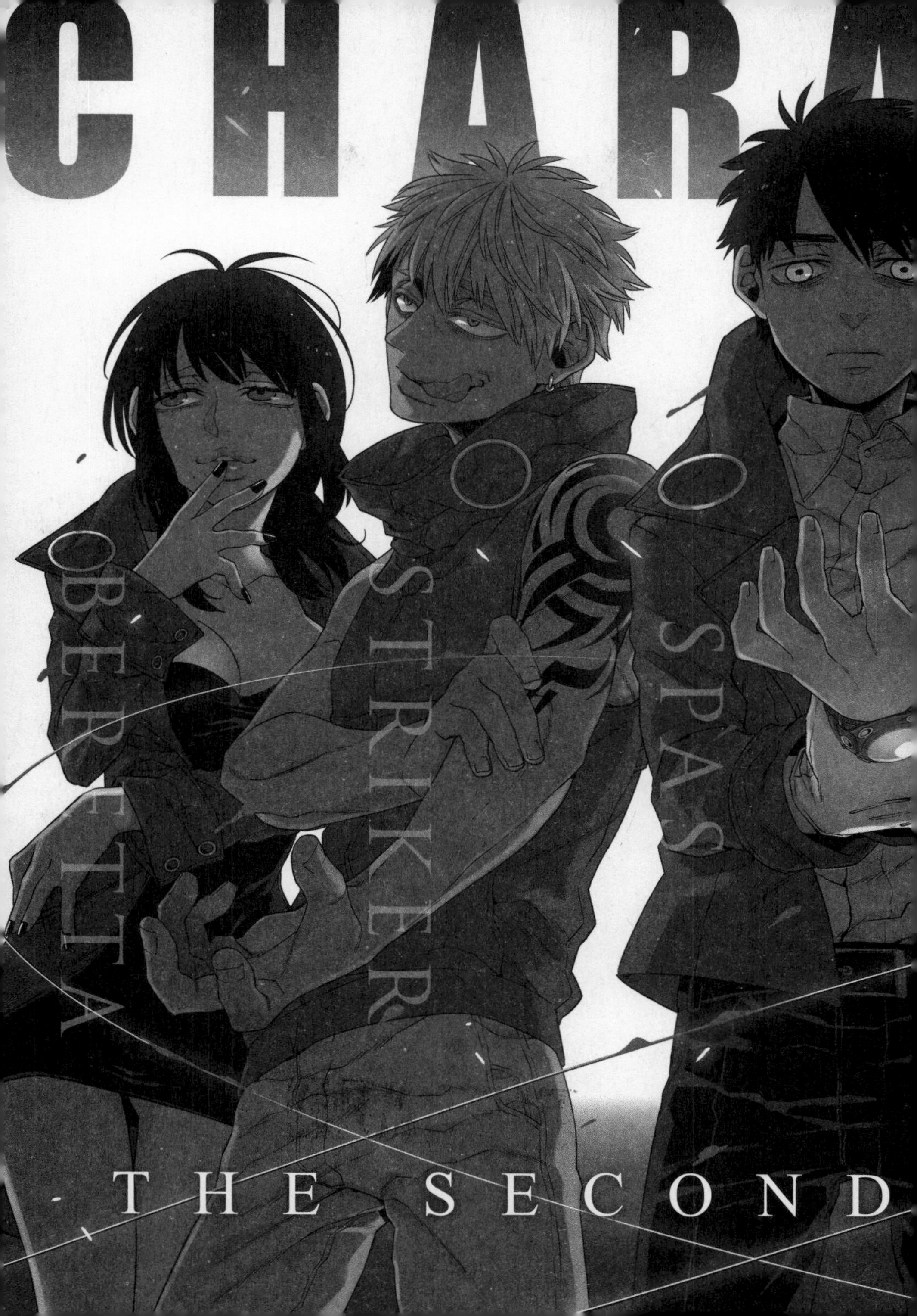
CHARA
BERETTA
STRIKER
SPAS
THE SECOND

CONTENTS

#04

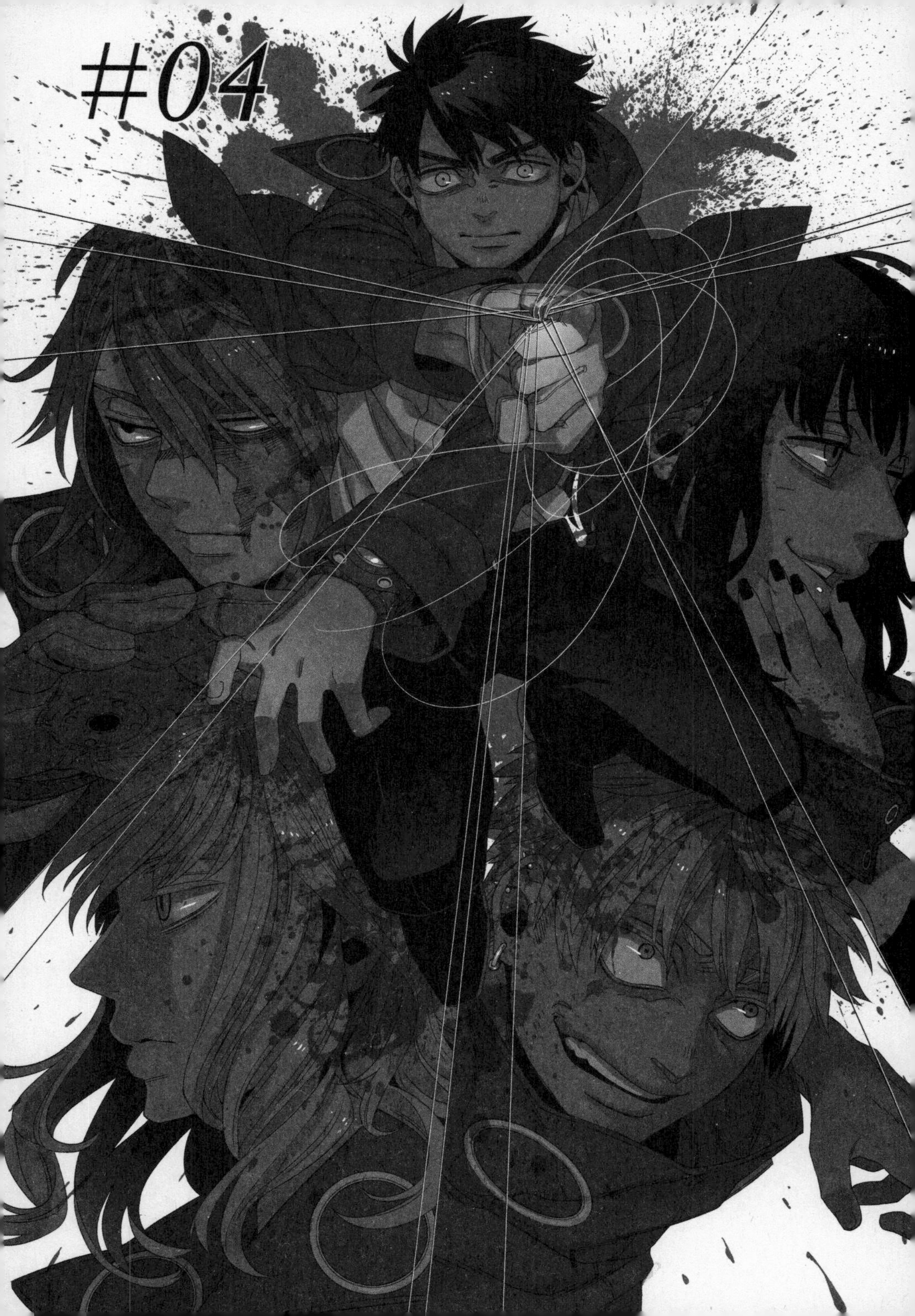

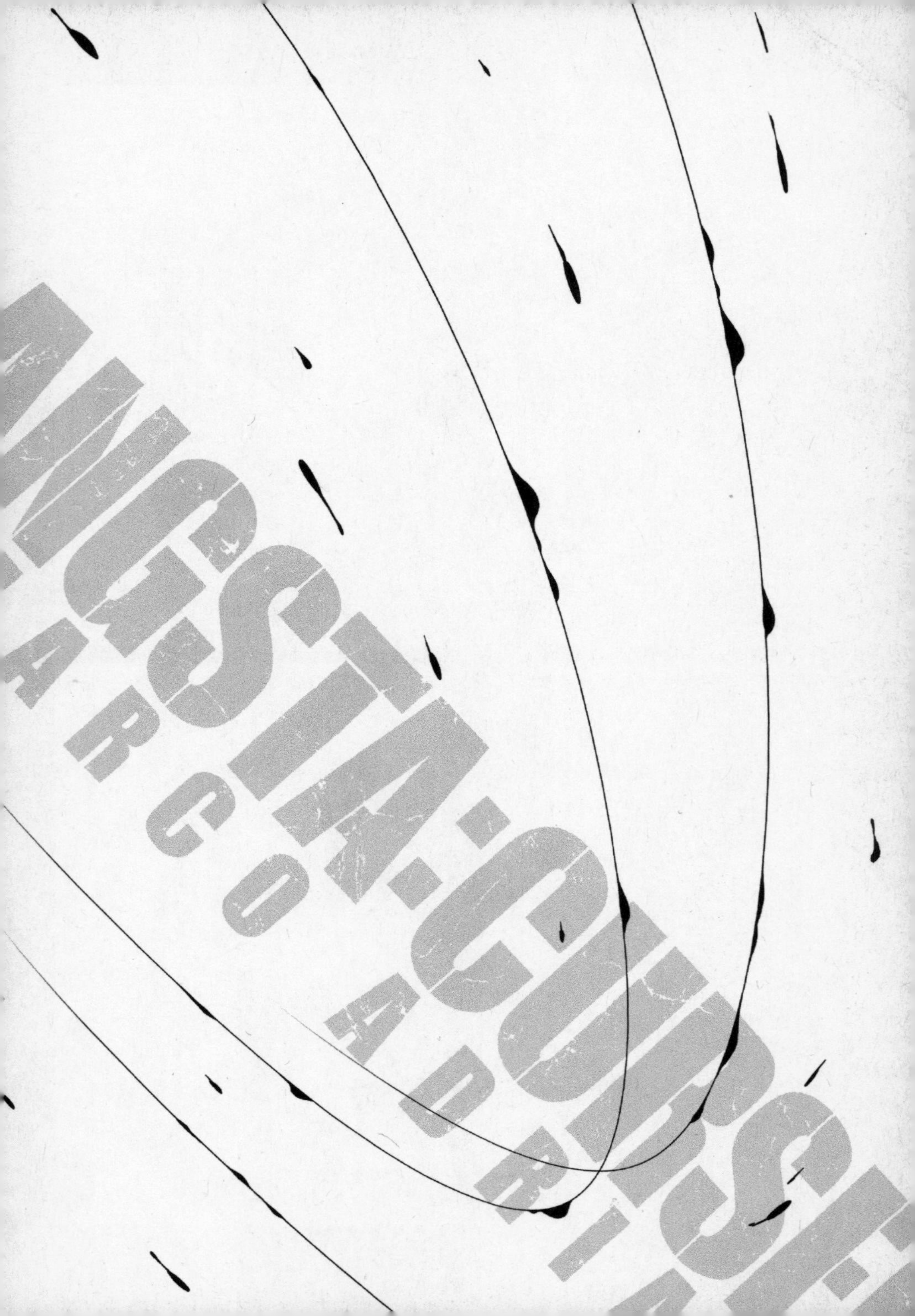

A long time ago, a young man was traveling the world on his own.

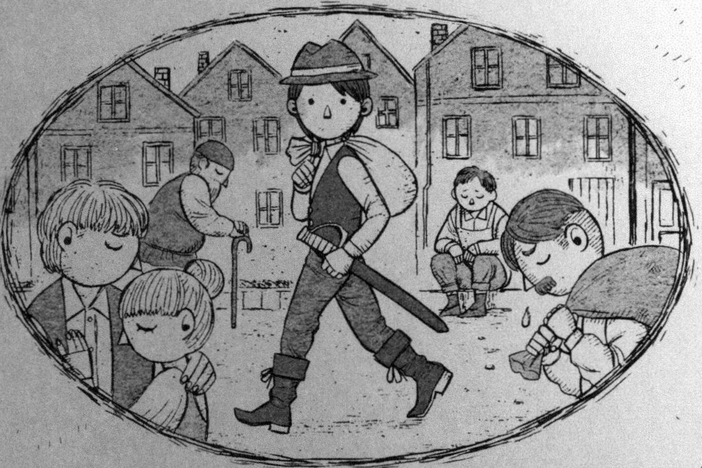

One day, he came upon a village where all the people looked sad.

The young man asked the villagers what was wrong. So a villager told him.

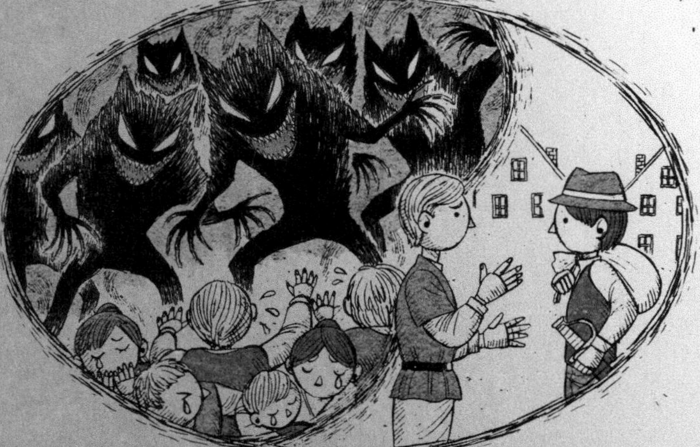

"In the neighboring forest, there are terrible monsters who come to our village and hurt us."

Hearing that, the young man went into the forest to teach the monsters a lesson.

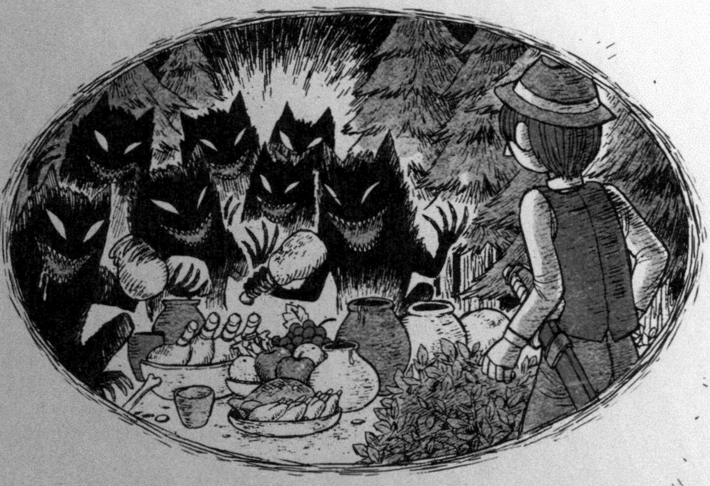

Upon arriving there, he saw many monsters having a grand feast, eating and drinking what they'd stolen from the village.

"You bad monsters!" the young man said. "Stop making trouble for the villagers!" But the monsters would not listen.

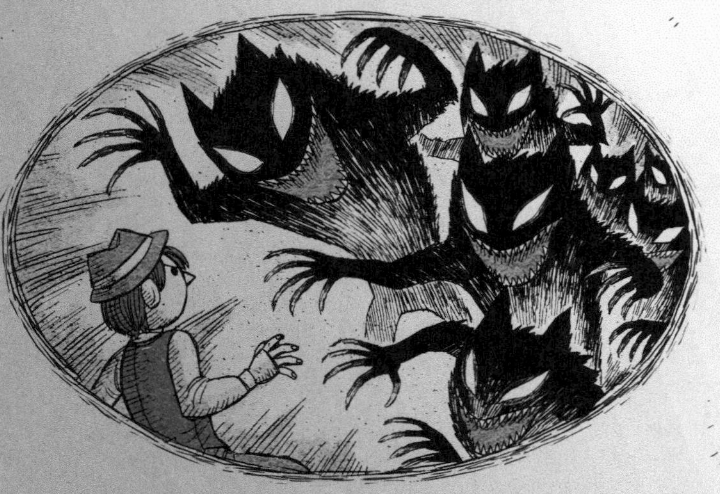

"If you try to stop us, we'll eat you!" they shouted. And then they attacked the young man.

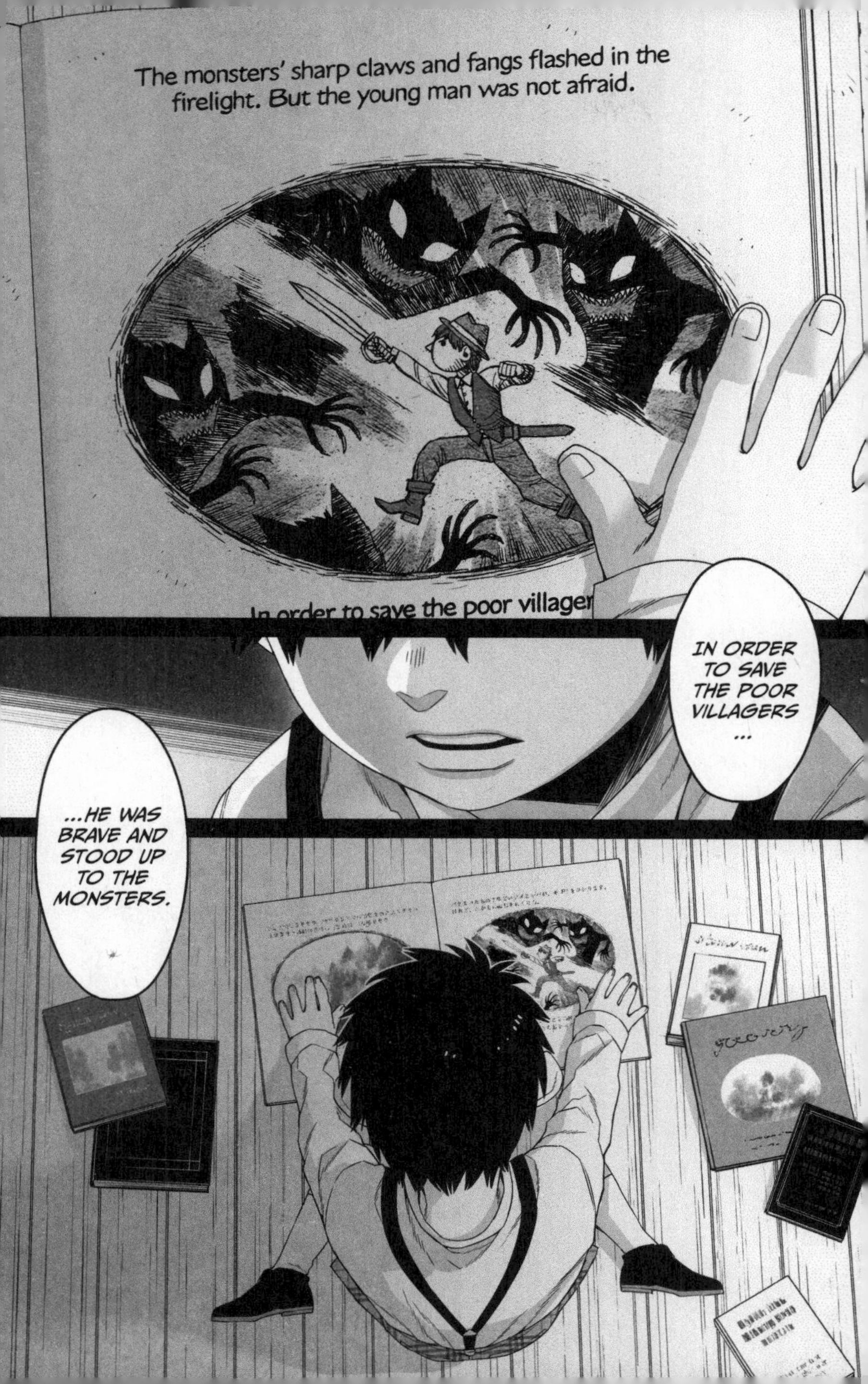
The monsters' sharp claws and fangs flashed in the firelight. But the young man was not afraid.
In order to save the poor villager
IN ORDER TO SAVE THE POOR VILLAGERS ...
...HE WAS BRAVE AND STOOD UP TO THE MONSTERS.

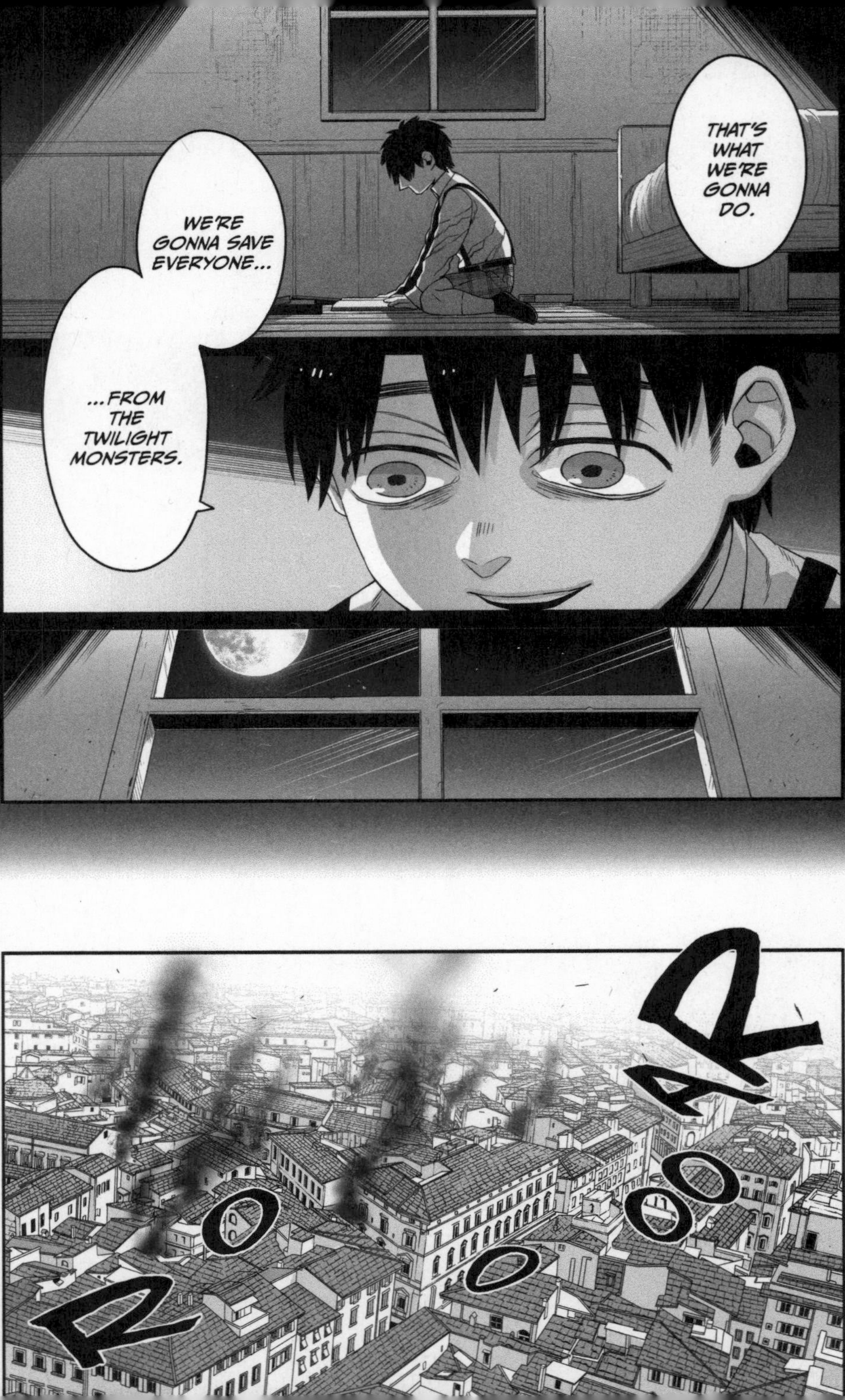
THAT'S WHAT WE'RE GONNA DO.
WE'RE GONNA SAVE EVERYONE...
...FROM THE TWILIGHT MONSTERS.
ROOOOAR

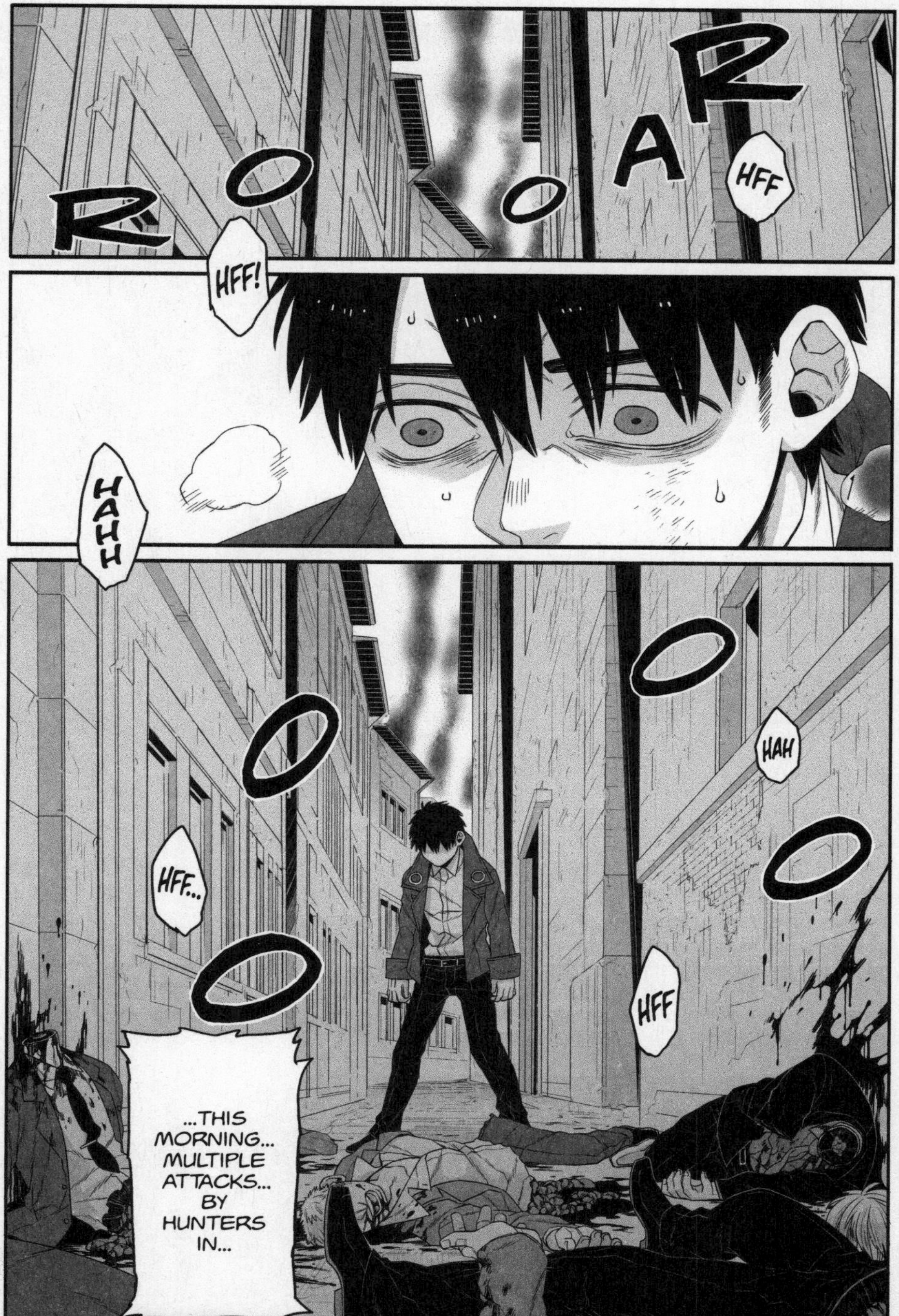
HFF
ROOAR
HFF!
HAHH
OOOOO
HAH
HFF
HFF...
...THIS MORNING... MULTIPLE ATTACKS... BY HUNTERS IN...

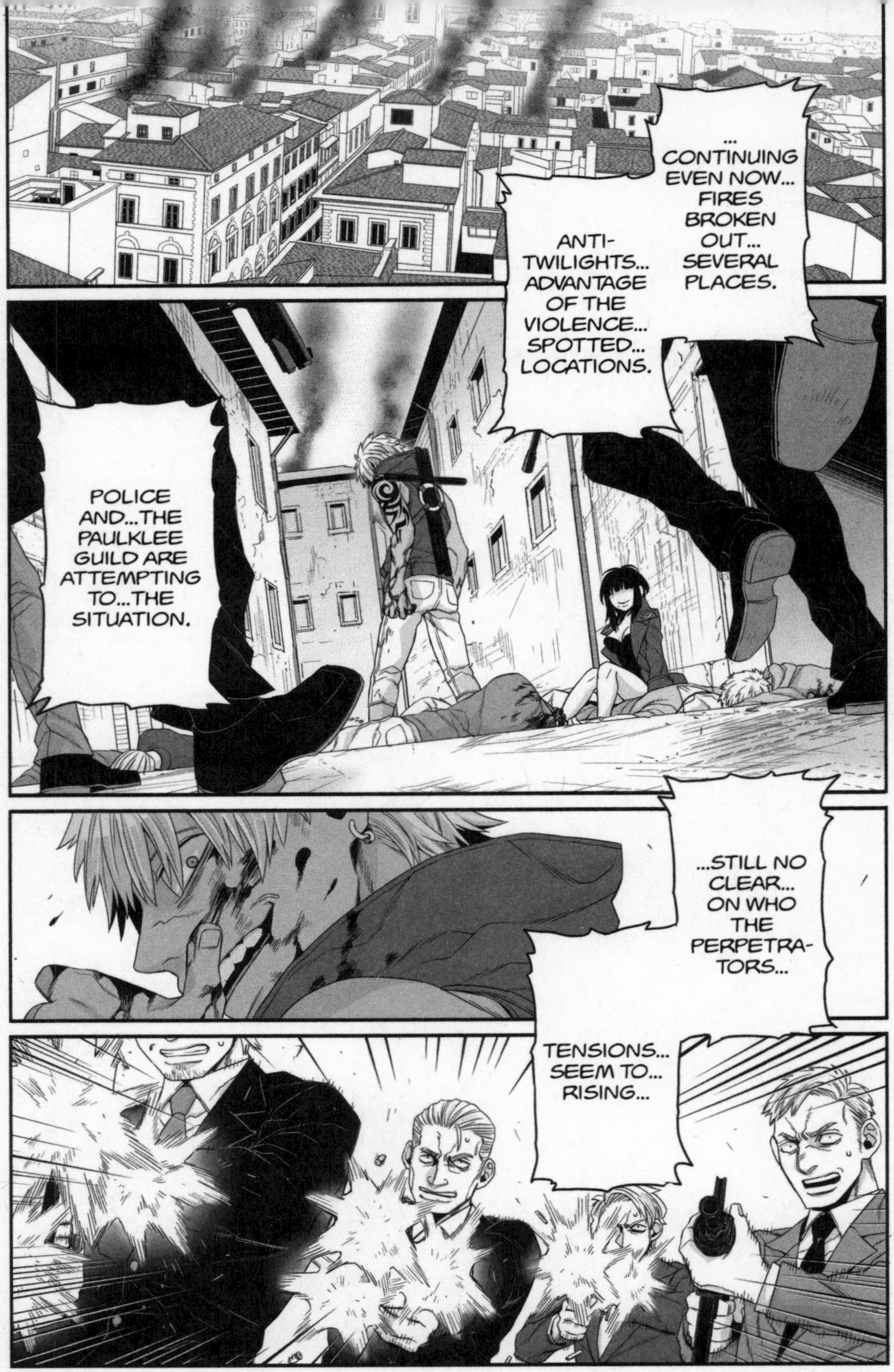
... CONTINUING EVEN NOW... FIRES BROKEN OUT... SEVERAL PLACES.
ANTI-TWILIGHTS... ADVANTAGE OF THE VIOLENCE... SPOTTED... LOCATIONS.
POLICE AND...THE PAULKLEE GUILD ARE ATTEMPTING TO...THE SITUATION.
...STILL NO CLEAR... ON WHO THE PERPETRATORS...
TENSIONS... SEEM TO... RISING...

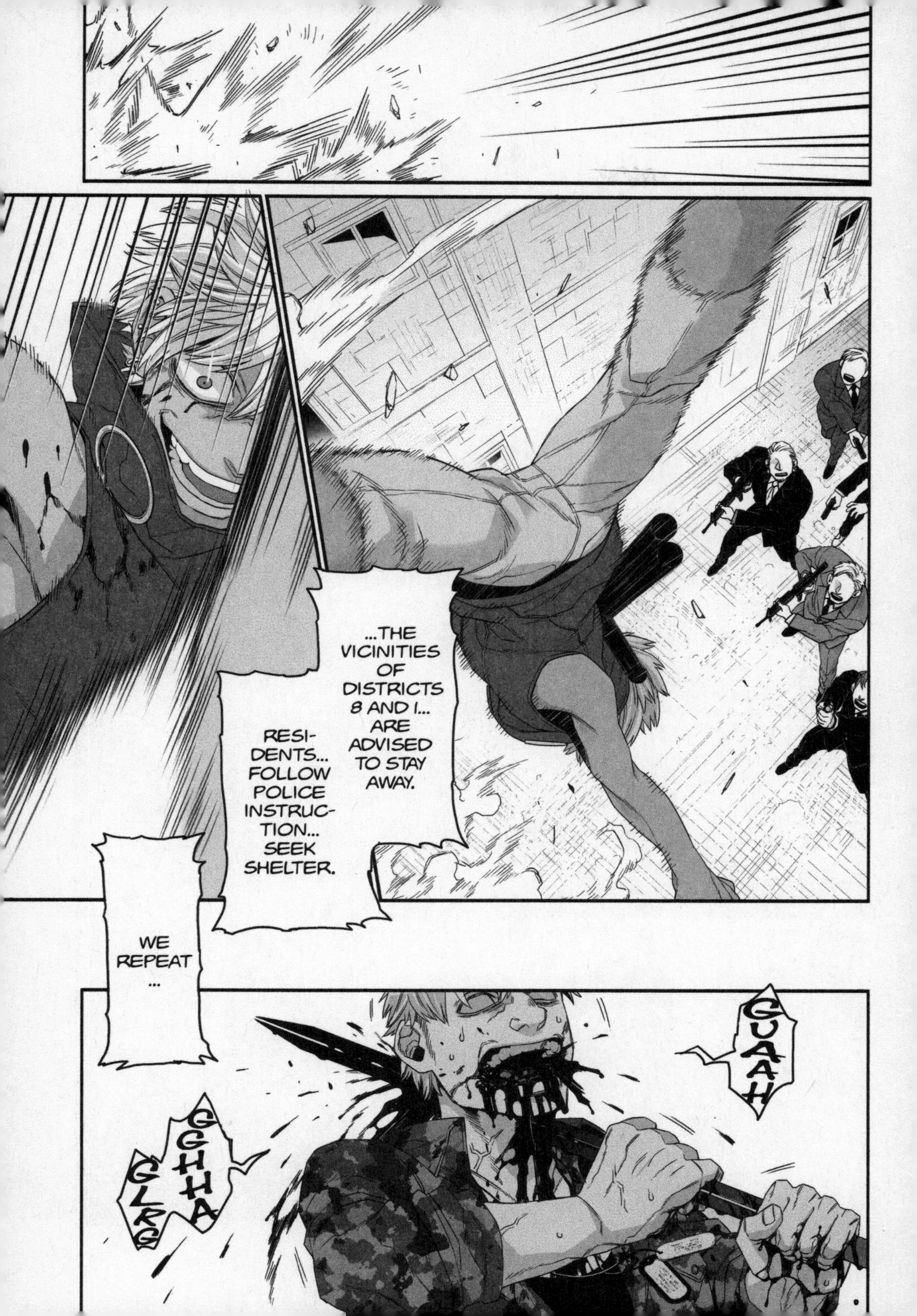
...THE VICINITIES OF DISTRICTS 8 AND 1... ARE ADVISED TO STAY AWAY.
RESIDENTS... FOLLOW POLICE INSTRUCTION... SEEK SHELTER.
WE REPEAT ...
GUAAH
GGHHA
GLRG

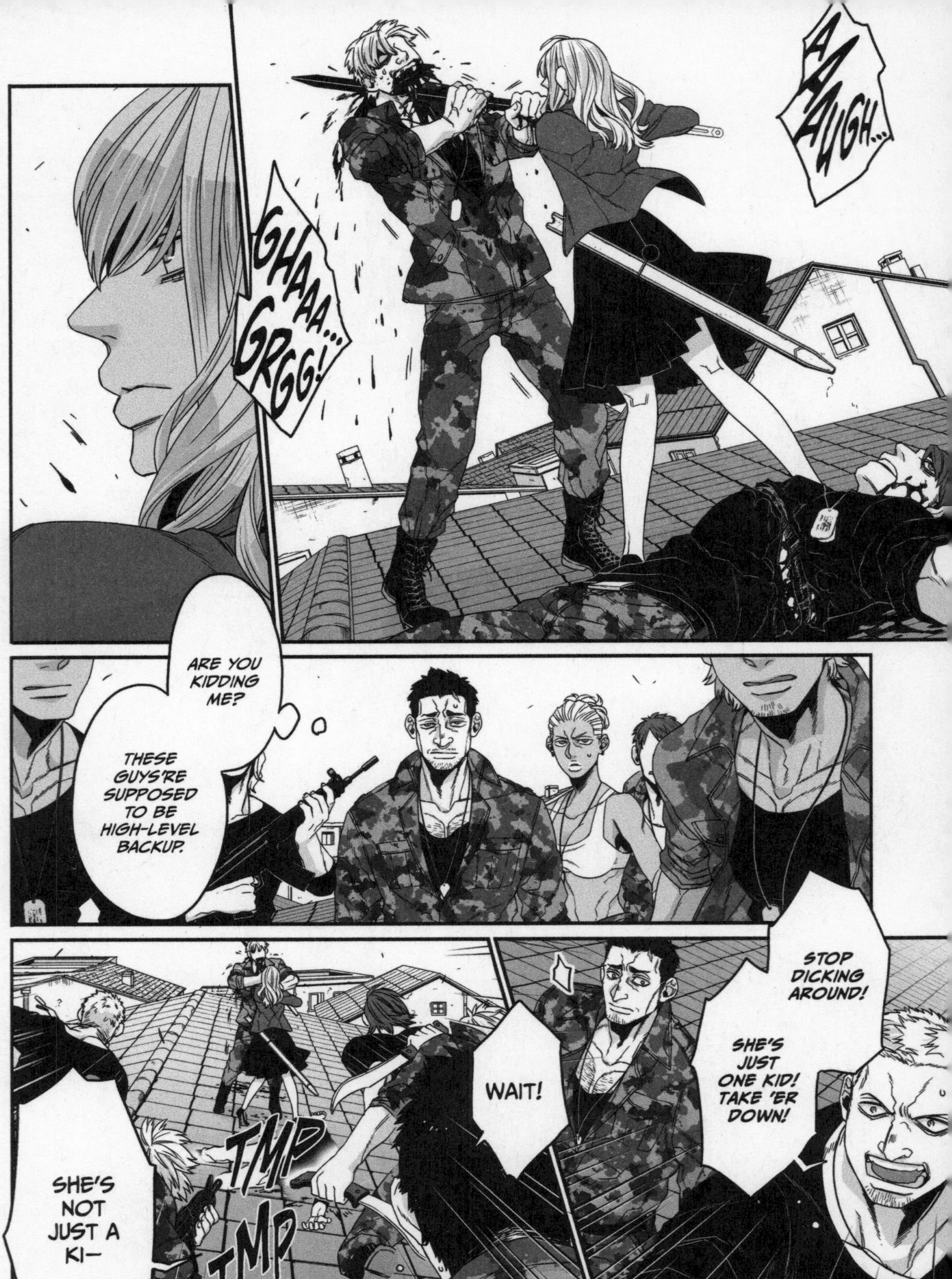
AAAUGH...
GHAAAA... GRGG!
ARE YOU KIDDING ME?
THESE GUYS'RE SUPPOSED TO BE HIGH-LEVEL BACKUP.
STOP DICKING AROUND!
SHE'S JUST ONE KID! TAKE 'ER DOWN!
WAIT!
TMP
TMP
TMP
SHE'S NOT JUST A KI—

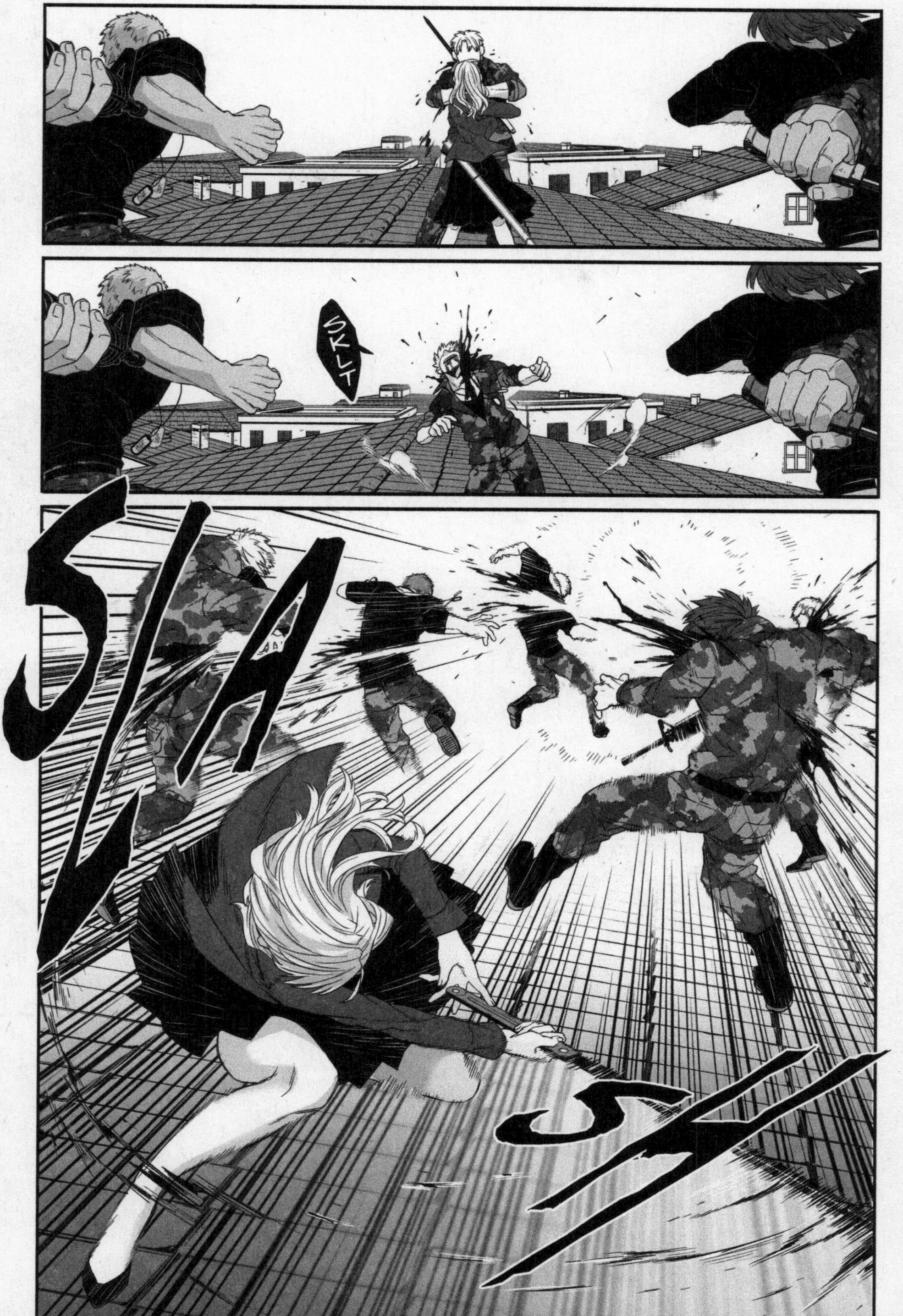
SKLT
SLA
SH

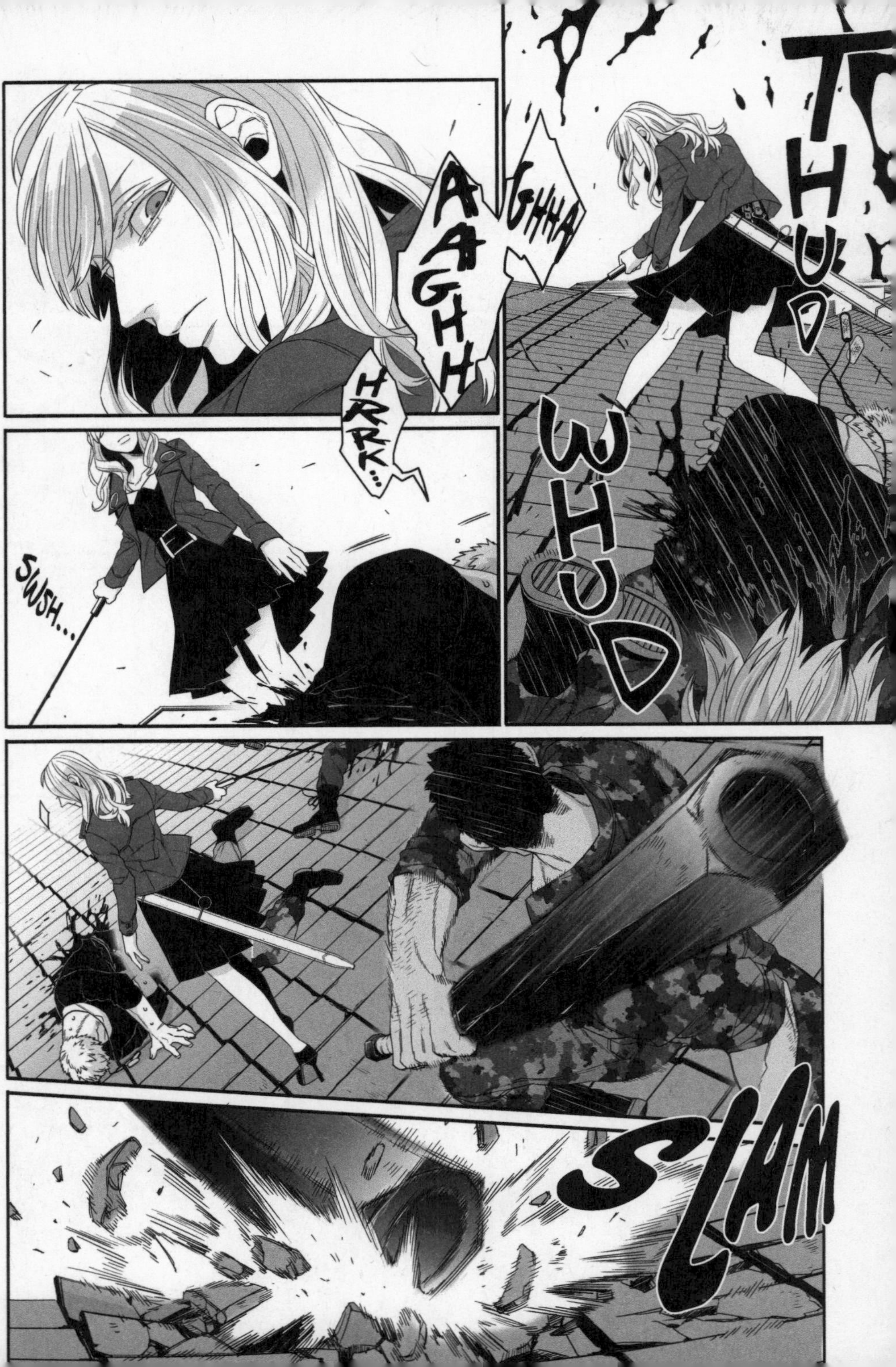
THUD
WHUD
GHHA
AAGHH
HRRK...
SWSH...
SLAM

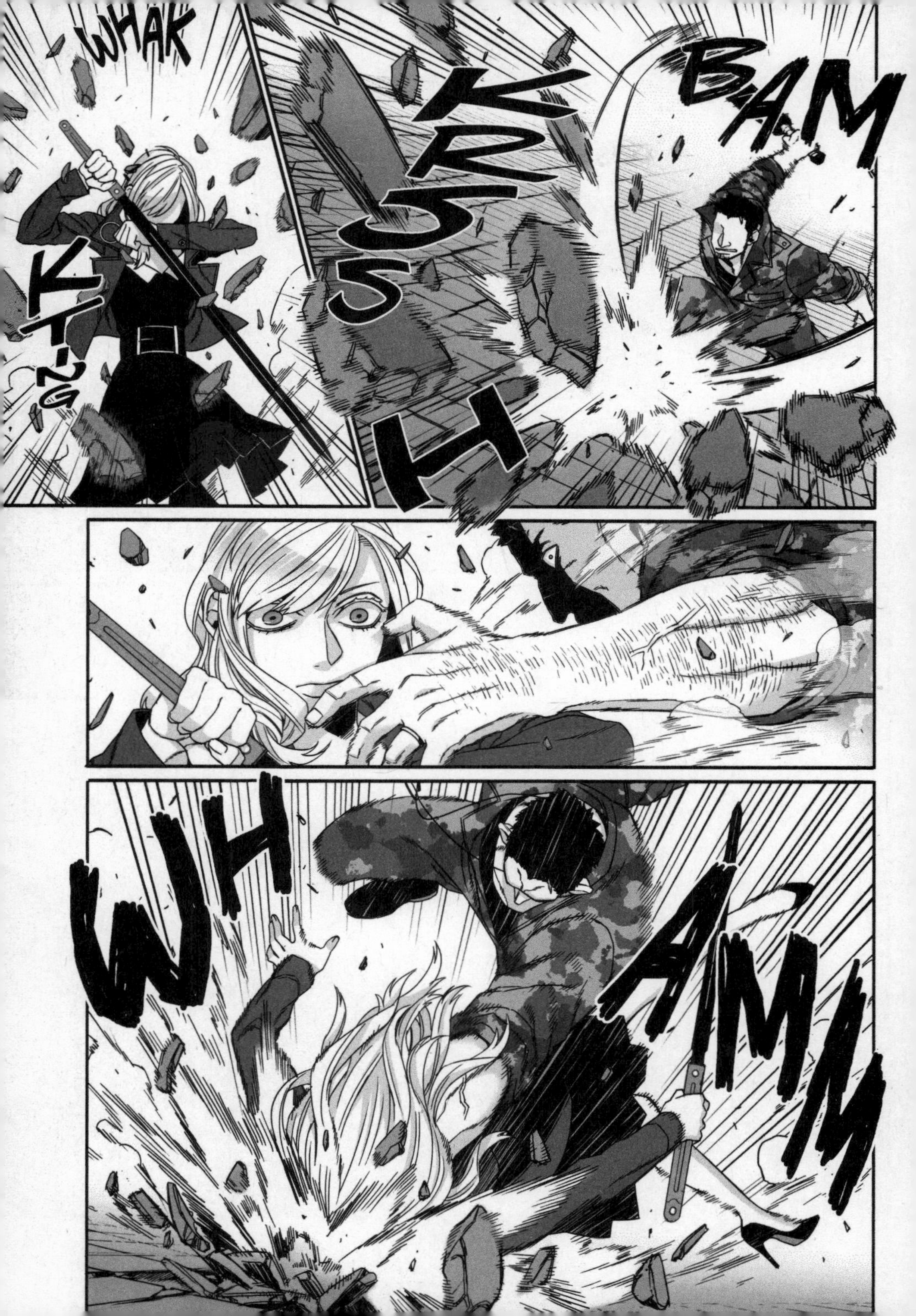
BAM
KRSSH
WHAK
KT-NG
WHAMM

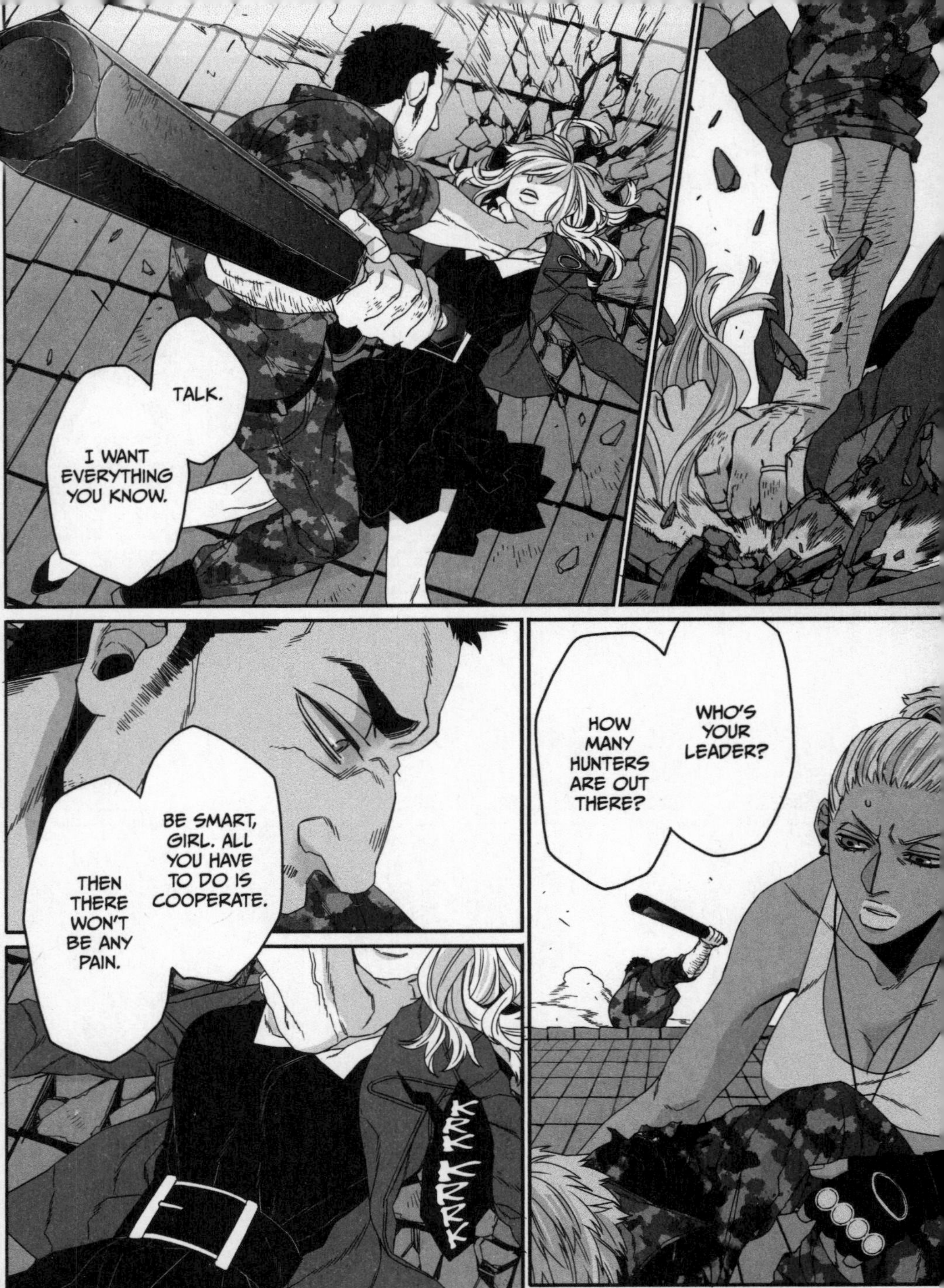
TALK.
I WANT EVERYTHING YOU KNOW.
WHO'S YOUR LEADER?
HOW MANY HUNTERS ARE OUT THERE?
BE SMART, GIRL. ALL YOU HAVE TO DO IS COOPERATE.
THEN THERE WON'T BE ANY PAIN.
KRRK KRRK

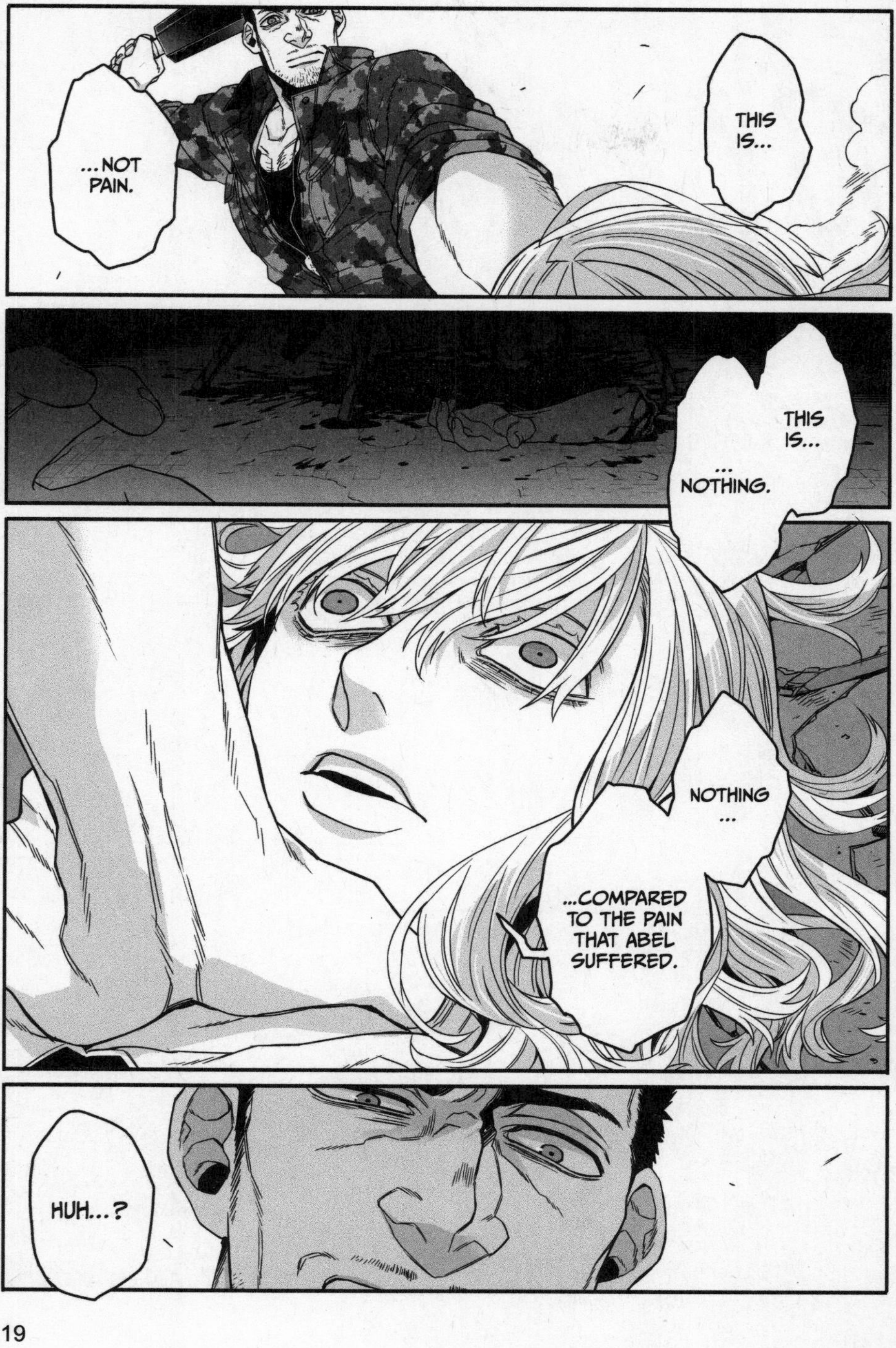
THIS IS...
...NOT PAIN.
THIS IS... ... NOTHING.
NOTHING ...
...COMPARED TO THE PAIN THAT ABEL SUFFERED.
HUH...?

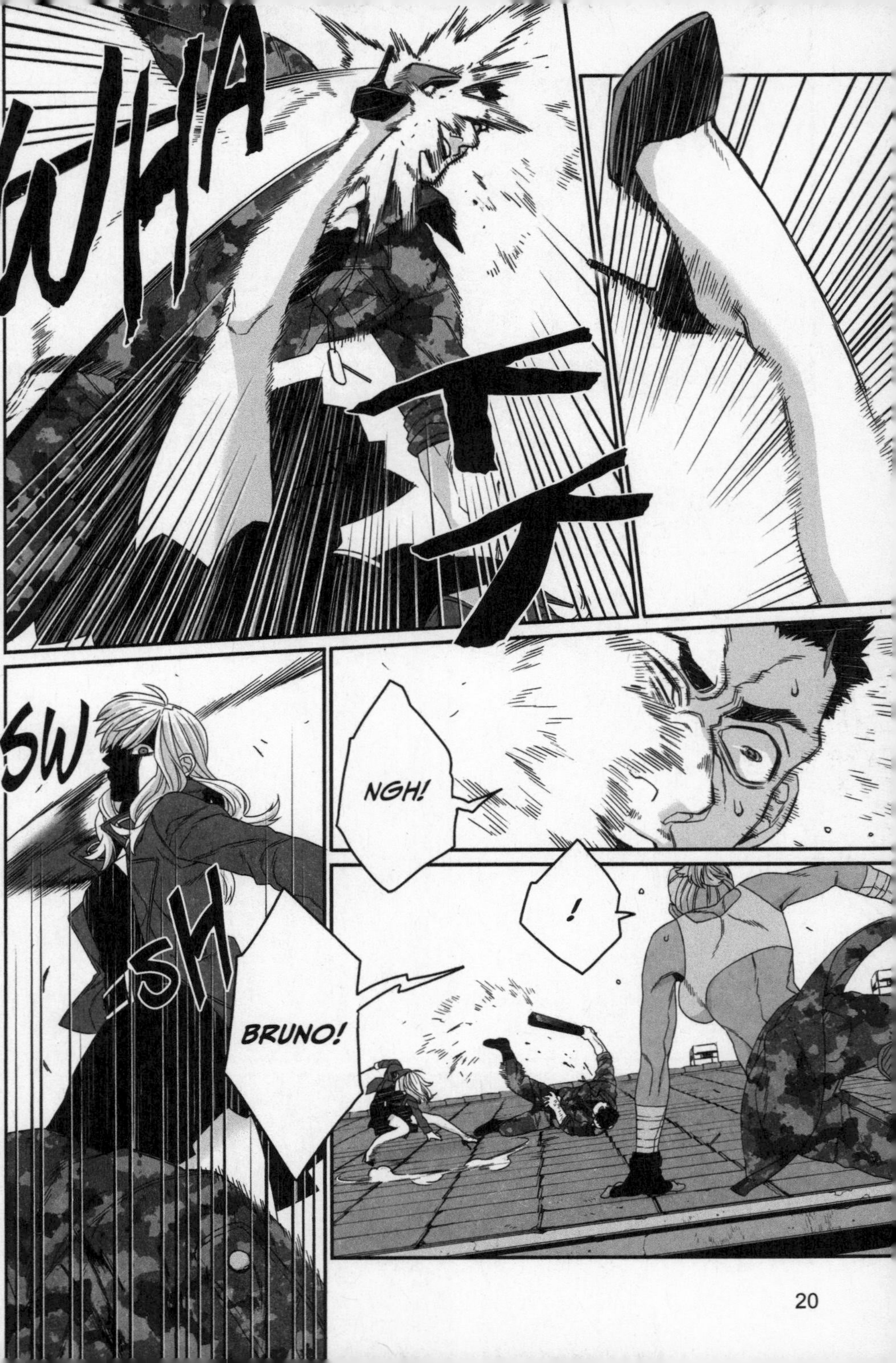
WHA
NGH!
!
SWISH
BRUNO!

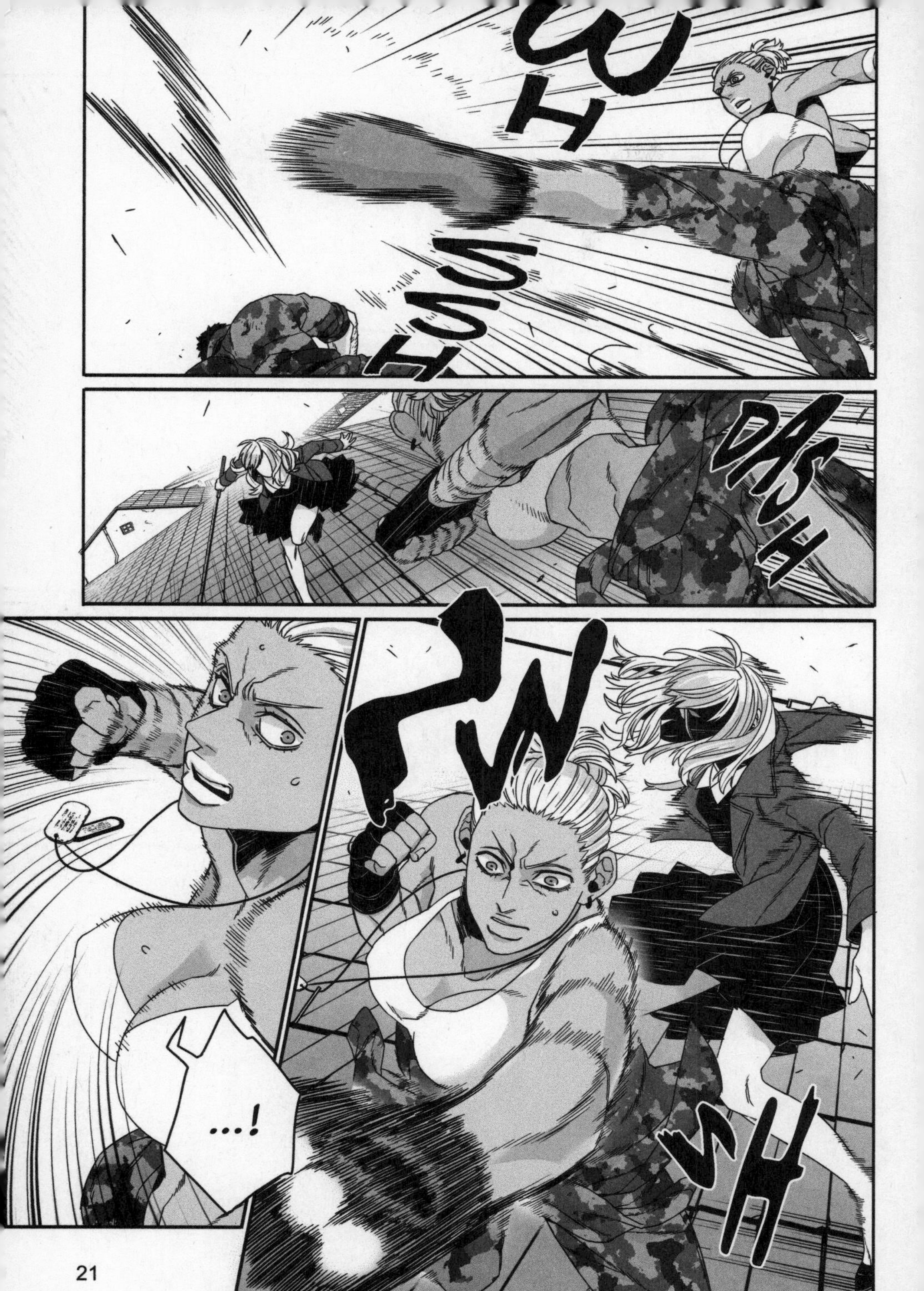
WHSSH
DASH
SWSH
...!

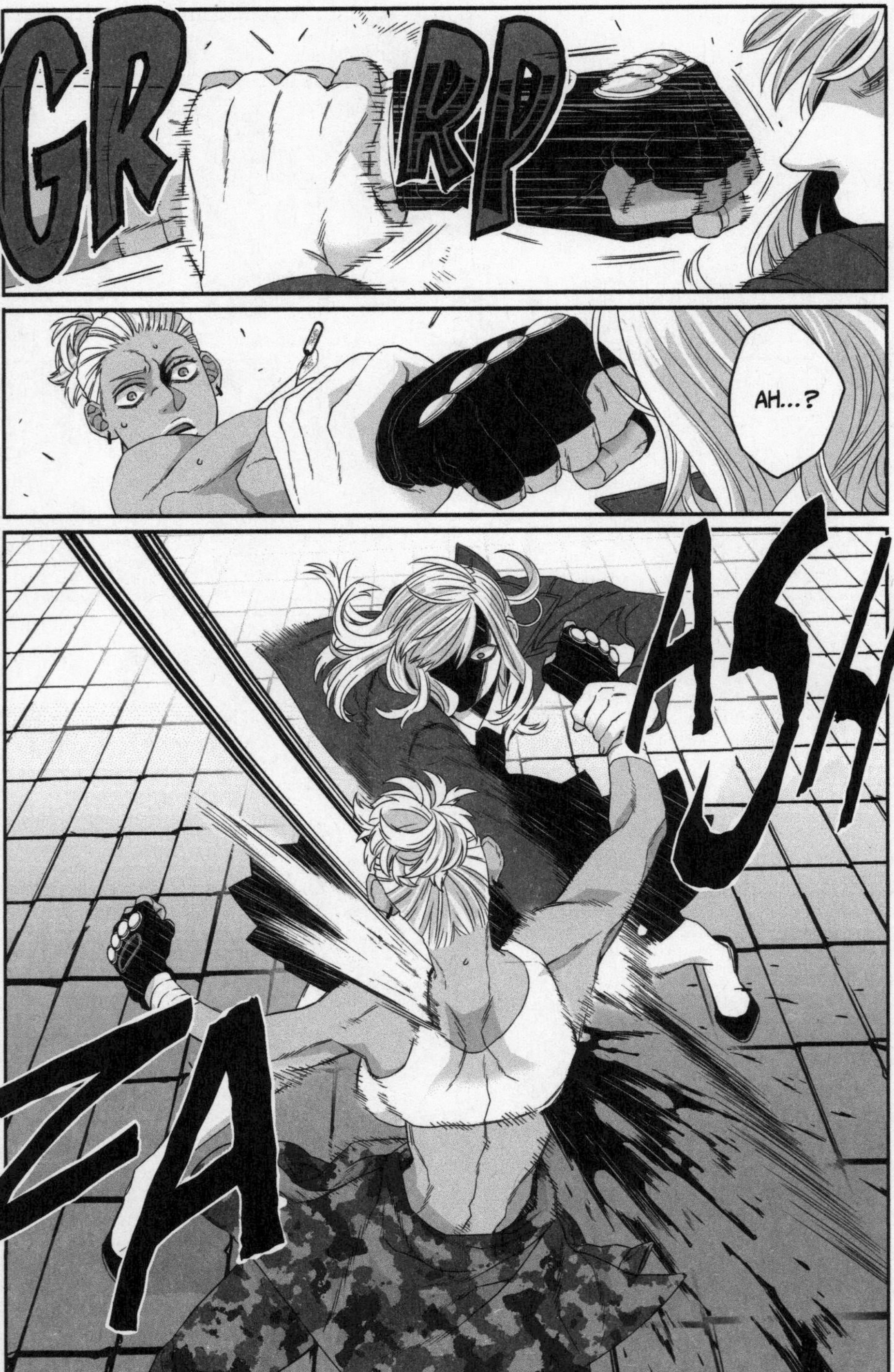
GR
RP
AH...?
ASH
ZA

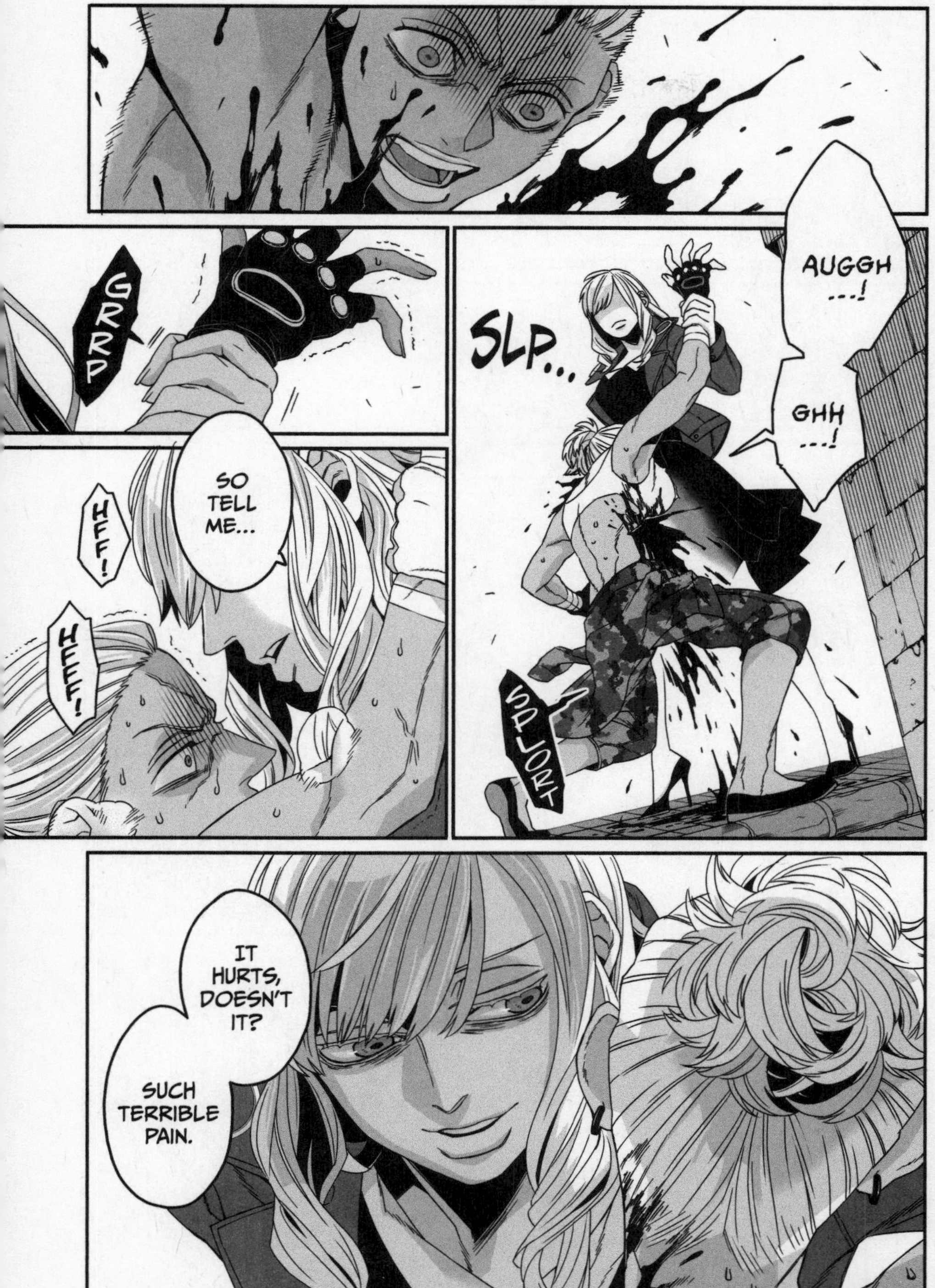
AUGGH...!
SLP...
GHH...!
SPLORT
GRRP
SO TELL ME...
HFF!
HFFF!
IT HURTS, DOESN'T IT?
SUCH TERRIBLE PAIN.

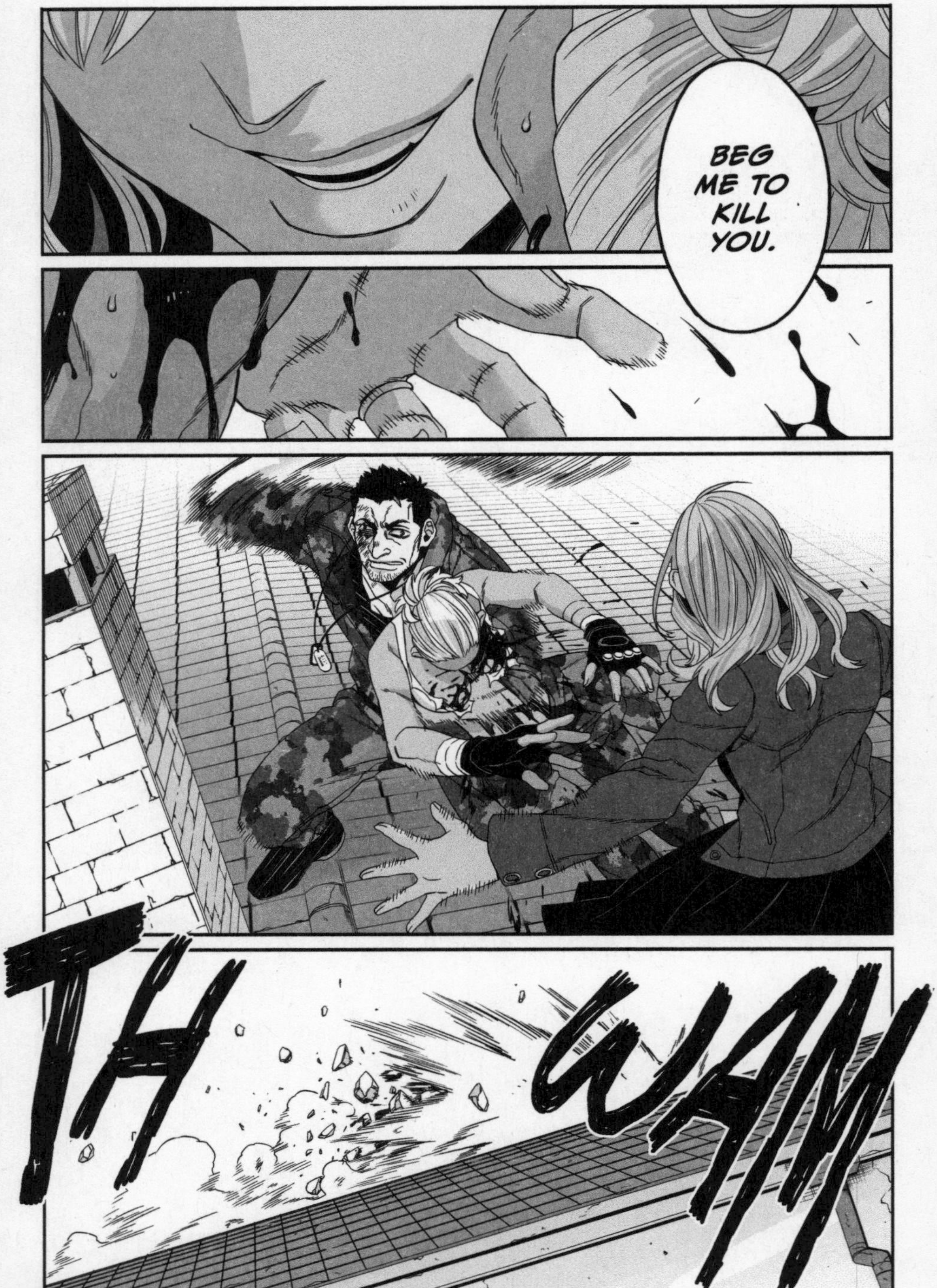
BEG ME TO KILL YOU.
TH WAM

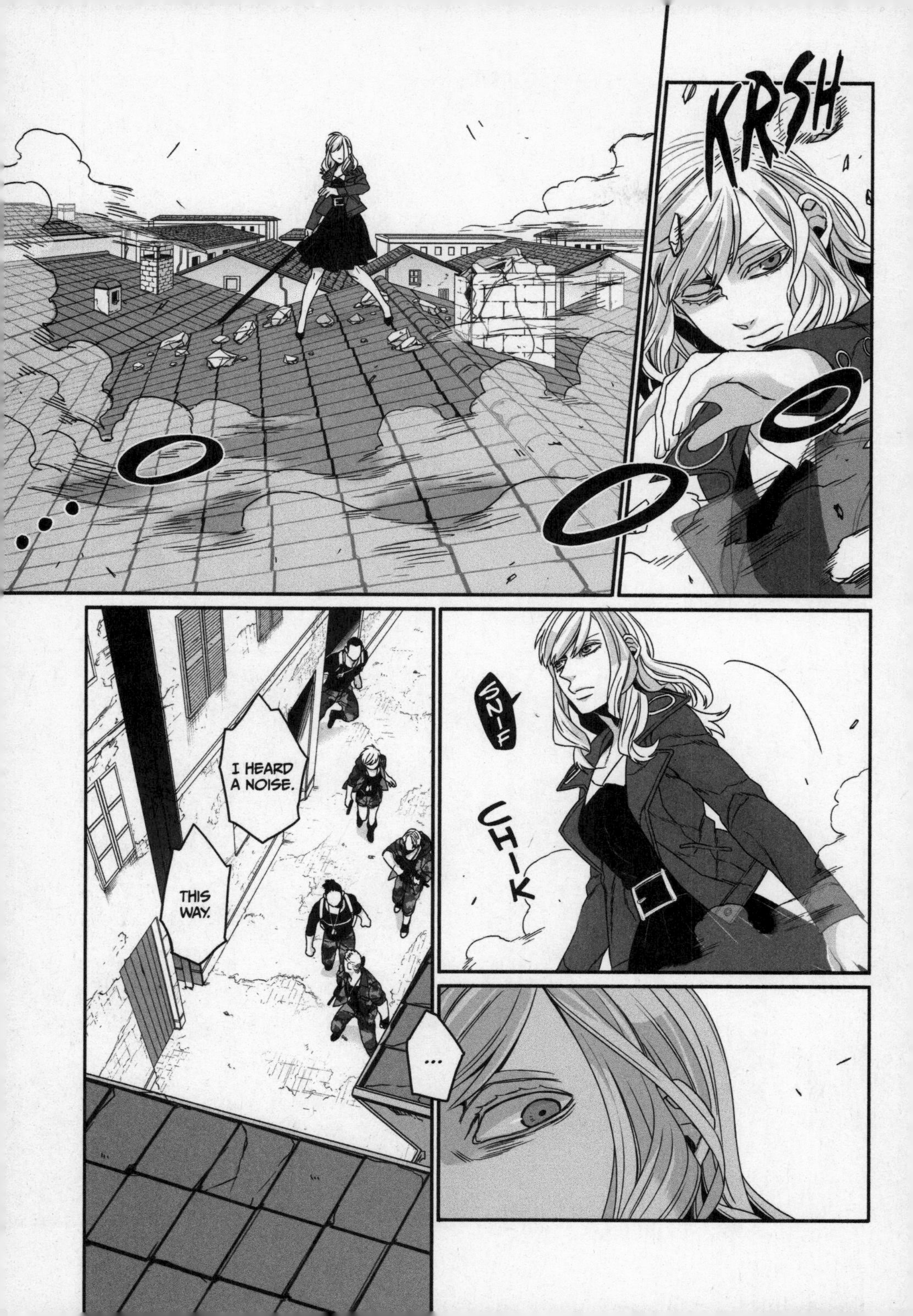
KRSH
...
SNIF
CHIK
I HEARD A NOISE.
THIS WAY.
...

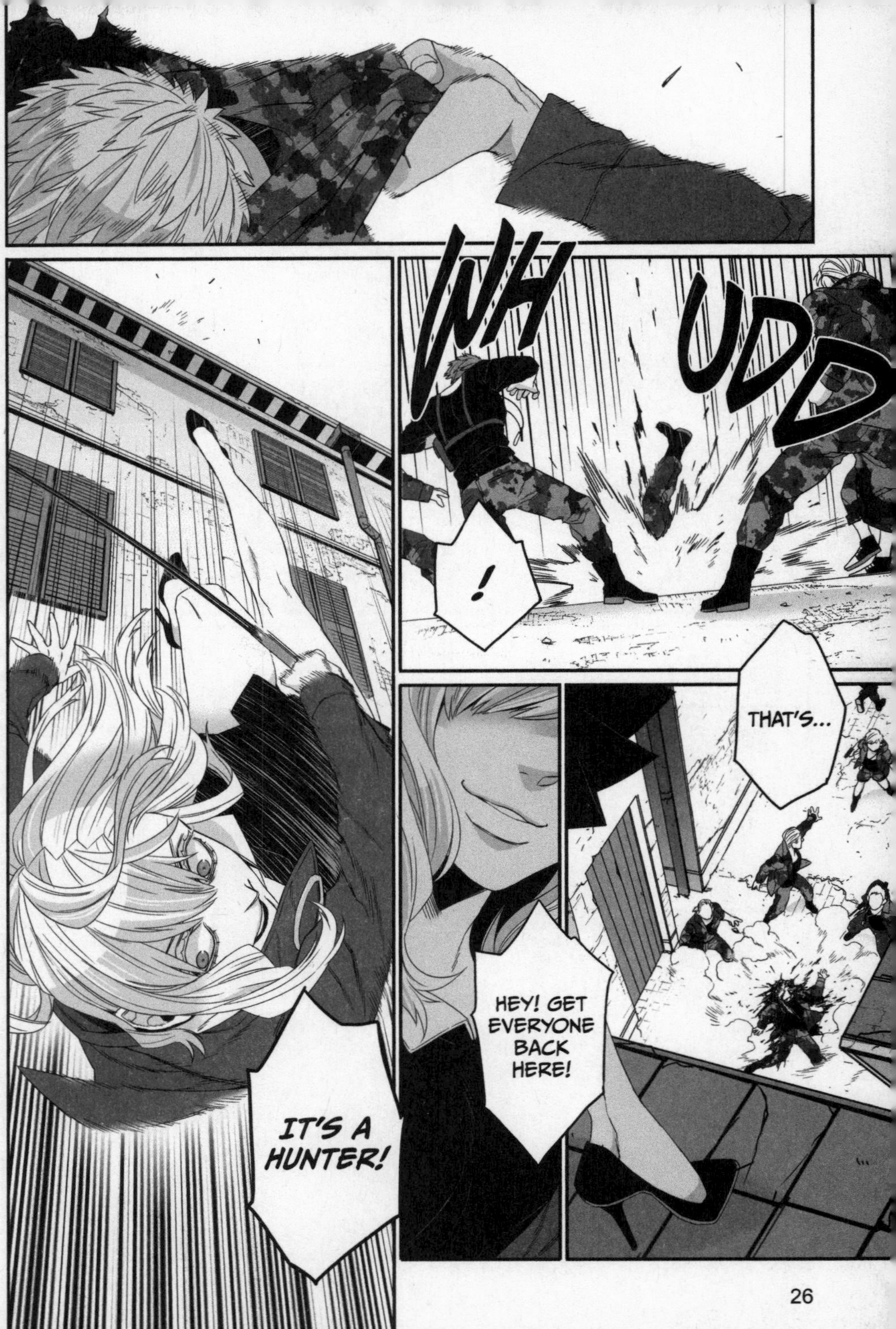
WHUDD
!
THAT'S...
HEY! GET EVERYONE BACK HERE!
IT'S A HUNTER!

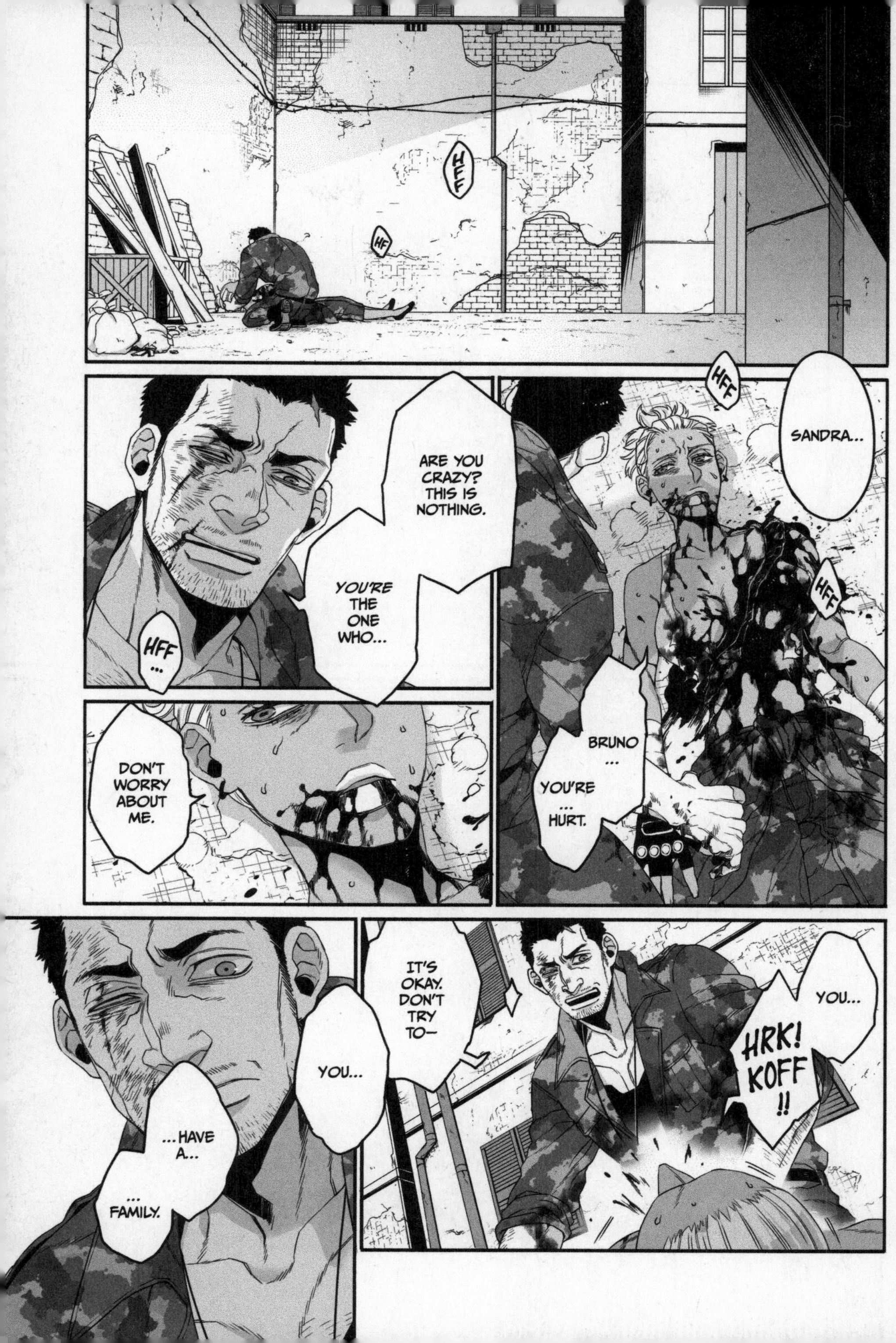
HFF
HF
SANDRA...
HFF
HFF
BRUNO... YOU'RE... HURT.
ARE YOU CRAZY? THIS IS NOTHING.
YOU'RE THE ONE WHO...
HFF...
DON'T WORRY ABOUT ME.
YOU...
HRK! KOFF!!
IT'S OKAY. DON'T TRY TO—
YOU...
...HAVE A...
...FAMILY.

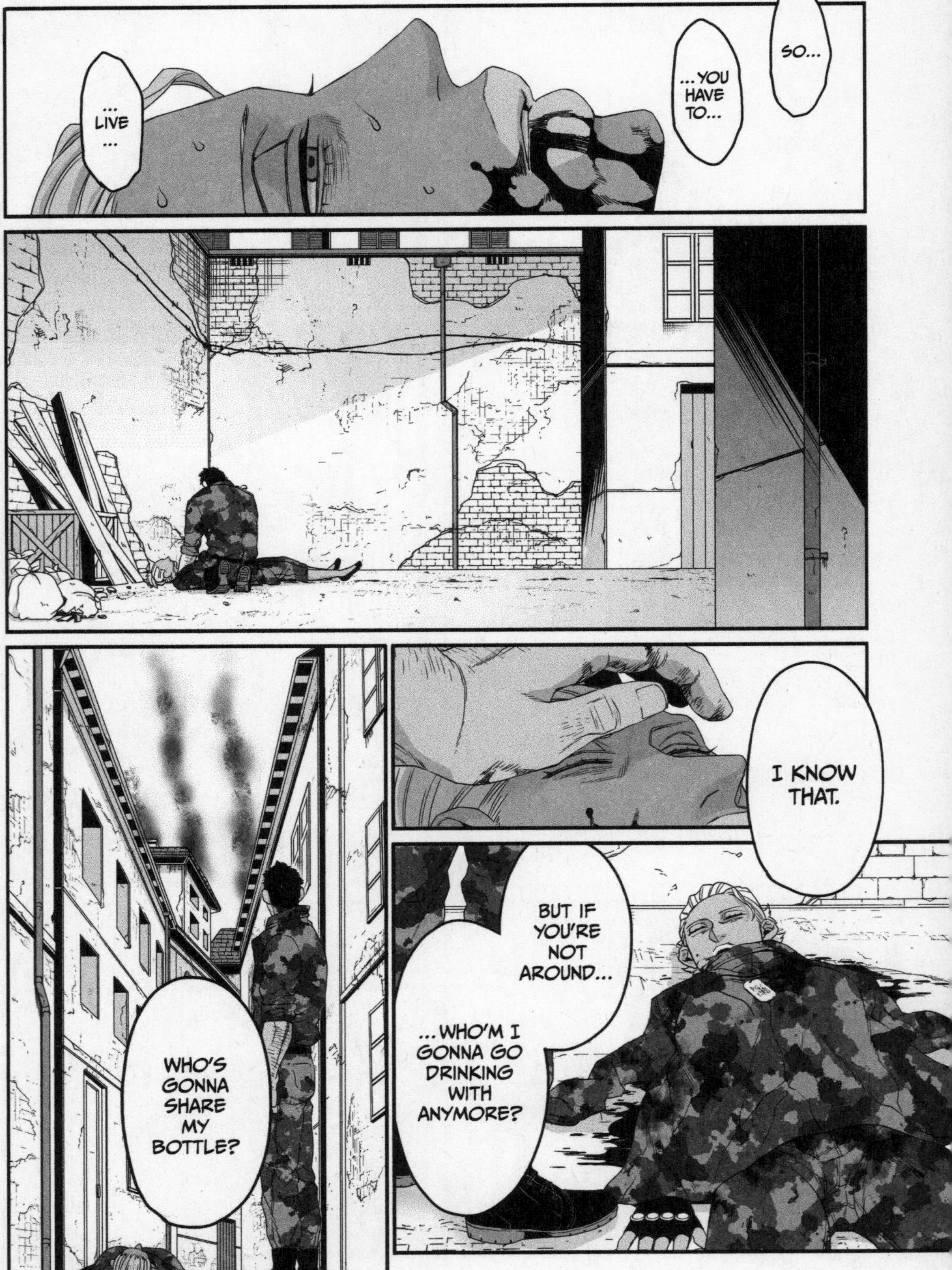
SO...
...YOU HAVE TO...
... LIVE ...
I KNOW THAT.
BUT IF YOU'RE NOT AROUND...
...WHO'M I GONNA GO DRINKING WITH ANYMORE?
WHO'S GONNA SHARE MY BOTTLE?

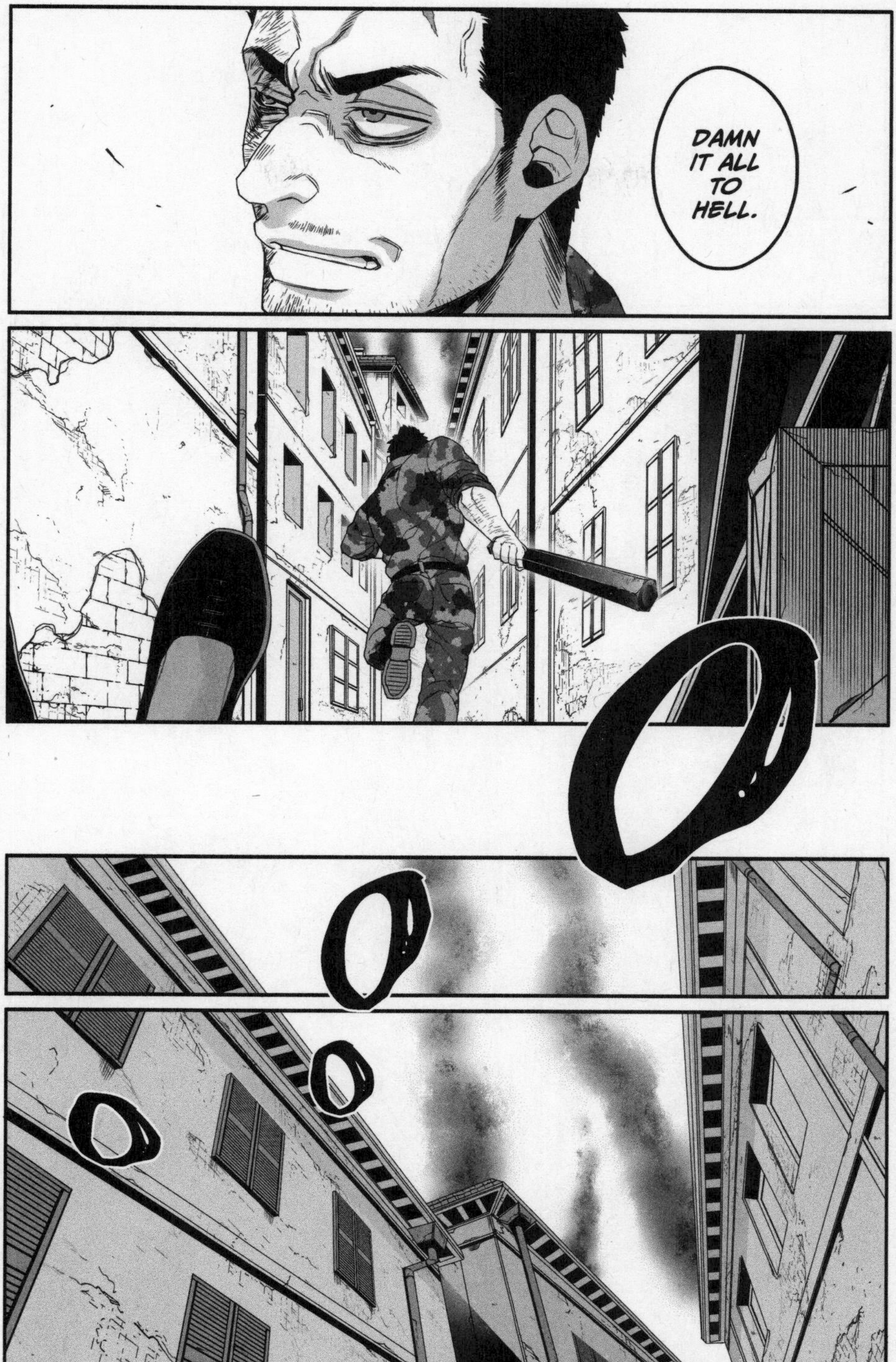
DAMN IT ALL TO HELL.

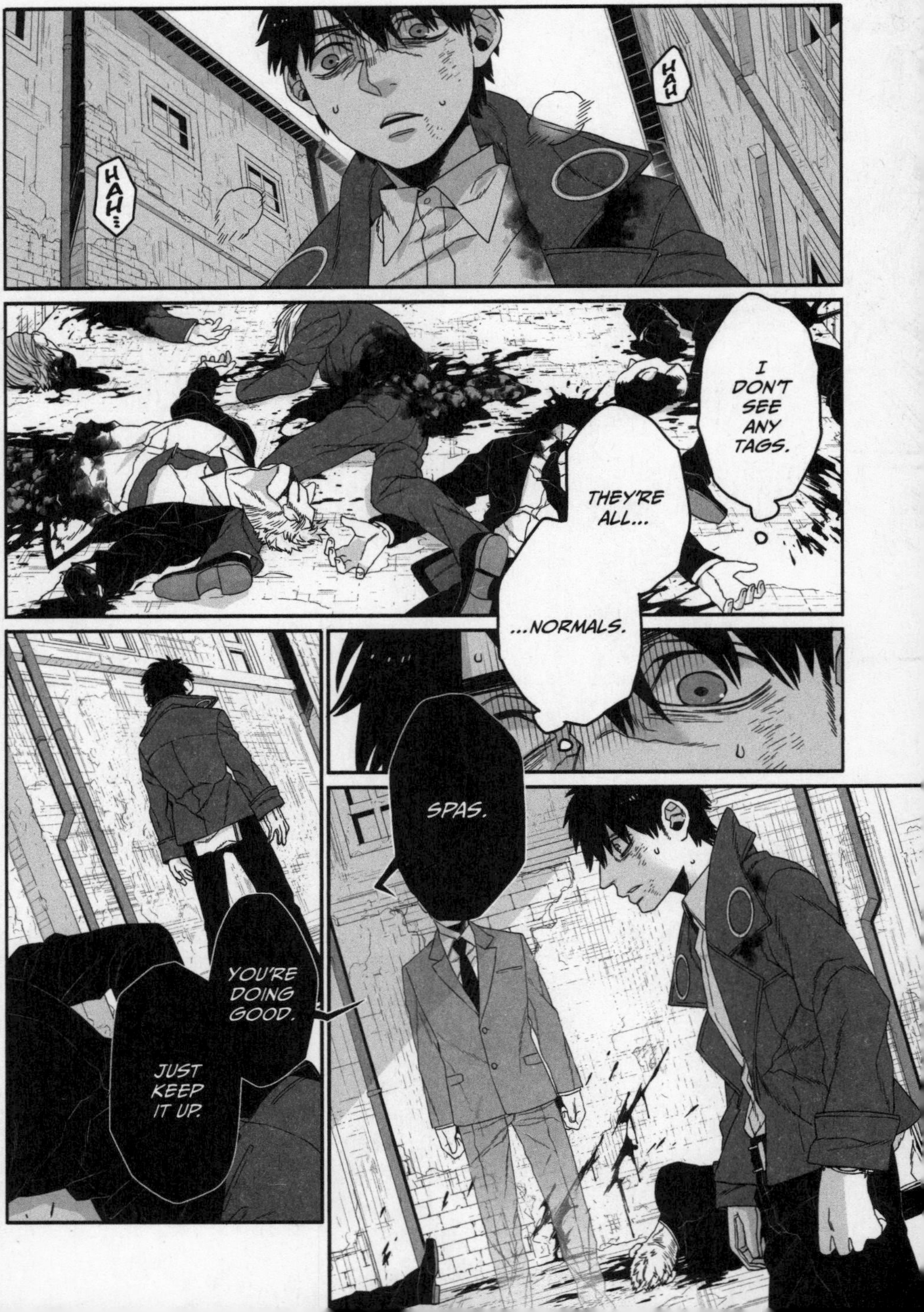
HAH
HAH...
I DON'T SEE ANY TAGS.
THEY'RE ALL...
...NORMALS.
...
SPAS.
YOU'RE DOING GOOD.
JUST KEEP IT UP.

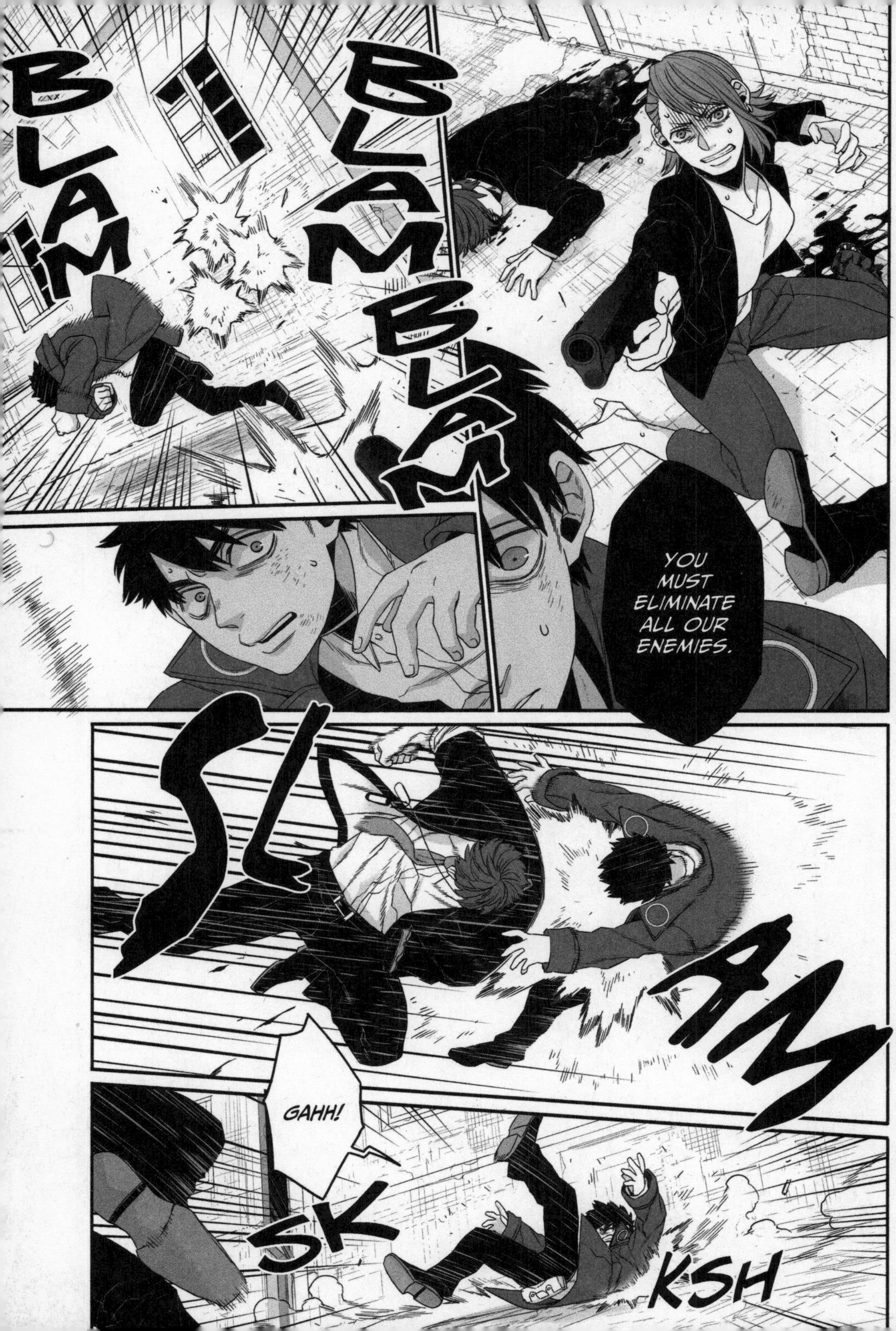
BLAM
BLAM
BLAM
YOU MUST ELIMINATE ALL OUR ENEMIES.
SLAM
GAHH!
KSH
SK

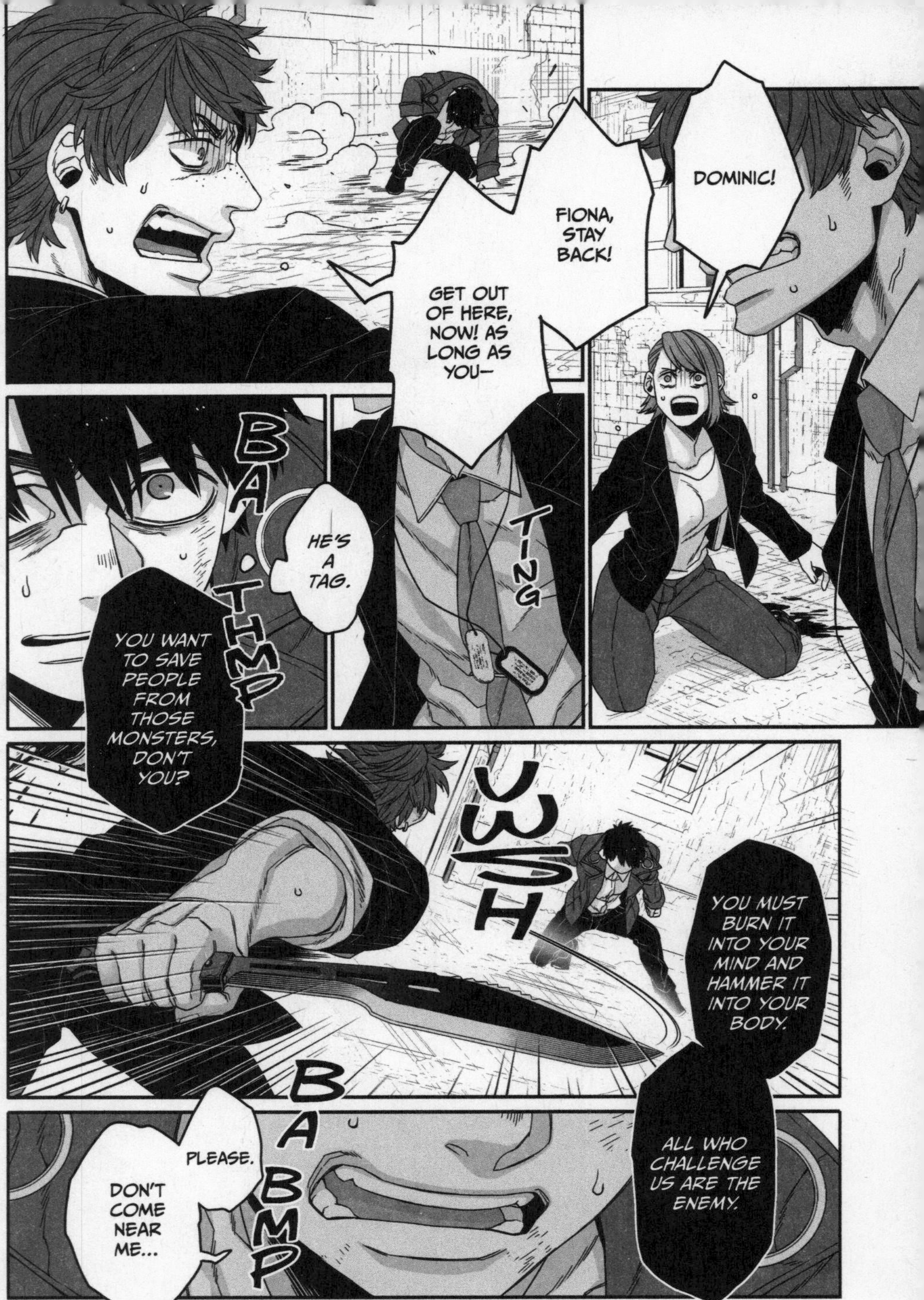
DOMINIC!
FIONA, STAY BACK!
GET OUT OF HERE, NOW! AS LONG AS YOU—
TING
HE'S A TAG.
BA THMP
YOU WANT TO SAVE PEOPLE FROM THOSE MONSTERS, DON'T YOU?
VWSH
YOU MUST BURN IT INTO YOUR MIND AND HAMMER IT INTO YOUR BODY.
ALL WHO CHALLENGE US ARE THE ENEMY.
BA BMP
PLEASE.
DON'T COME NEAR ME...

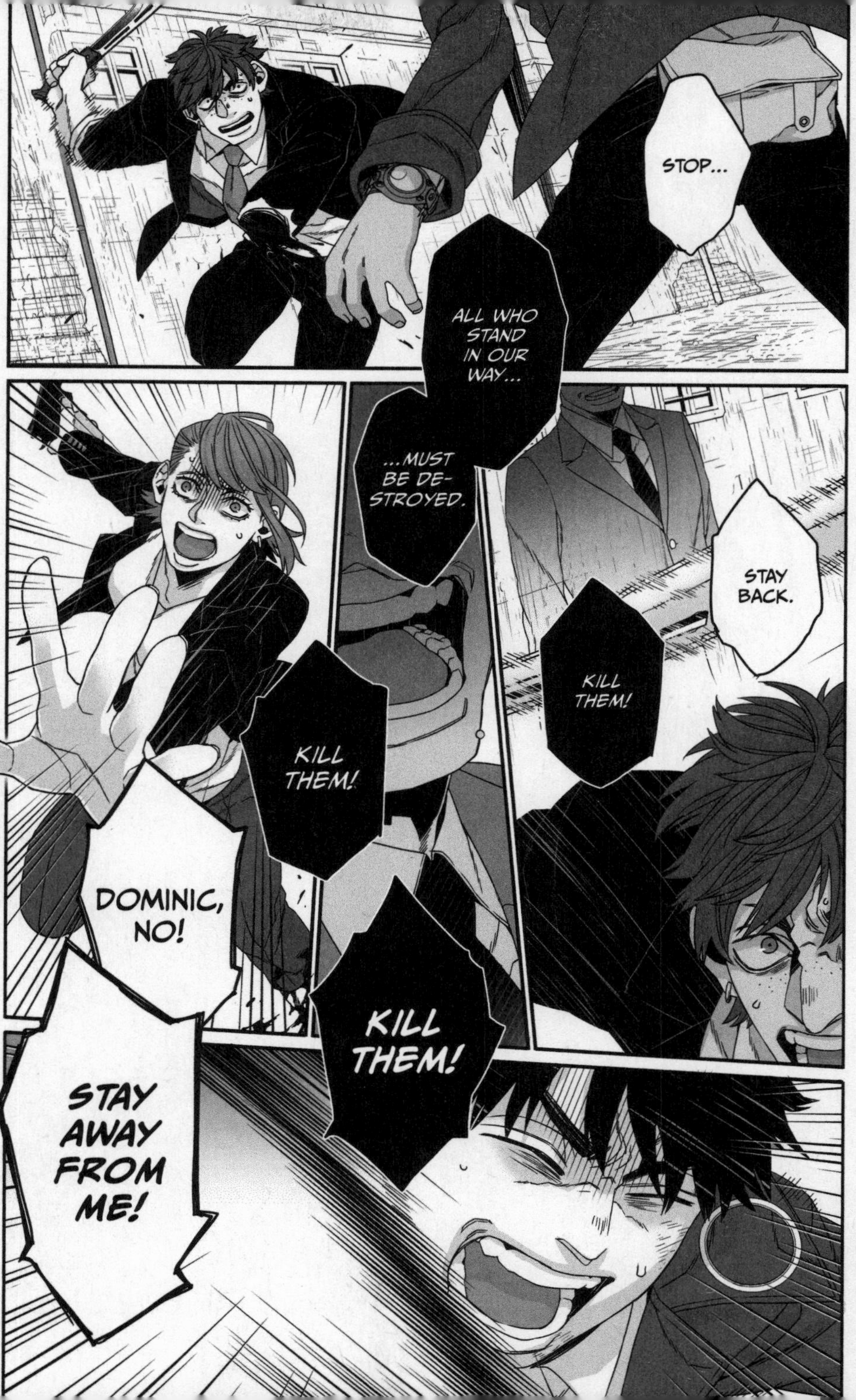
STOP...
ALL WHO STAND IN OUR WAY...
STAY BACK.
KILL THEM!
...MUST BE DE-STROYED.
KILL THEM!
DOMINIC, NO!
KILL THEM!
STAY AWAY FROM ME!

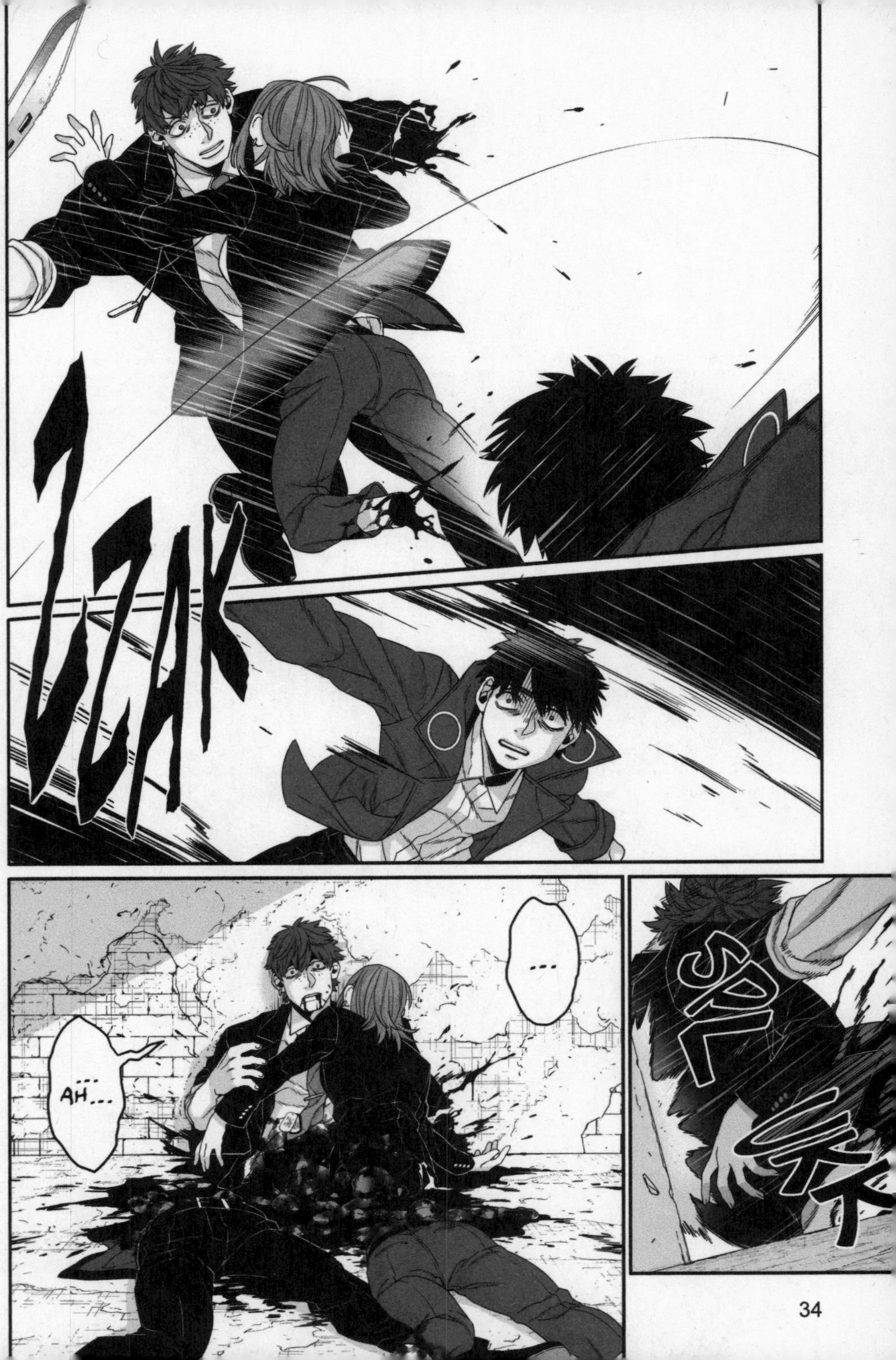
ZZAK
SPLUK
...
...AH...

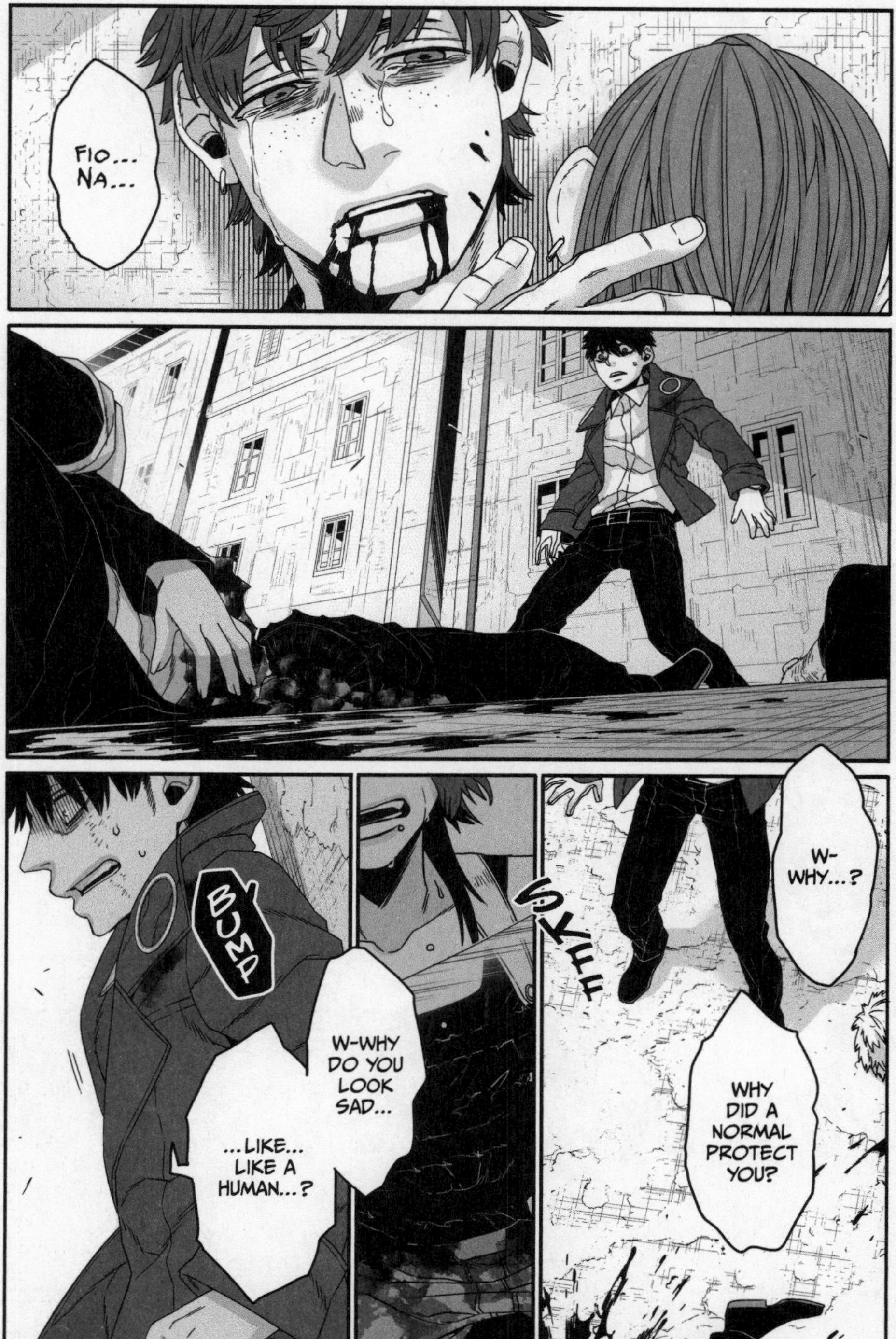
FIO... NA...
W- WHY...?
SKFF
WHY DID A NORMAL PROTECT YOU?
W-WHY DO YOU LOOK SAD...
...LIKE... LIKE A HUMAN...?
BUMP

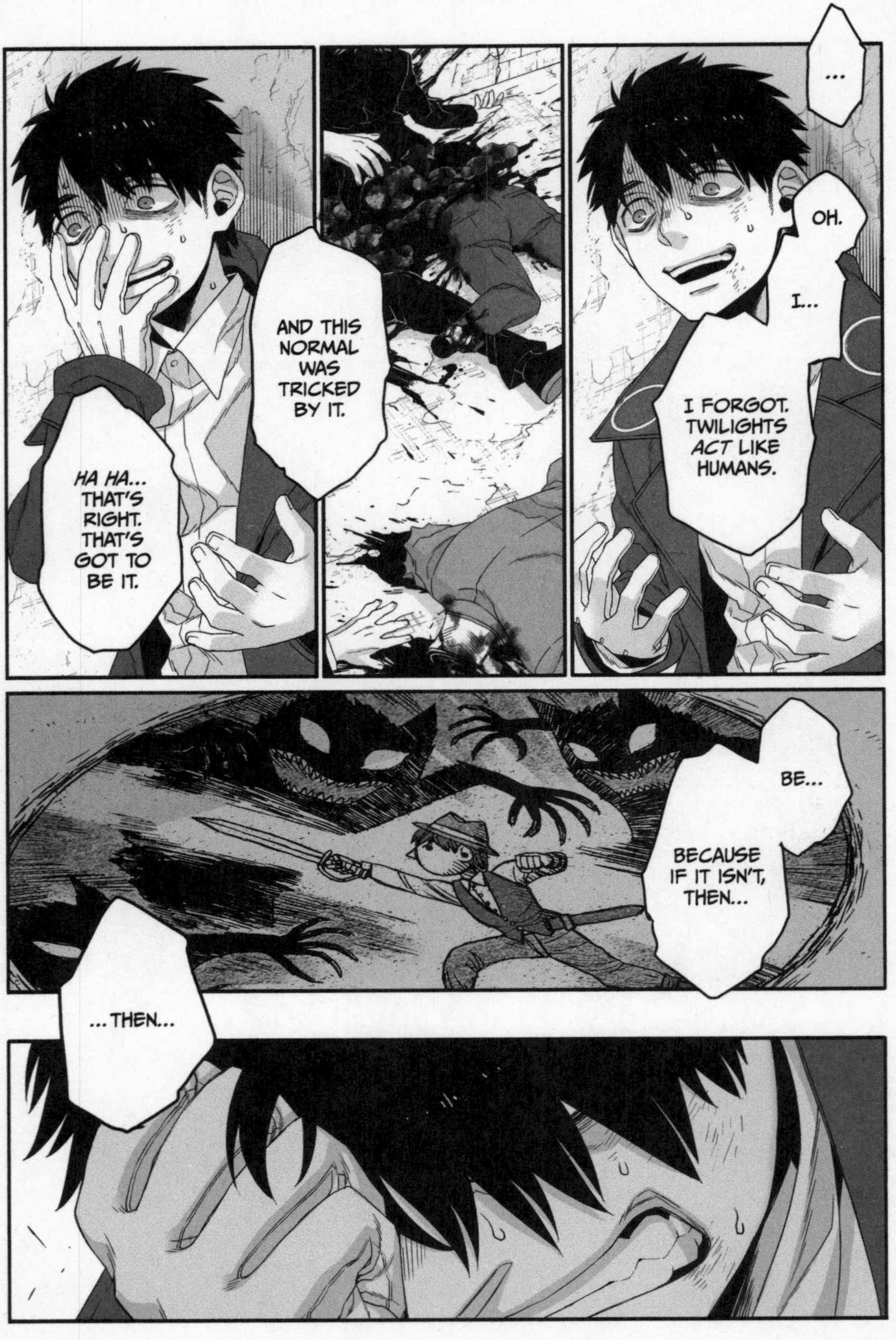
...
OH.
I...
I FORGOT. TWILIGHTS *ACT* LIKE HUMANS.
AND THIS NORMAL WAS TRICKED BY IT.
HA HA... THAT'S RIGHT. THAT'S GOT TO BE IT.
BE...
BECAUSE IF IT ISN'T, THEN...
...THEN...

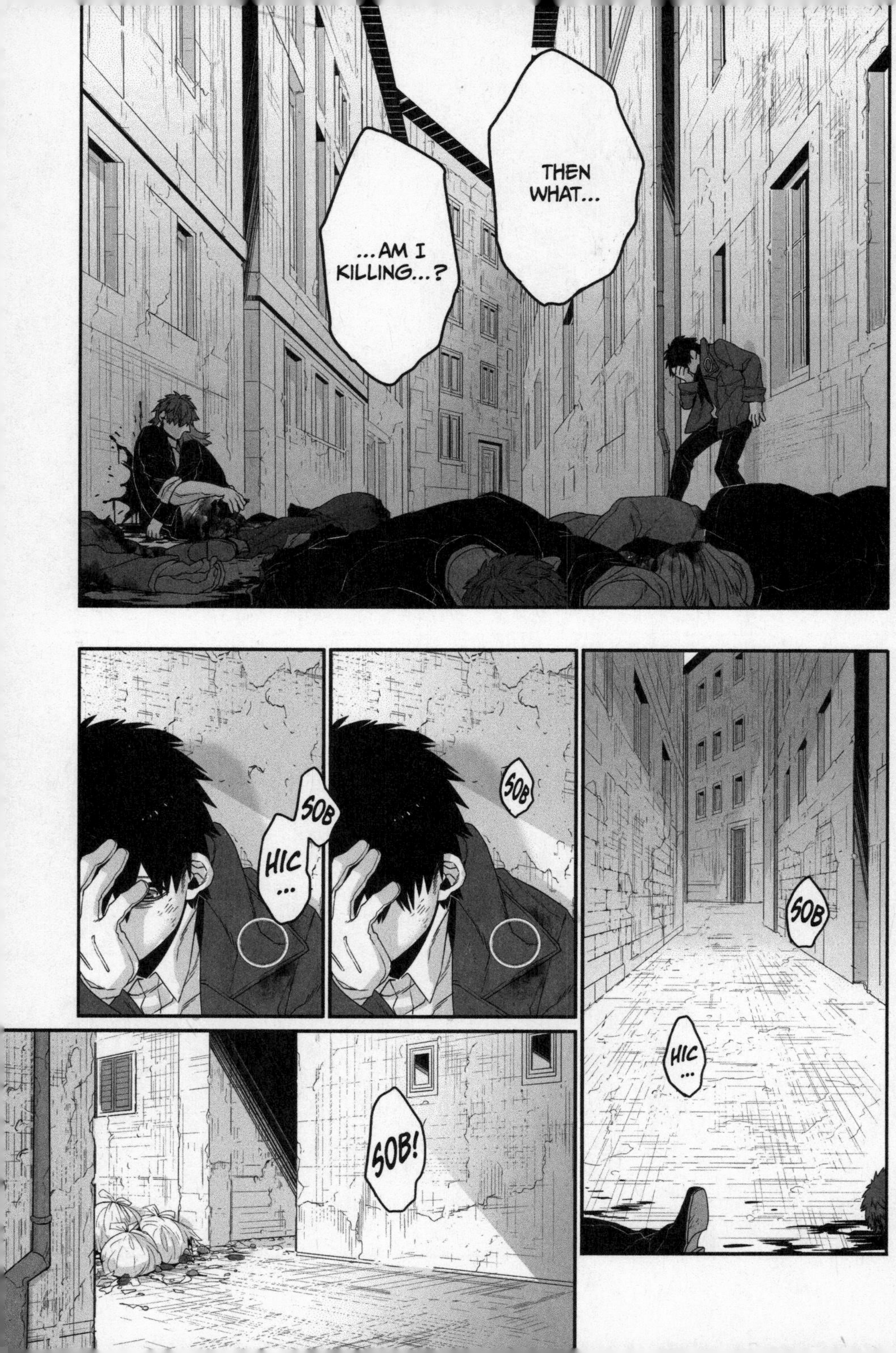
THEN WHAT...
...AM I KILLING...?
SOB
HIC ...
SOB
SOB
HIC ...
SOB!

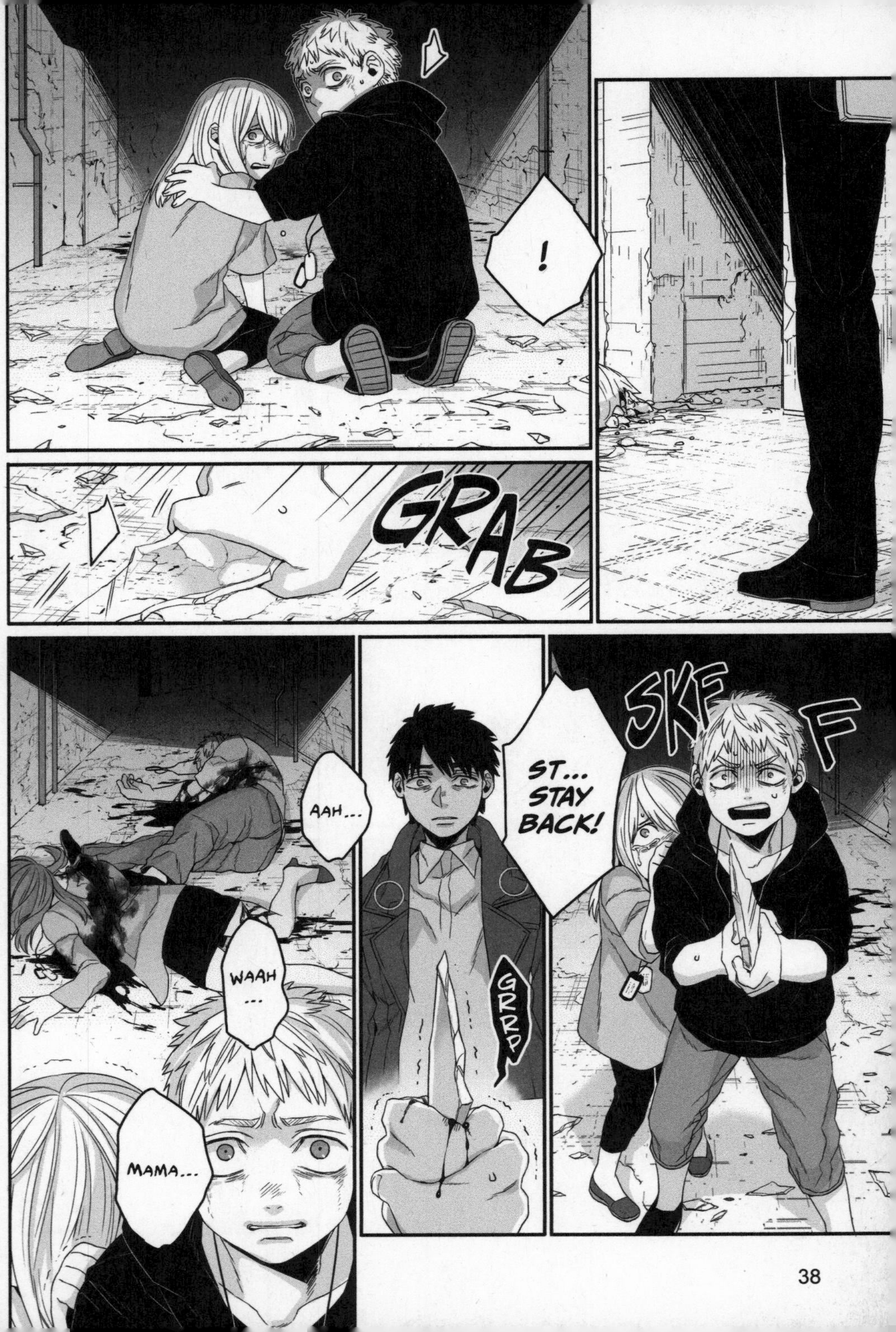
!
GRAB
SKFF
ST... STAY BACK!
GRRP
AAH...
WAAH ...
MAMA...

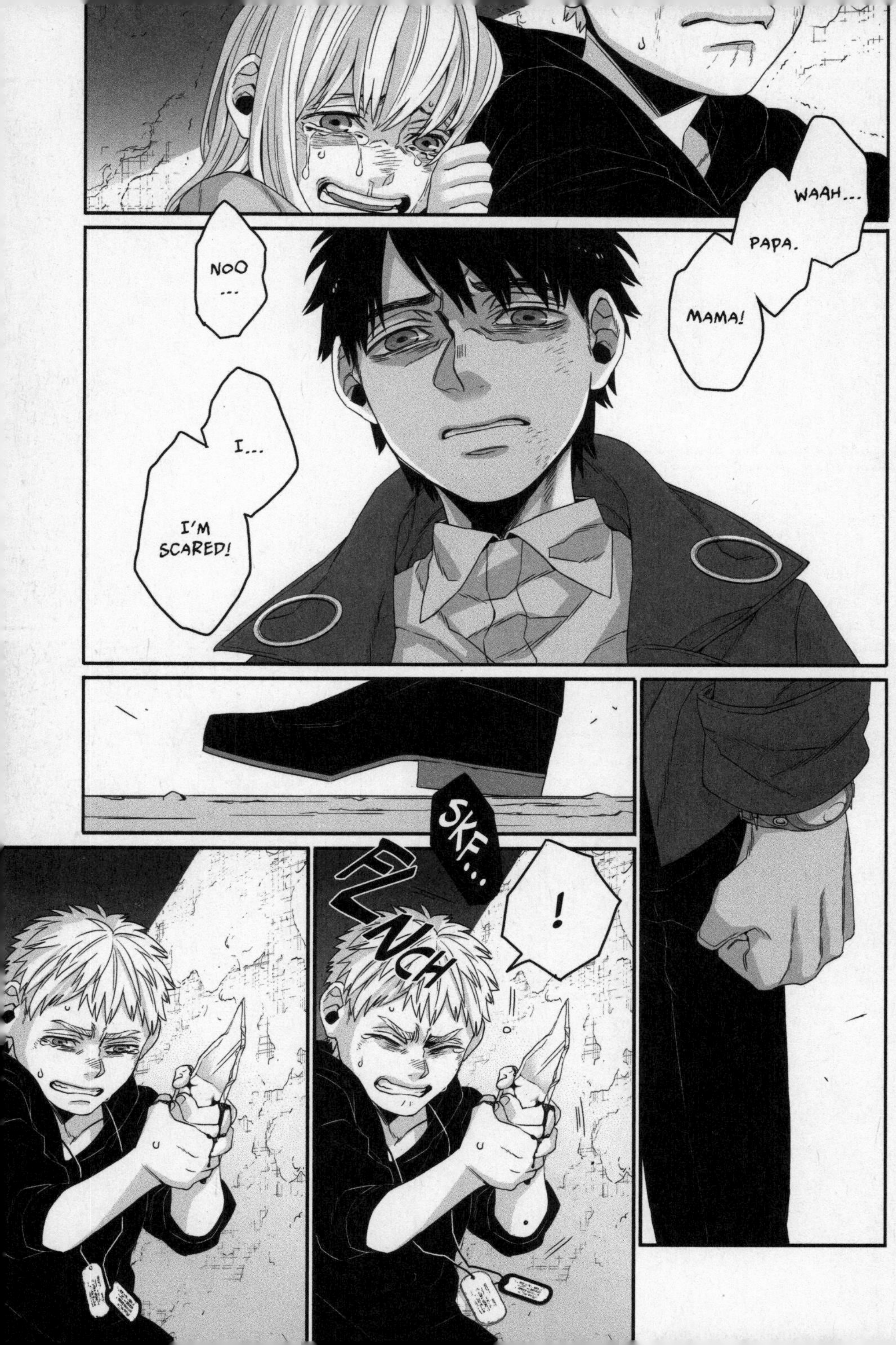
WAAH...
PAPA.
MAMA!
NOO ...
I...
I'M SCARED!
SKF...
FLINCH
!

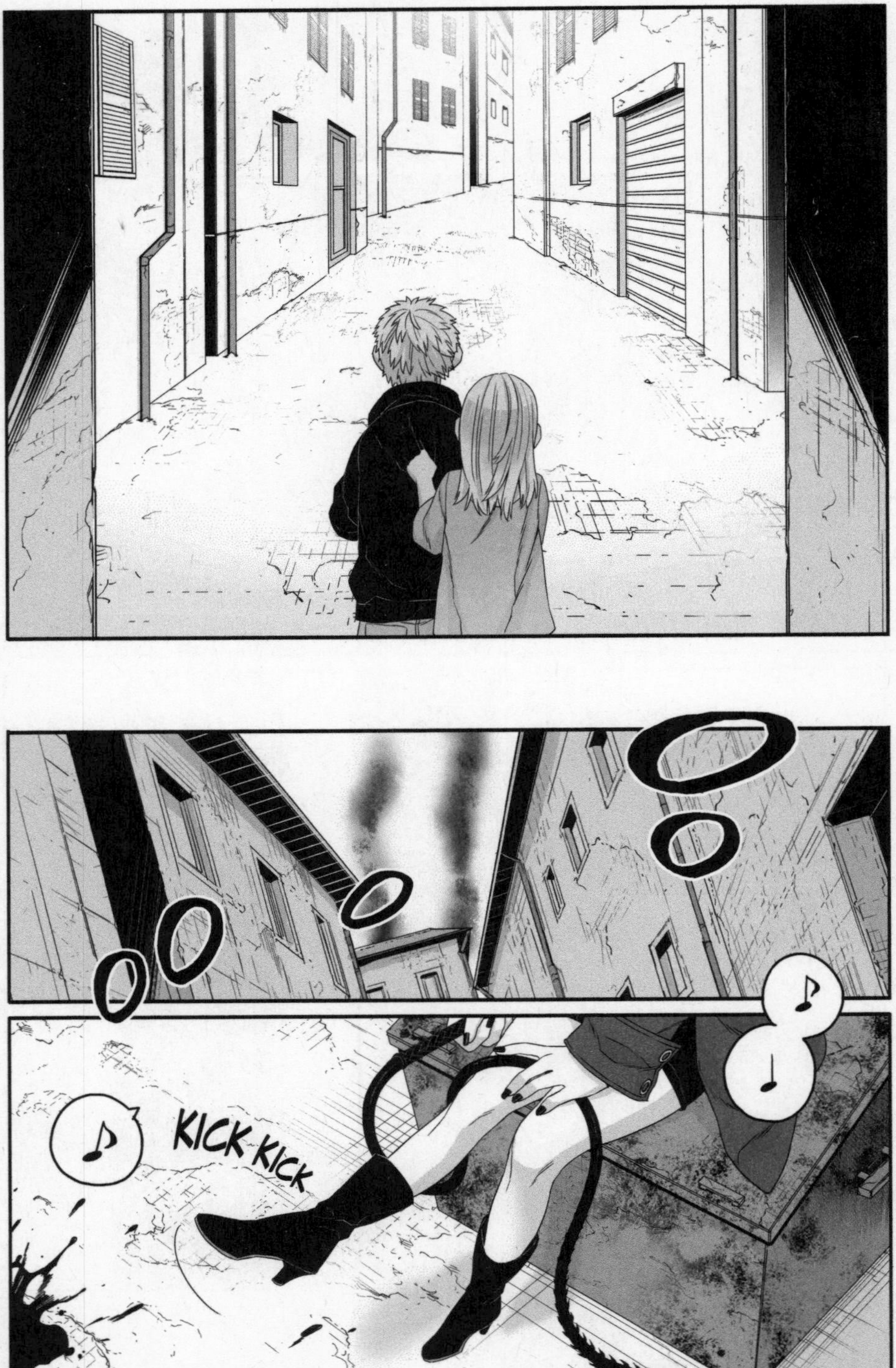
♪
♪
KICK KICK
♪

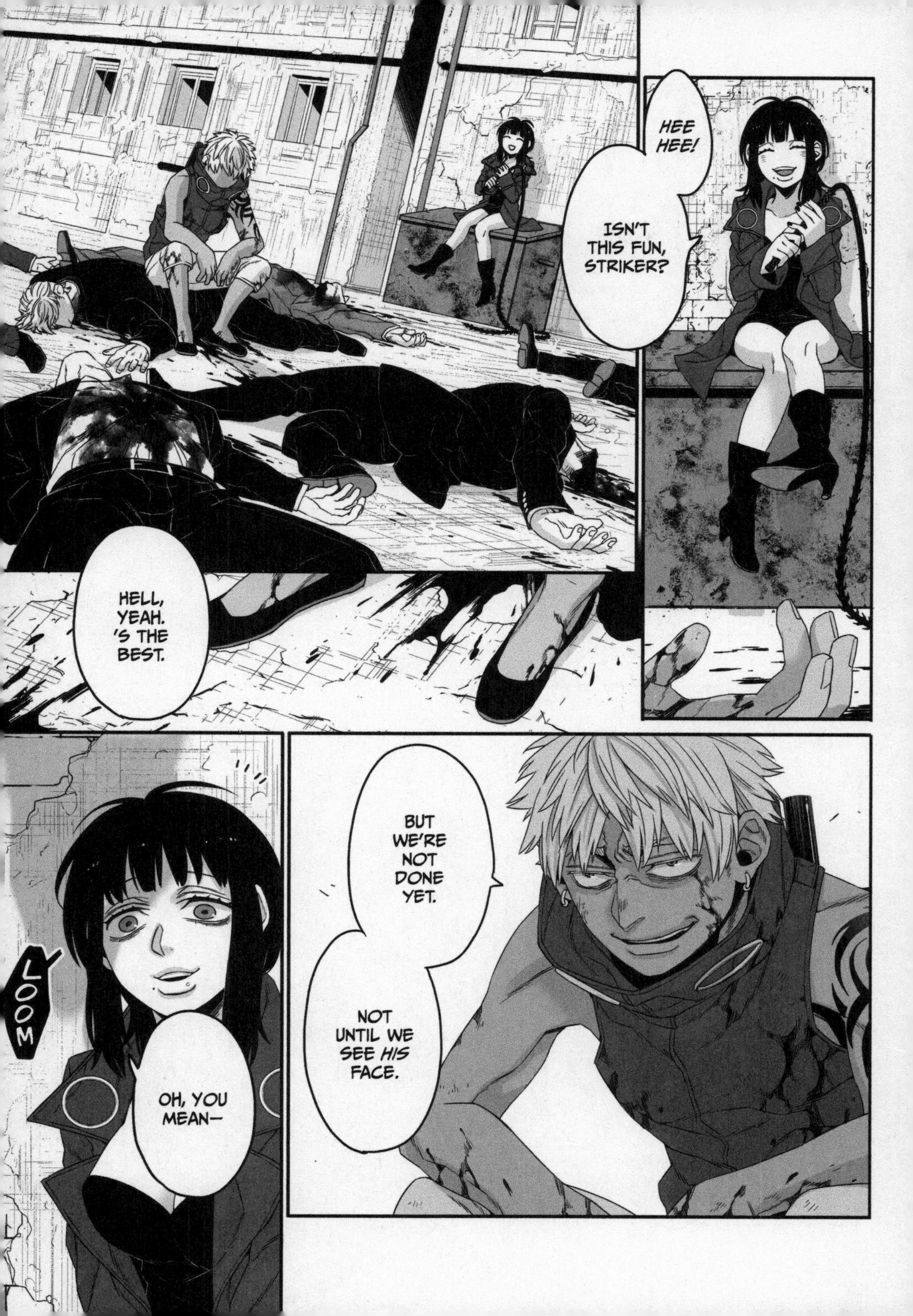
HEE HEE!
ISN'T THIS FUN, STRIKER?
HELL, YEAH. 'S THE BEST.
BUT WE'RE NOT DONE YET.
NOT UNTIL WE SEE *HIS* FACE.
LOOM
OH, YOU MEAN—

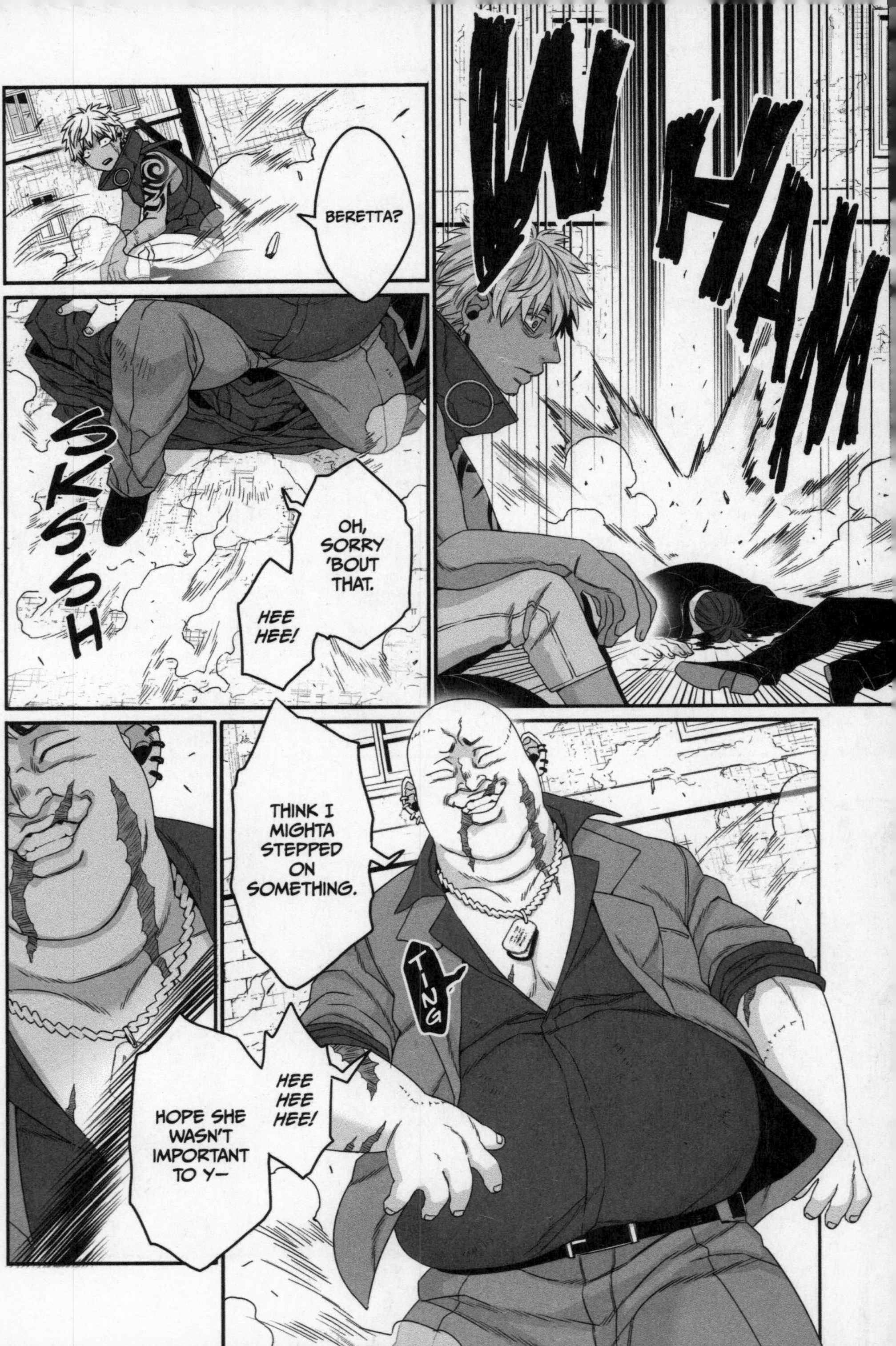
WHAM
BERETTA?
SKSSH
OH, SORRY 'BOUT THAT.
HEE HEE!
THINK I MIGHTA STEPPED ON SOMETHING.
TING
HEE HEE HEE!
HOPE SHE WASN'T IMPORTANT TO Y—

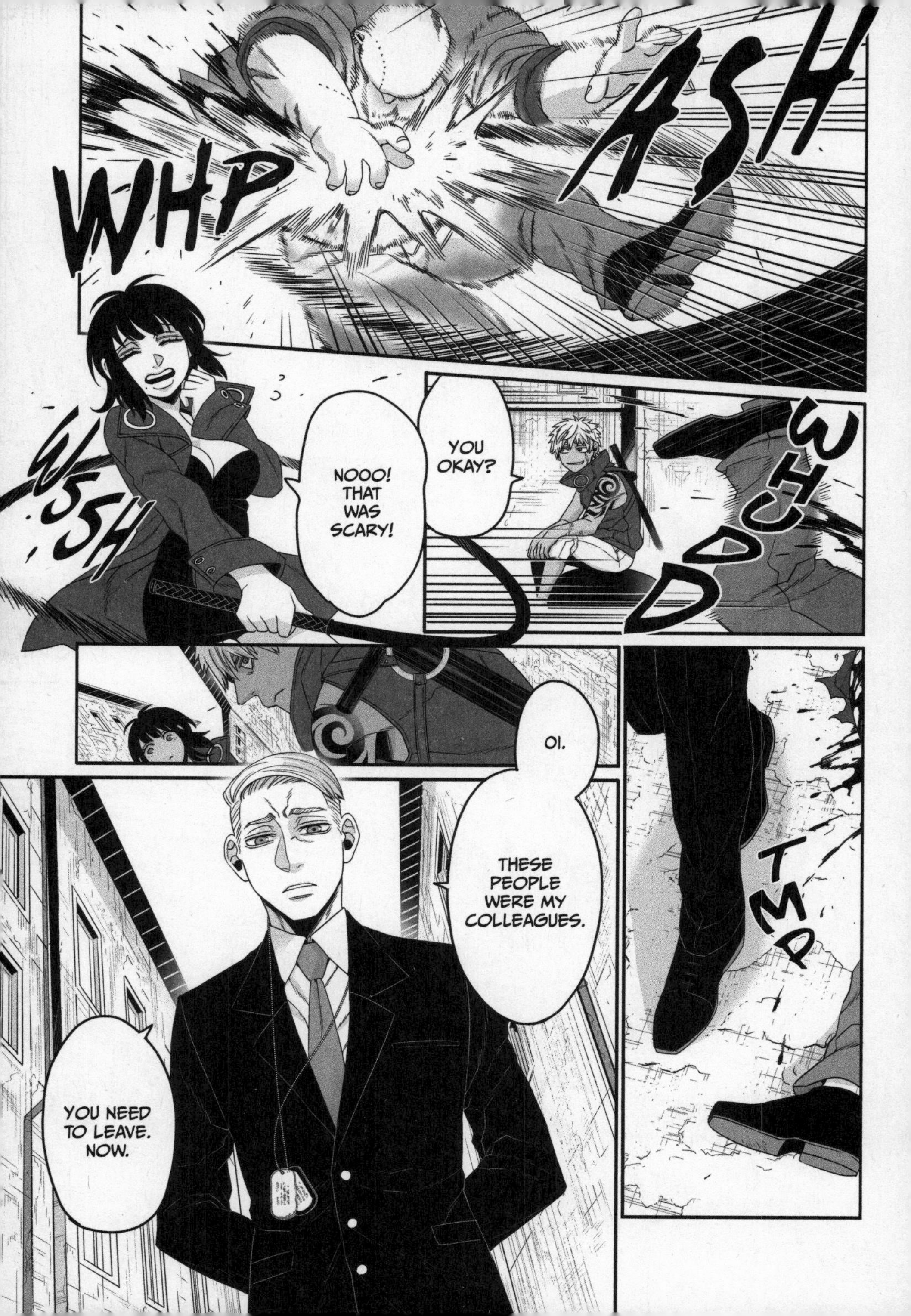
ASH
WHP
WHUDDD
YOU OKAY?
NOOO! THAT WAS SCARY!
WSSH
TMP
OI.
THESE PEOPLE WERE MY COLLEAGUES.
YOU NEED TO LEAVE. NOW.

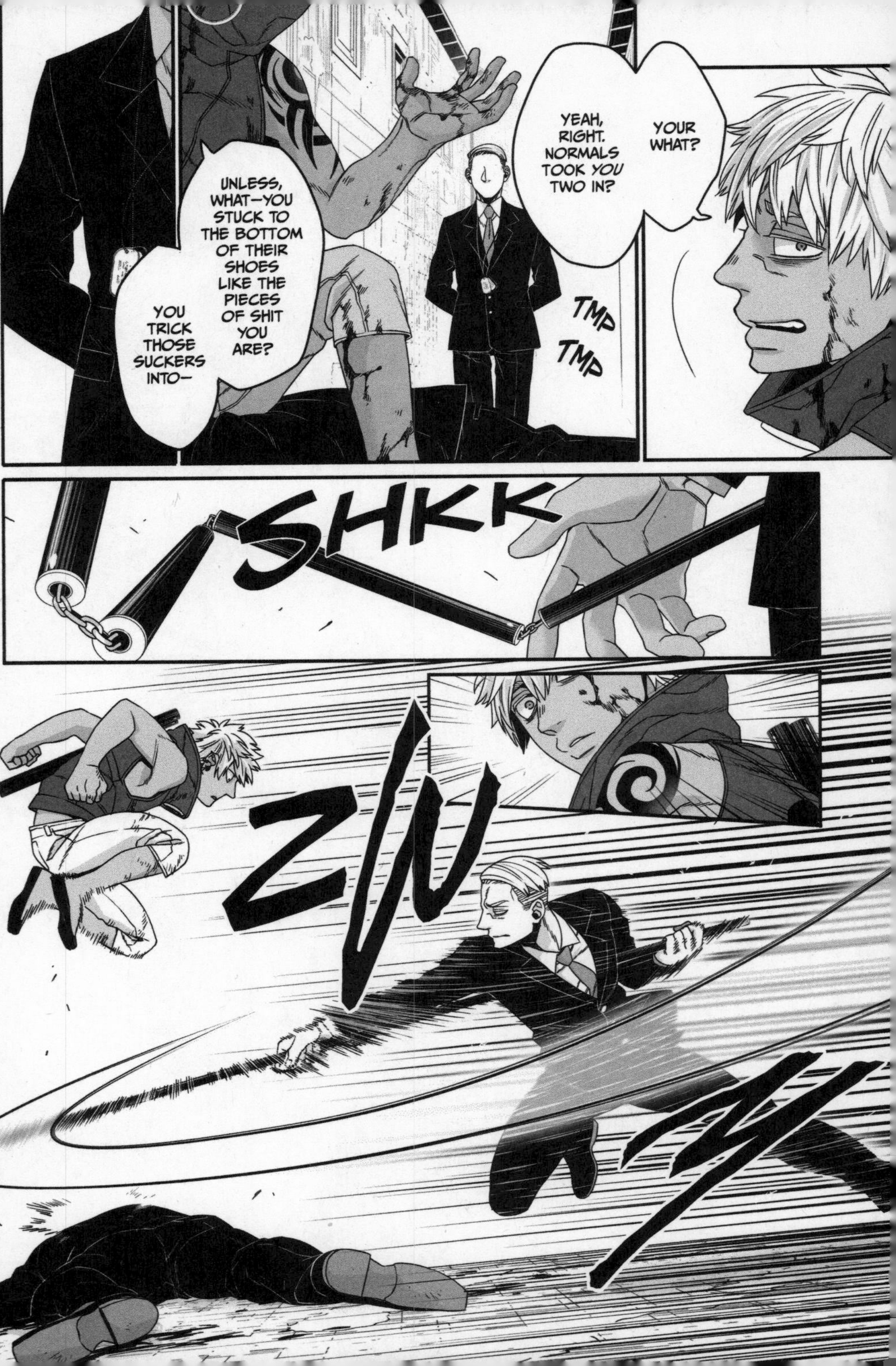
YOUR WHAT?
TMP
TMP
YEAH, RIGHT. NORMALS TOOK *YOU* TWO IN?
UNLESS, WHAT—YOU STUCK TO THE BOTTOM OF THEIR SHOES LIKE THE PIECES OF SHIT YOU ARE?
YOU TRICK THOSE SUCKERS INTO—
SHKK

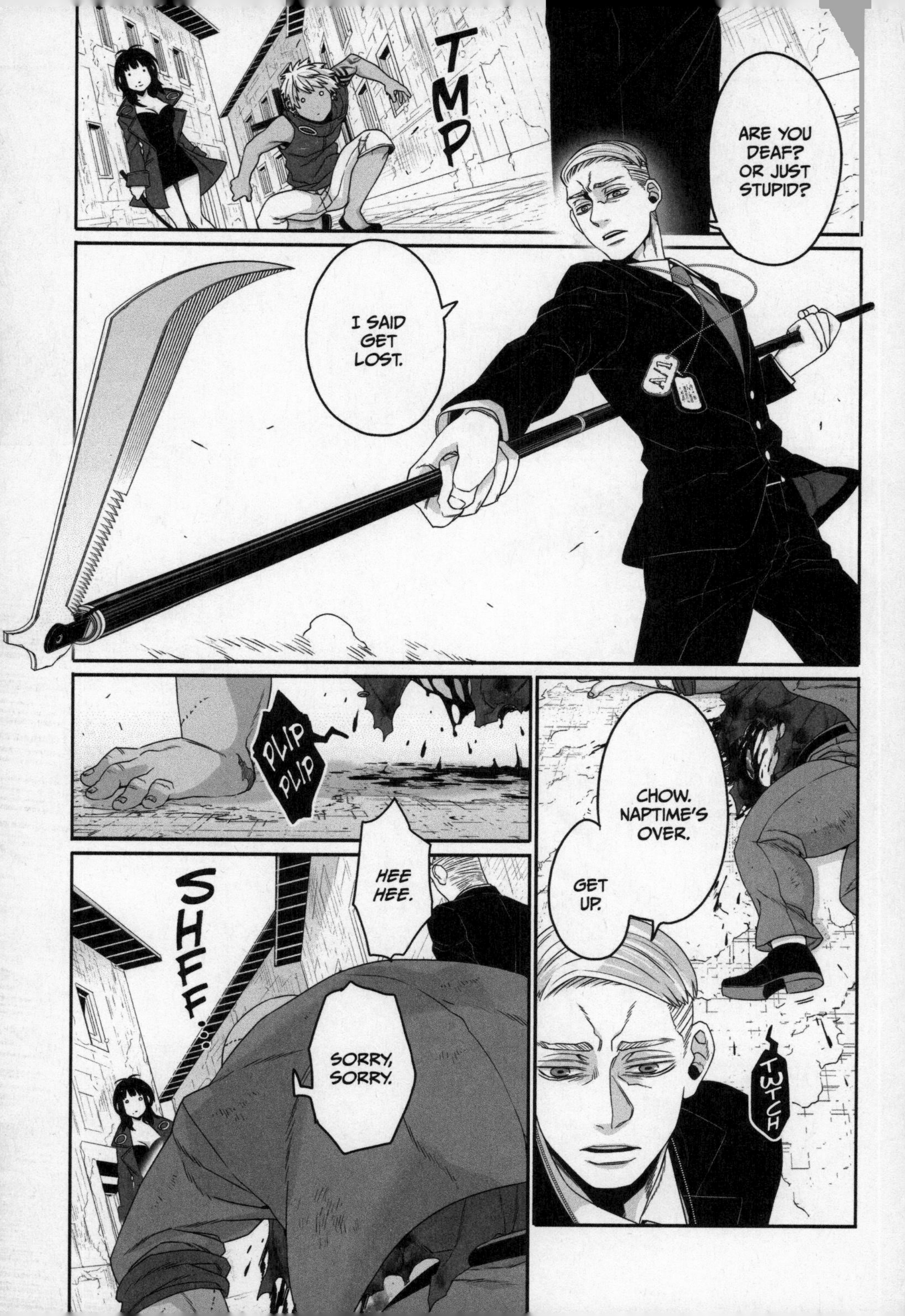
ARE YOU DEAF? OR JUST STUPID?
TMP
I SAID GET LOST.
CHOW. NAPTIME'S OVER.
GET UP.
TWTCH
PLIP PLIP
HEE HEE.
SHFF...
SORRY, SORRY.

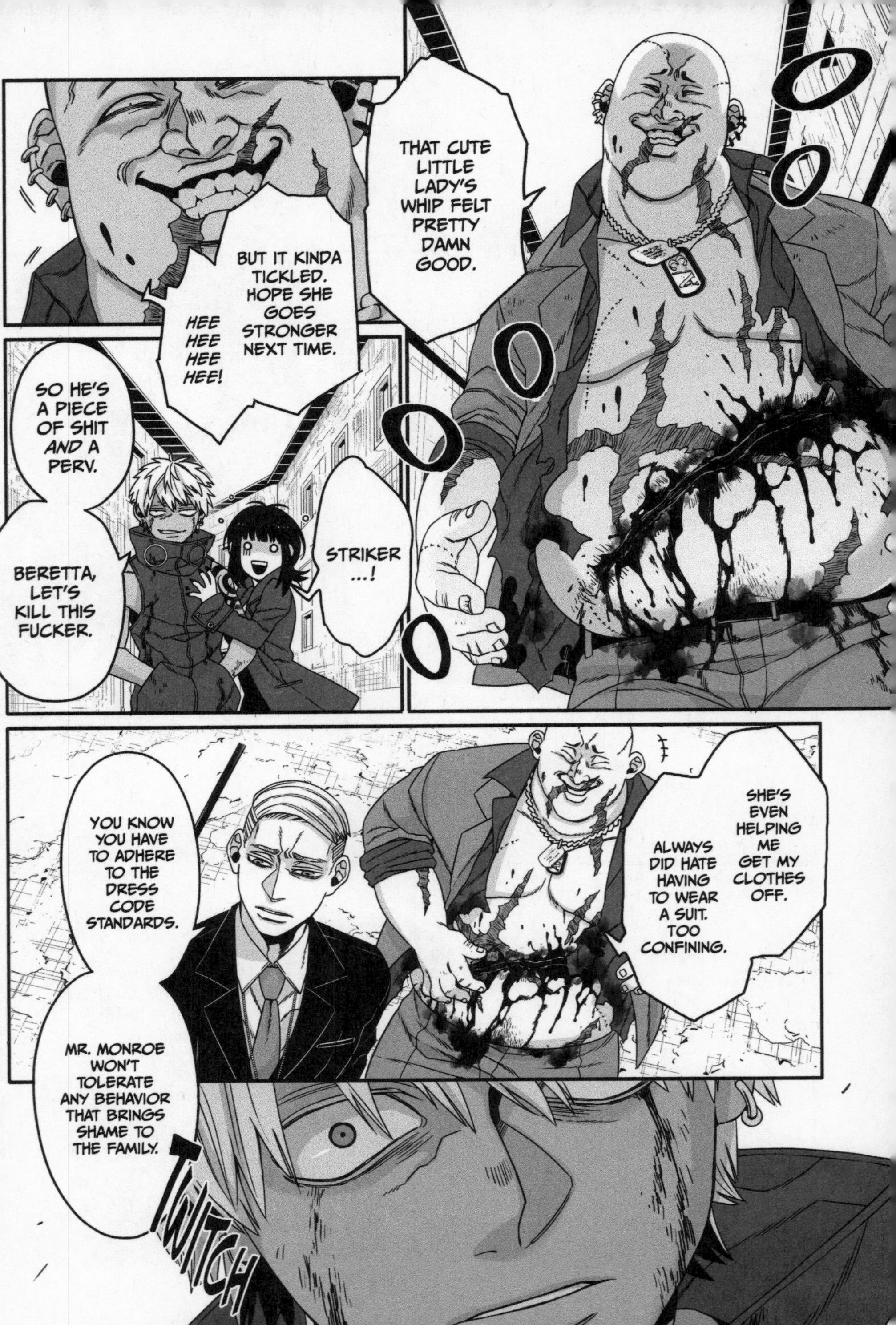
THAT CUTE LITTLE LADY'S WHIP FELT PRETTY DAMN GOOD.
BUT IT KINDA TICKLED. HOPE SHE GOES STRONGER NEXT TIME.
HEE HEE HEE HEE!
STRIKER ...!
SO HE'S A PIECE OF SHIT AND A PERV.
BERETTA, LET'S KILL THIS FUCKER.
SHE'S EVEN HELPING ME GET MY CLOTHES OFF.
ALWAYS DID HATE HAVING TO WEAR A SUIT. TOO CONFINING.
YOU KNOW YOU HAVE TO ADHERE TO THE DRESS CODE STANDARDS.
MR. MONROE WON'T TOLERATE ANY BEHAVIOR THAT BRINGS SHAME TO THE FAMILY.
TWITCH

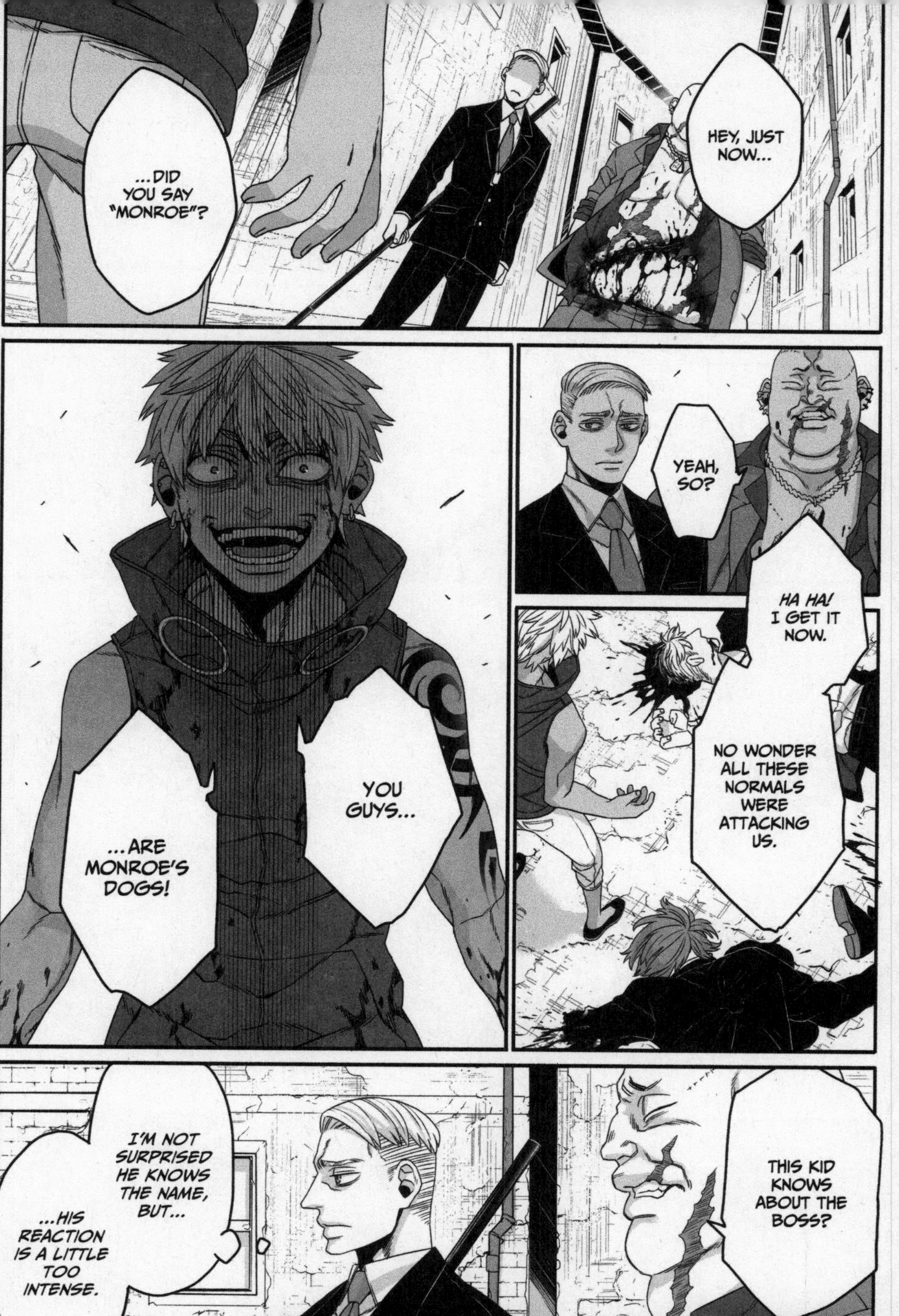
HEY, JUST NOW...
...DID YOU SAY "MONROE"?
YEAH, SO?
HA HA! I GET IT NOW.
NO WONDER ALL THESE NORMALS WERE ATTACKING US.
YOU GUYS...
...ARE MONROE'S DOGS!
THIS KID KNOWS ABOUT THE BOSS?
I'M NOT SURPRISED HE KNOWS THE NAME, BUT...
...HIS REACTION IS A LITTLE TOO INTENSE.

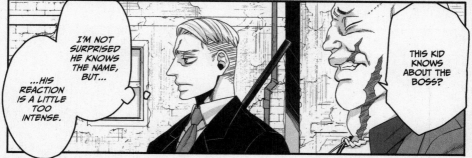

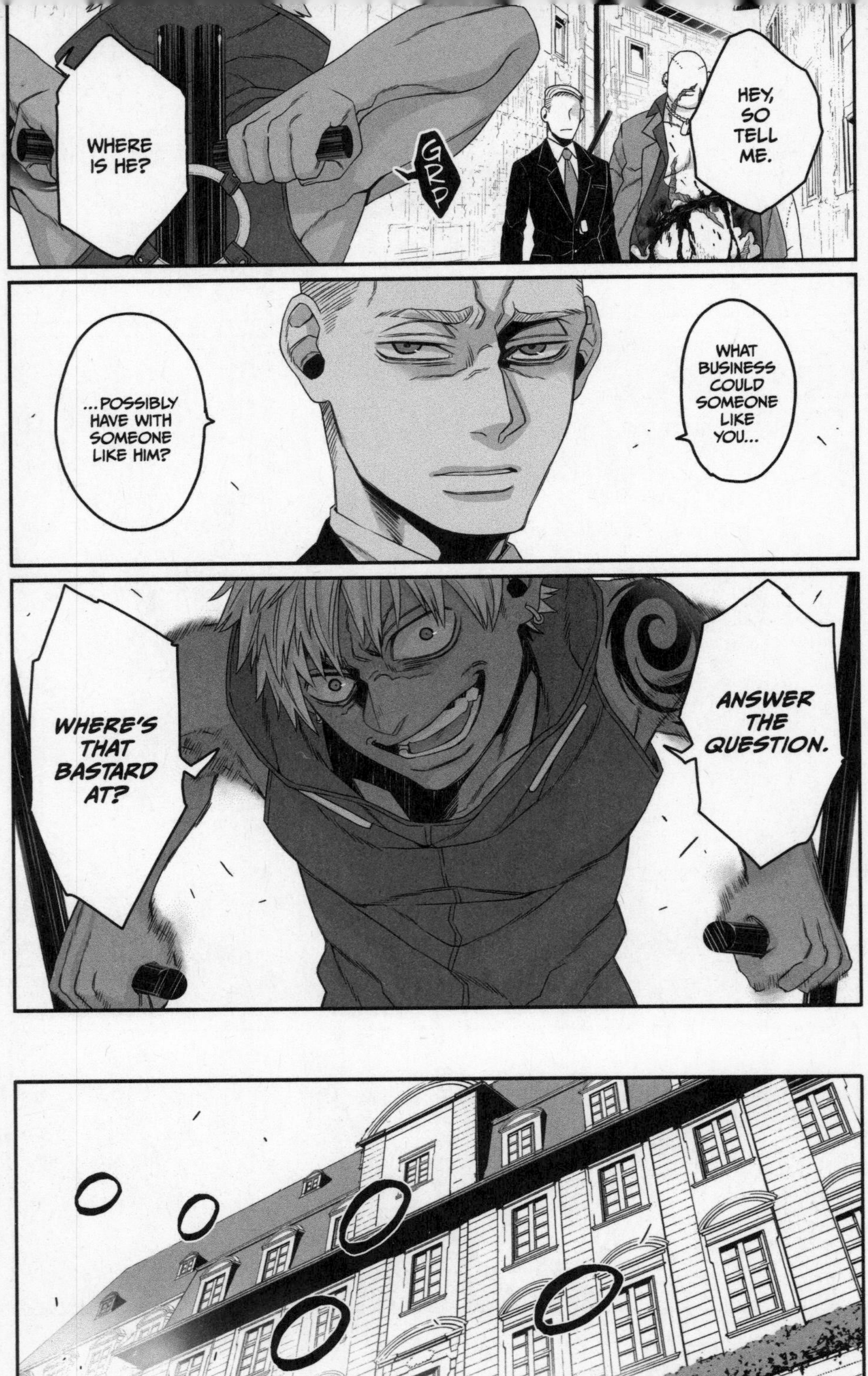
HEY, SO TELL ME.
GRP
WHERE IS HE?
WHAT BUSINESS COULD SOMEONE LIKE YOU...
...POSSIBLY HAVE WITH SOMEONE LIKE HIM?
ANSWER THE QUESTION.
WHERE'S THAT BASTARD AT?

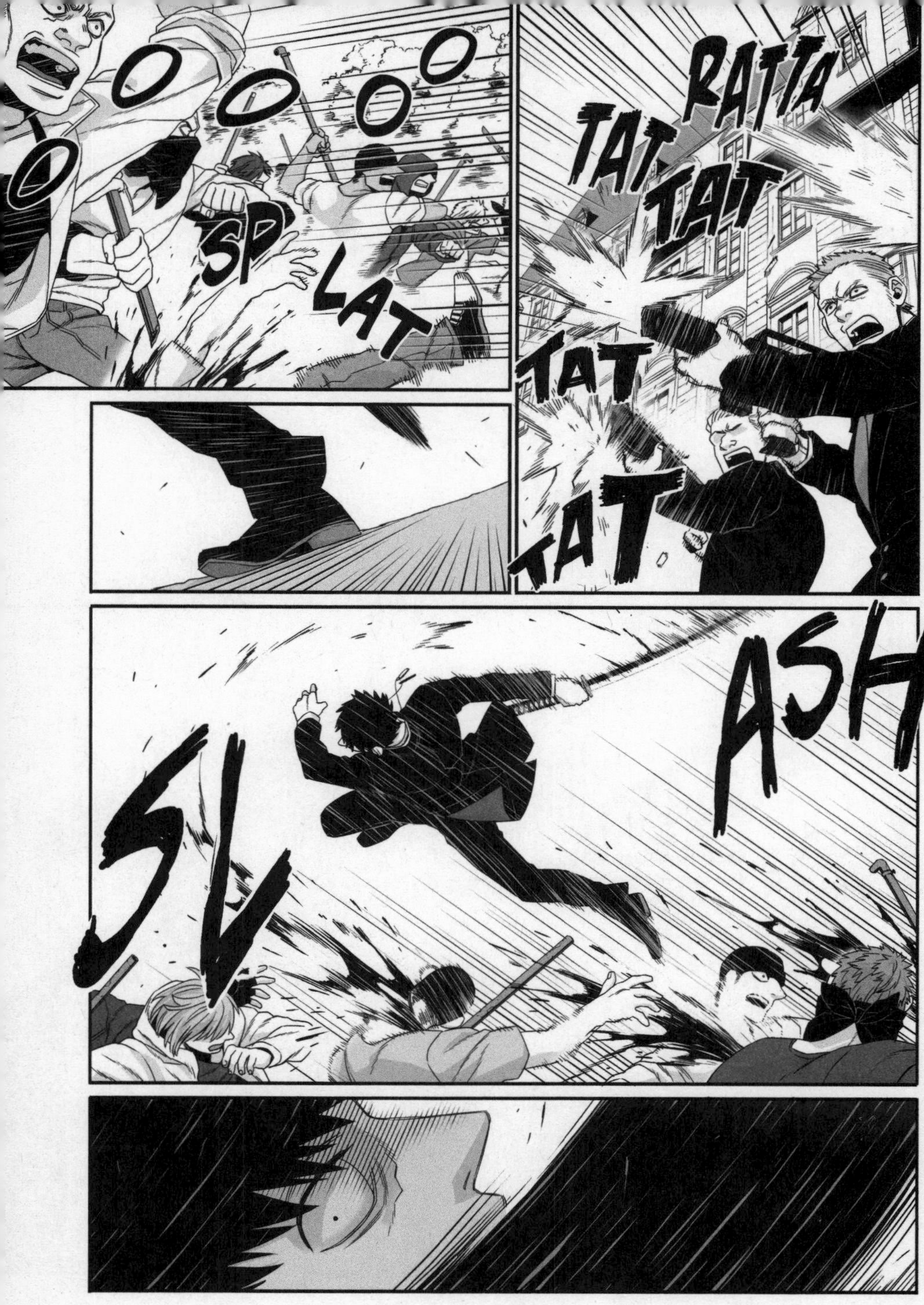
RATTA
TAT TAT
TAT
TAT TAT
OOOOOO
SPLAT
SLASH

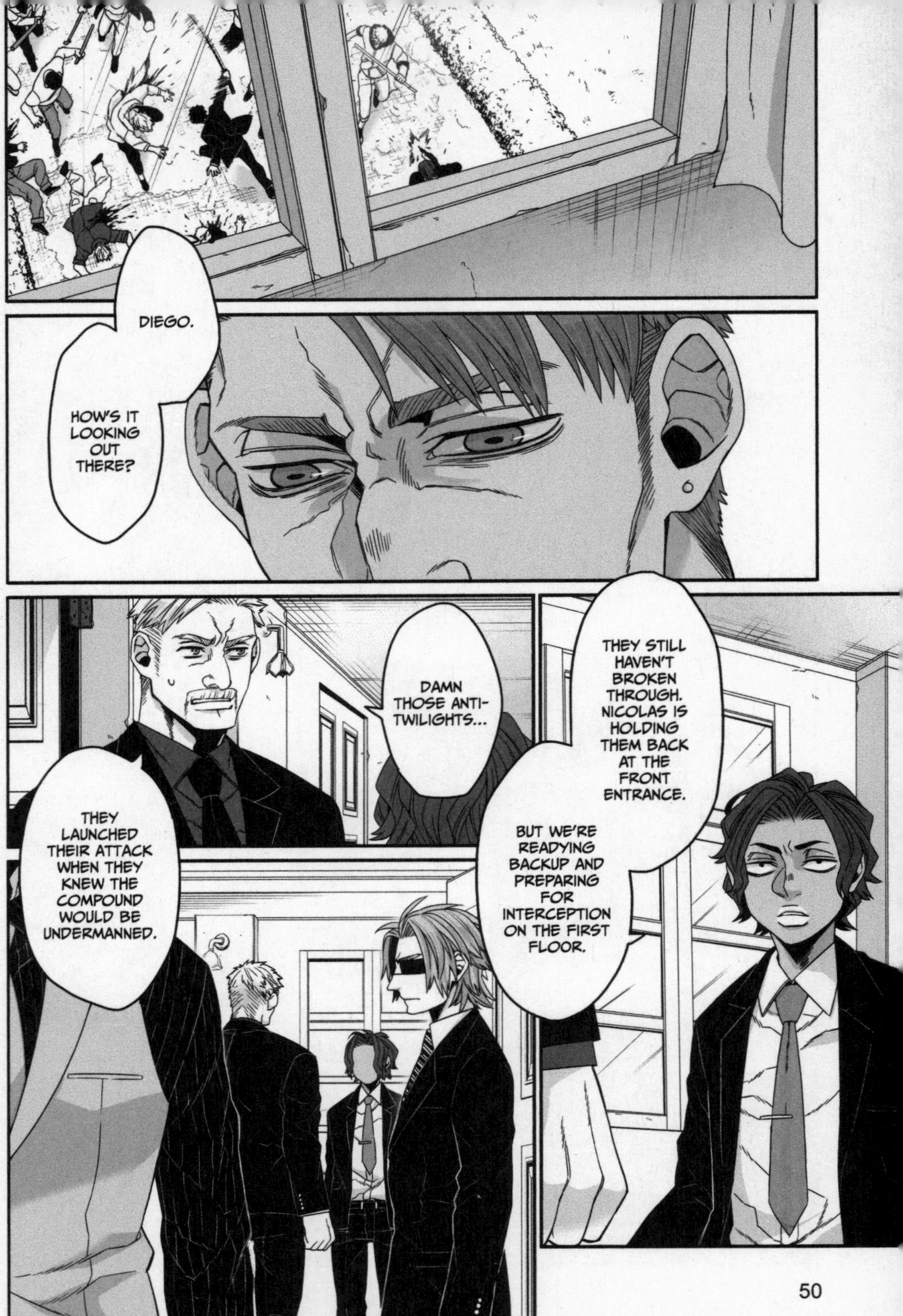
DIEGO.
HOW'S IT LOOKING OUT THERE?
THEY STILL HAVEN'T BROKEN THROUGH. NICOLAS IS HOLDING THEM BACK AT THE FRONT ENTRANCE.
BUT WE'RE READYING BACKUP AND PREPARING FOR INTERCEPTION ON THE FIRST FLOOR.
DAMN THOSE ANTI-TWILIGHTS...
THEY LAUNCHED THEIR ATTACK WHEN THEY KNEW THE COMPOUND WOULD BE UNDERMANNED.

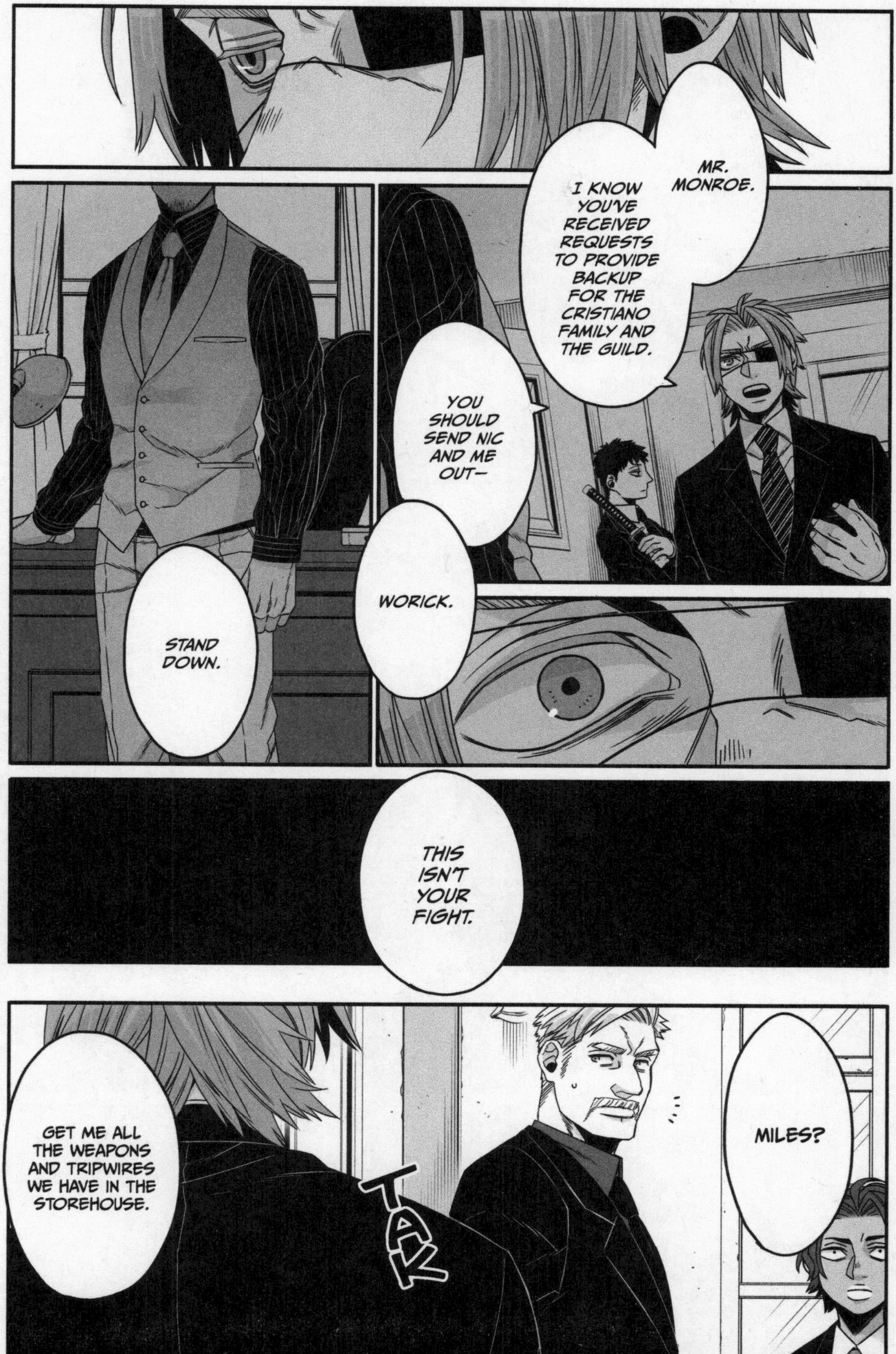
MR. MONROE. I KNOW YOU'VE RECEIVED REQUESTS TO PROVIDE BACKUP FOR THE CRISTIANO FAMILY AND THE GUILD.
YOU SHOULD SEND NIC AND ME OUT—
WORICK.
STAND DOWN.
THIS ISN'T YOUR FIGHT.
MILES?
GET ME ALL THE WEAPONS AND TRIPWIRES WE HAVE IN THE STOREHOUSE.
TAK

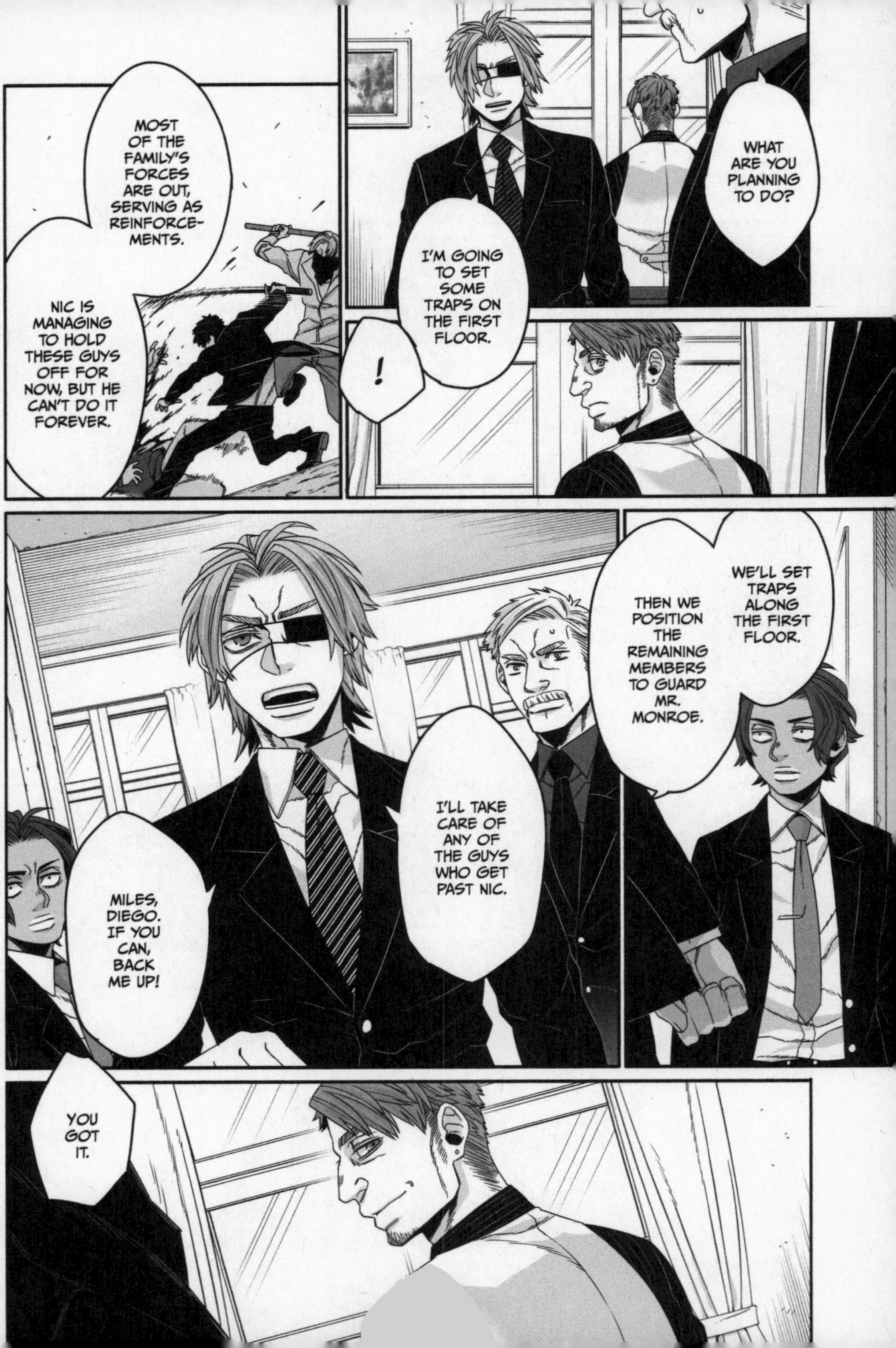
WHAT ARE YOU PLANNING TO DO?
I'M GOING TO SET SOME TRAPS ON THE FIRST FLOOR.
!
MOST OF THE FAMILY'S FORCES ARE OUT, SERVING AS REINFORCE-MENTS.
NIC IS MANAGING TO HOLD THESE GUYS OFF FOR NOW, BUT HE CAN'T DO IT FOREVER.
WE'LL SET TRAPS ALONG THE FIRST FLOOR.
THEN WE POSITION THE REMAINING MEMBERS TO GUARD MR. MONROE.
I'LL TAKE CARE OF ANY OF THE GUYS WHO GET PAST NIC.
MILES, DIEGO. IF YOU CAN, BACK ME UP!
YOU GOT IT.

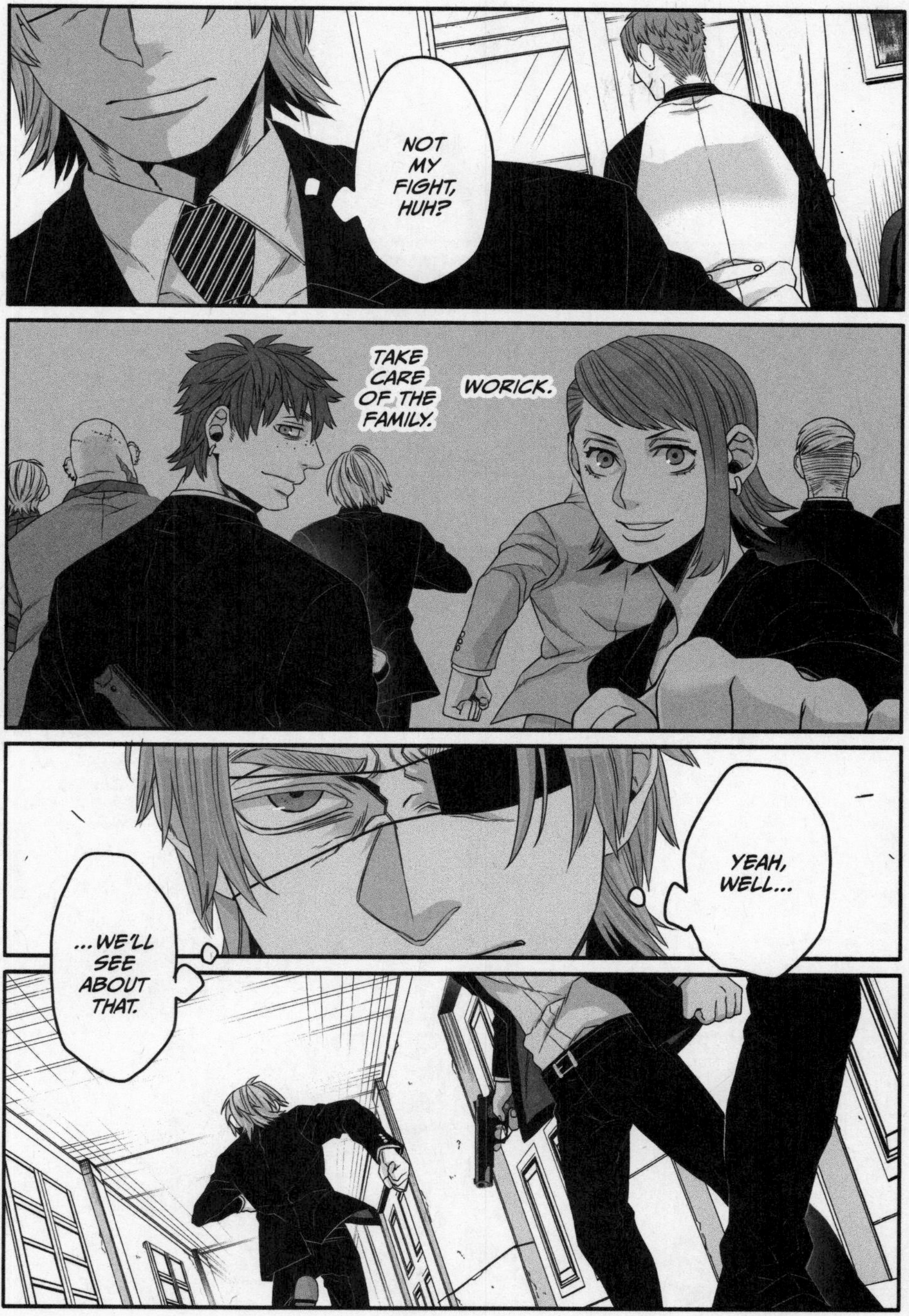
NOT MY FIGHT, HUH?
WORICK.
TAKE CARE OF THE FAMILY.
YEAH, WELL...
...WE'LL SEE ABOUT THAT.

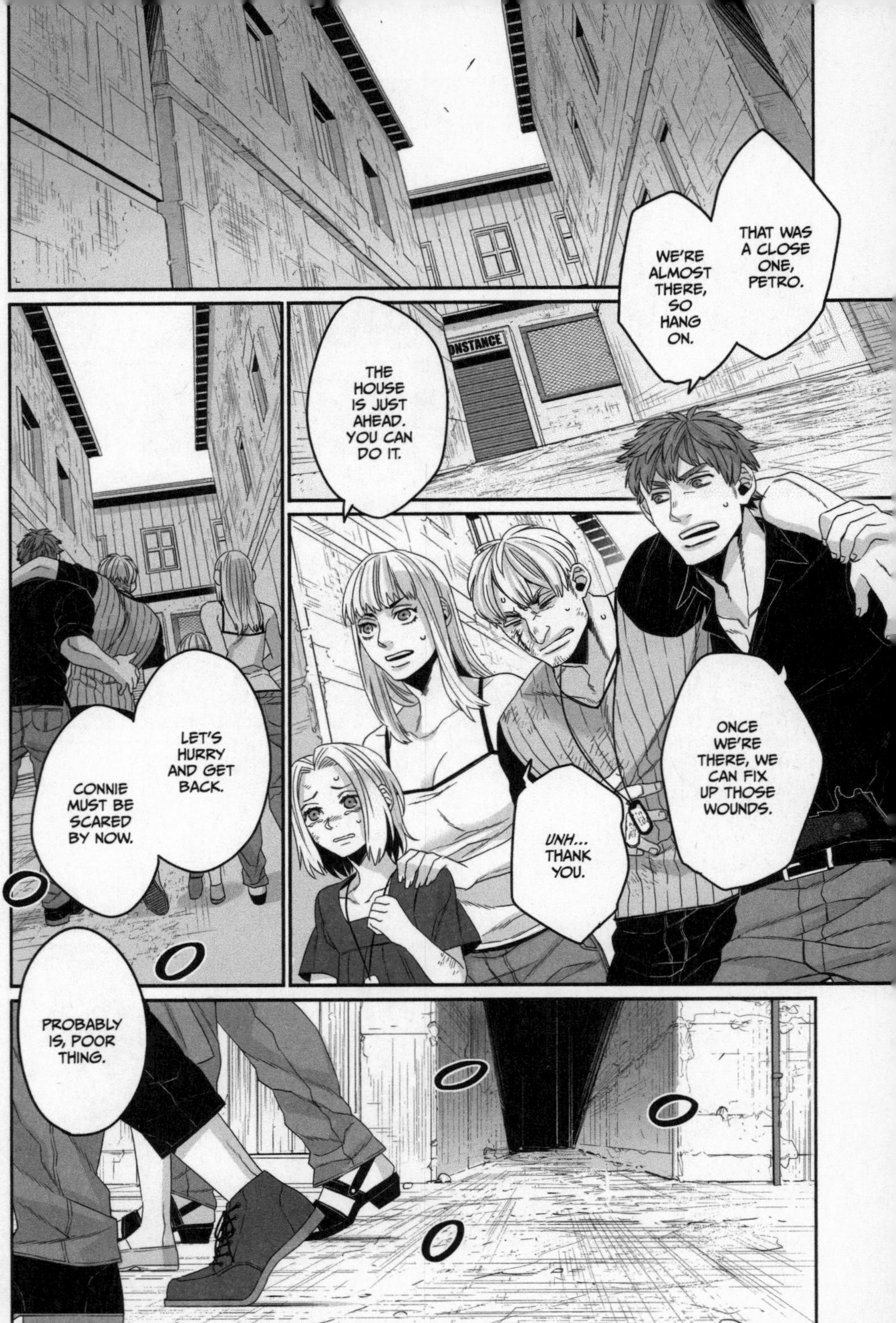
THAT WAS A CLOSE ONE, PETRO.
WE'RE ALMOST THERE, SO HANG ON.
ONSTANCE
THE HOUSE IS JUST AHEAD. YOU CAN DO IT.
ONCE WE'RE THERE, WE CAN FIX UP THOSE WOUNDS.
UNH... THANK YOU.
LET'S HURRY AND GET BACK.
CONNIE MUST BE SCARED BY NOW.
PROBABLY IS, POOR THING.

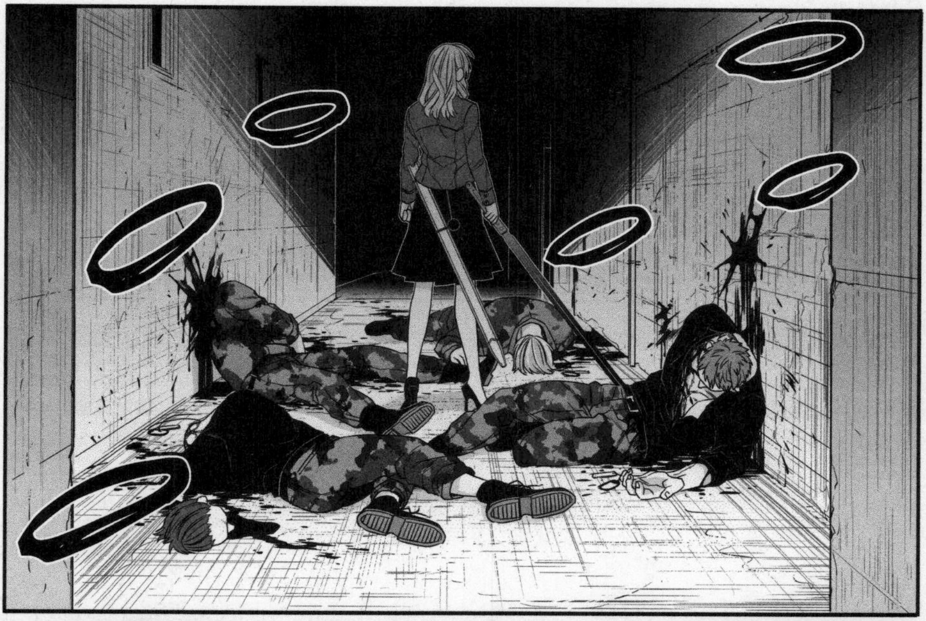

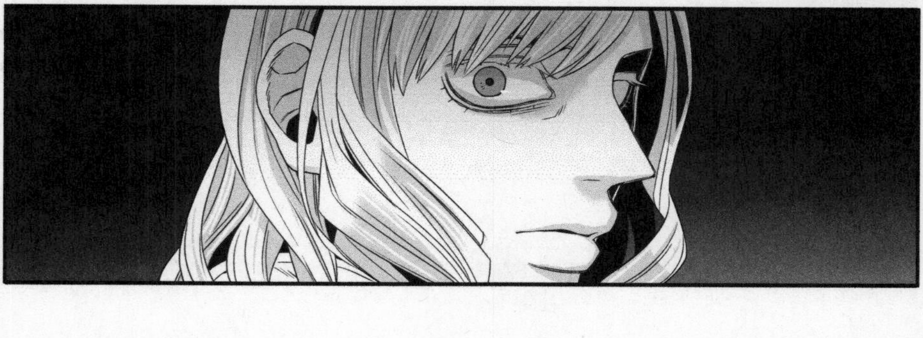

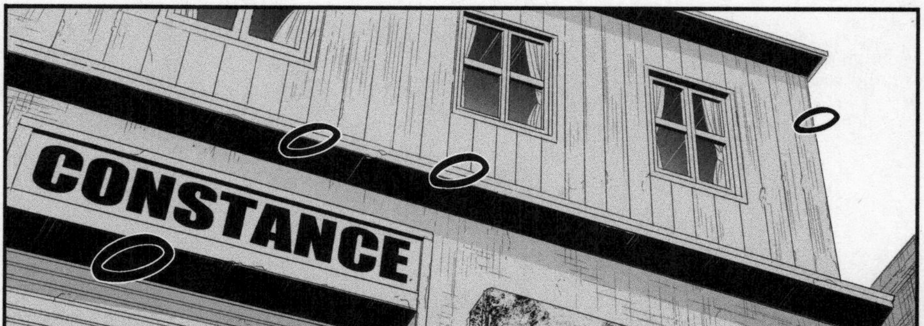
CONSTANCE

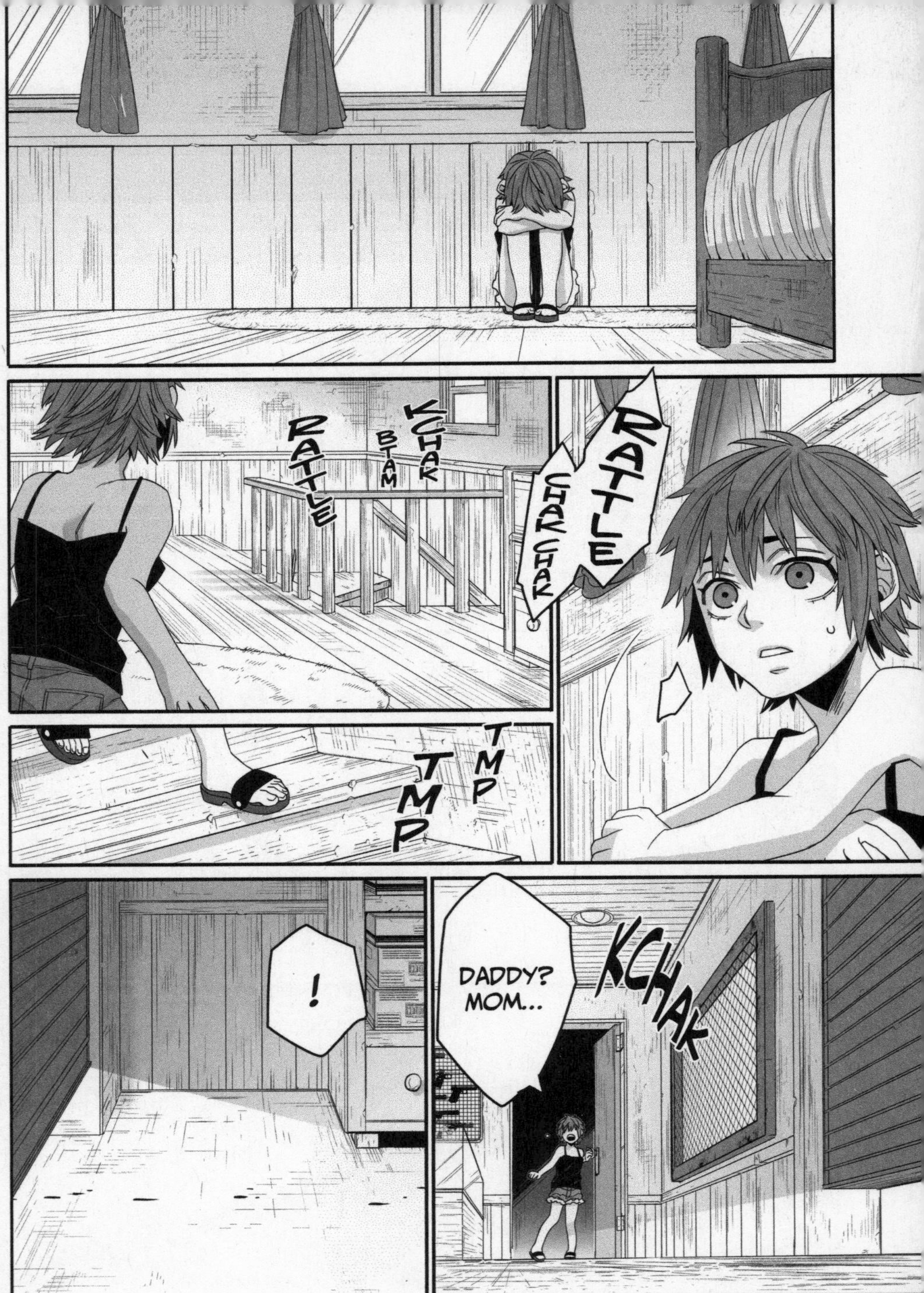
RATTLE
CHAK CHAK
KCHAK
BTAM
RATTLE
TMP
TMP
KCHAK
DADDY? MOM...
!

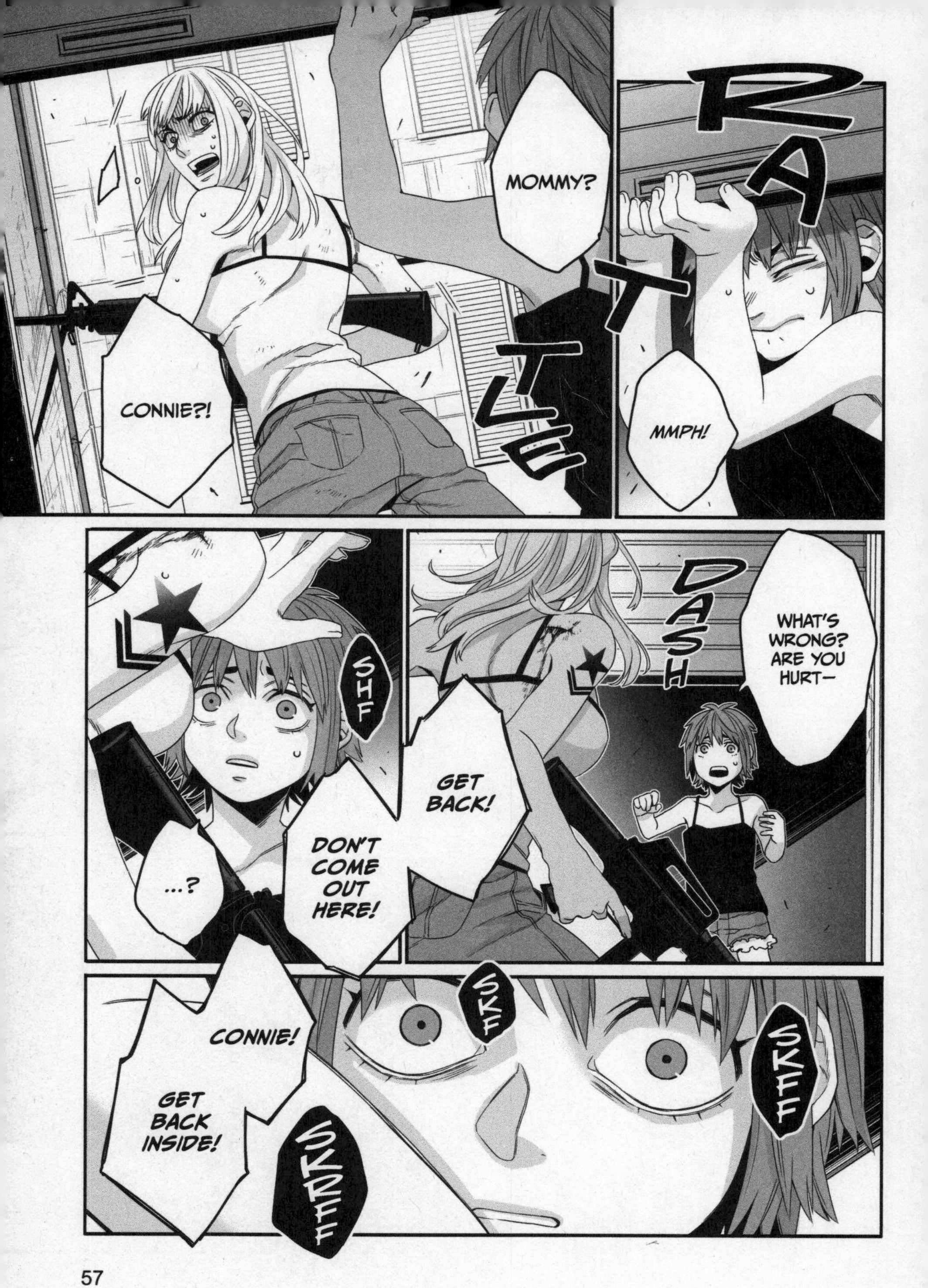
RATTLE
MMPH!
MOMMY?
CONNIE?!
DASH
WHAT'S WRONG? ARE YOU HURT—
GET BACK!
DON'T COME OUT HERE!
SHF
...?
SKFF
SKF
CONNIE!
GET BACK INSIDE!
SKRFF

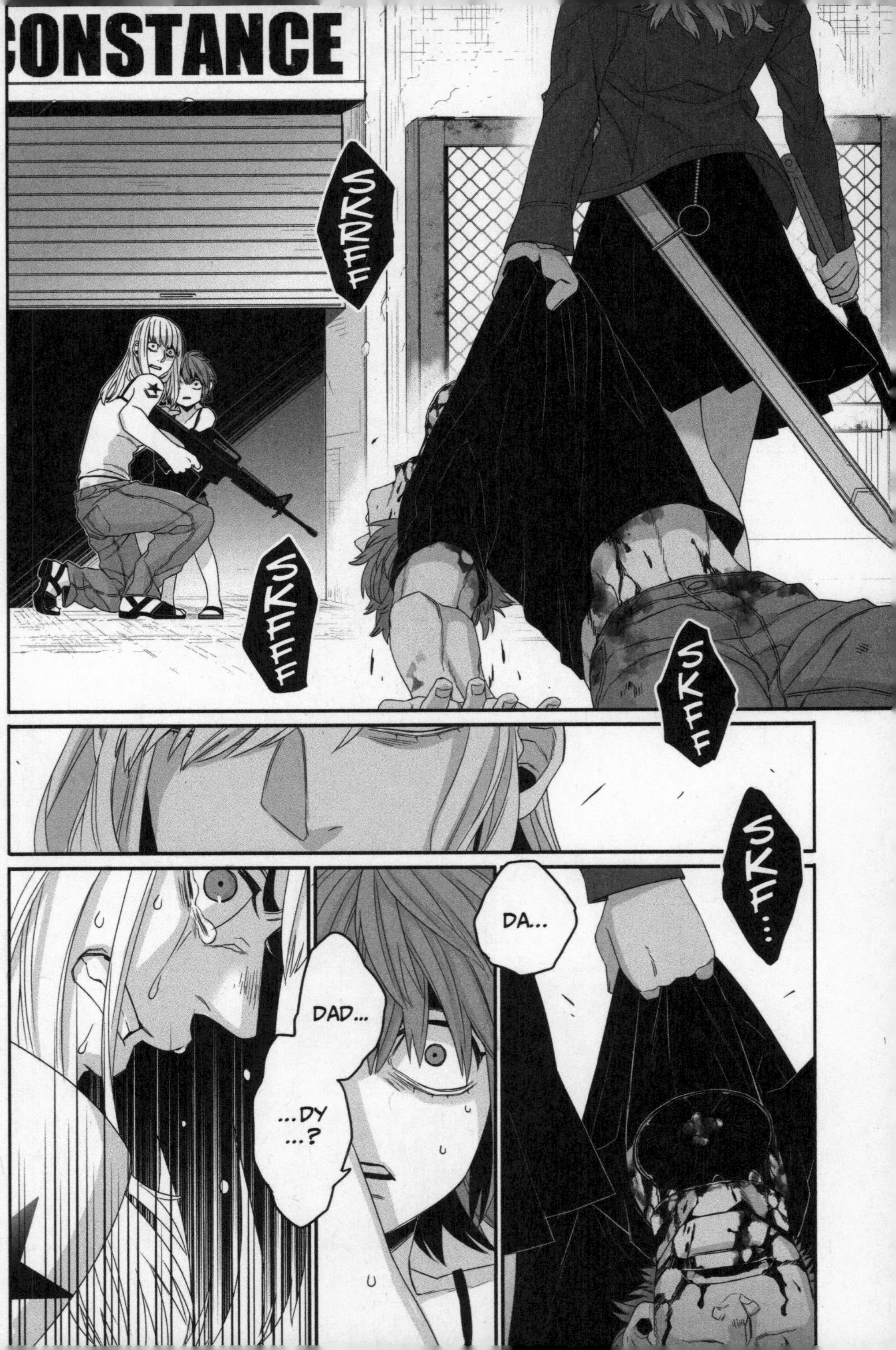
CONSTANCE
SKREFF
SKFFF
SKFF
SKF...
DA...
DAD...
...DY
...?

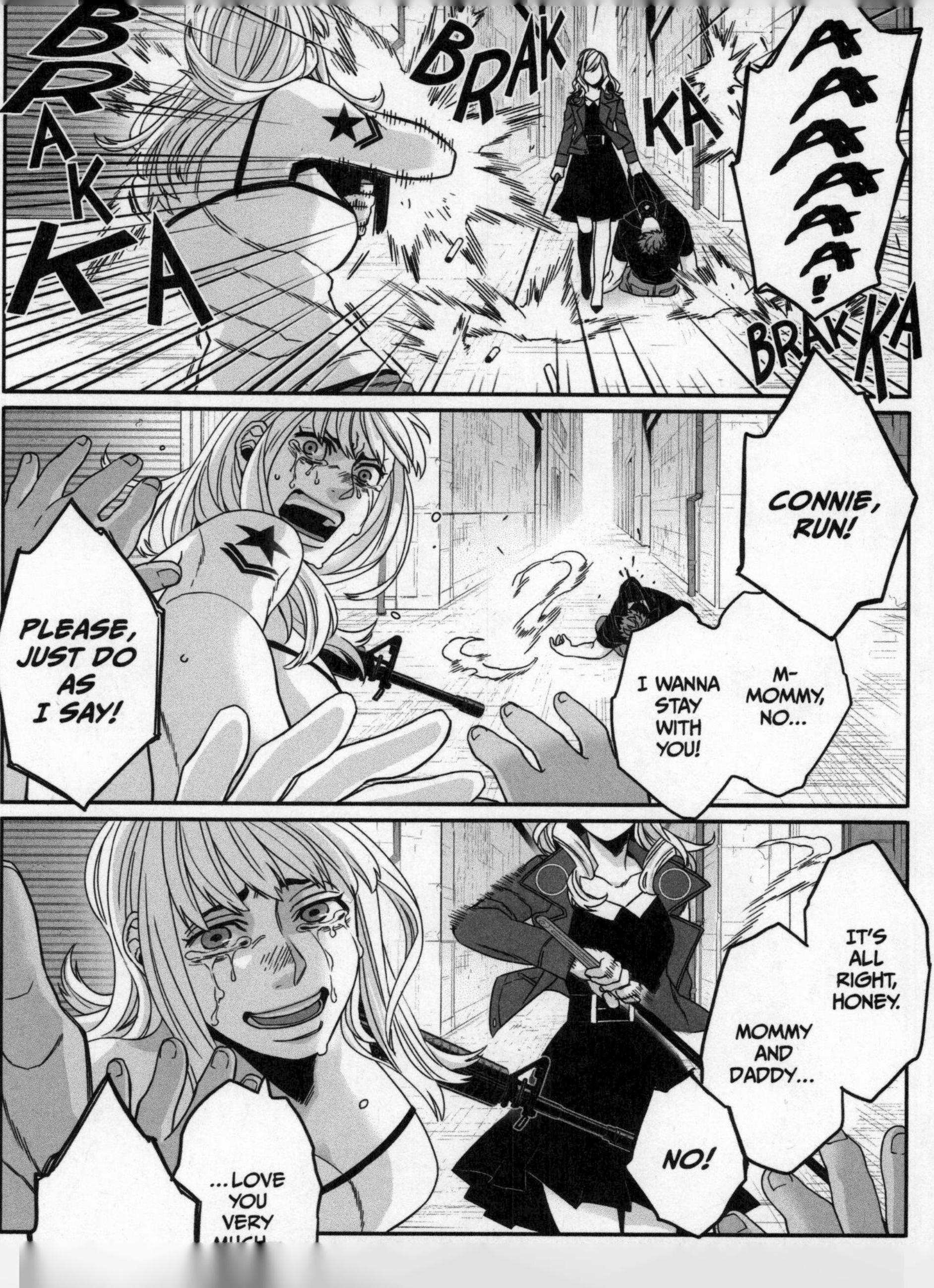
AAAAAAA!
BRAKKA
BRÄK KA
BRAKKA
CONNIE, RUN!
M-MOMMY, NO...
I WANNA STAY WITH YOU!
PLEASE, JUST DO AS I SAY!
IT'S ALL RIGHT, HONEY.
MOMMY AND DADDY...
NO!
...LOVE YOU VERY

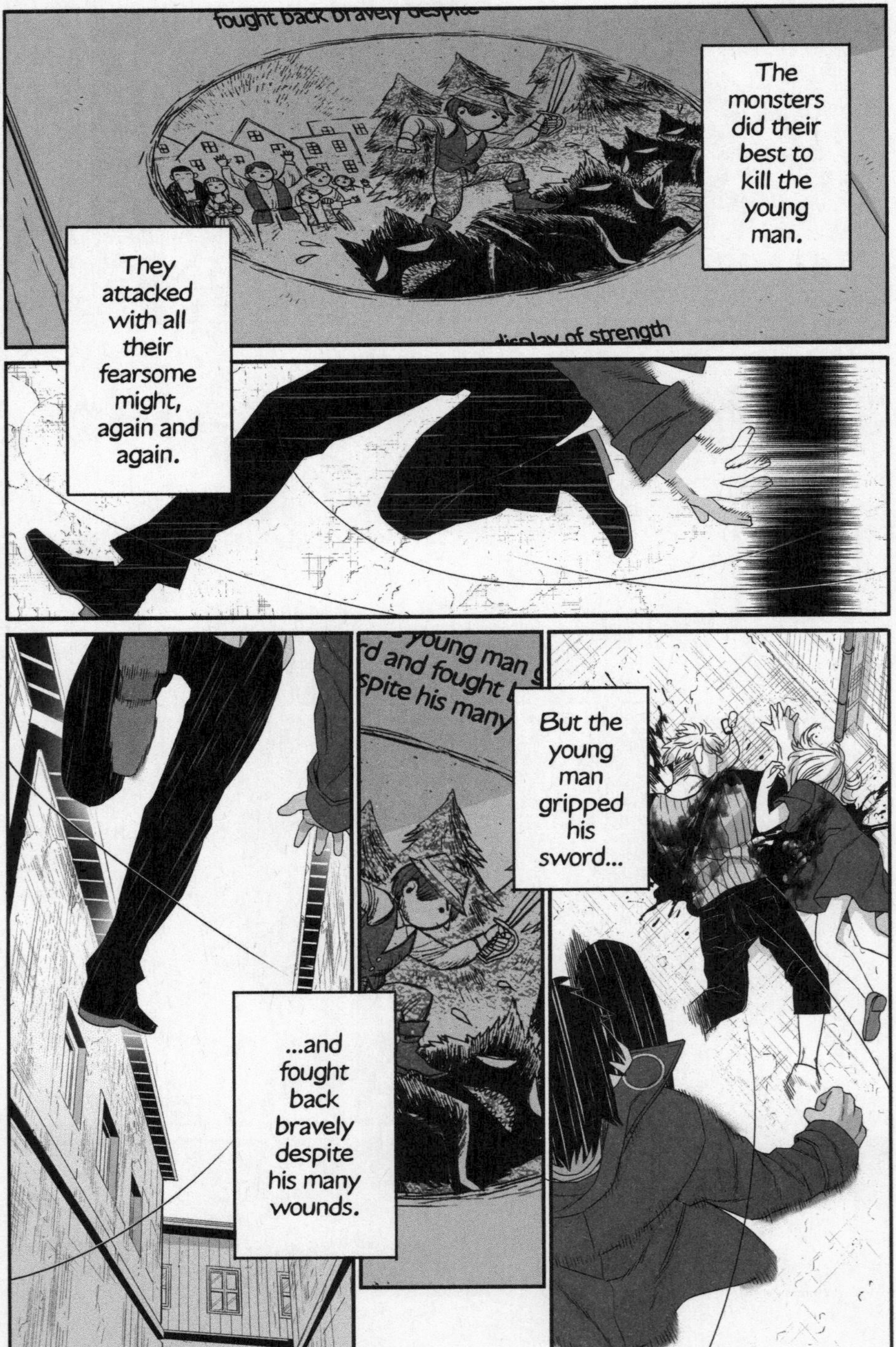
The monsters did their best to kill the young man.
fought back bravely despite
They attacked with all their fearsome might, again and again.
display of strength
But the young man gripped his sword...
young man
and fought
his many
...and fought back bravely despite his many wounds.

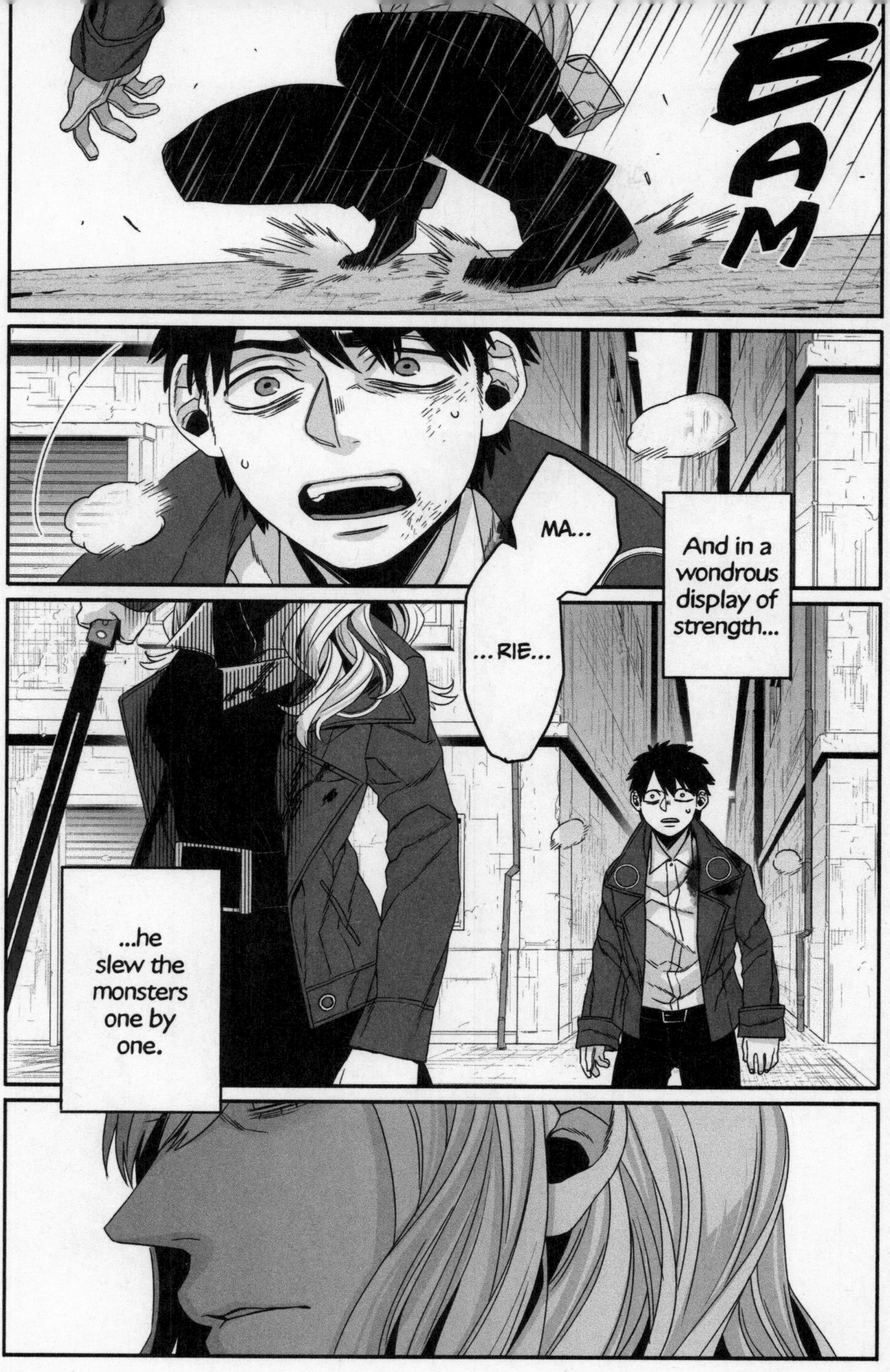
BAM
MA...
And in a wondrous display of strength...
...RIE...
...he slew the monsters one by one.

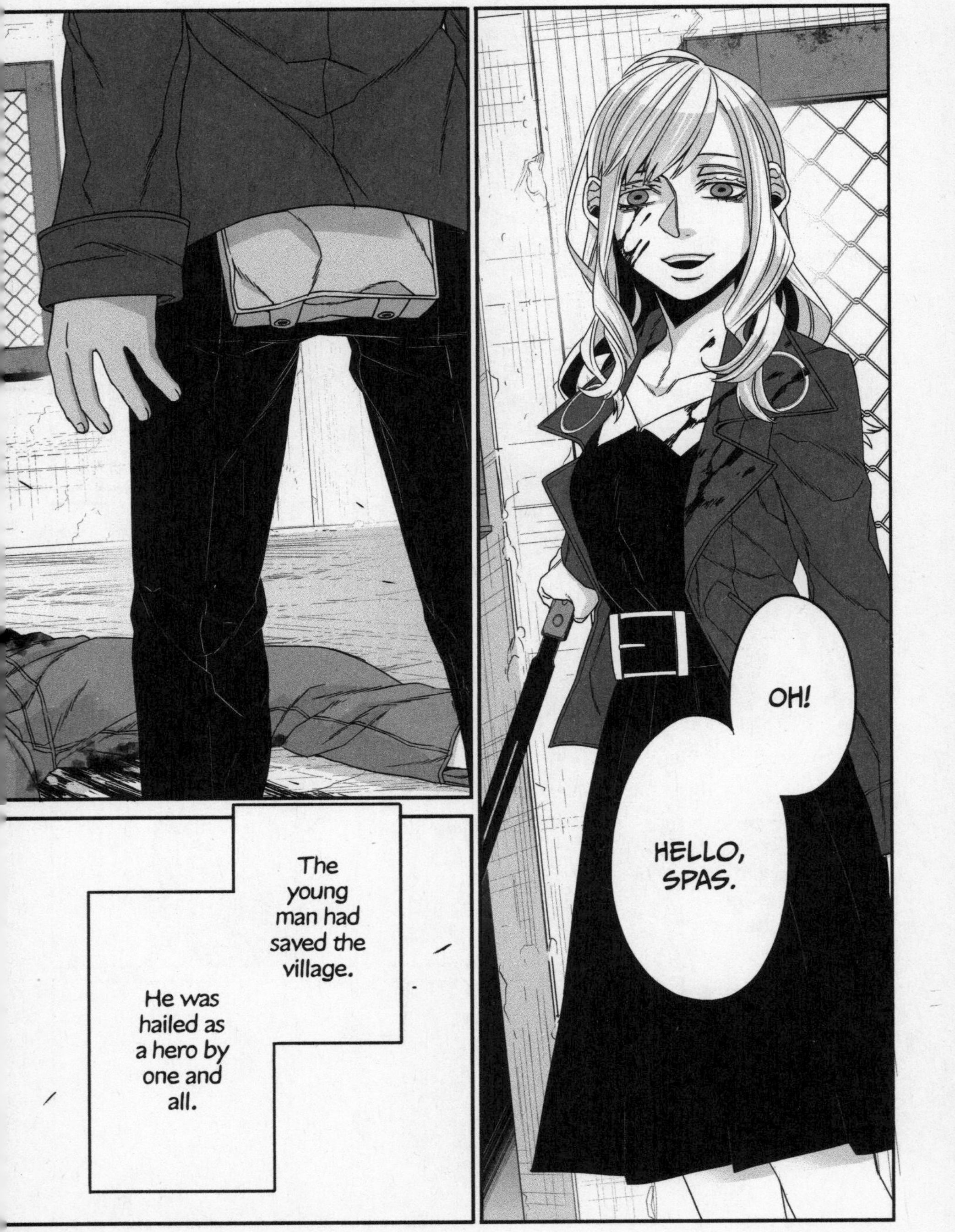
OH!
HELLO, SPAS.
The young man had saved the village.
He was hailed as a hero by one and all.

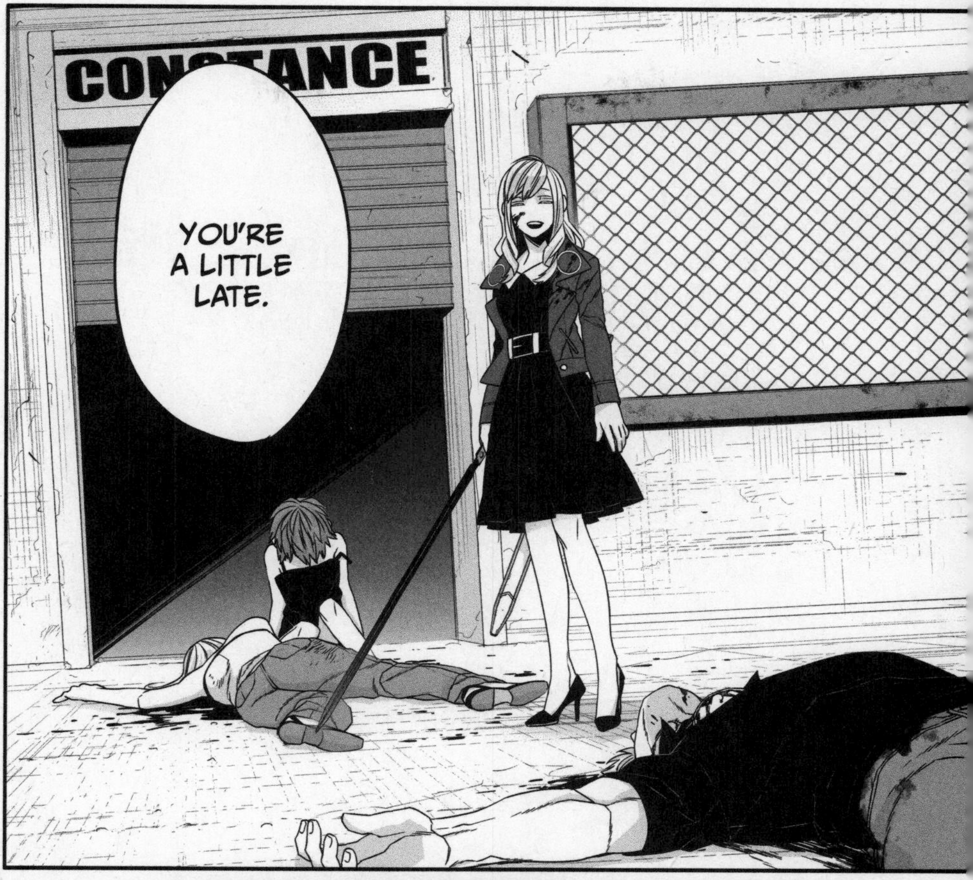
CONSTANCE
YOU'RE A LITTLE LATE.
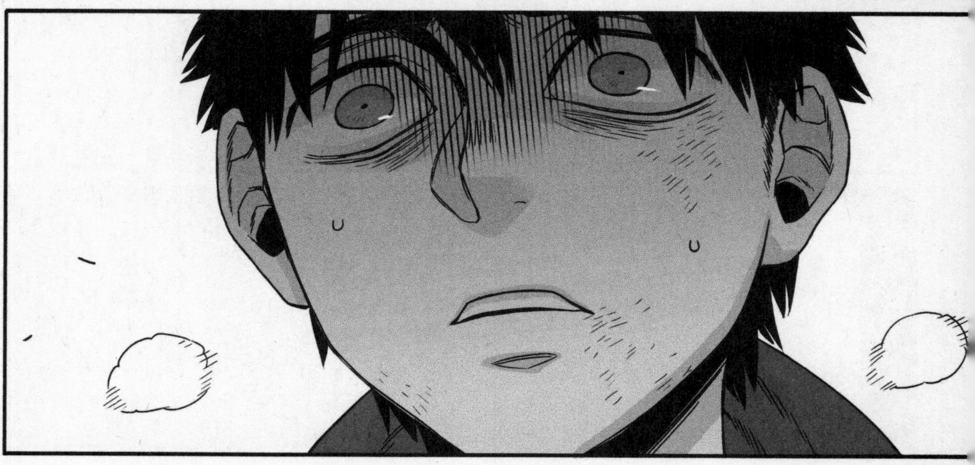

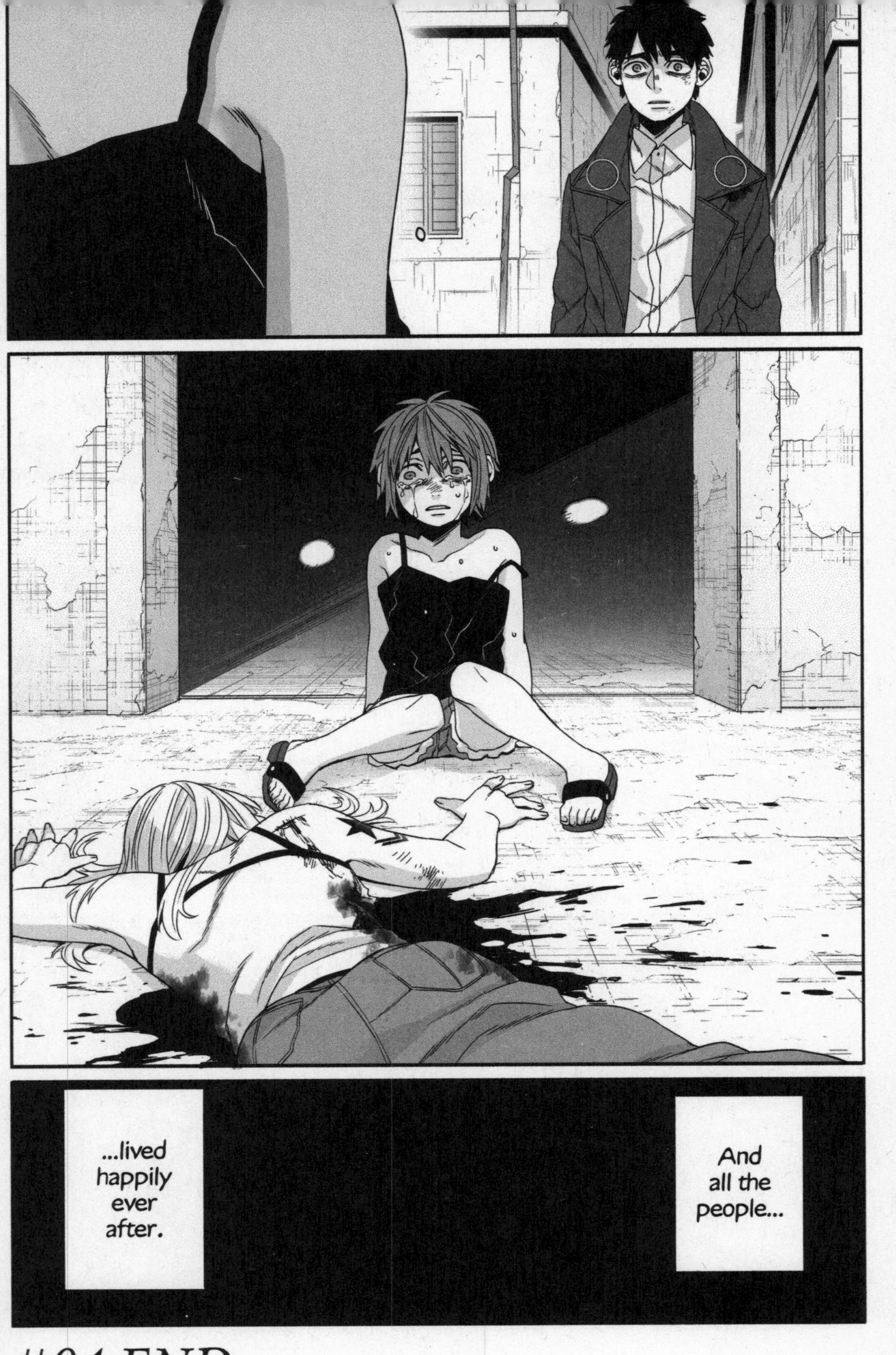
And all the people...
...lived happily ever after.

#04 END

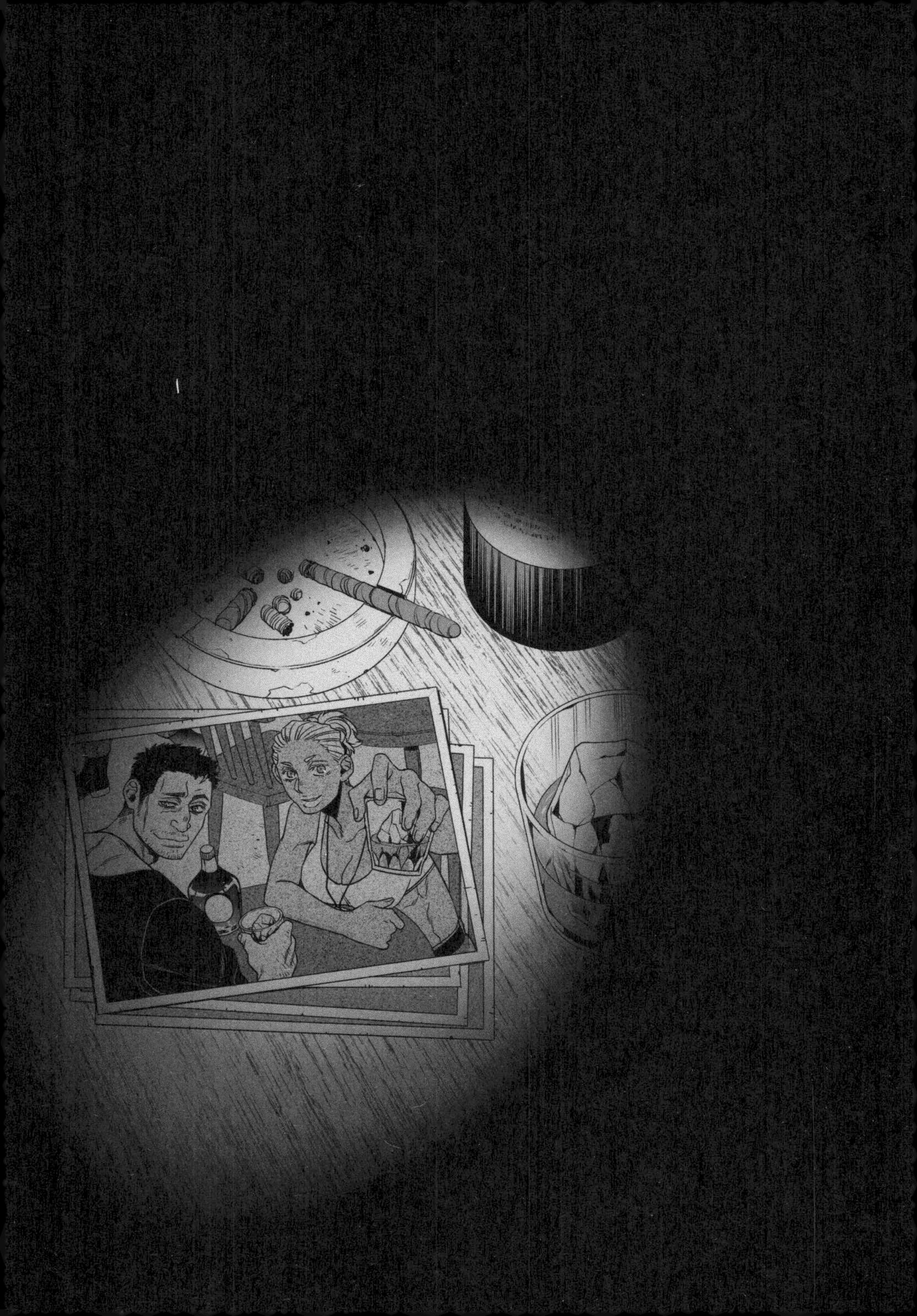

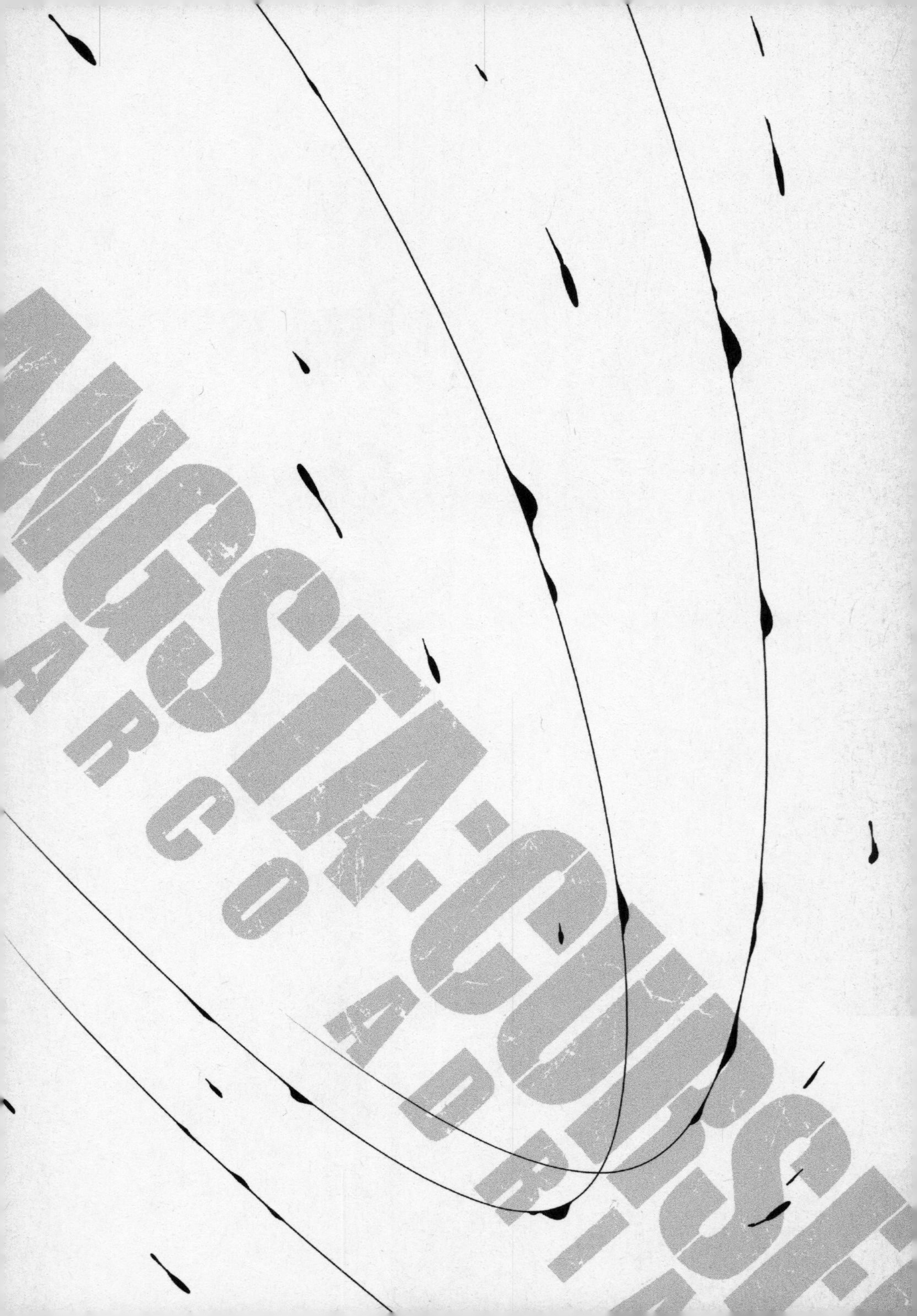
A R C O

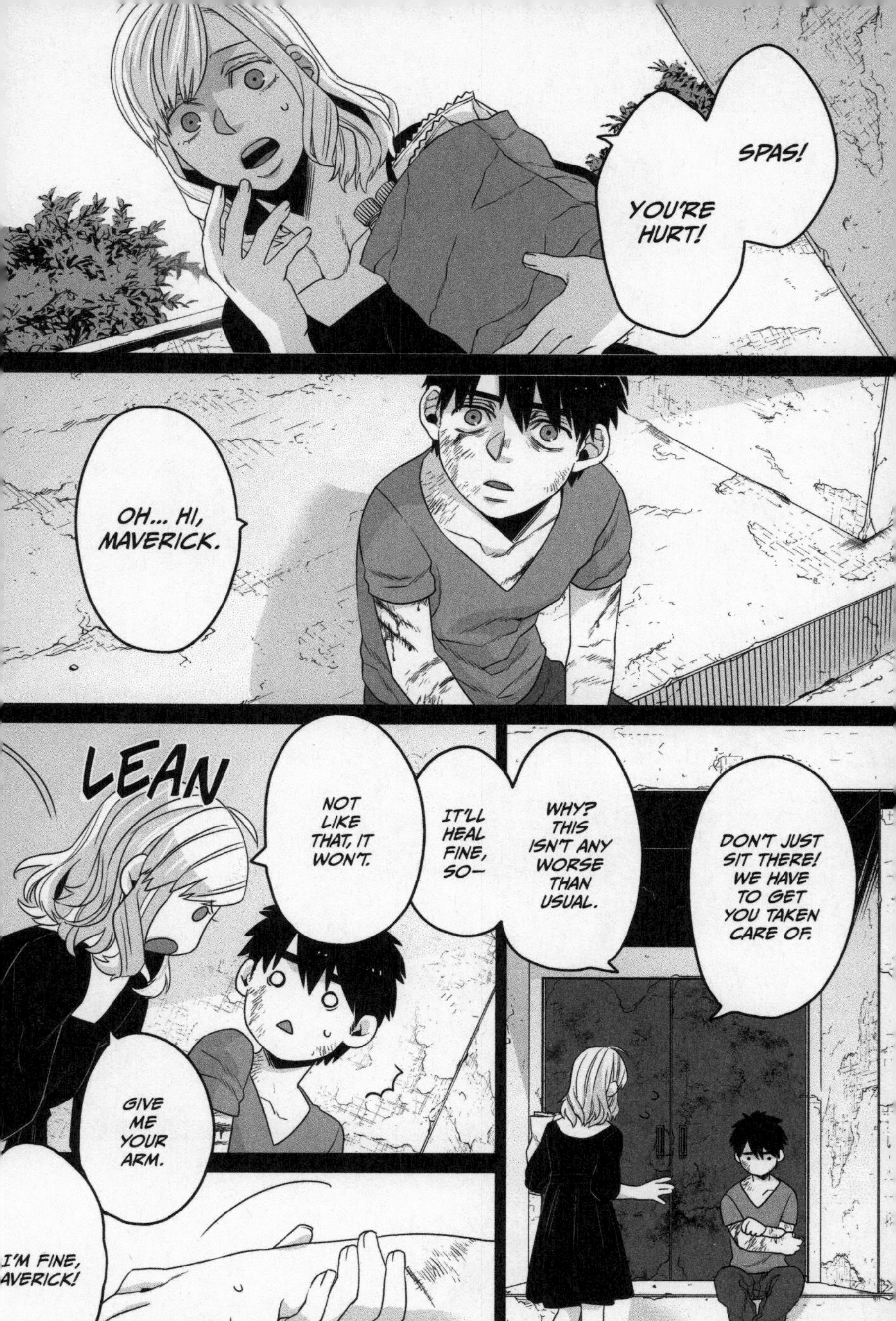
SPAS!
YOU'RE HURT!
OH... HI, MAVERICK.
DON'T JUST SIT THERE! WE HAVE TO GET YOU TAKEN CARE OF.
WHY? THIS ISN'T ANY WORSE THAN USUAL.
IT'LL HEAL FINE, SO—
LEAN
NOT LIKE THAT, IT WON'T.
GIVE ME YOUR ARM.
I'M FINE, AVERICK!

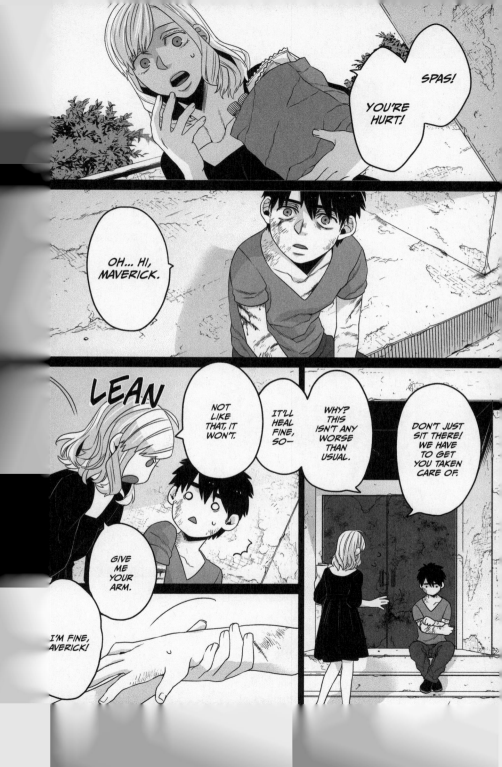

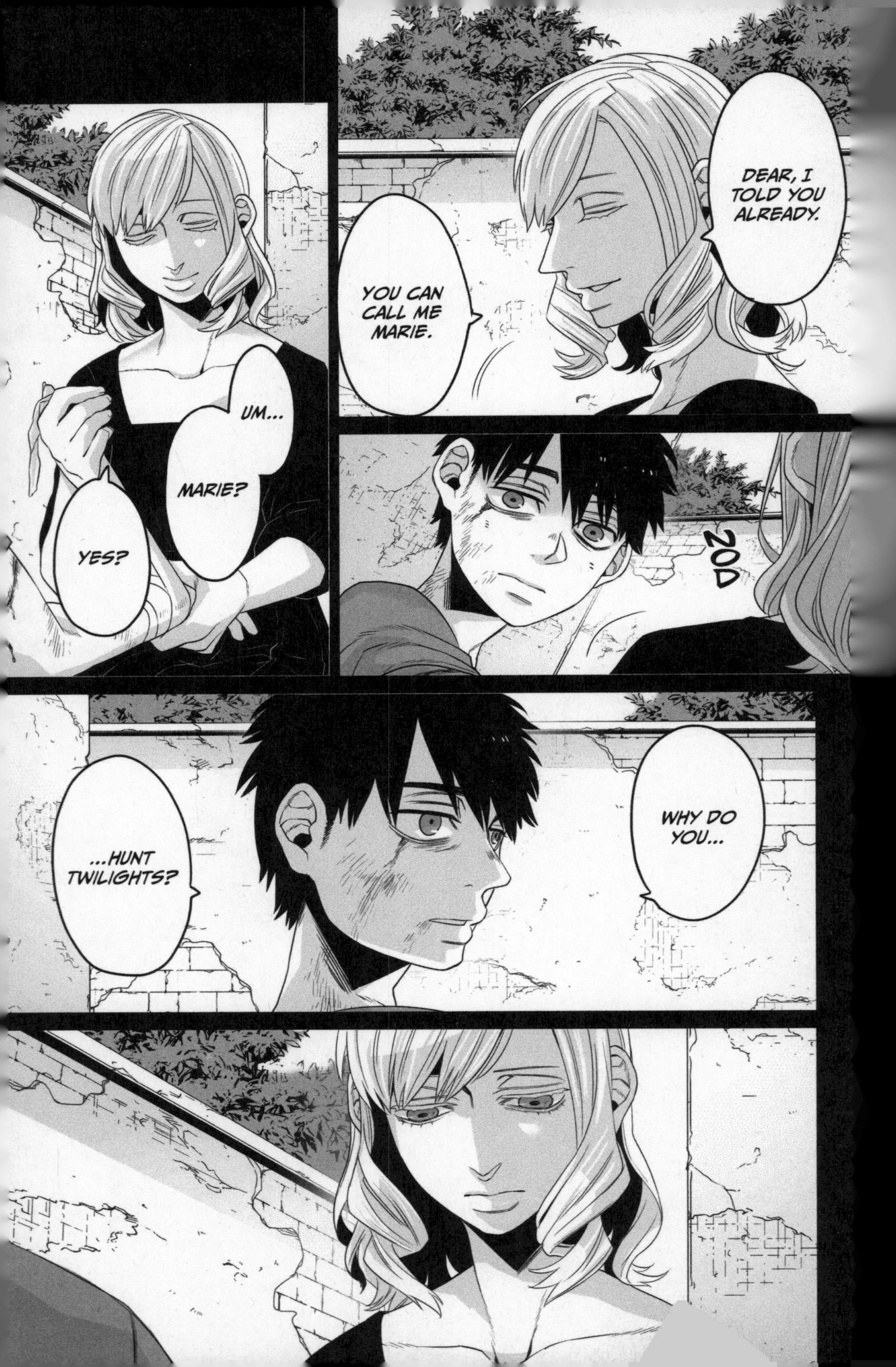
DEAR, I TOLD YOU ALREADY.
YOU CAN CALL ME MARIE.
ZOD
UM...
MARIE?
YES?
WHY DO YOU...
...HUNT TWILIGHTS?

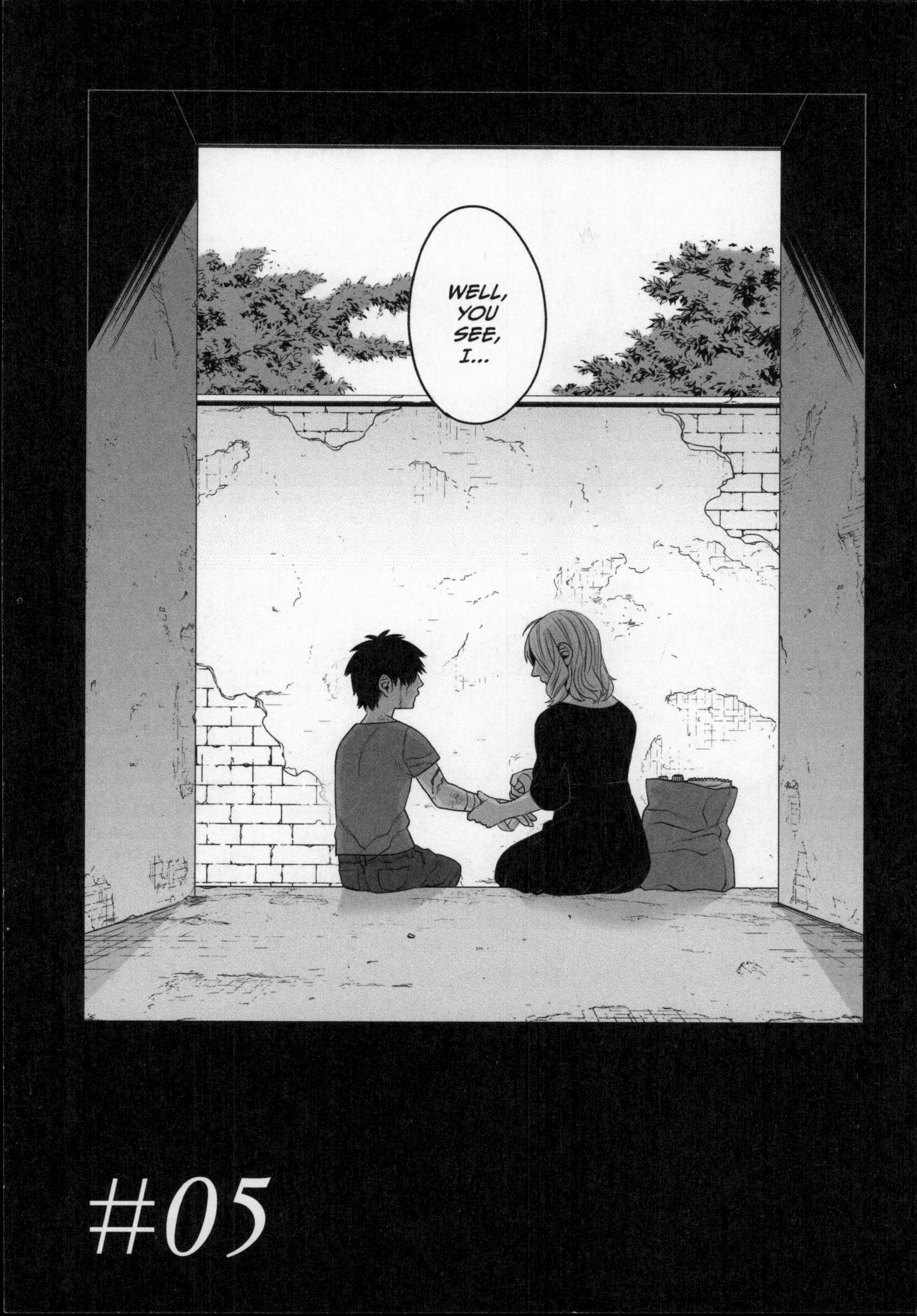
WELL, YOU SEE, I...

#05

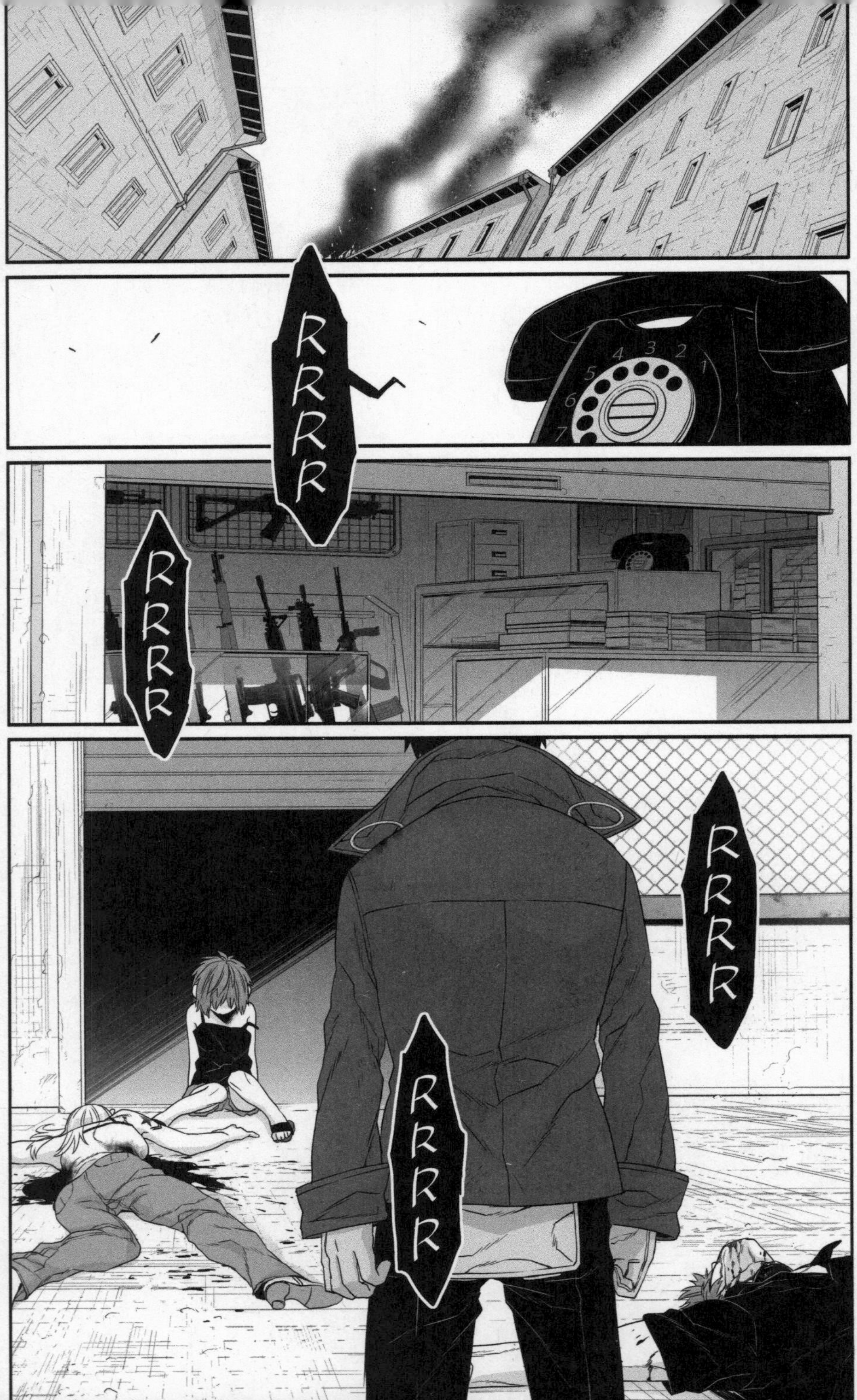
RRRR
RRRR
RRRR
RRRR

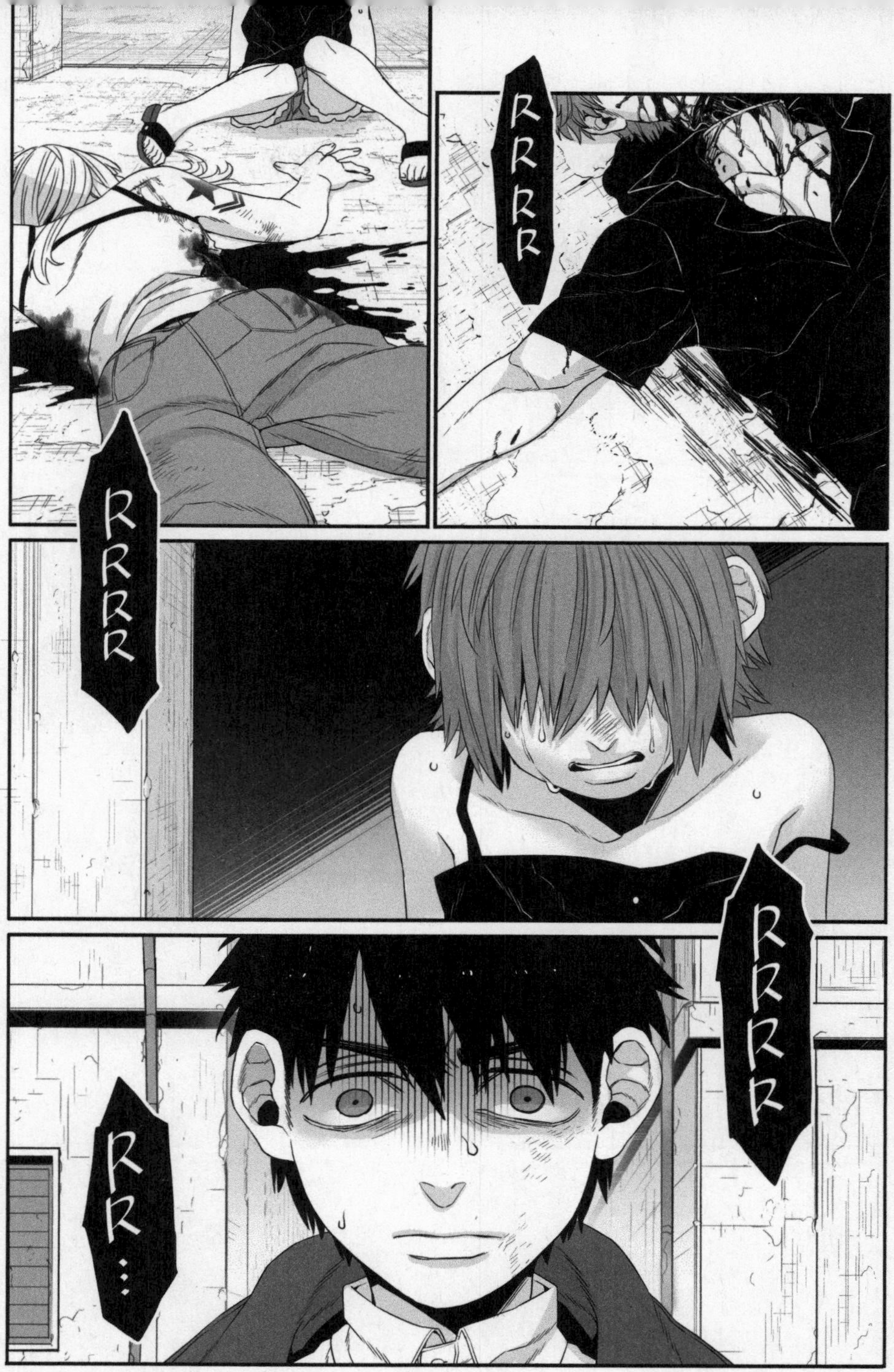
RRRR
RRRR
RRRR
RR...

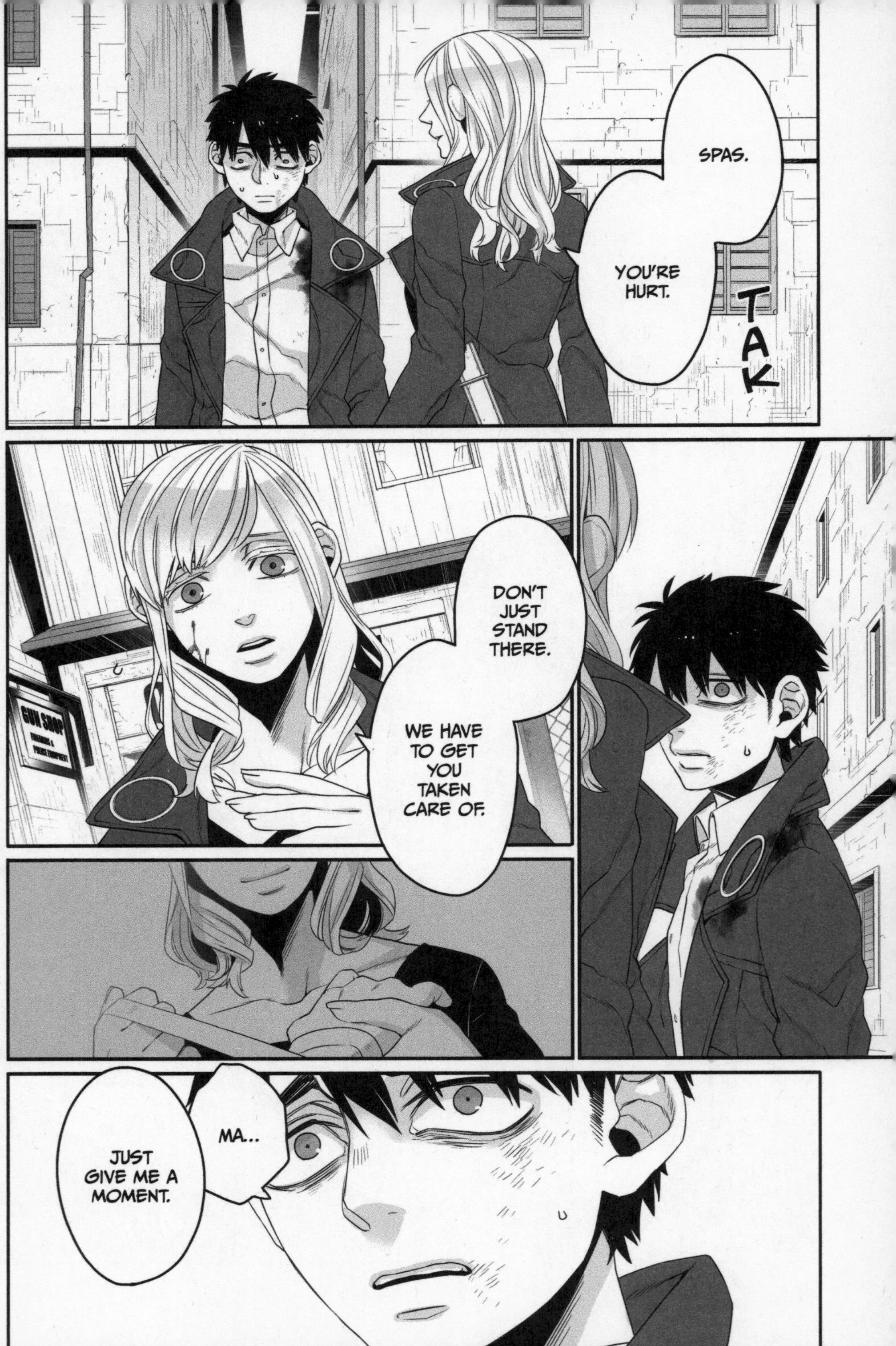
SPAS.
YOU'RE HURT.
TAK
DON'T JUST STAND THERE.
WE HAVE TO GET YOU TAKEN CARE OF.
GUN SHOP
MA...
JUST GIVE ME A MOMENT.

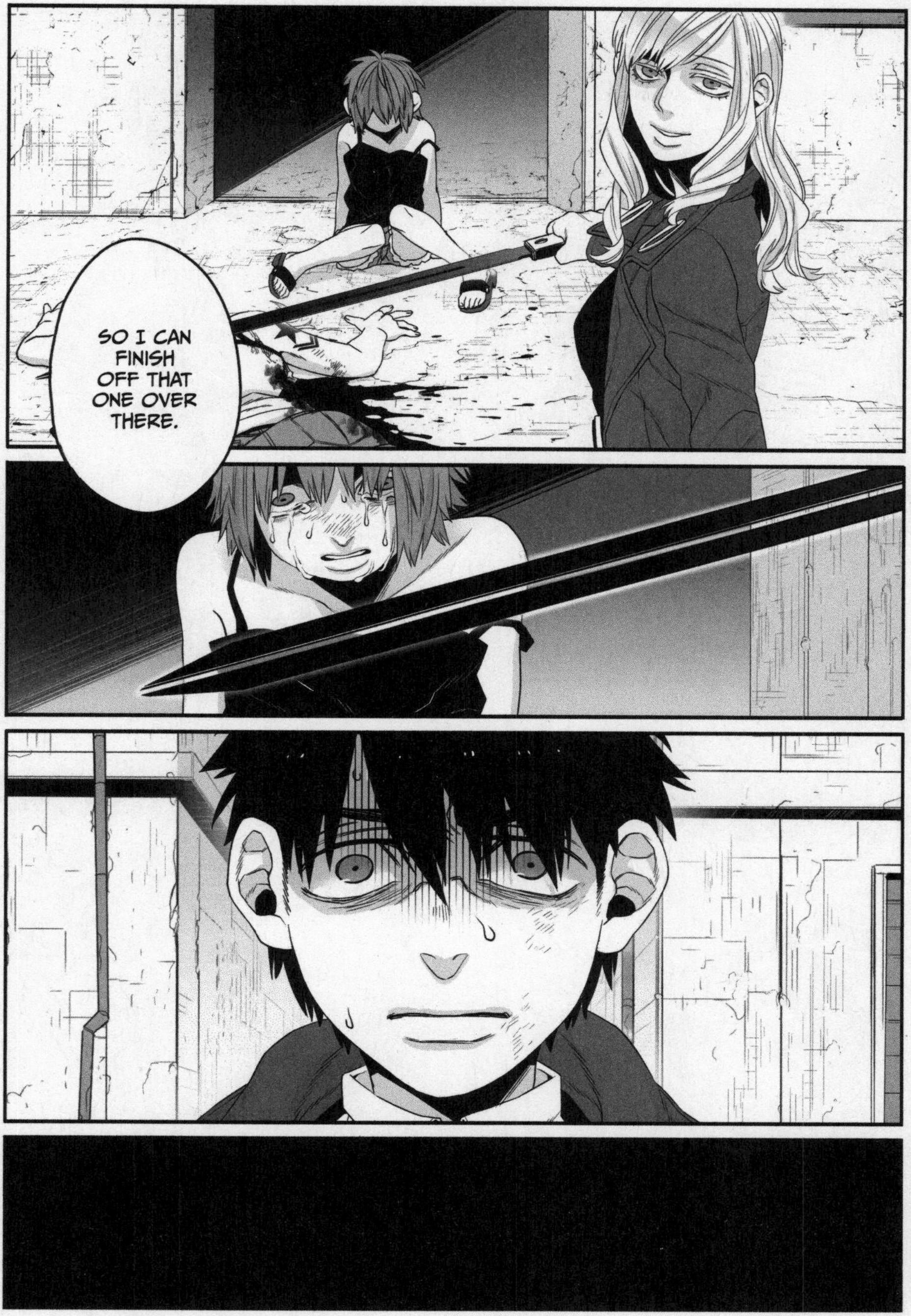
SO I CAN FINISH OFF THAT ONE OVER THERE.

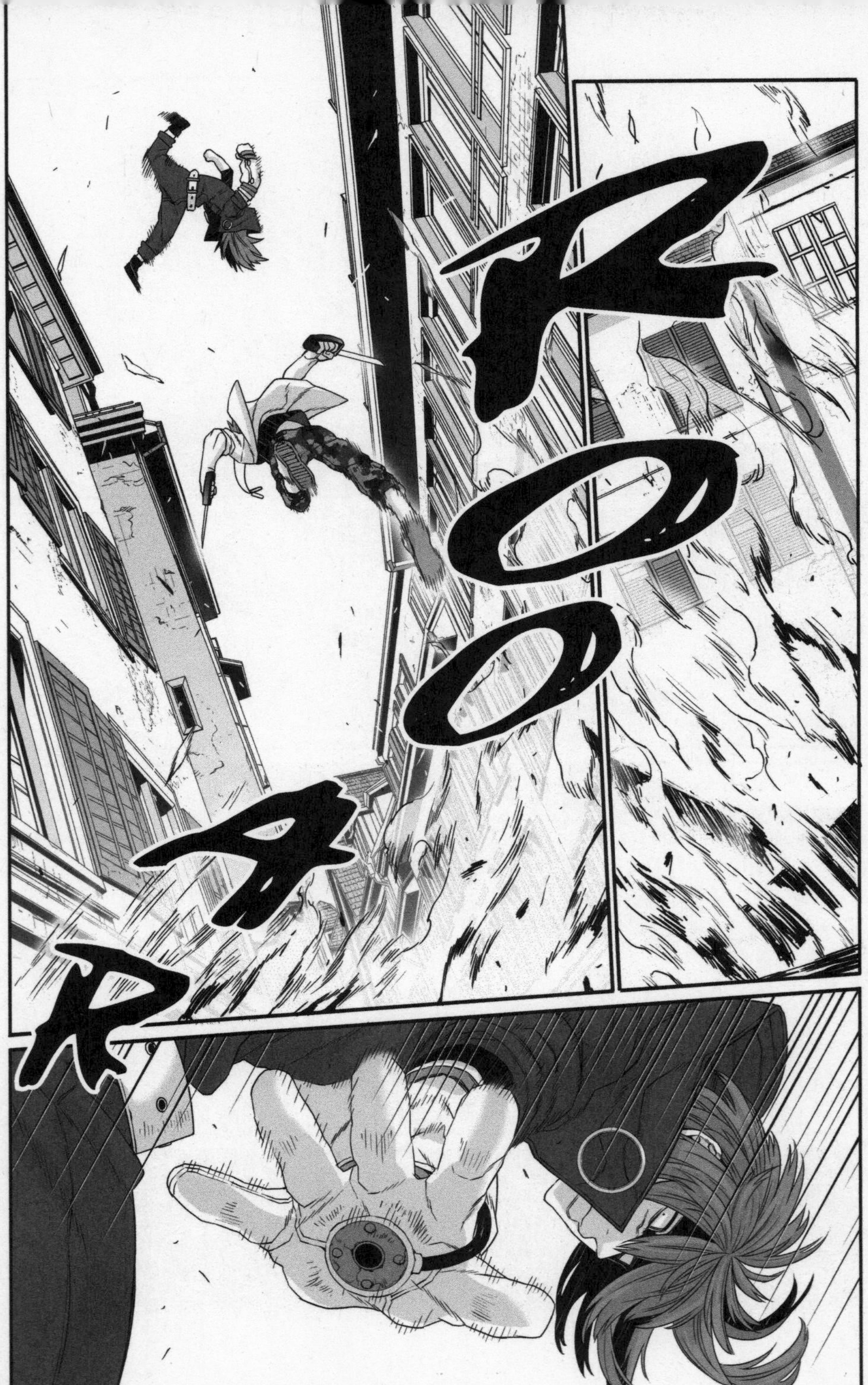
ROOAR

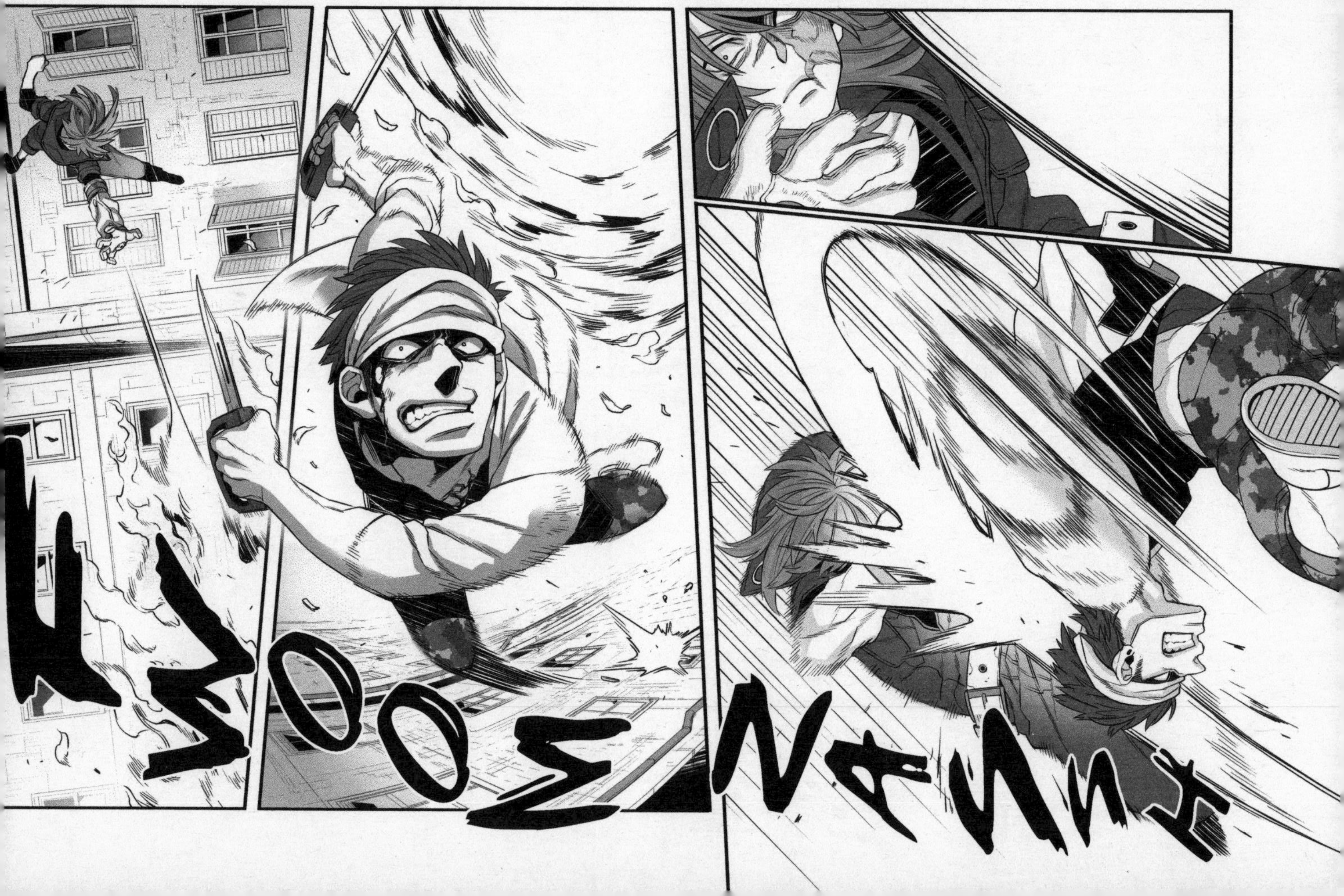
FWOOOM
WASH

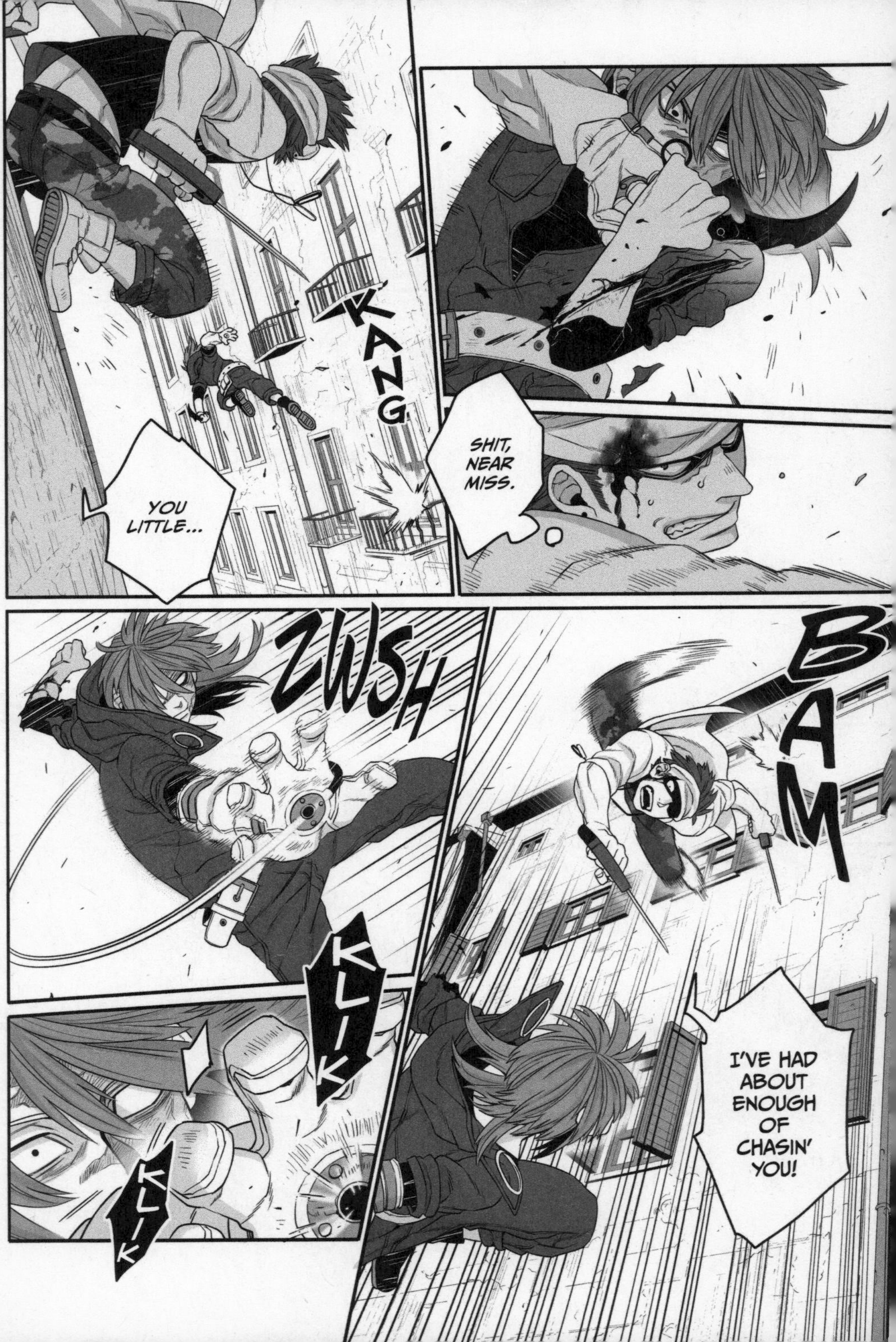
SHIT, NEAR MISS.
KANG
YOU LITTLE...
BAM
ZWSH
I'VE HAD ABOUT ENOUGH OF CHASIN' YOU!
KLIK
KLIK
KLIK

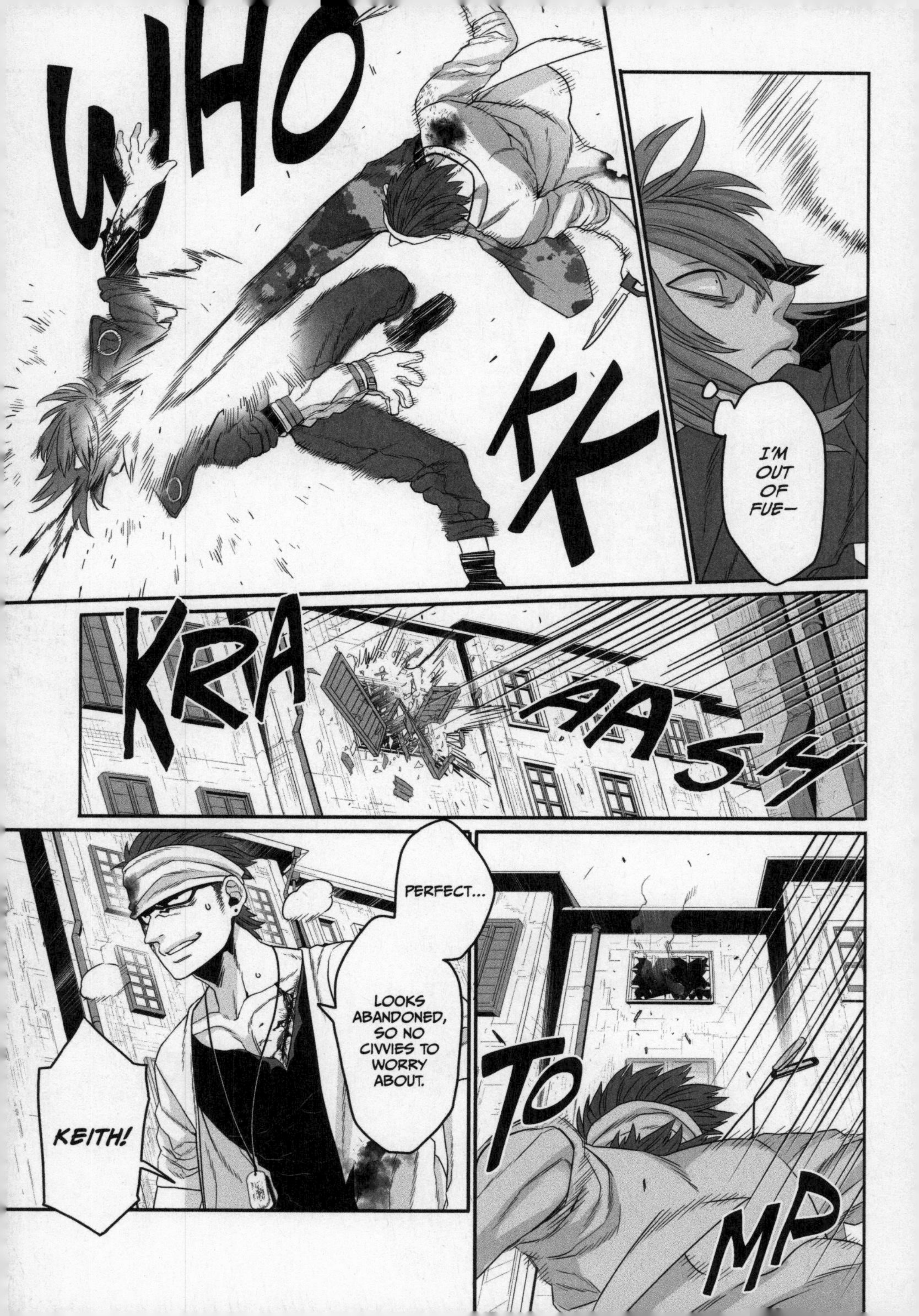
I'M OUT OF FUE—
WHO
KK
KRA
AASH
TO
MP
PERFECT...
LOOKS ABANDONED, SO NO CIVVIES TO WORRY ABOUT.
KEITH!

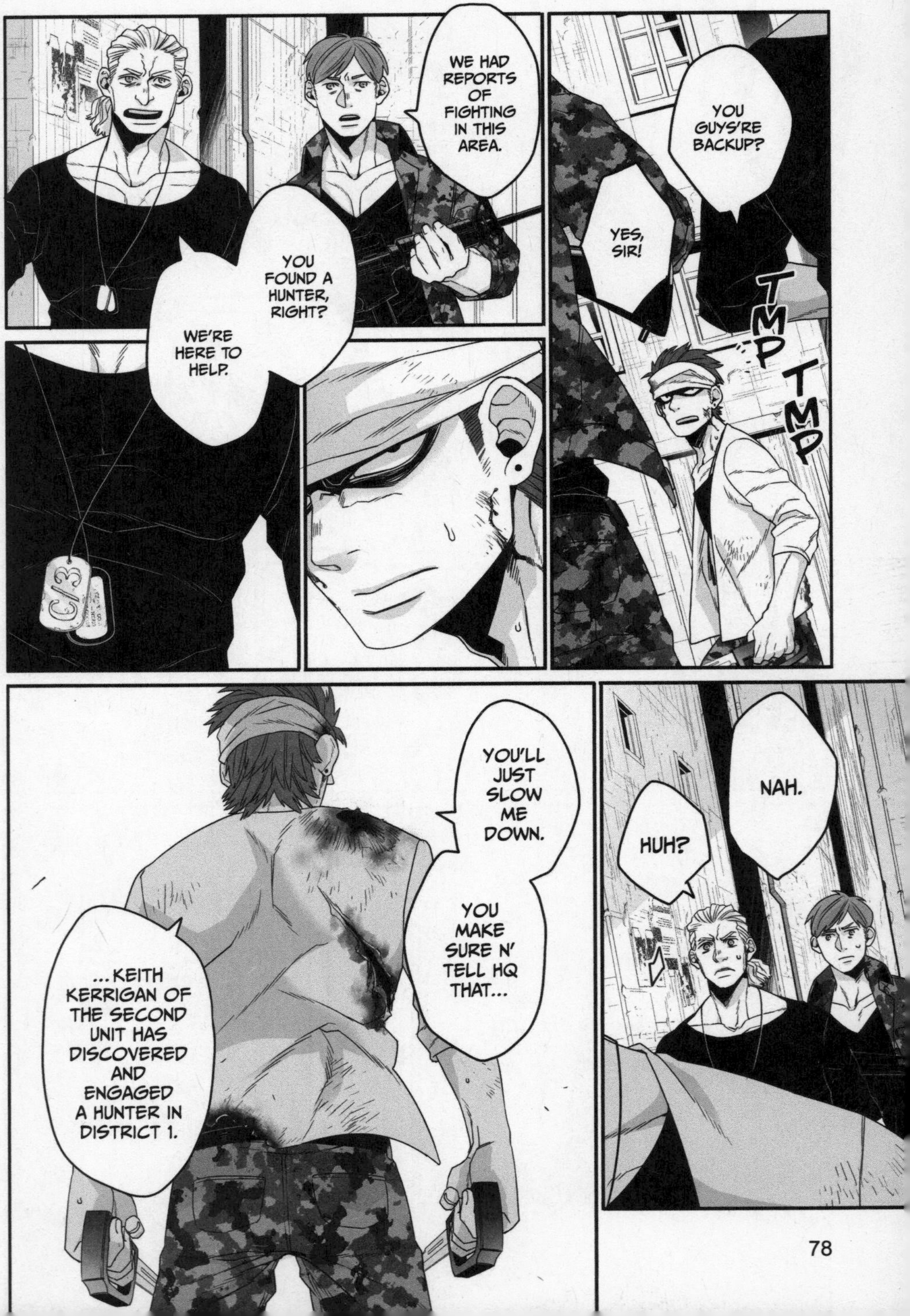
YOU GUYS'RE BACKUP?
YES, SIR!
TMP
TMP
TMP
TMP
WE HAD REPORTS OF FIGHTING IN THIS AREA.
YOU FOUND A HUNTER, RIGHT?
WE'RE HERE TO HELP.
NAH.
HUH?
YOU'LL JUST SLOW ME DOWN.
YOU MAKE SURE N' TELL HQ THAT...
...KEITH KERRIGAN OF THE SECOND UNIT HAS DISCOVERED AND ENGAGED A HUNTER IN DISTRICT 1.

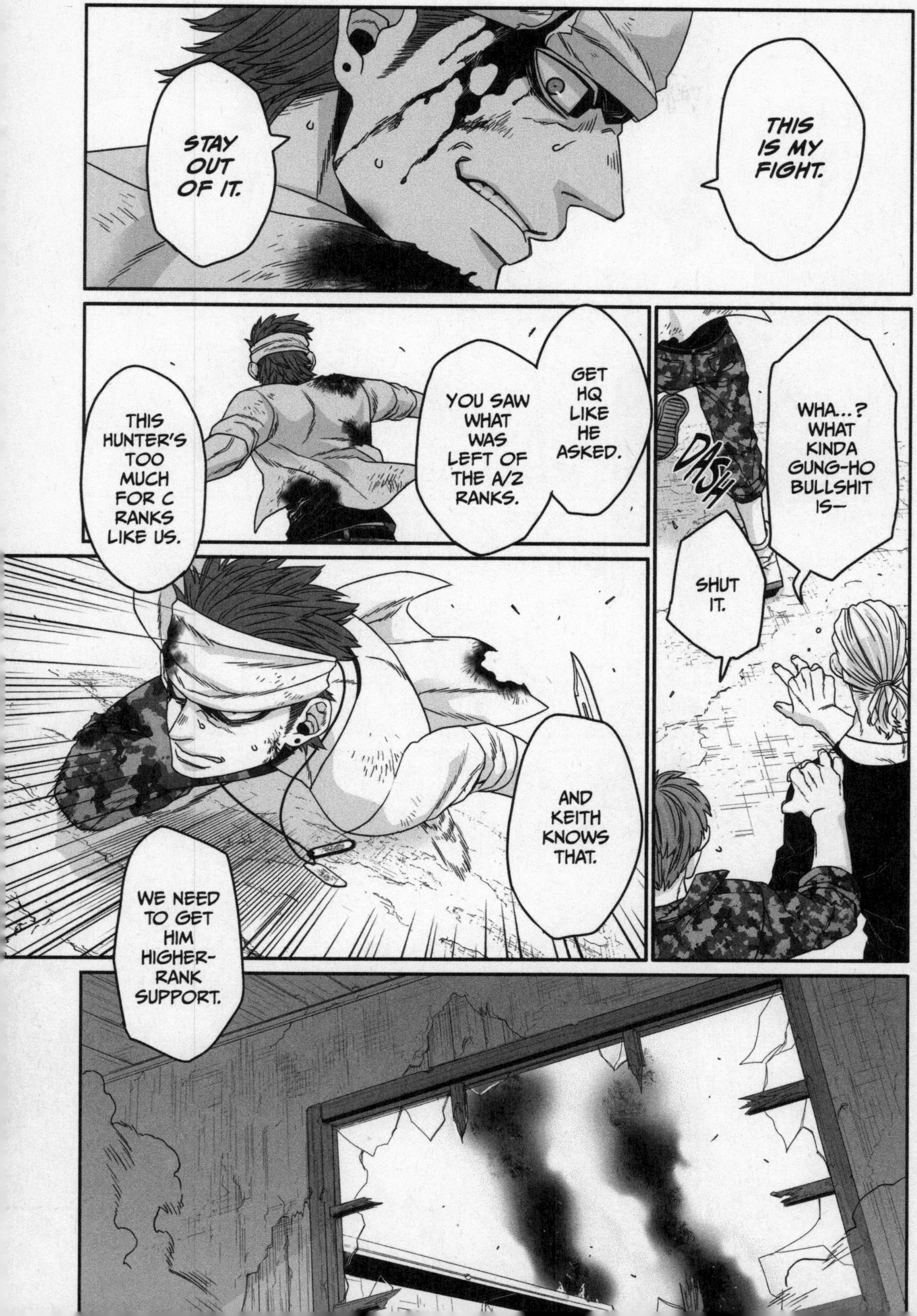
THIS IS MY FIGHT.
STAY OUT OF IT.
WHA...? WHAT KINDA GUNG-HO BULLSHIT IS—
DASH
SHUT IT.
GET HQ LIKE HE ASKED.
YOU SAW WHAT WAS LEFT OF THE A/2 RANKS.
THIS HUNTER'S TOO MUCH FOR C RANKS LIKE US.
AND KEITH KNOWS THAT.
WE NEED TO GET HIM HIGHER-RANK SUPPORT.

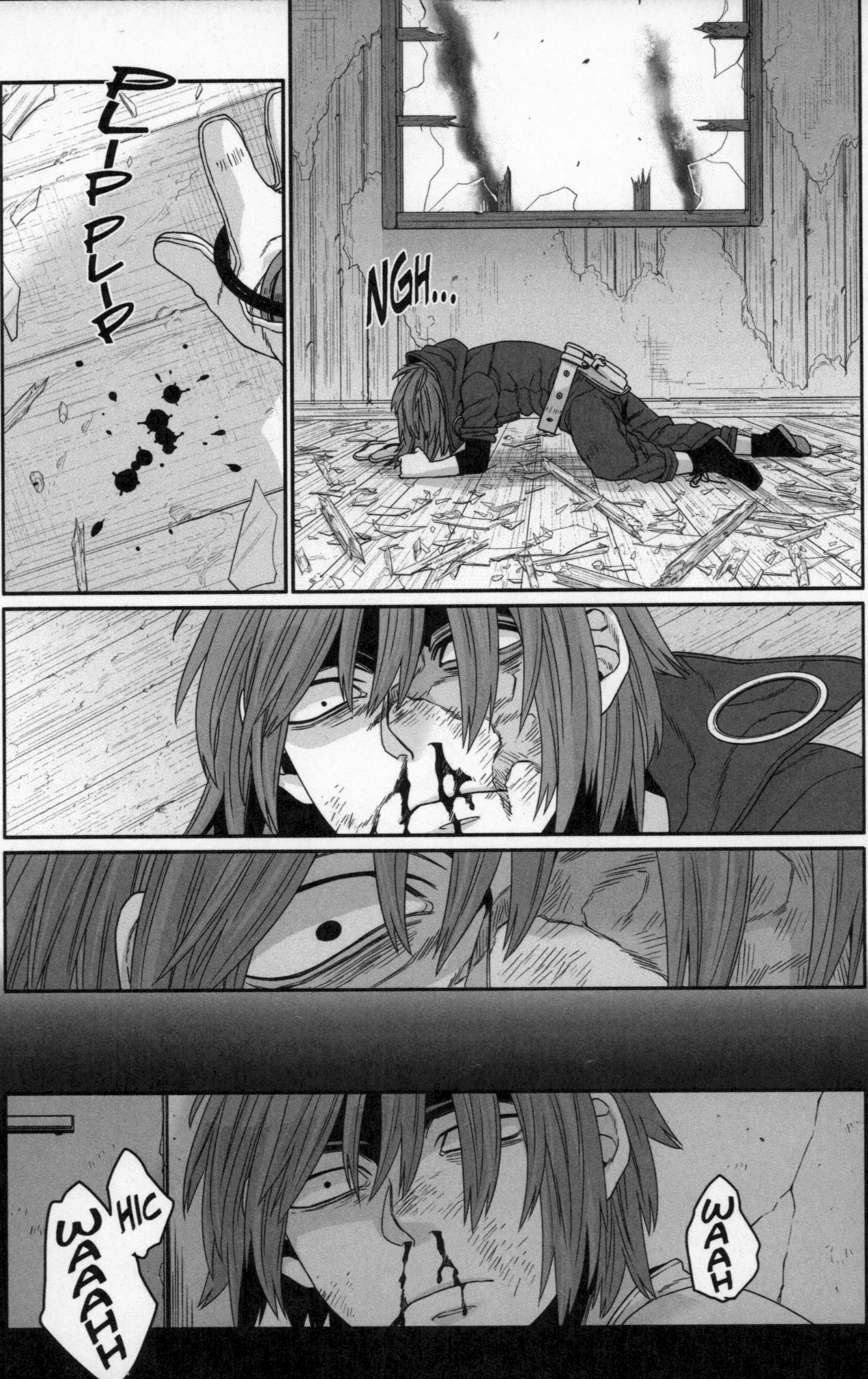
NGH...
PLIP PLIP PLIP
HIC
WAAAHH
WAAH

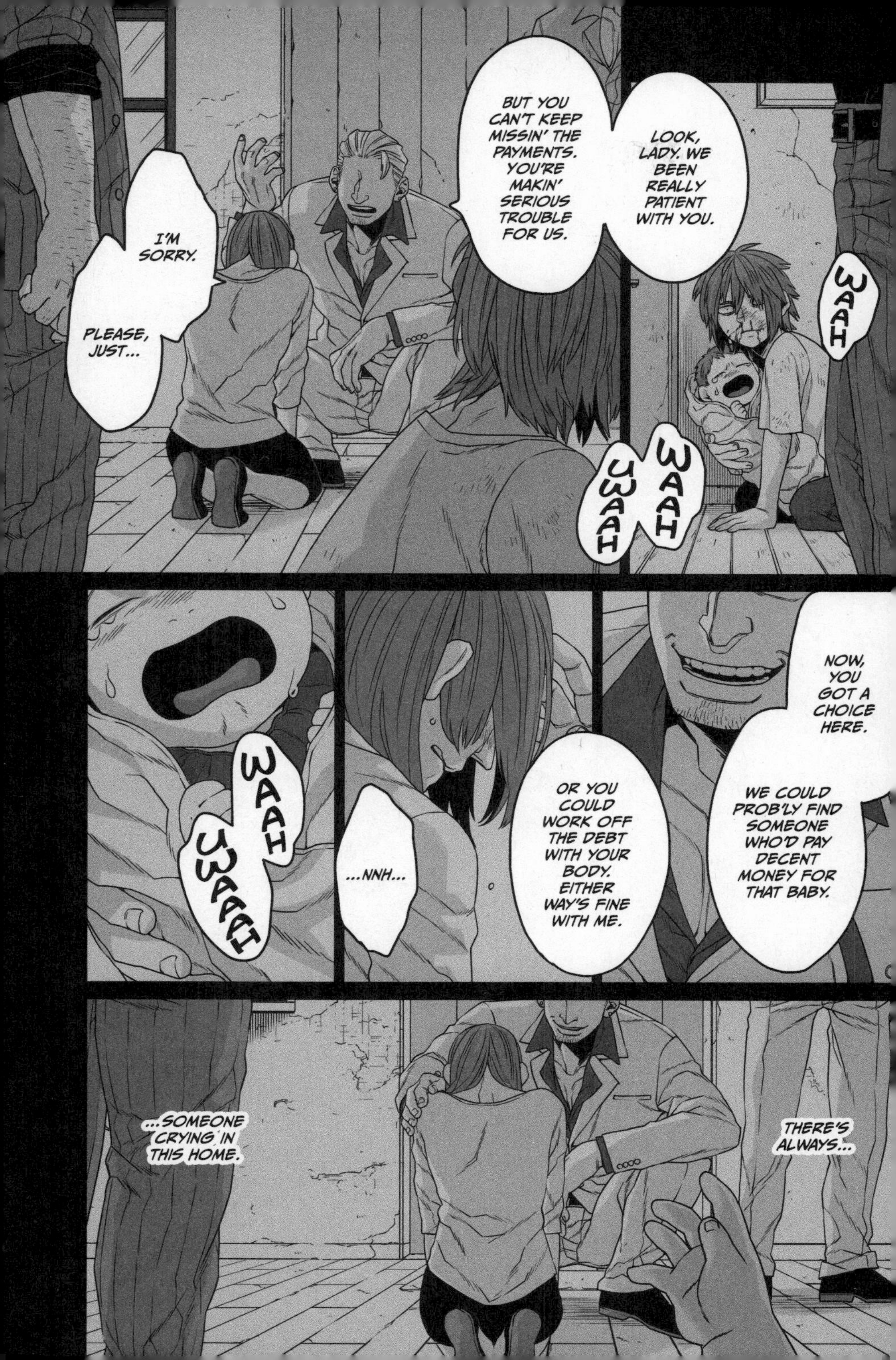
WAAH
LOOK, LADY. WE BEEN REALLY PATIENT WITH YOU.
WAAH
UWAAH
BUT YOU CAN'T KEEP MISSIN' THE PAYMENTS. YOU'RE MAKIN' SERIOUS TROUBLE FOR US.
I'M SORRY.
PLEASE, JUST...
NOW, YOU GOT A CHOICE HERE.
WE COULD PROB'LY FIND SOMEONE WHO'D PAY DECENT MONEY FOR THAT BABY.
OR YOU COULD WORK OFF THE DEBT WITH YOUR BODY. EITHER WAY'S FINE WITH ME.
...NNH...
WAAH
UWAAAH
THERE'S ALWAYS...
...SOMEONE CRYING IN THIS HOME.

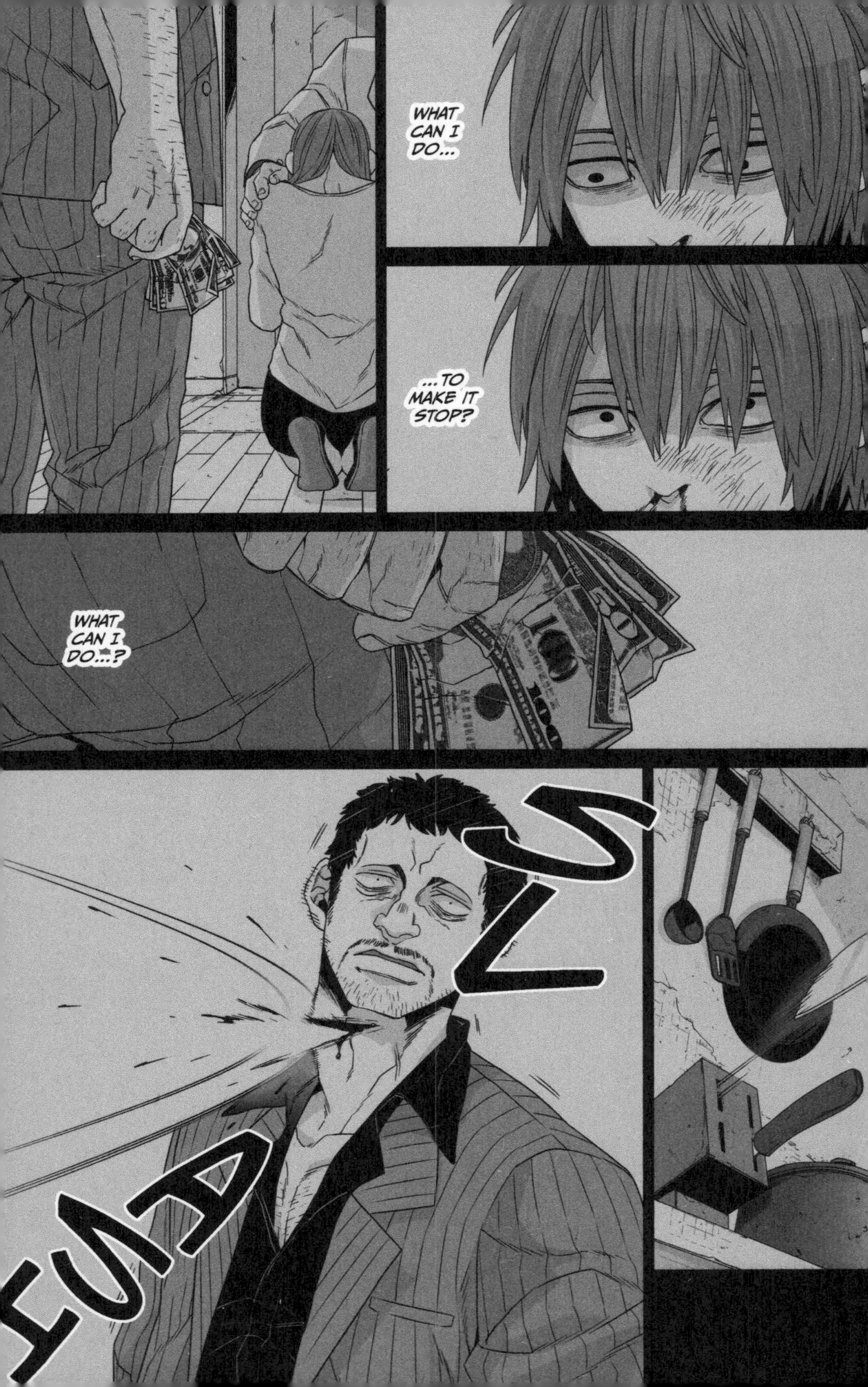
WHAT CAN I DO...
...TO MAKE IT STOP?
WHAT CAN I DO...?

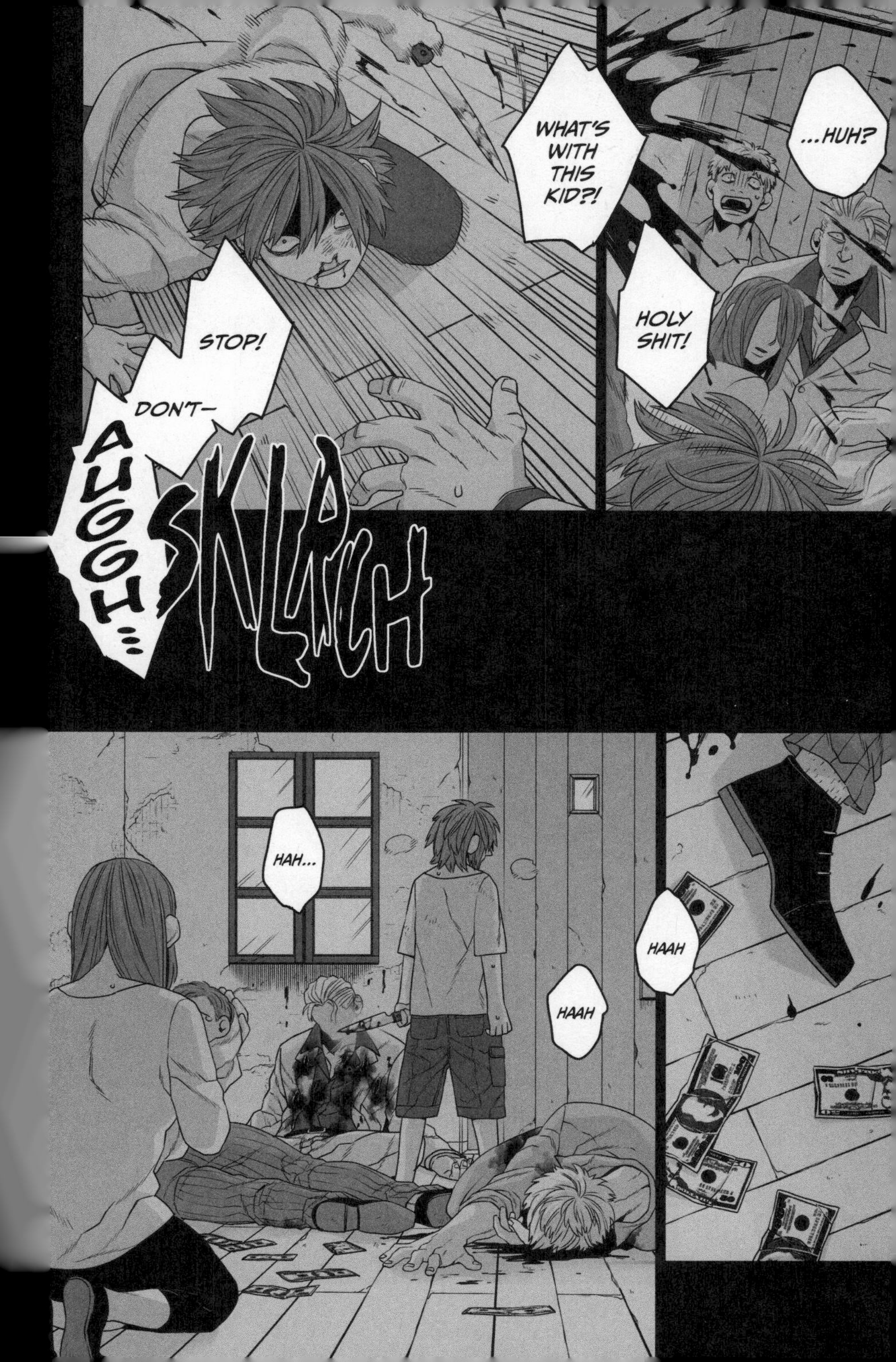
...HUH?
WHAT'S WITH THIS KID?!
HOLY SHIT!
STOP!
DON'T—
AUGGGH...
SKLRCH
HAAH
HAAH
HAH...

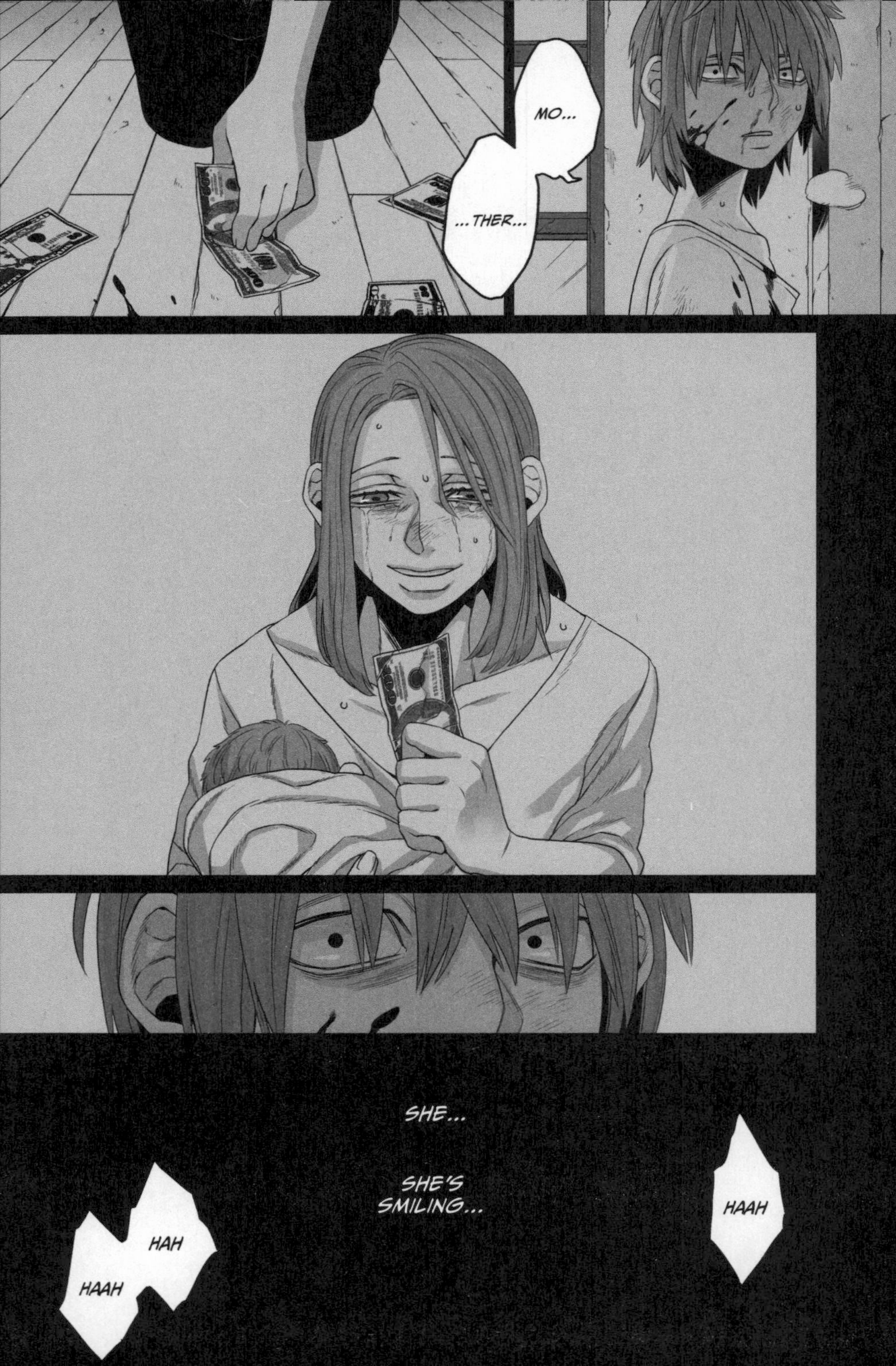
MO...
...THER...
SHE...
SHE'S SMILING...
HAAH
HAH
HAAH

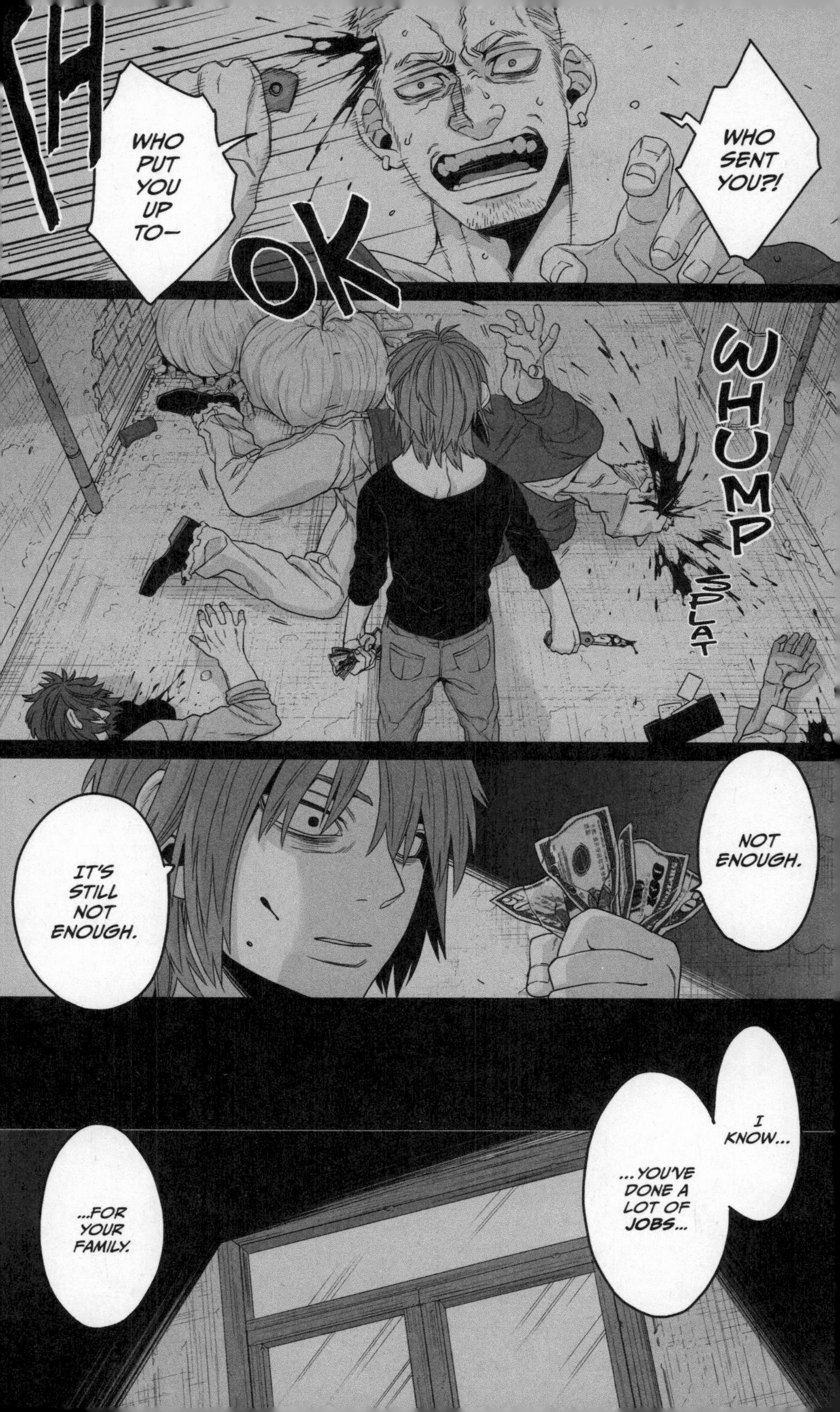
WHO SENT YOU?!
WHO PUT YOU UP TO—
OK
WHUMP
SPLAT
NOT ENOUGH.
IT'S STILL NOT ENOUGH.
I KNOW...
...YOU'VE DONE A LOT OF JOBS...
...FOR YOUR FAMILY.

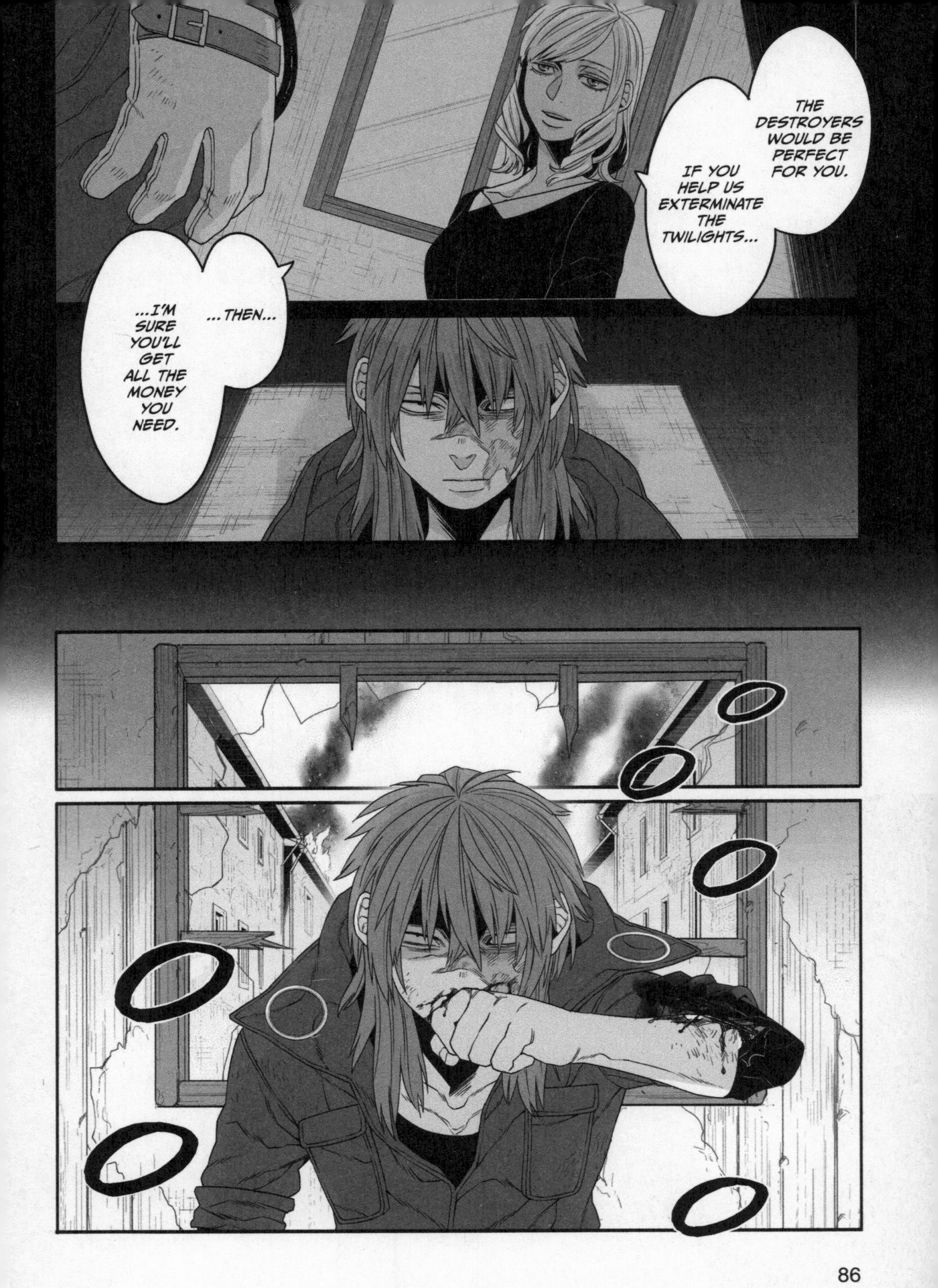
THE DESTROYERS WOULD BE PERFECT FOR YOU.
IF YOU HELP US EXTERMINATE THE TWILIGHTS...
...THEN...
...I'M SURE YOU'LL GET ALL THE MONEY YOU NEED.

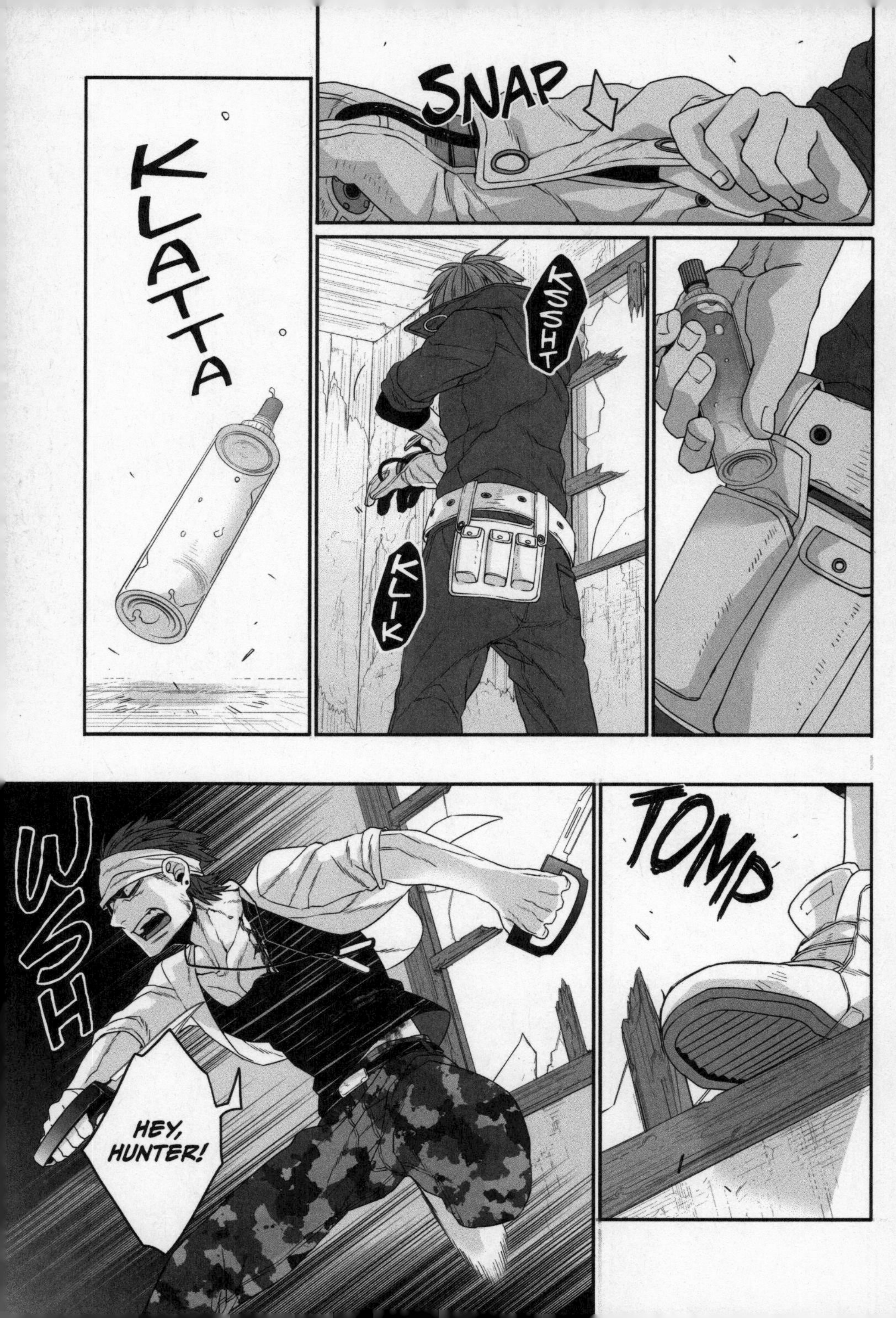
SNAP
KSSHT
KLIK
KLATTA
TOMP
WSH
HEY, HUNTER!

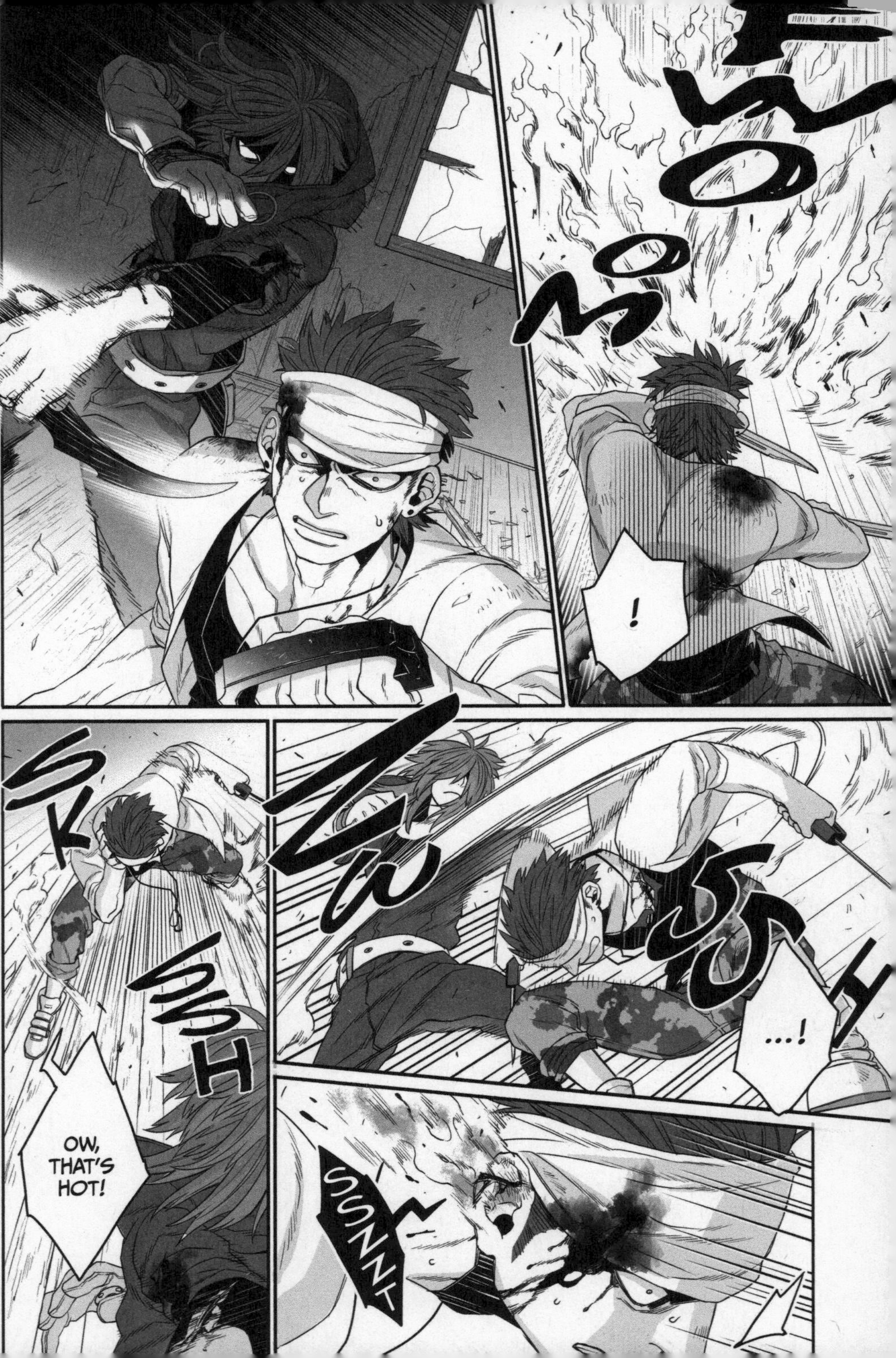
FWOOM
!
...!
OW, THAT'S HOT!
SSNNT

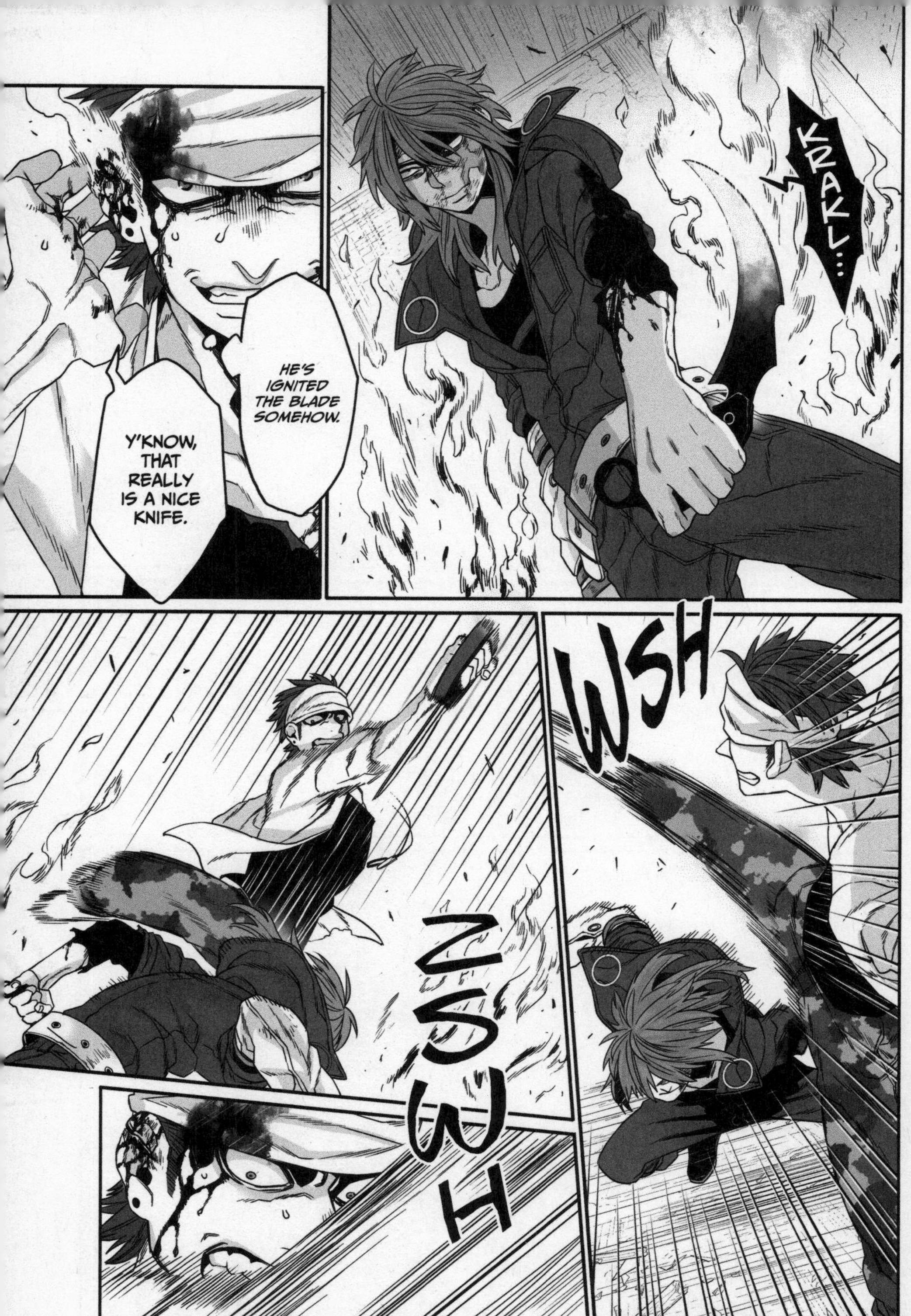
KRAKL...
HE'S IGNITED THE BLADE SOMEHOW.
Y'KNOW, THAT REALLY IS A NICE KNIFE.
WSH

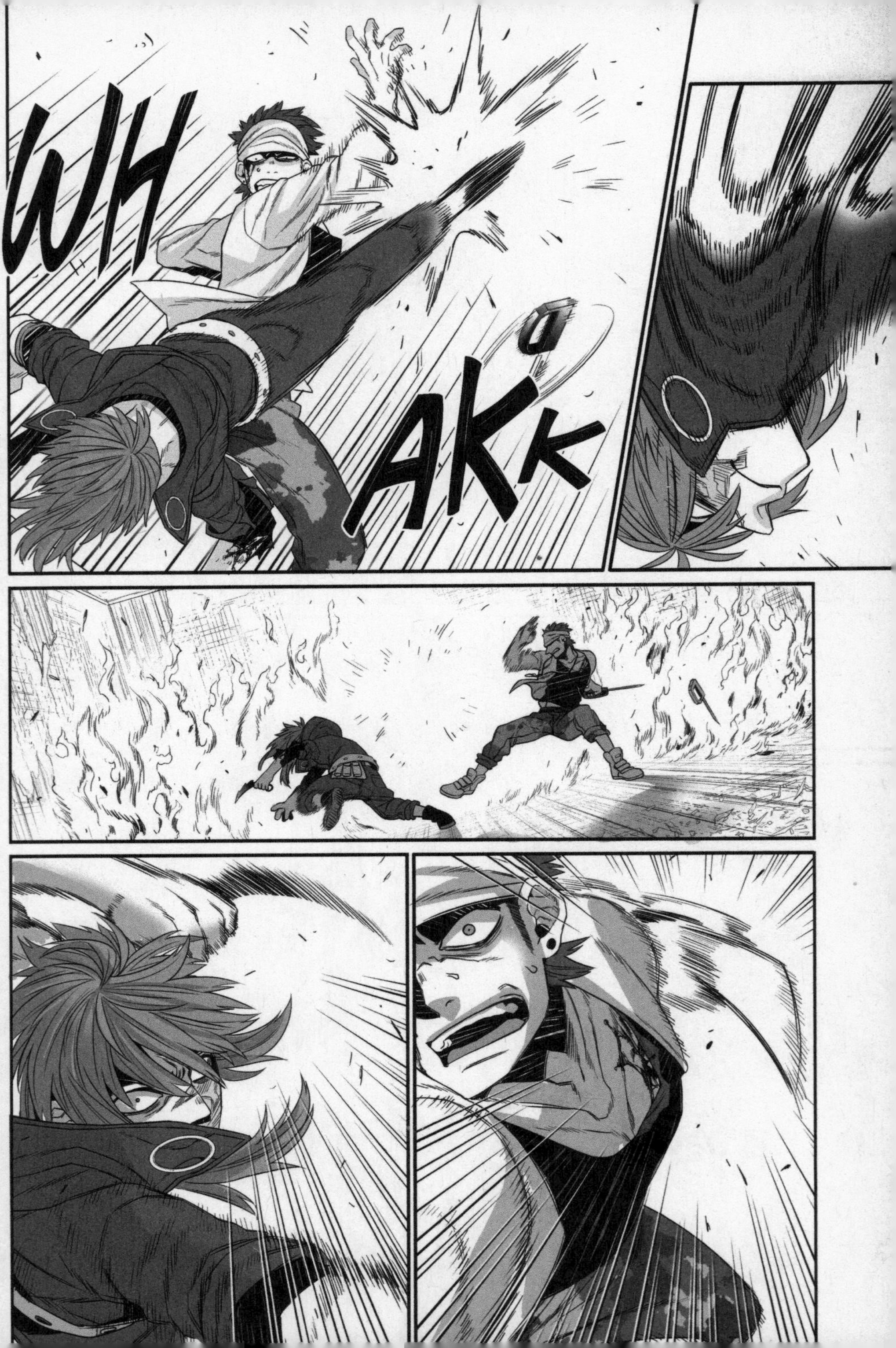
UH
WH
AKK

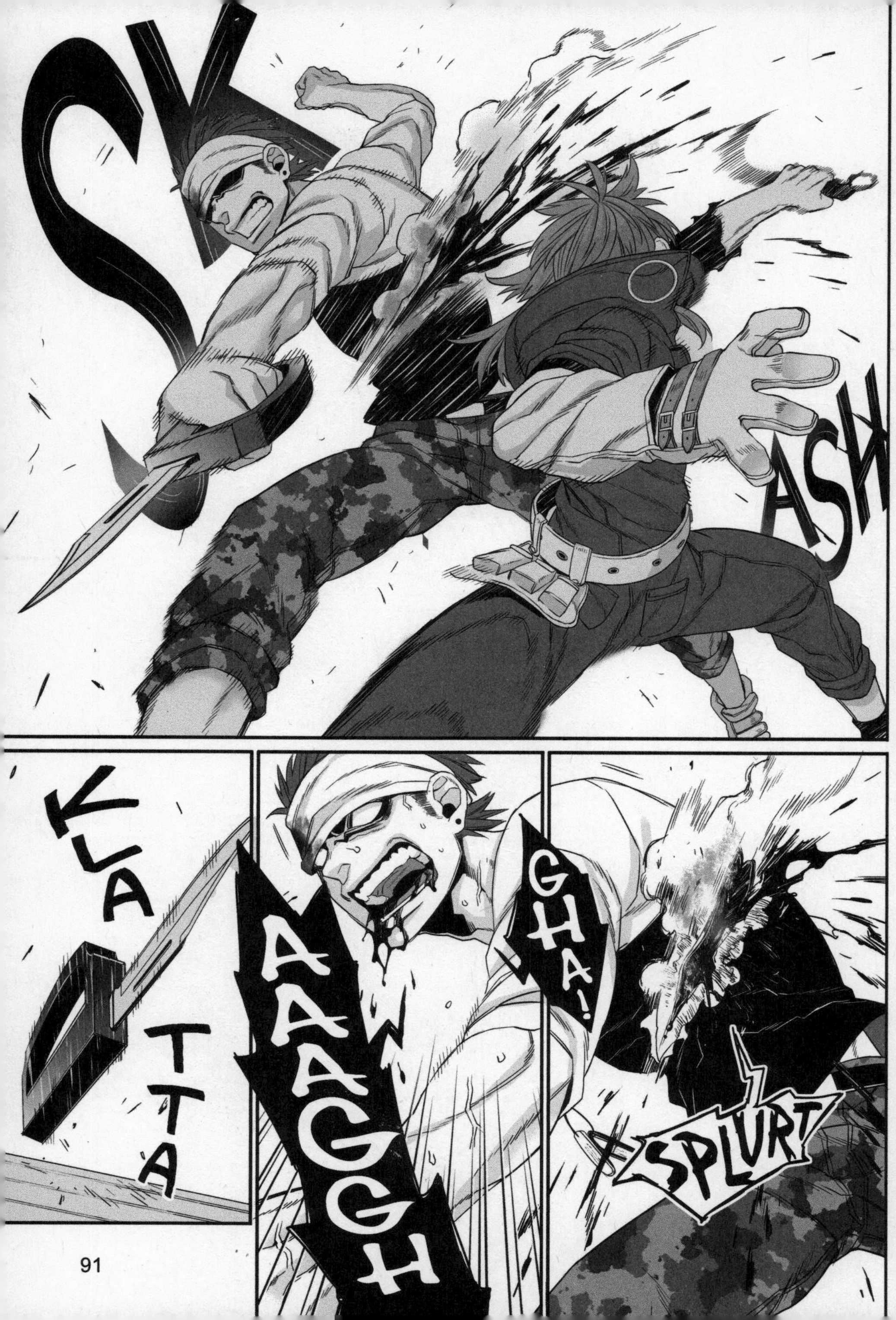
SK
ASH
SPLURT
GHA!
AAGGH
KLA
TTA

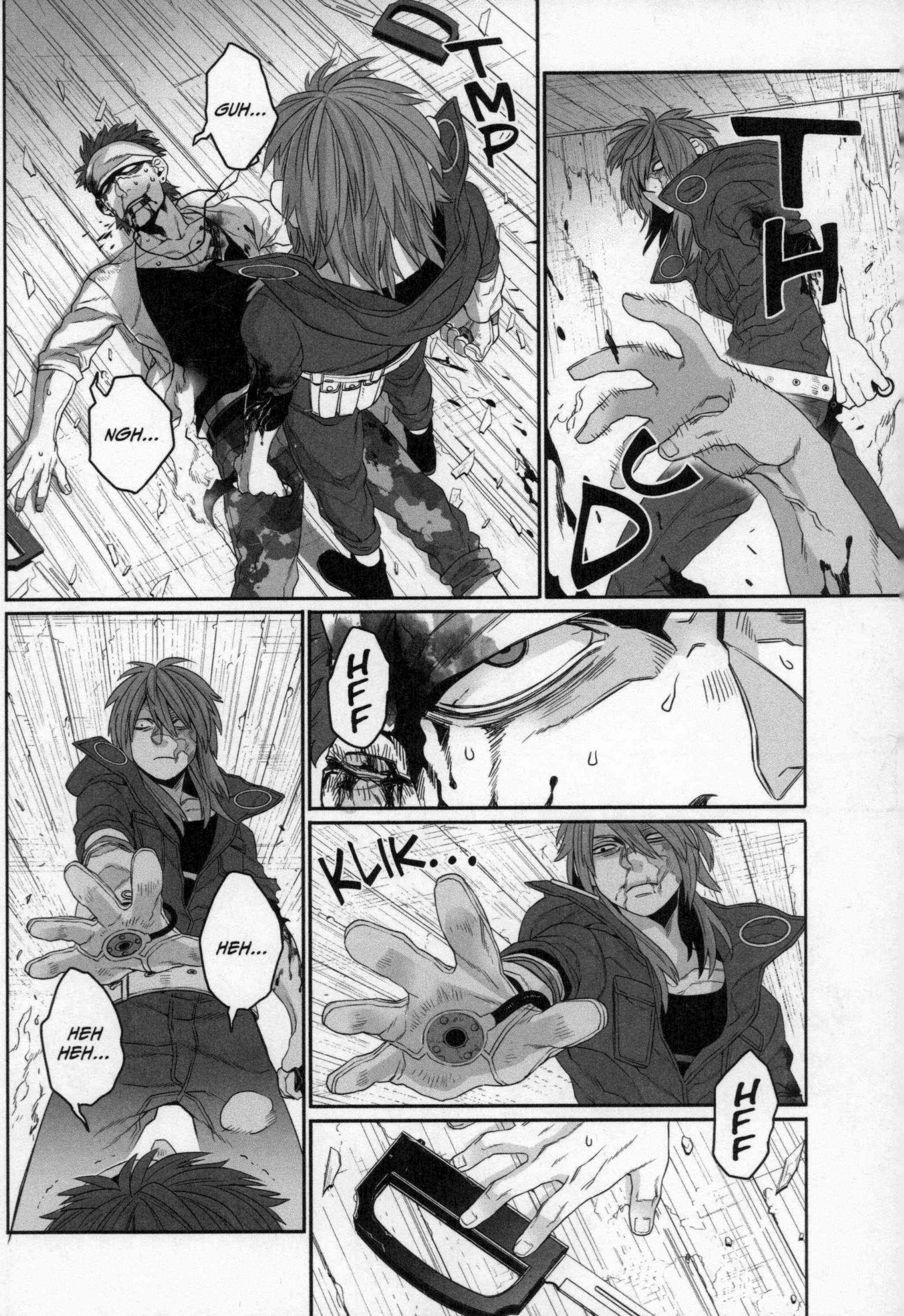
THUD
TMP
GUH...
NGH...
HFF
KLIK...
HFF
HEH...
HEH
HEH...

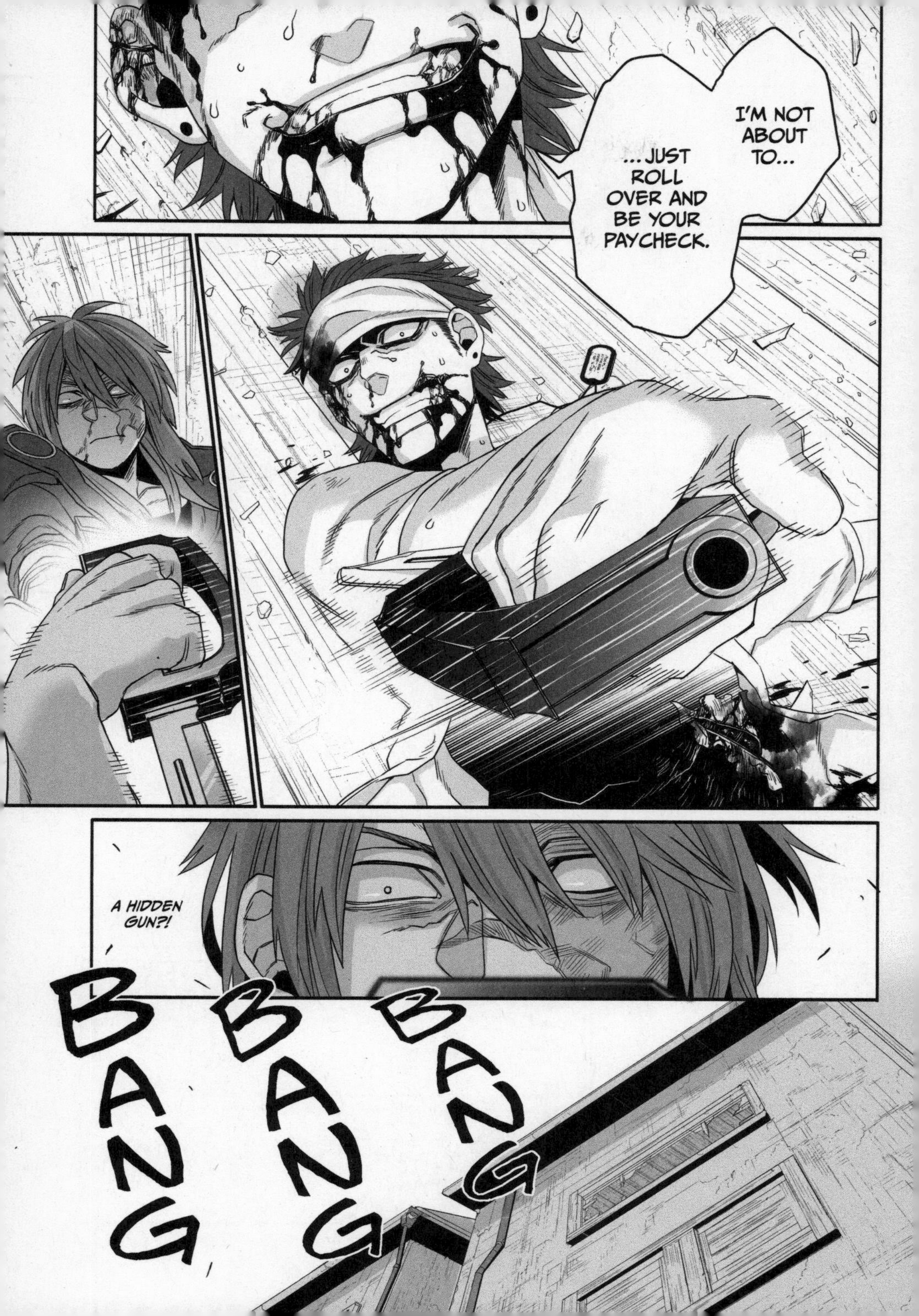
I'M NOT ABOUT TO...
...JUST ROLL OVER AND BE YOUR PAYCHECK.
A HIDDEN GUN?!
BANG
BANG
BANG

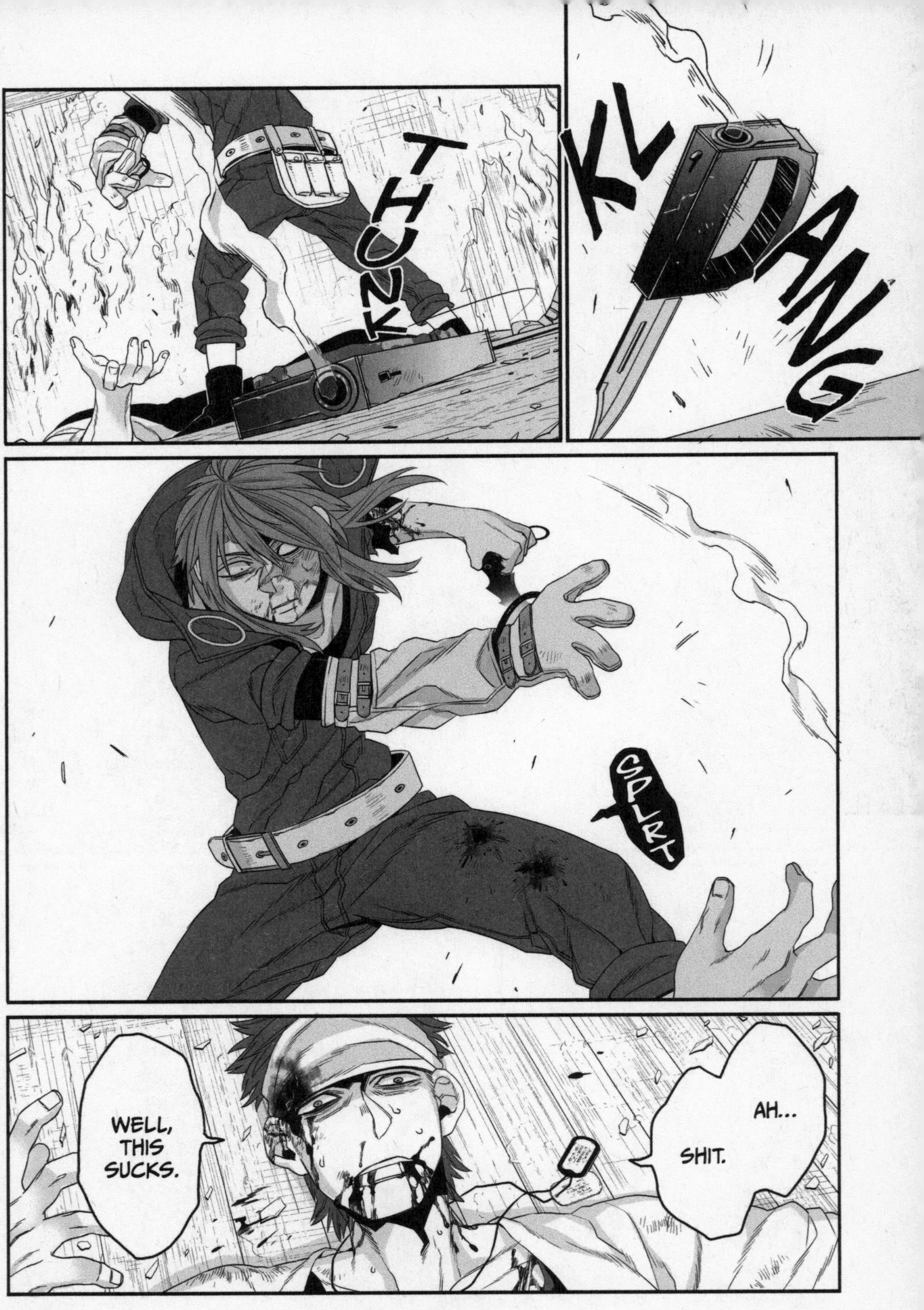
KLDANG
THUNK
SPLRT
AH... SHIT.
WELL, THIS SUCKS.

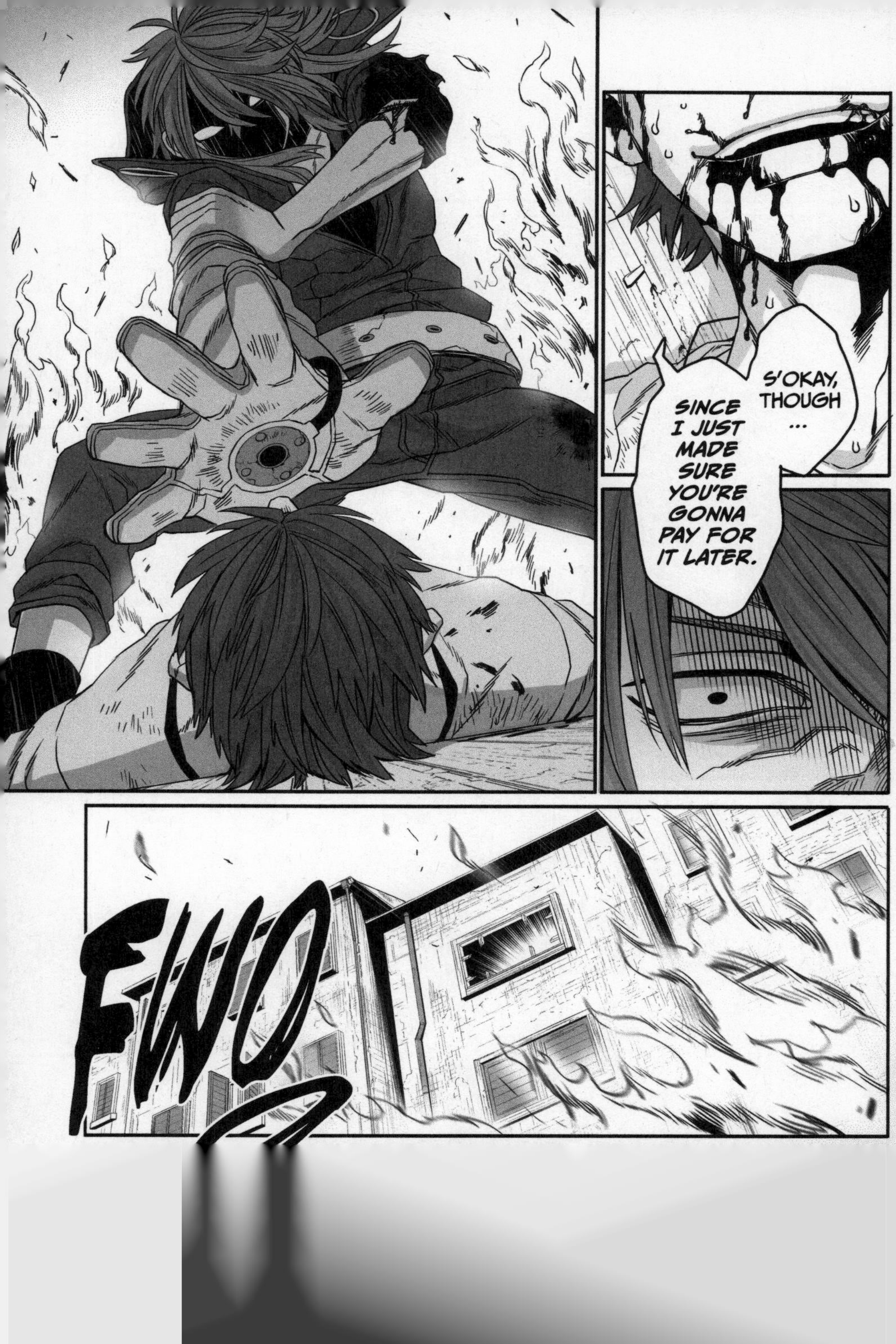
S'OKAY, THOUGH ...
SINCE I JUST MADE SURE YOU'RE GONNA PAY FOR IT LATER.
FWO

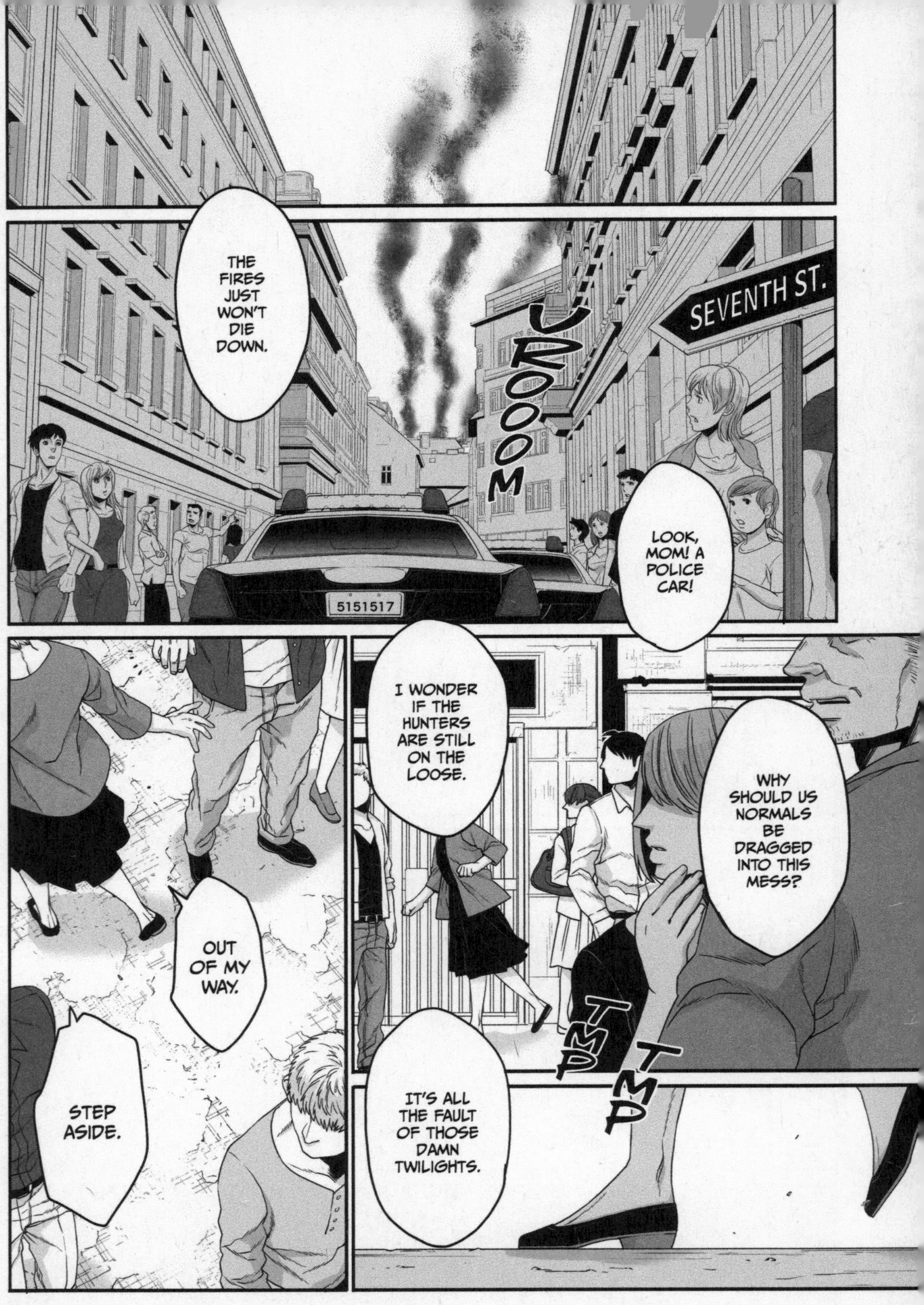
SEVENTH ST.
THE FIRES JUST WON'T DIE DOWN.
UROOOM
LOOK, MOM! A POLICE CAR!
WHY SHOULD US NORMALS BE DRAGGED INTO THIS MESS?
I WONDER IF THE HUNTERS ARE STILL ON THE LOOSE.
TMP TMP
IT'S ALL THE FAULT OF THOSE DAMN TWILIGHTS.
OUT OF MY WAY.
STEP ASIDE.

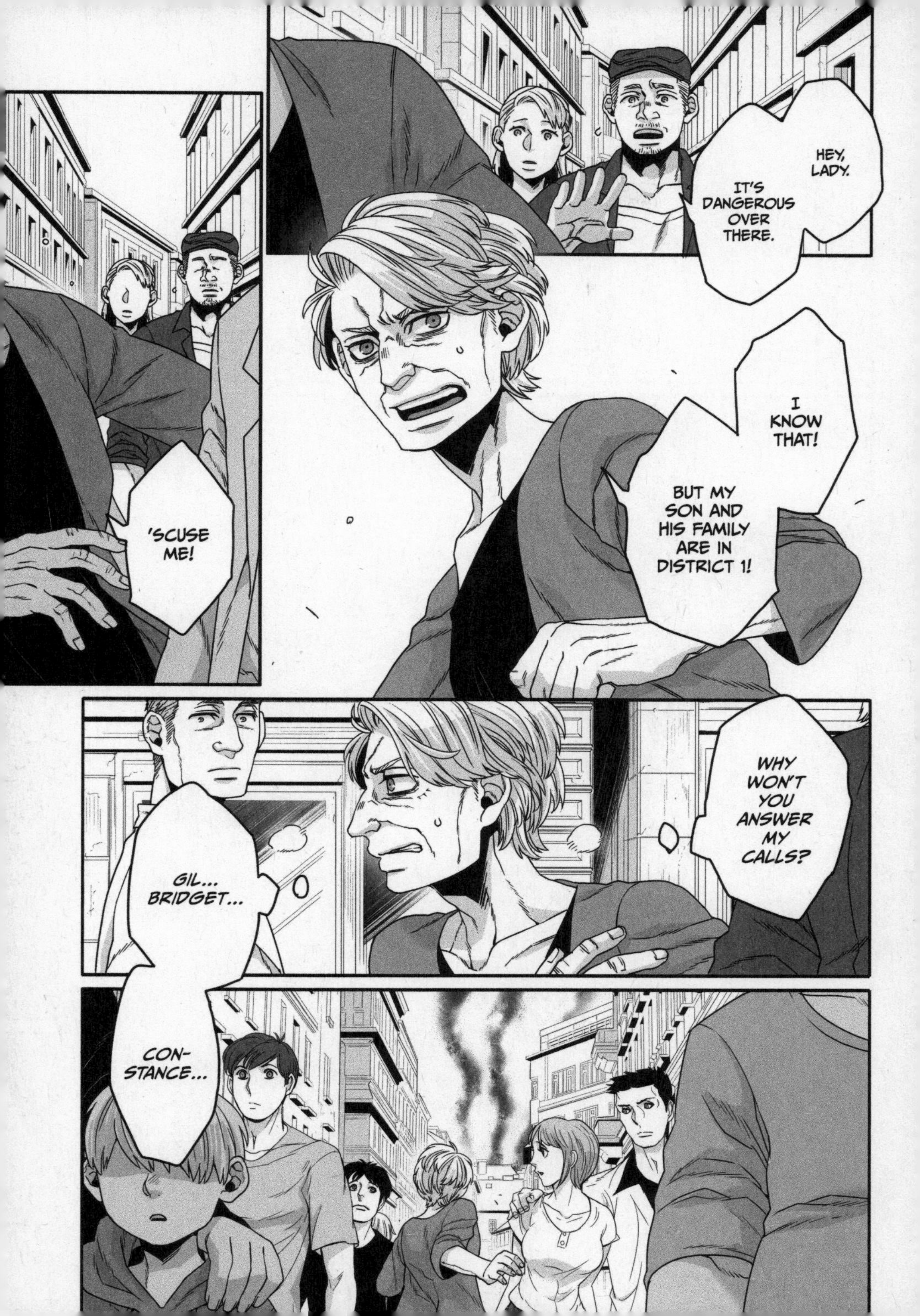
HEY, LADY.
IT'S DANGEROUS OVER THERE.
I KNOW THAT!
BUT MY SON AND HIS FAMILY ARE IN DISTRICT 1!
'SCUSE ME!
WHY WON'T YOU ANSWER MY CALLS?
GIL... BRIDGET...
CON-STANCE...

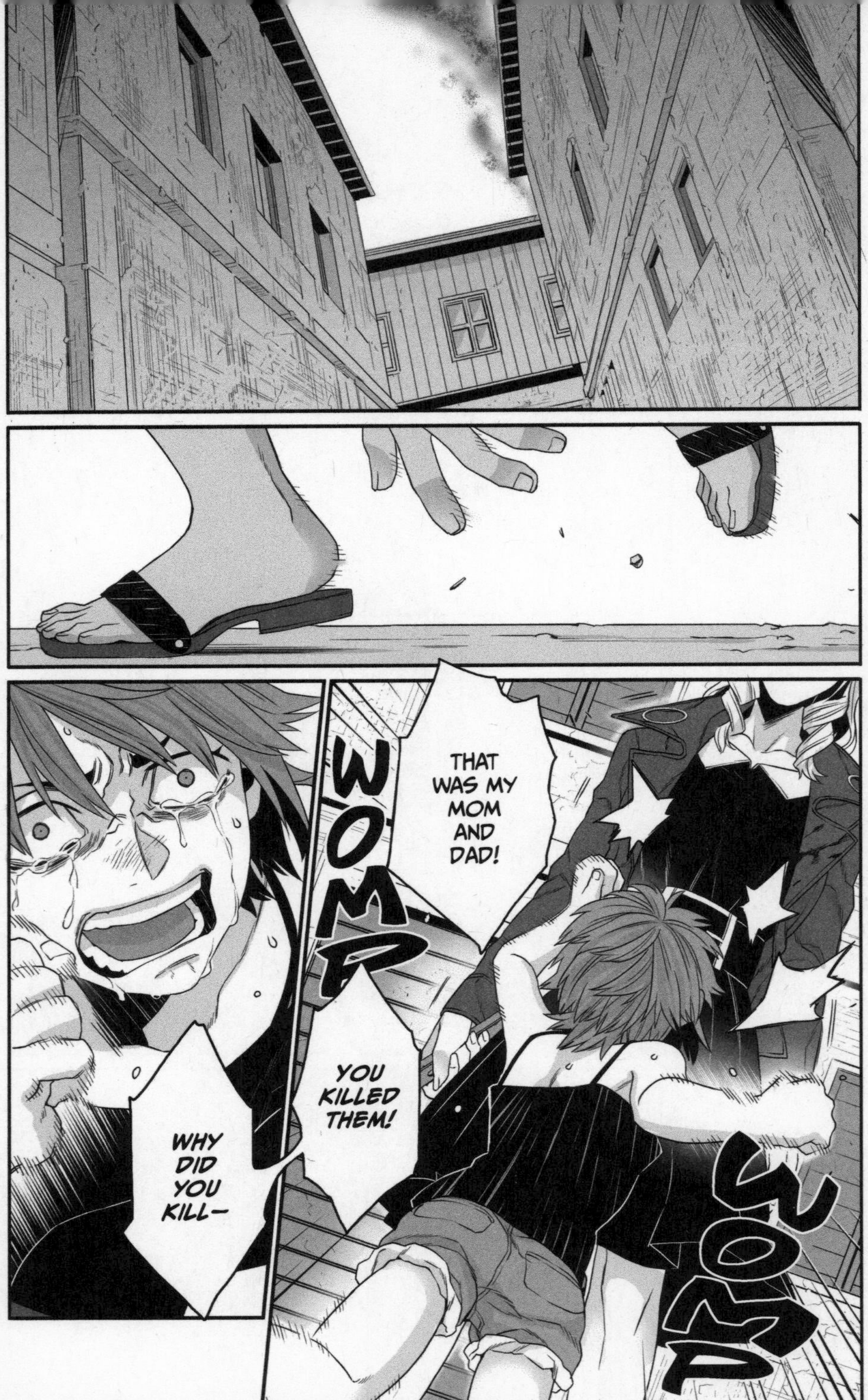
THAT WAS MY MOM AND DAD!
WOMP
YOU KILLED THEM!
WOMP
WHY DID YOU KILL—

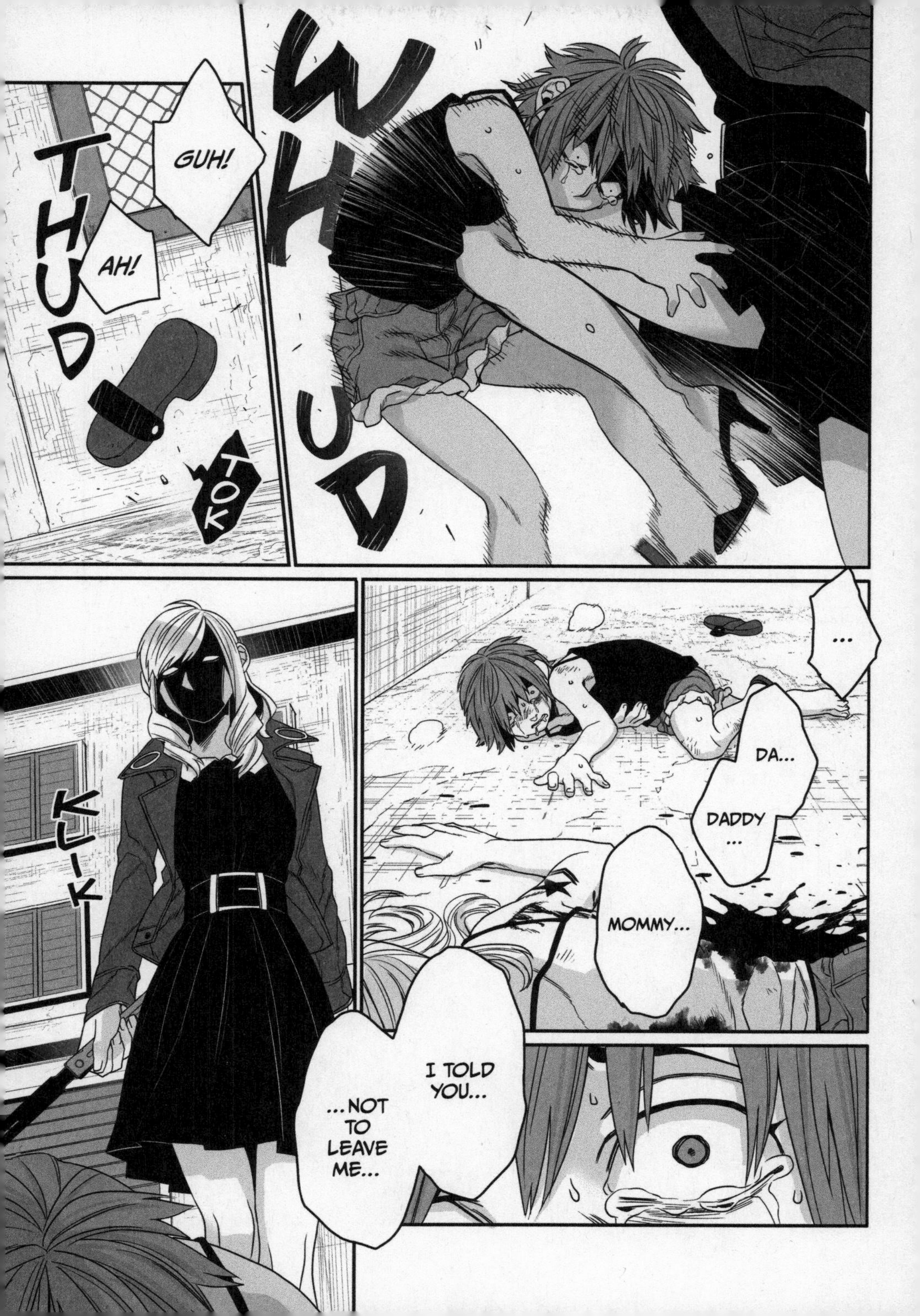
WHUD
GUH!
AH!
THUD
TOK
...
DA...
DADDY ...
MOMMY...
I TOLD YOU...
...NOT TO LEAVE ME...
KLIK

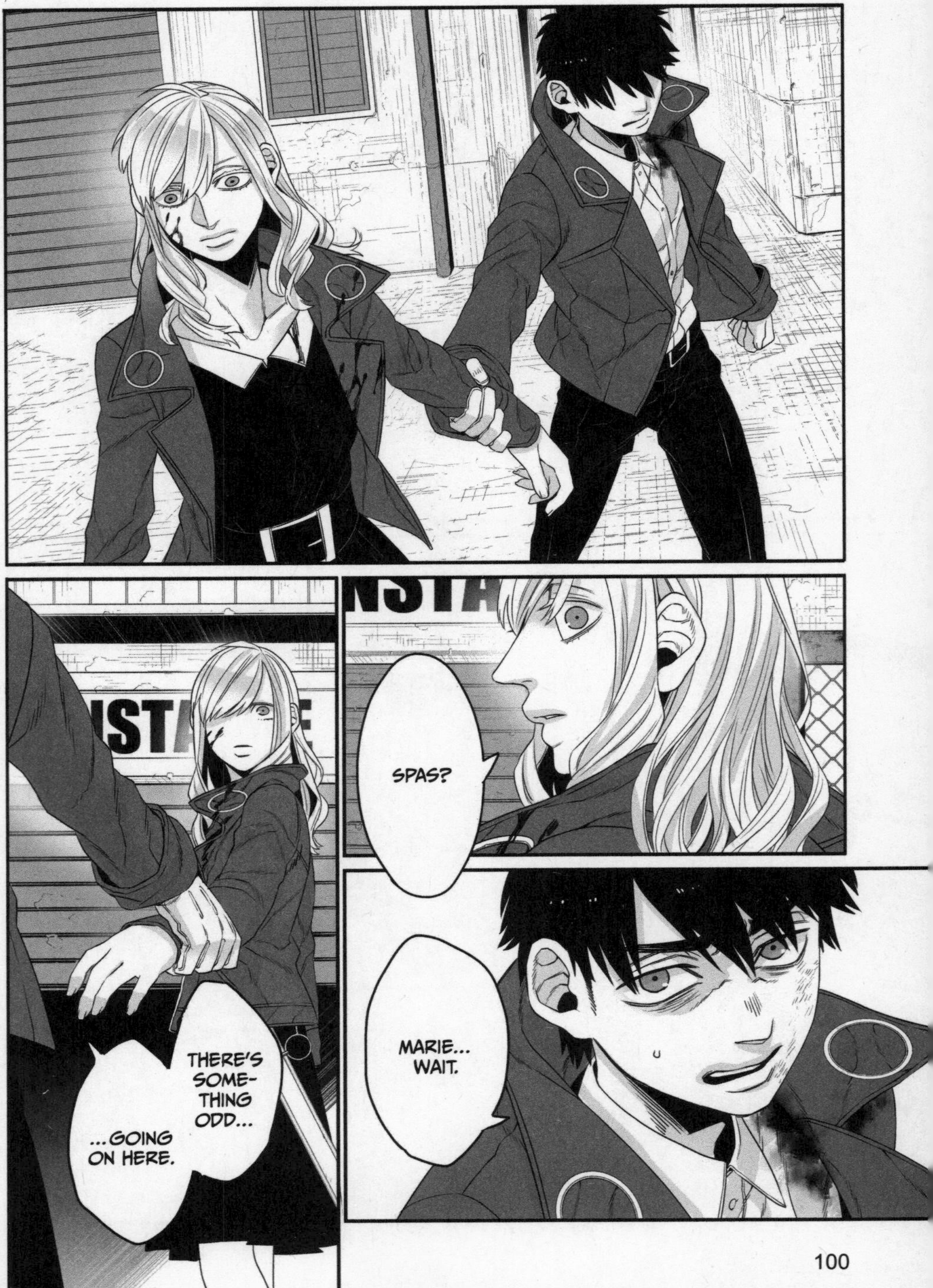
SPAS?
MARIE... WAIT.
THERE'S SOME-THING ODD...
...GOING ON HERE.

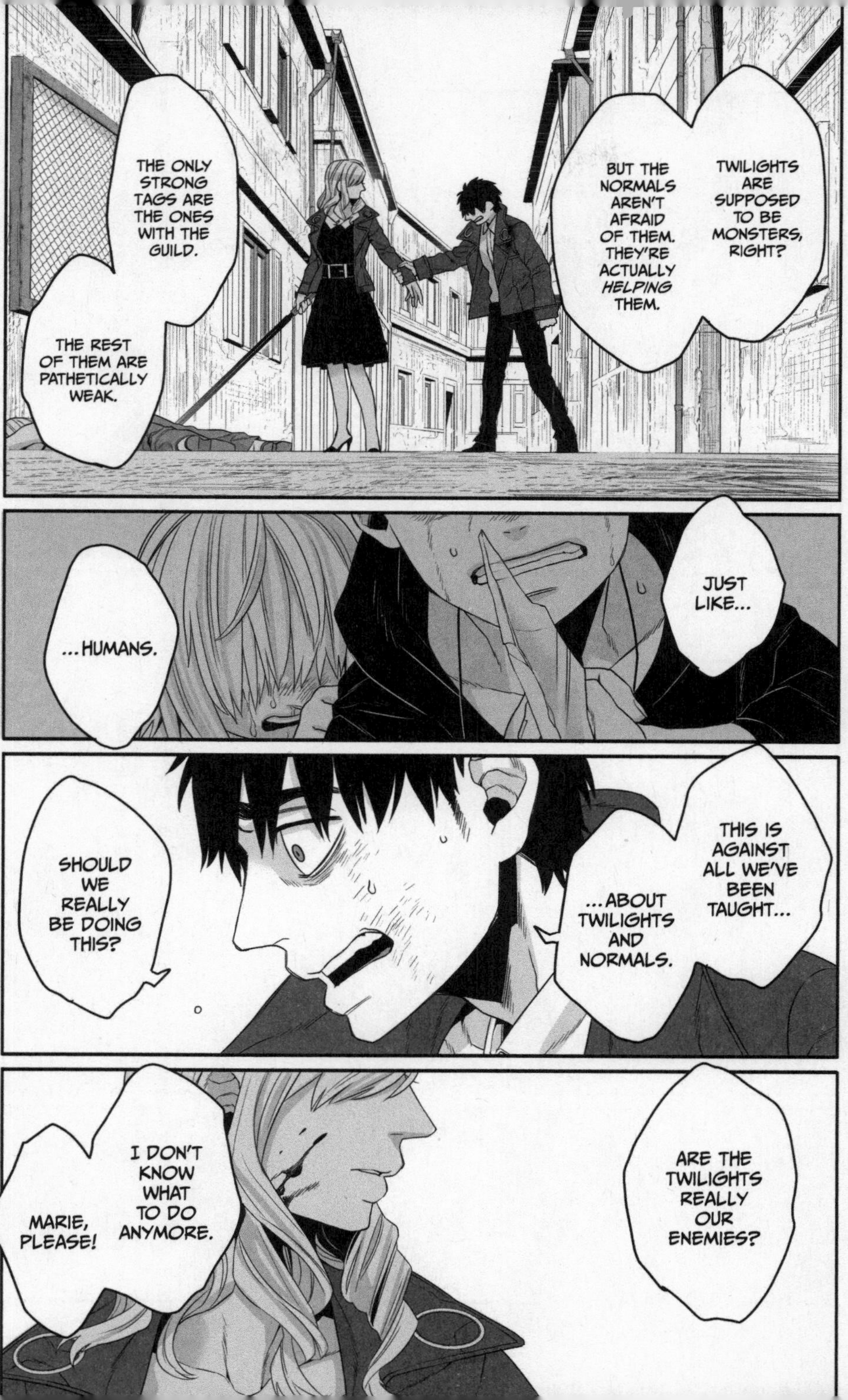
TWILIGHTS ARE SUPPOSED TO BE MONSTERS, RIGHT?
BUT THE NORMALS AREN'T AFRAID OF THEM. THEY'RE ACTUALLY *HELPING* THEM.
THE ONLY STRONG TAGS ARE THE ONES WITH THE GUILD.
THE REST OF THEM ARE PATHETICALLY WEAK.
JUST LIKE...
...HUMANS.
THIS IS AGAINST ALL WE'VE BEEN TAUGHT...
...ABOUT TWILIGHTS AND NORMALS.
SHOULD WE REALLY BE DOING THIS?
ARE THE TWILIGHTS REALLY OUR ENEMIES?
I DON'T KNOW WHAT TO DO ANYMORE.
MARIE, PLEASE!

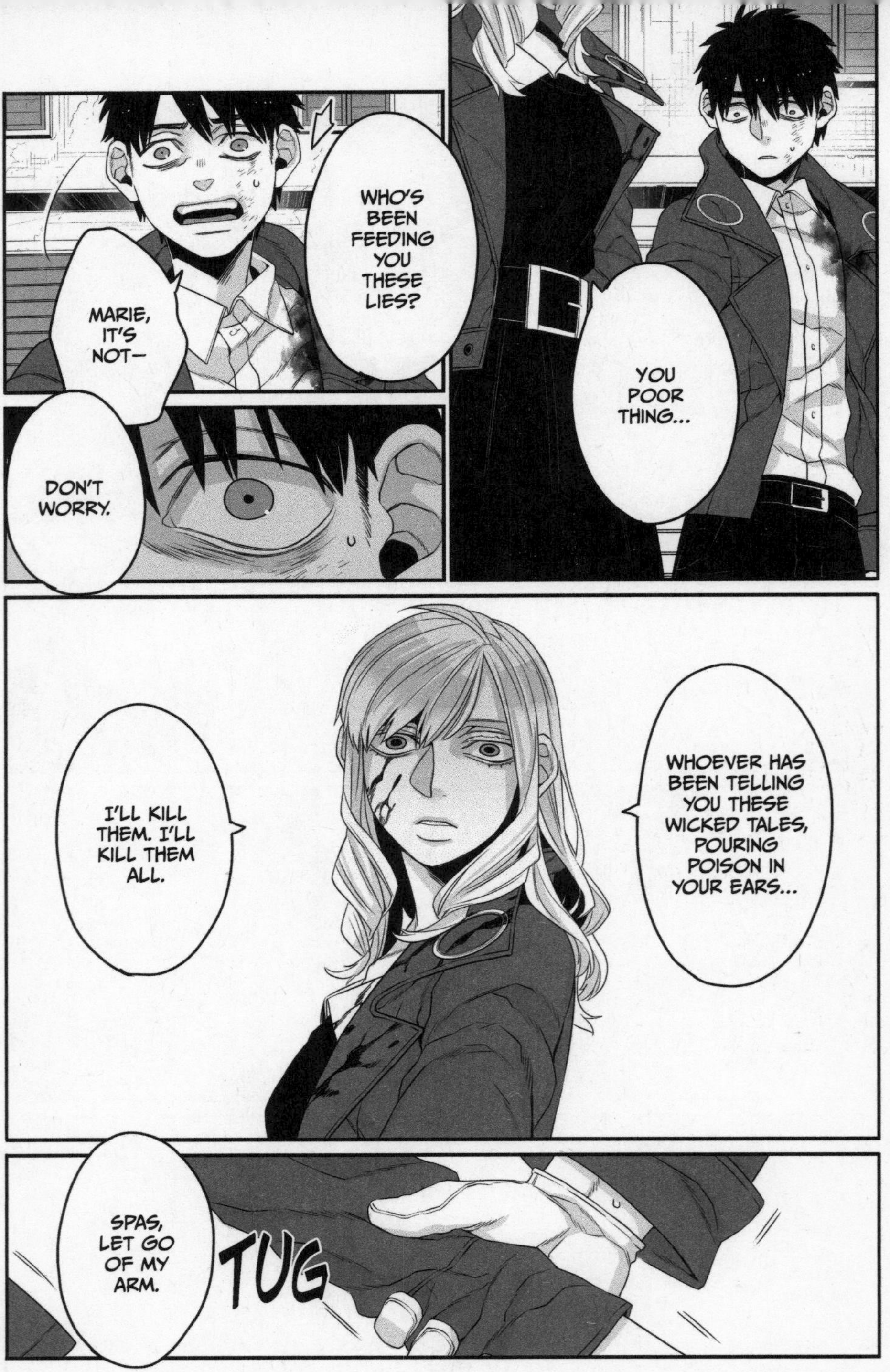
YOU POOR THING...
WHO'S BEEN FEEDING YOU THESE LIES?
MARIE, IT'S NOT—
DON'T WORRY.
WHOEVER HAS BEEN TELLING YOU THESE WICKED TALES, POURING POISON IN YOUR EARS...
I'LL KILL THEM. I'LL KILL THEM ALL.
SPAS, LET GO OF MY ARM.
TUG

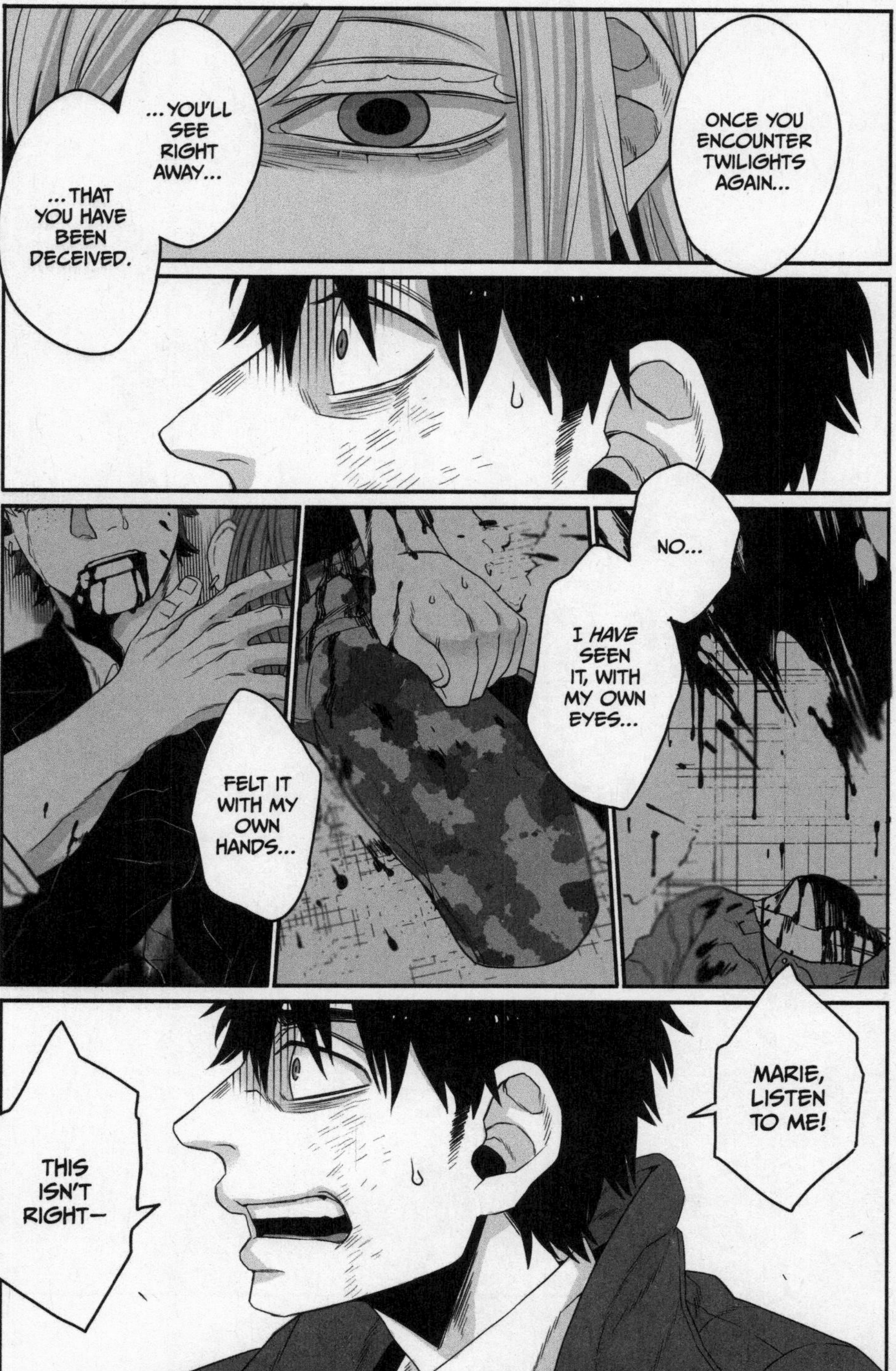
ONCE YOU ENCOUNTER TWILIGHTS AGAIN...
...YOU'LL SEE RIGHT AWAY...
...THAT YOU HAVE BEEN DECEIVED.
NO...
I *HAVE* SEEN IT, WITH MY OWN EYES...
FELT IT WITH MY OWN HANDS...
MARIE, LISTEN TO ME!
THIS ISN'T RIGHT—

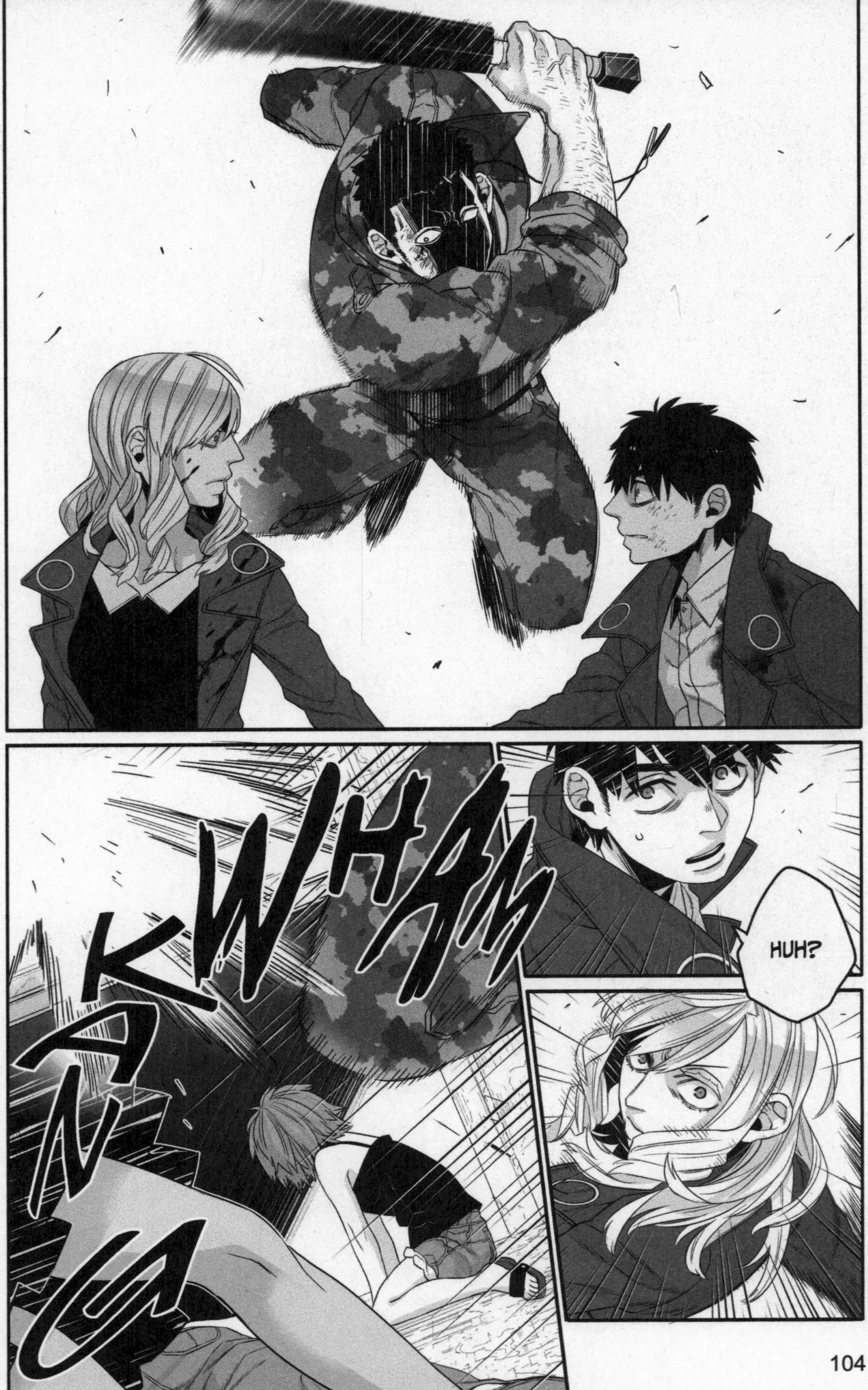
HUH?
WHAM
KANG

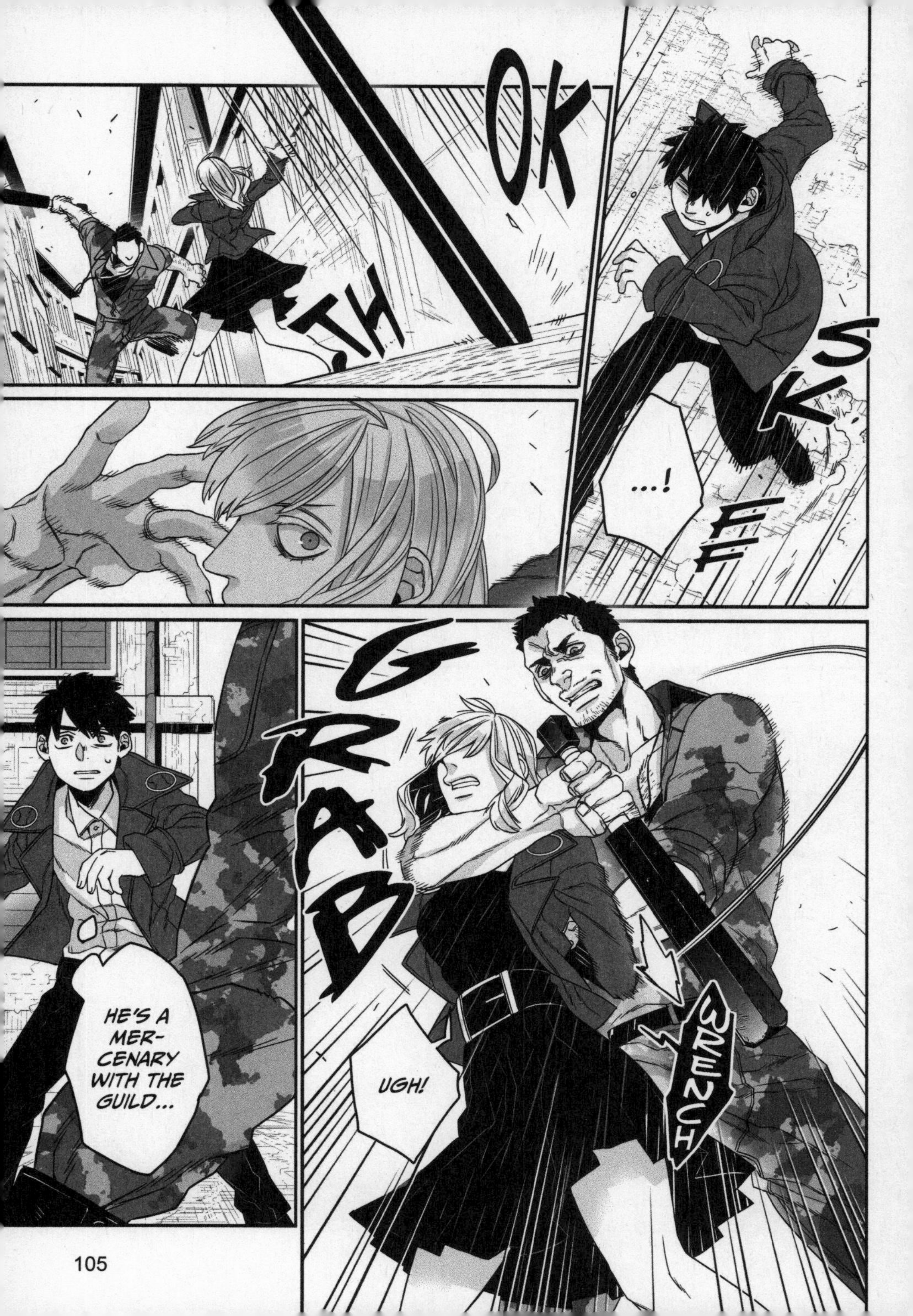
SK
...!
FF
THOK
GRAB
UGH!
WRENCH
HE'S A MERCENARY WITH THE GUILD...

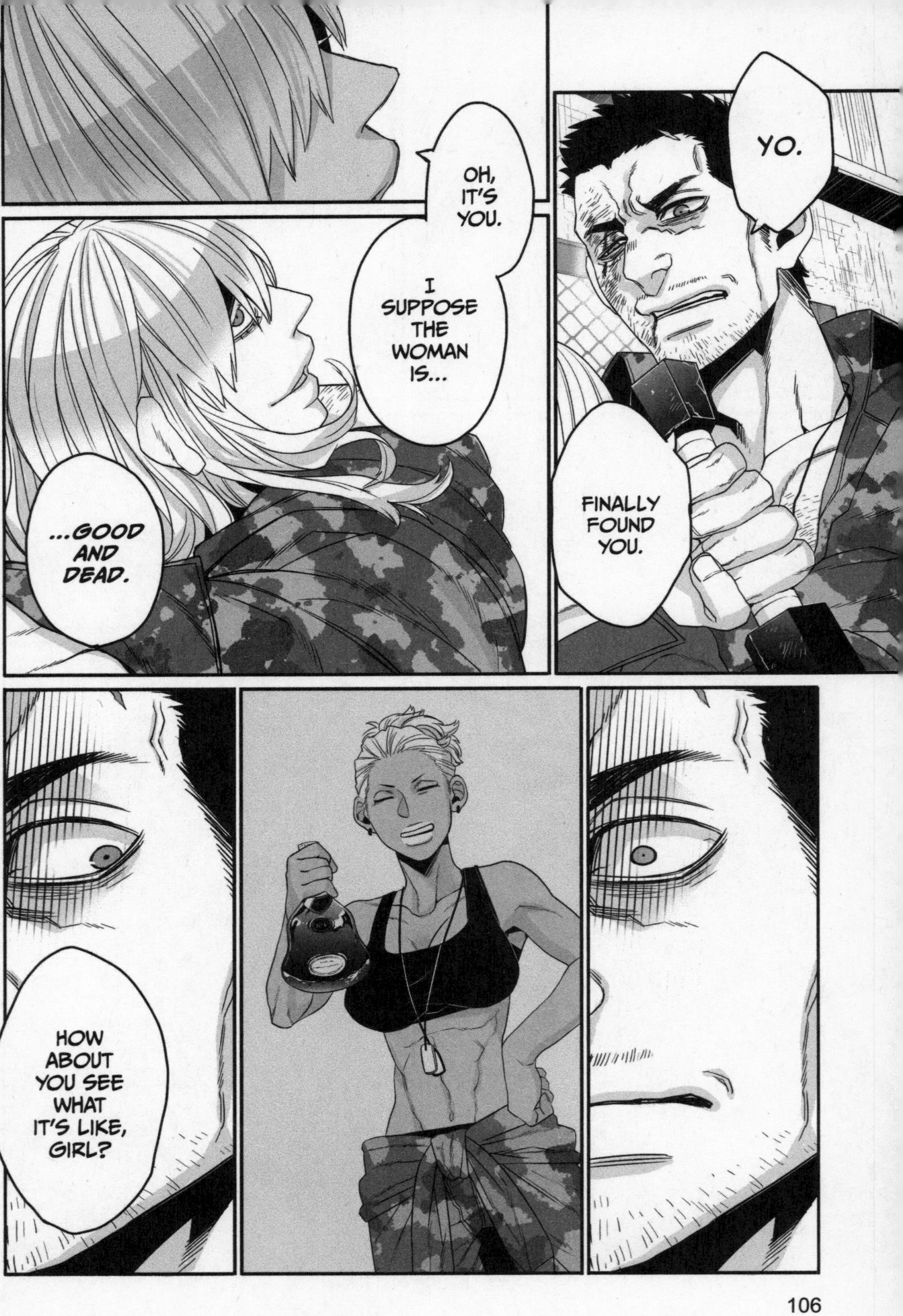
YO.
FINALLY FOUND YOU.
OH, IT'S YOU.
I SUPPOSE THE WOMAN IS...
...GOOD AND DEAD.
HOW ABOUT YOU SEE WHAT IT'S LIKE, GIRL?

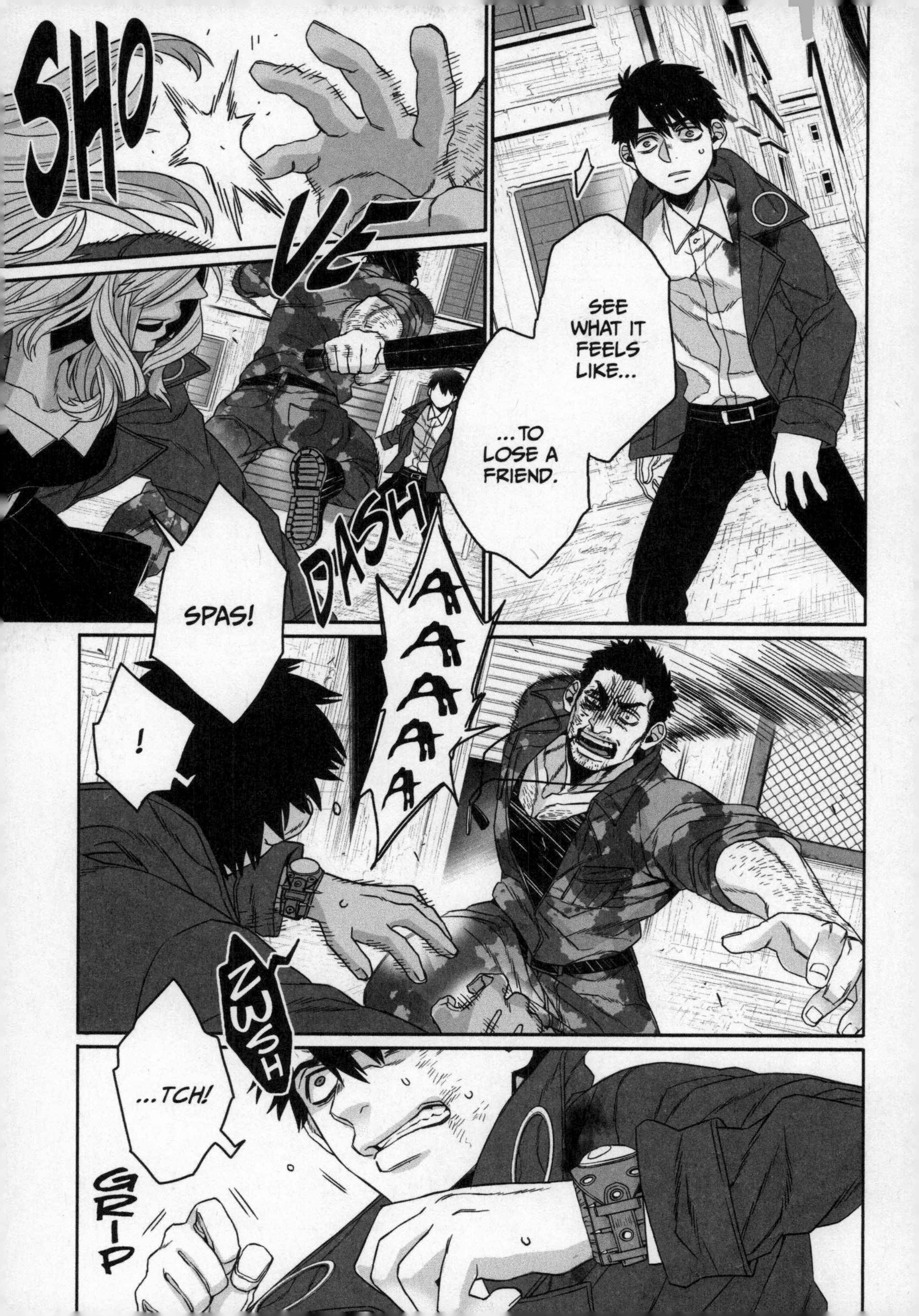
SEE WHAT IT FEELS LIKE...
...TO LOSE A FRIEND.
SHOVE
DASH
AAAAAA
SPAS!
!
NUSH
...TCH!
GRIP

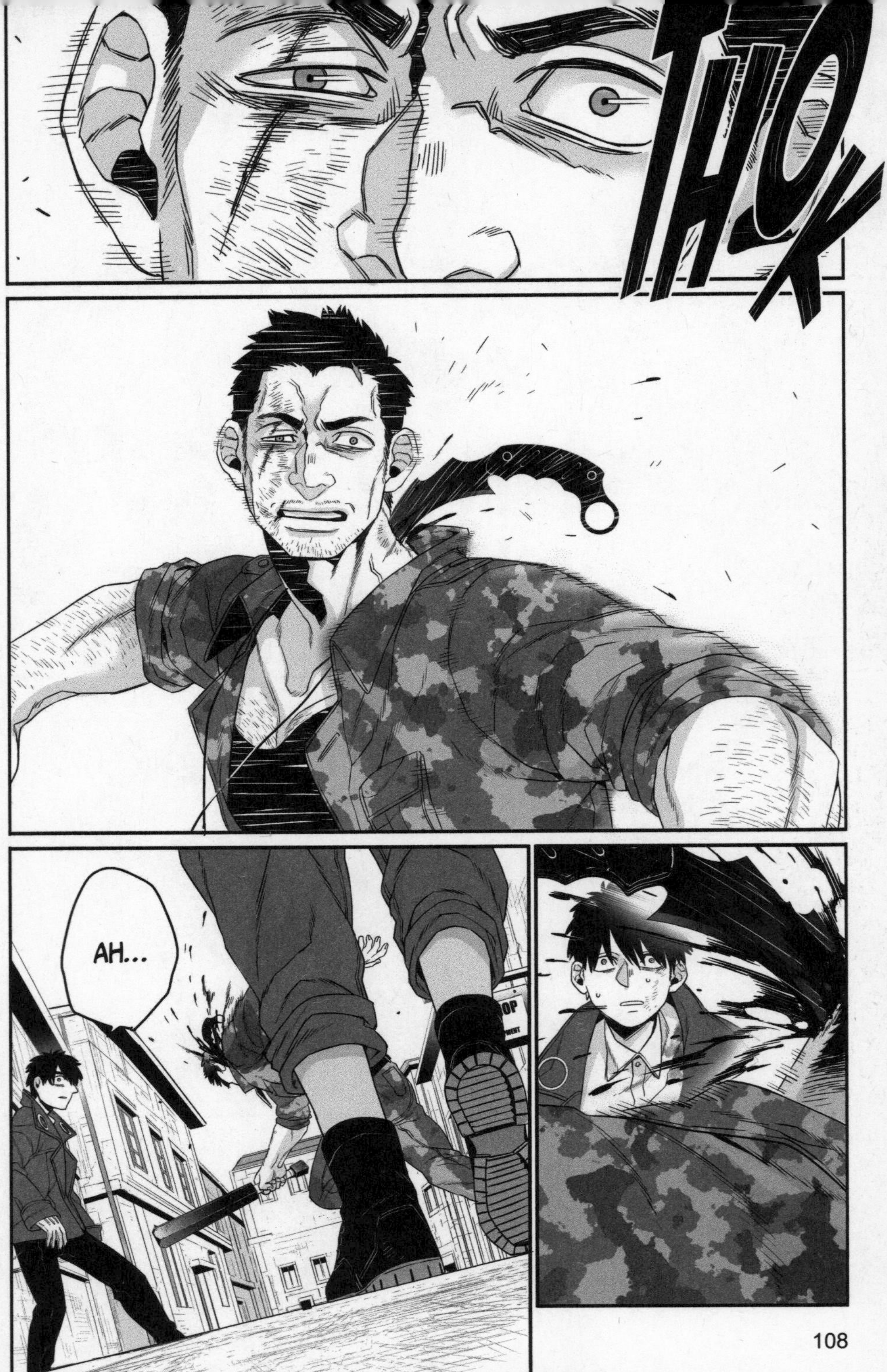
THOK
AH...

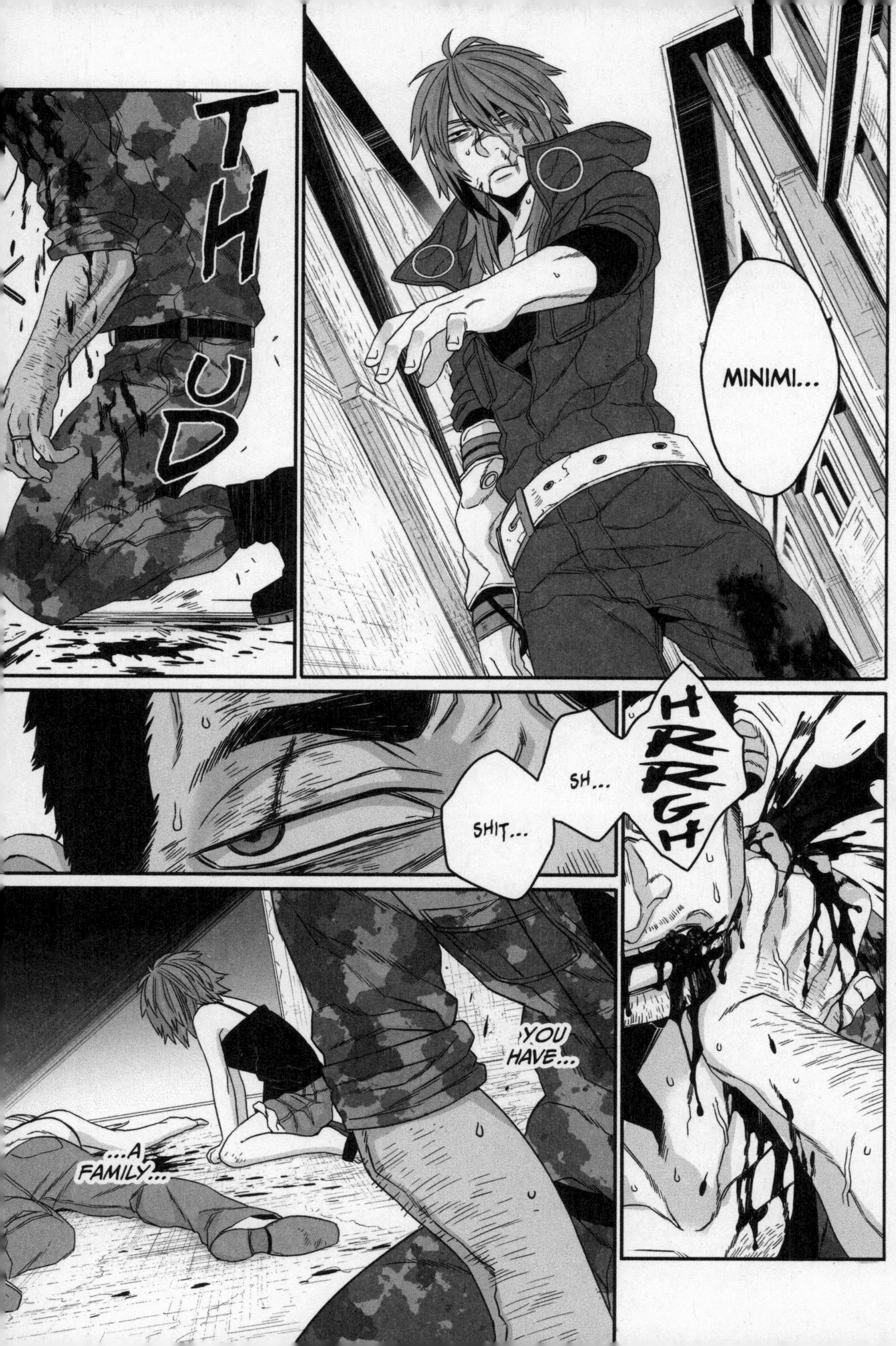
MINIMI...
THUD
HRRGH
SH...
SHIT...
YOU HAVE...
...A FAMILY...

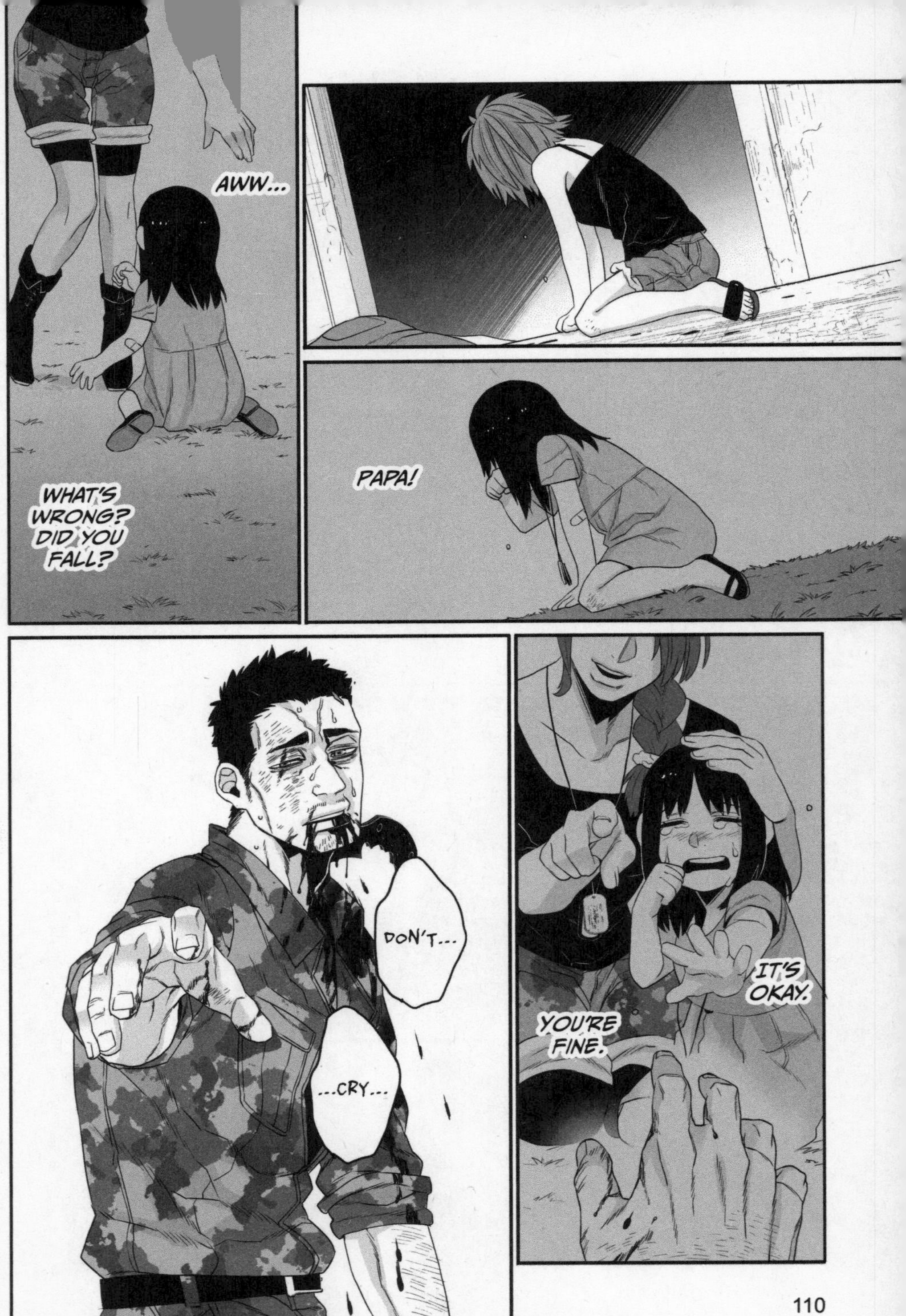
PAPA!
AWW...
WHAT'S WRONG? DID YOU FALL?
IT'S OKAY.
YOU'RE FINE.
DON'T...
...CRY...

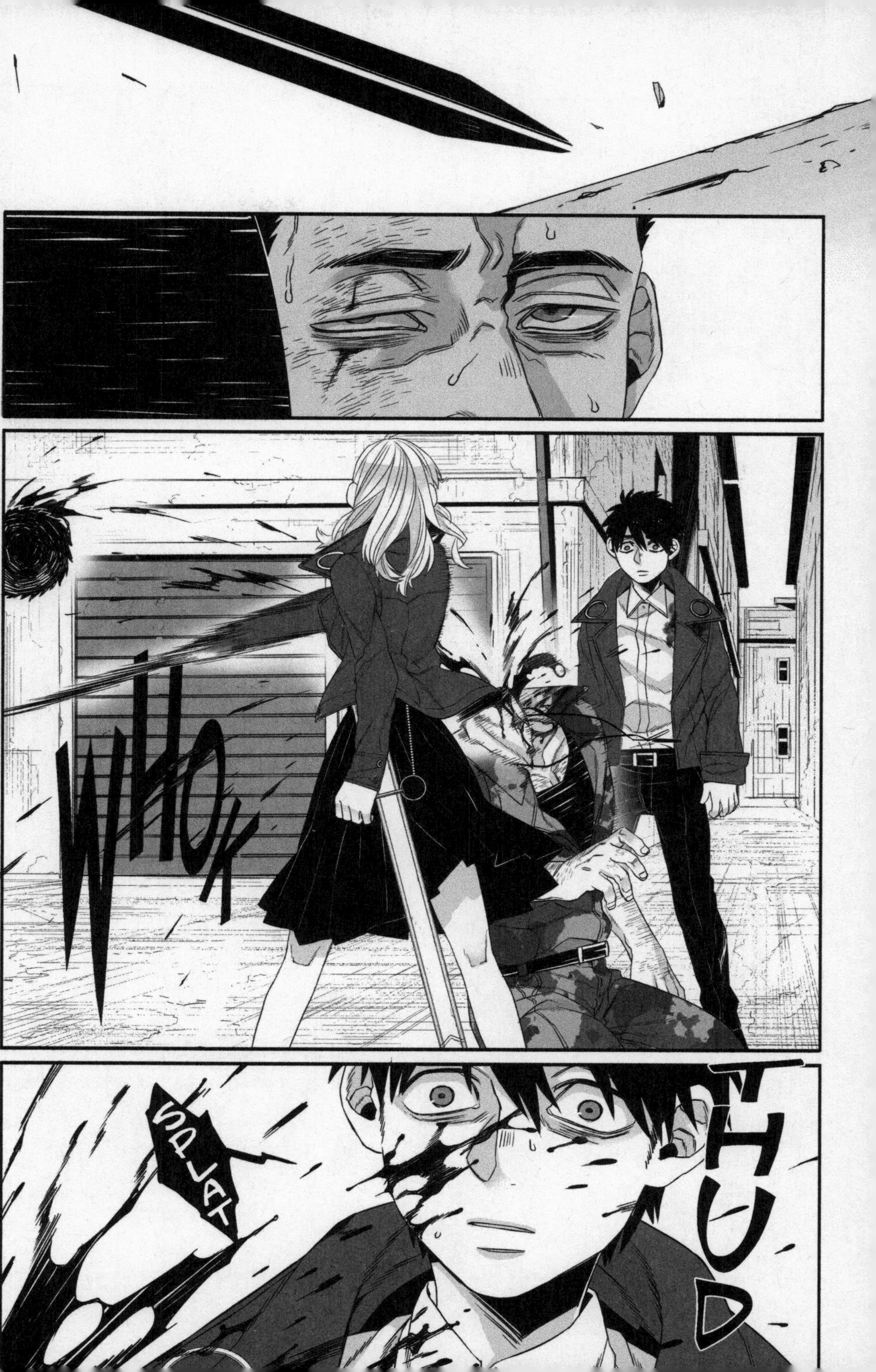
WHOK
THUD
SPLAT

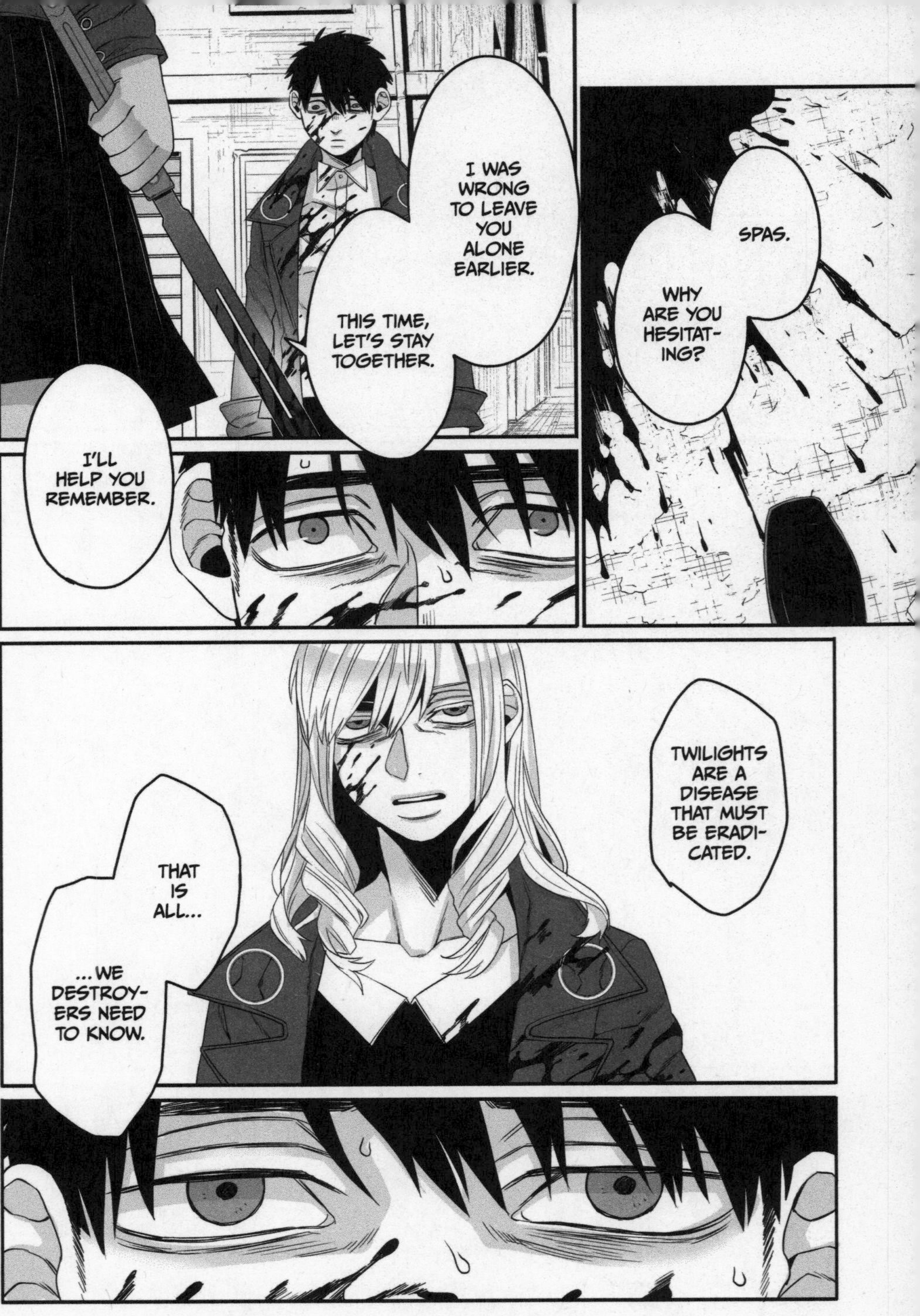
SPAS.
WHY ARE YOU HESITATING?
I WAS WRONG TO LEAVE YOU ALONE EARLIER.
THIS TIME, LET'S STAY TOGETHER.
I'LL HELP YOU REMEMBER.
TWILIGHTS ARE A DISEASE THAT MUST BE ERADICATED.
THAT IS ALL...
...WE DESTROYERS NEED TO KNOW.

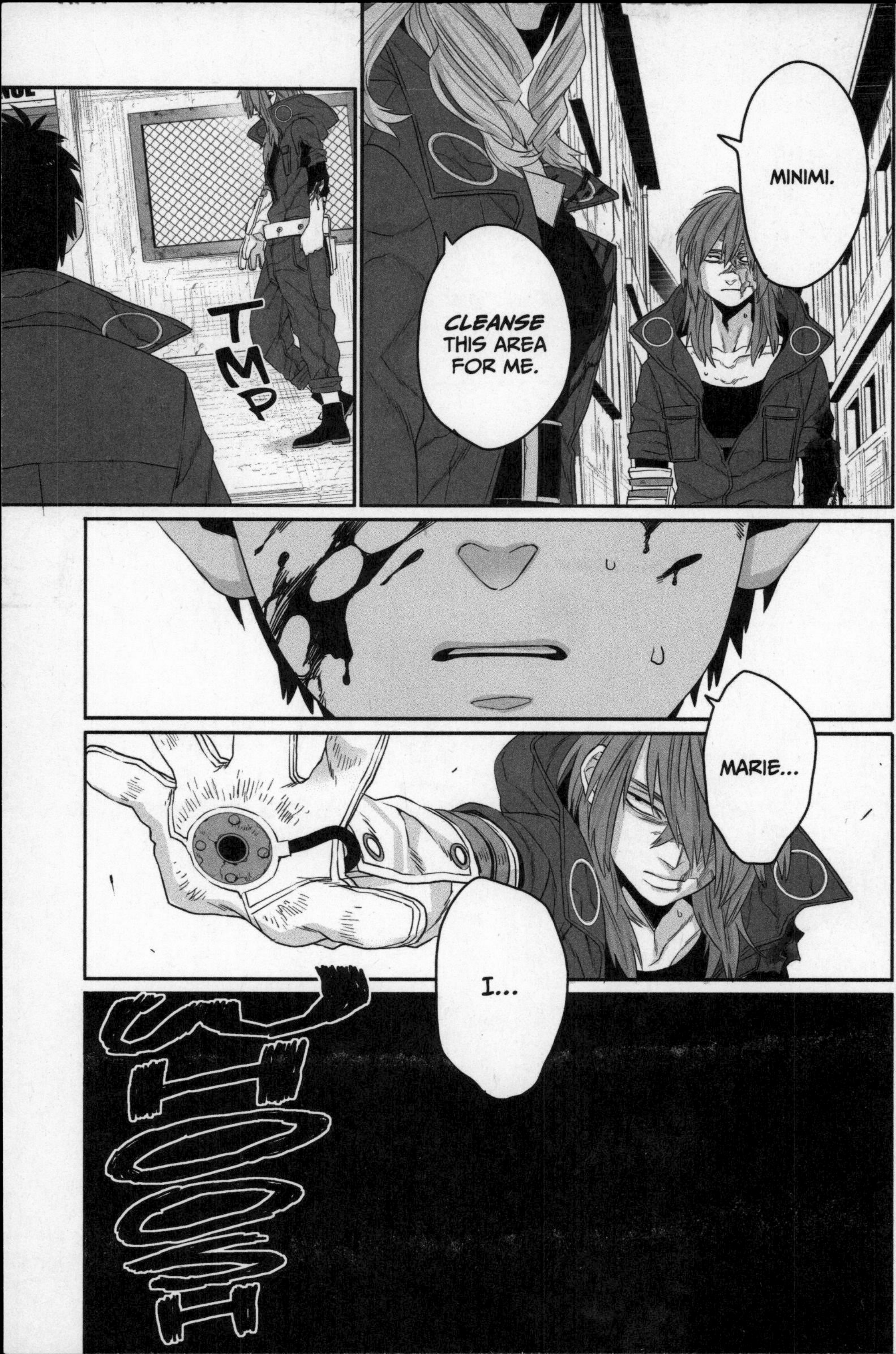
MINIMI.
CLEANSE THIS AREA FOR ME.
TMP
MARIE...
I...

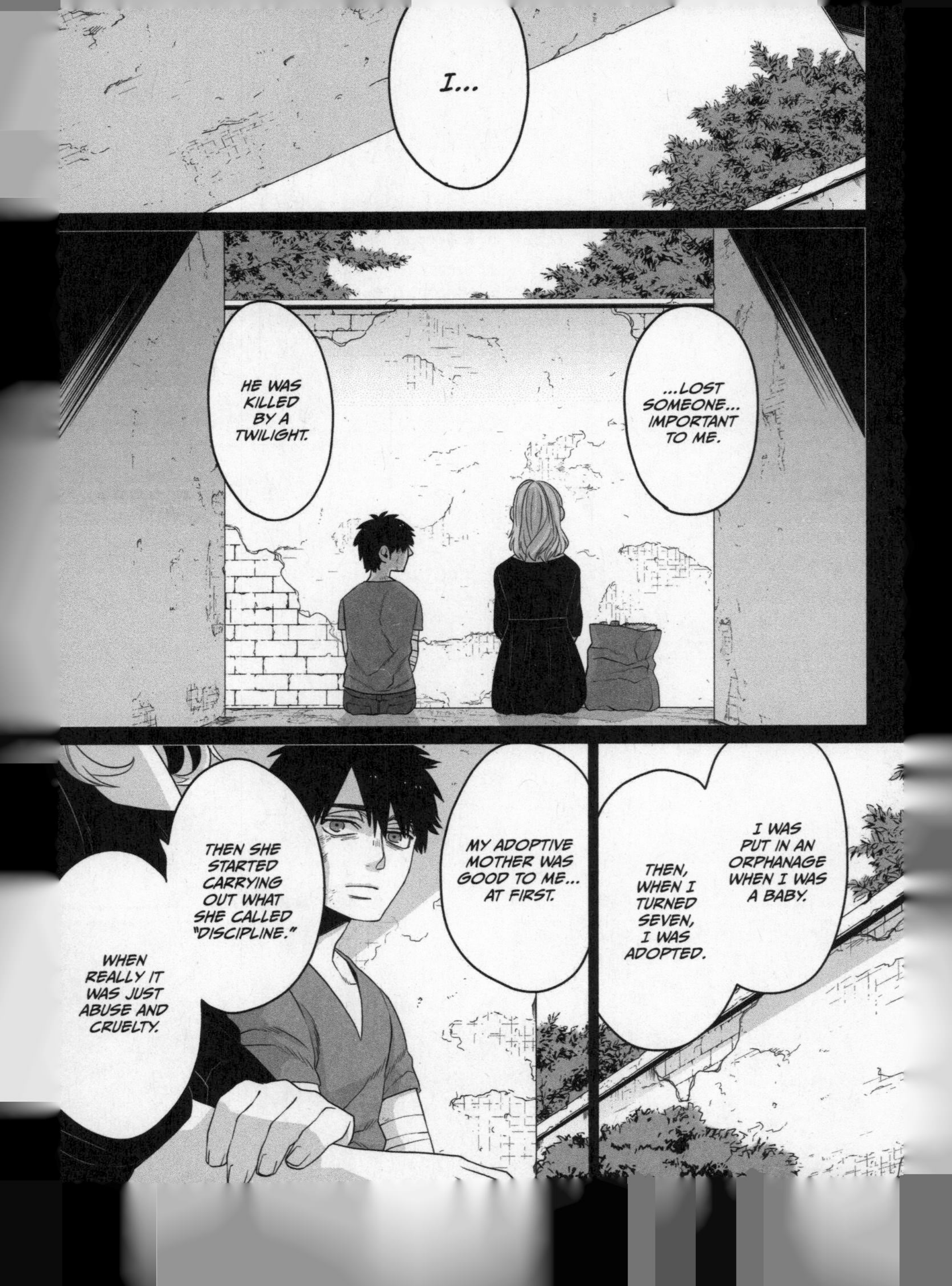
I...
...LOST SOMEONE... IMPORTANT TO ME.
HE WAS KILLED BY A TWILIGHT.
I WAS PUT IN AN ORPHANAGE WHEN I WAS A BABY.
THEN, WHEN I TURNED SEVEN, I WAS ADOPTED.
MY ADOPTIVE MOTHER WAS GOOD TO ME... AT FIRST.
THEN SHE STARTED CARRYING OUT WHAT SHE CALLED "DISCIPLINE."
WHEN REALLY IT WAS JUST ABUSE AND CRUELTY.

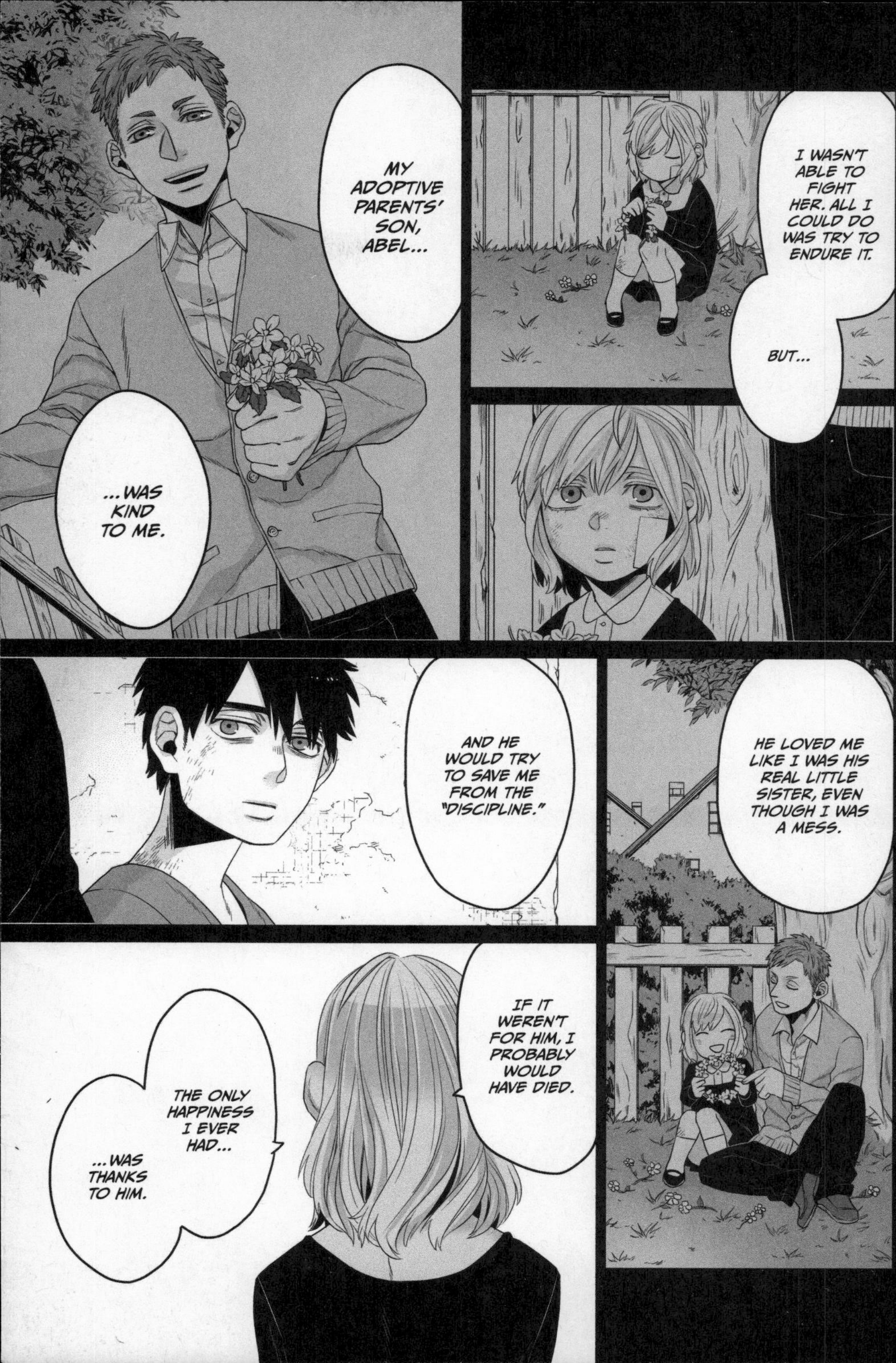
I WASN'T ABLE TO FIGHT HER. ALL I COULD DO WAS TRY TO ENDURE IT.
BUT...
MY ADOPTIVE PARENTS' SON, ABEL...
...WAS KIND TO ME.
HE LOVED ME LIKE I WAS HIS REAL LITTLE SISTER, EVEN THOUGH I WAS A MESS.
AND HE WOULD TRY TO SAVE ME FROM THE "DISCIPLINE."
IF IT WEREN'T FOR HIM, I PROBABLY WOULD HAVE DIED.
THE ONLY HAPPINESS I EVER HAD...
...WAS THANKS TO HIM.

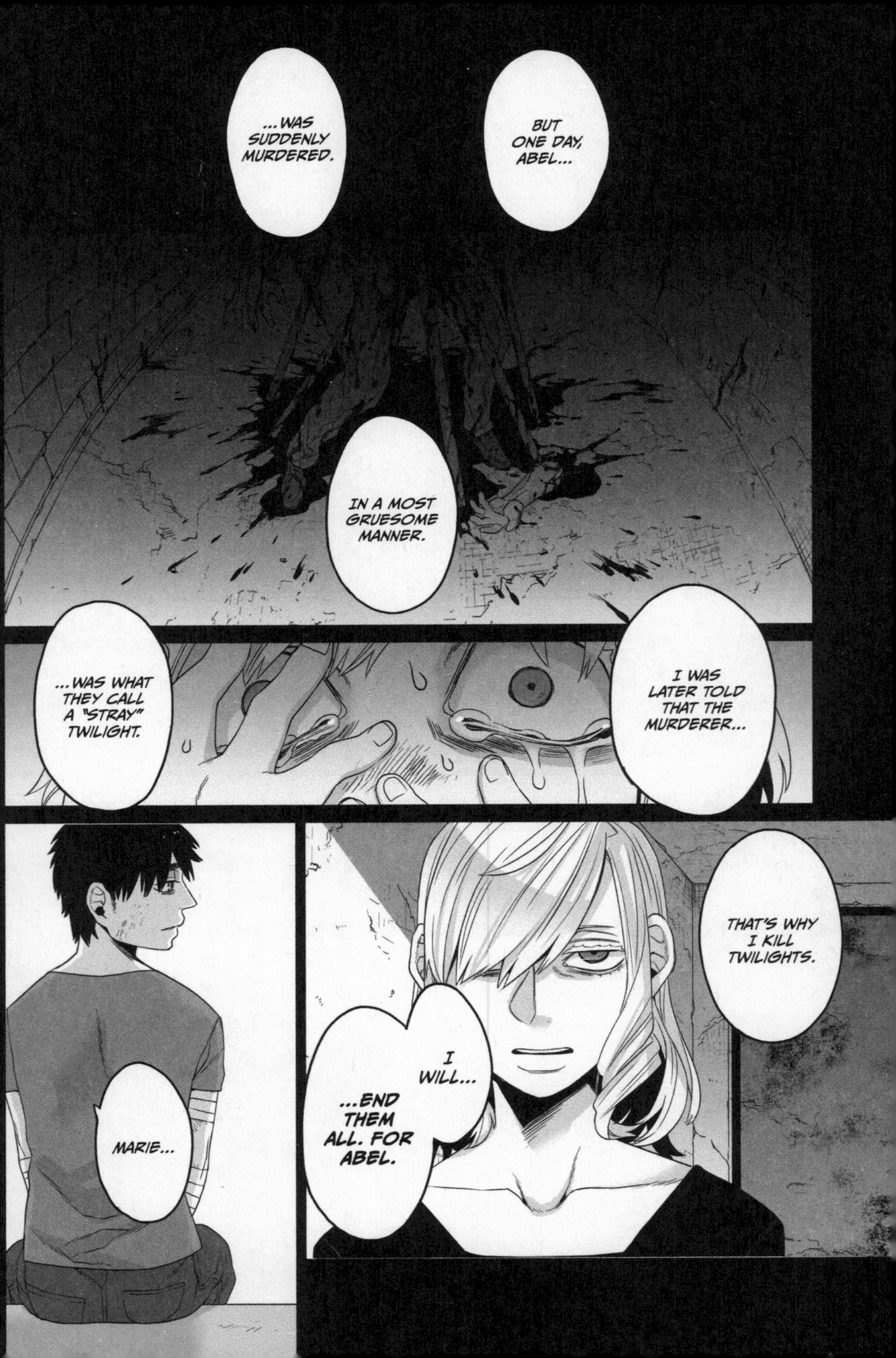
BUT ONE DAY, ABEL...
...WAS SUDDENLY MURDERED.
IN A MOST GRUESOME MANNER.
I WAS LATER TOLD THAT THE MURDERER...
...WAS WHAT THEY CALL A "STRAY" TWILIGHT.
THAT'S WHY I KILL TWILIGHTS.
I WILL...
...END THEM ALL. FOR ABEL.
MARIE...

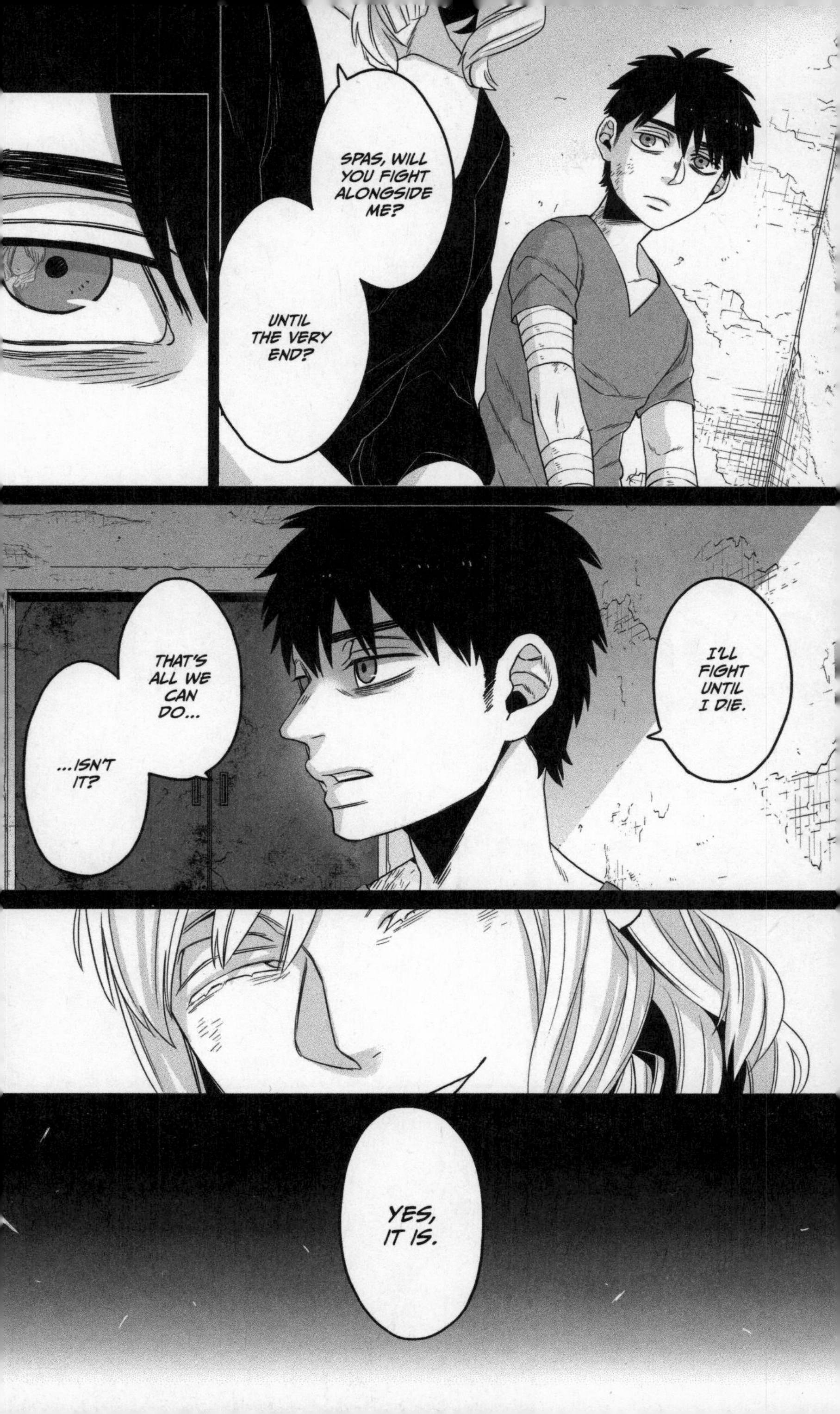
SPAS, WILL YOU FIGHT ALONGSIDE ME?
UNTIL THE VERY END?
I'LL FIGHT UNTIL I DIE.
THAT'S ALL WE CAN DO...
...ISN'T IT?
YES, IT IS.

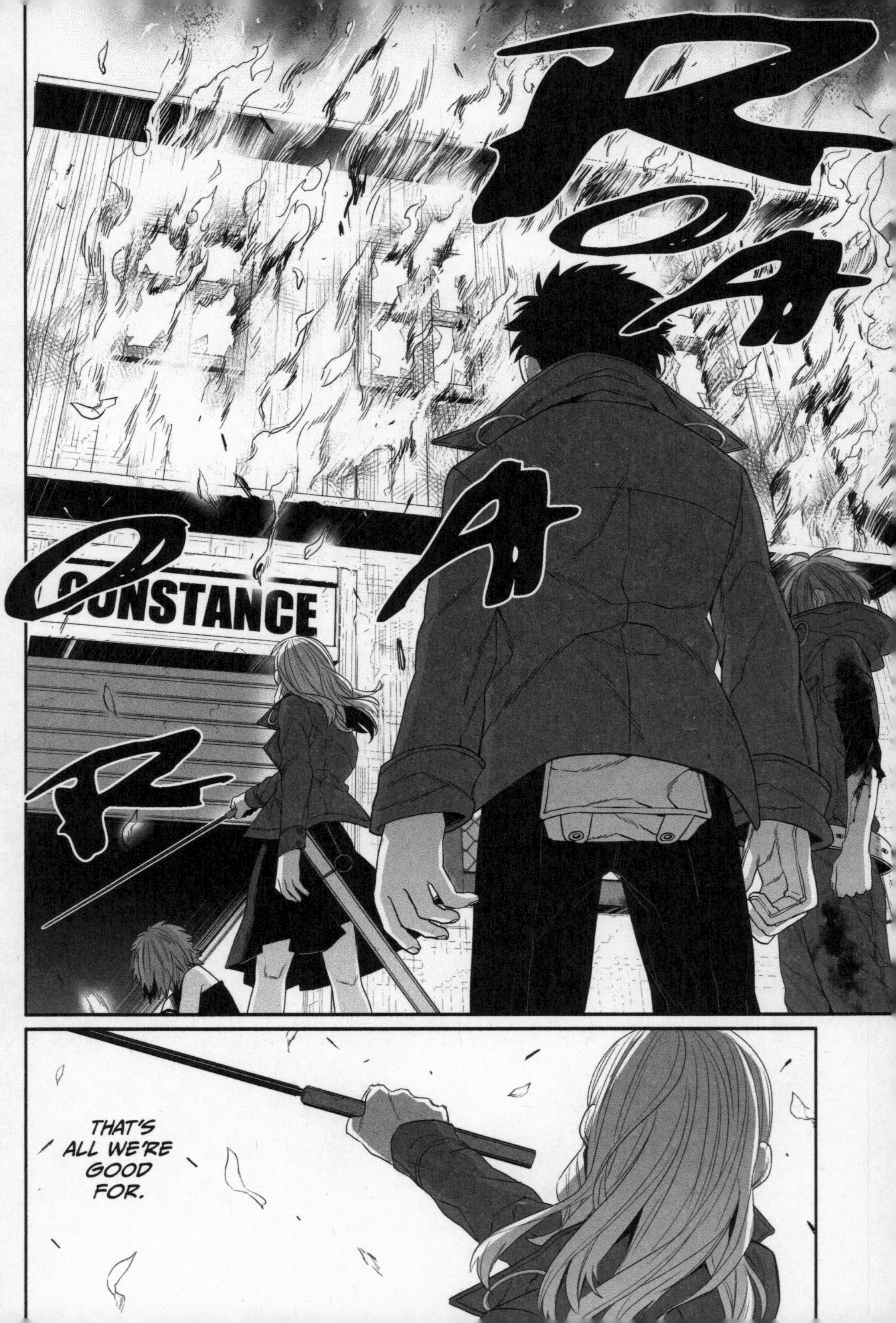
CONSTANCE
THAT'S ALL WE'RE GOOD FOR.

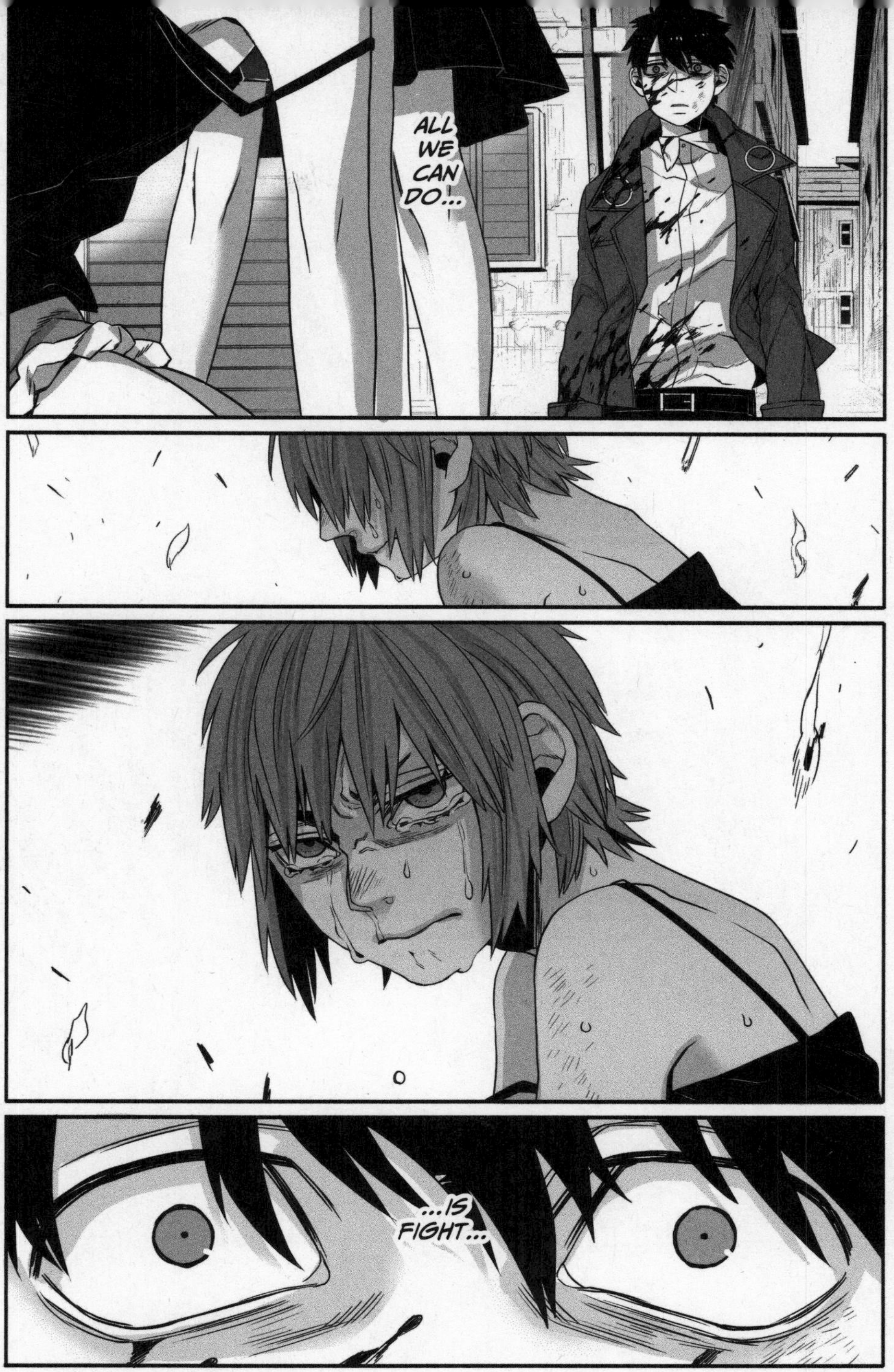
ALL WE CAN DO...
...IS FIGHT...

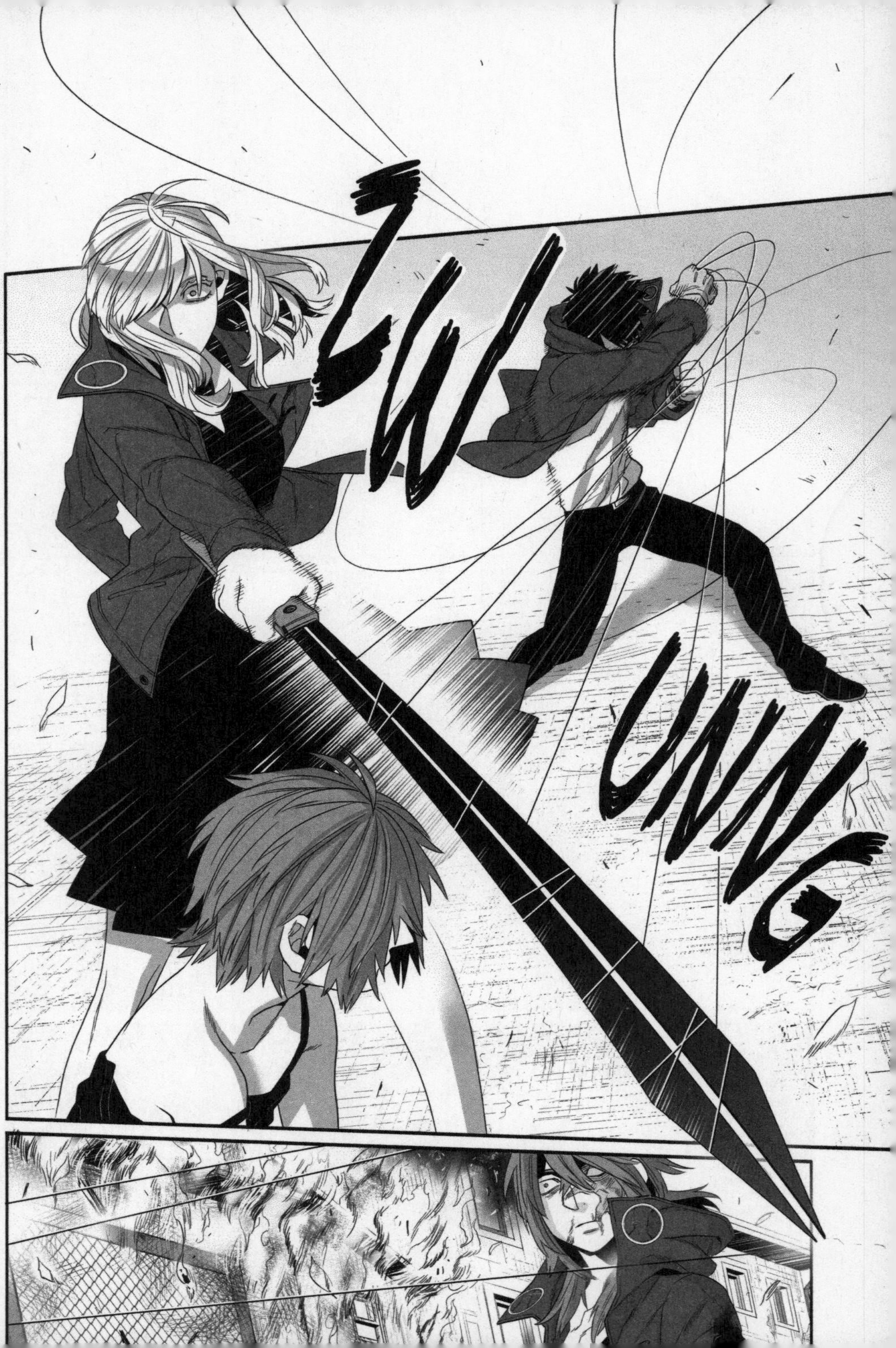
ZWUNNG

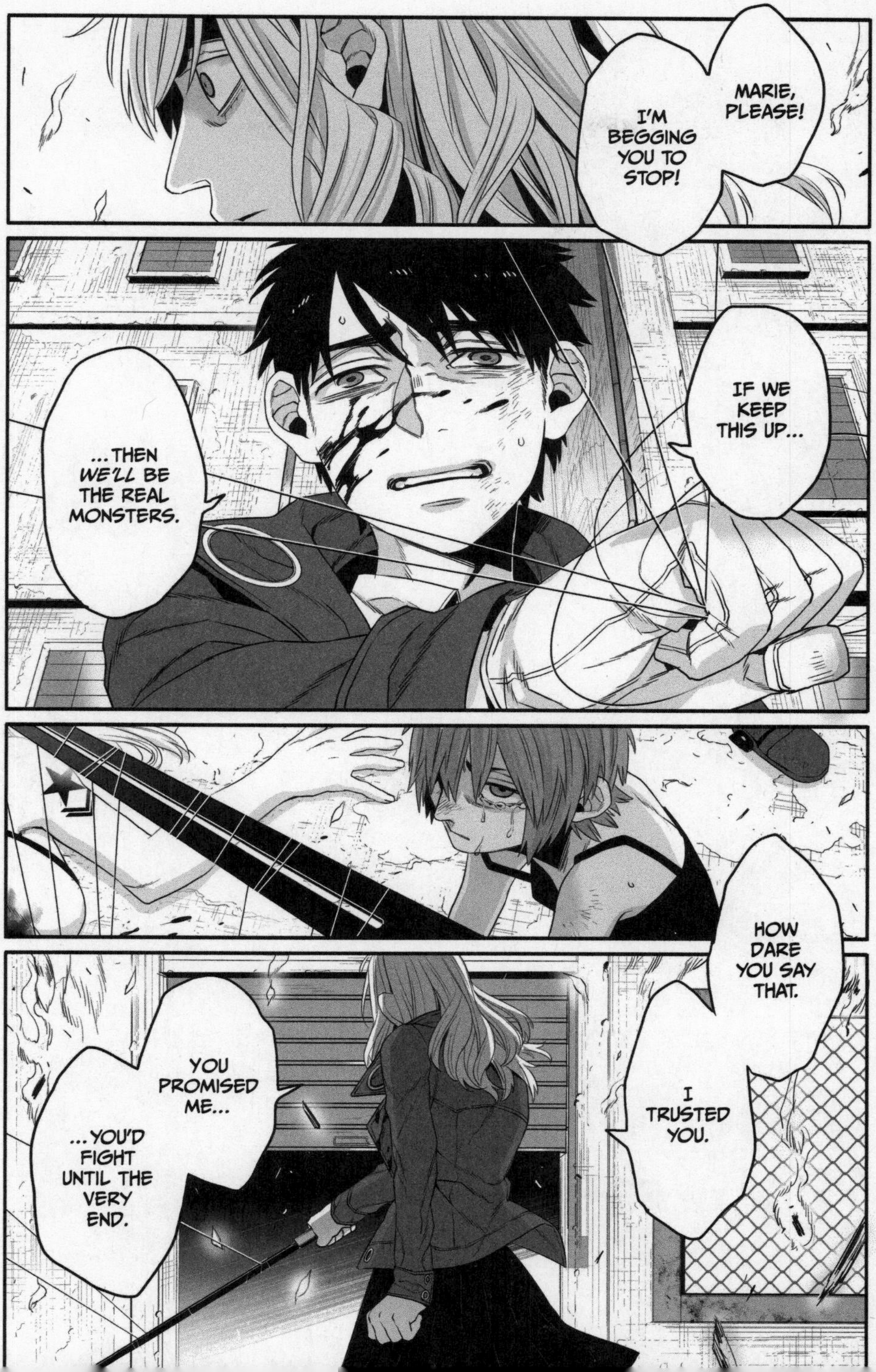
MARIE, PLEASE!
I'M BEGGING YOU TO STOP!
IF WE KEEP THIS UP...
...THEN WE'LL BE THE REAL MONSTERS.
HOW DARE YOU SAY THAT.
I TRUSTED YOU.
YOU PROMISED ME...
...YOU'D FIGHT UNTIL THE VERY END.

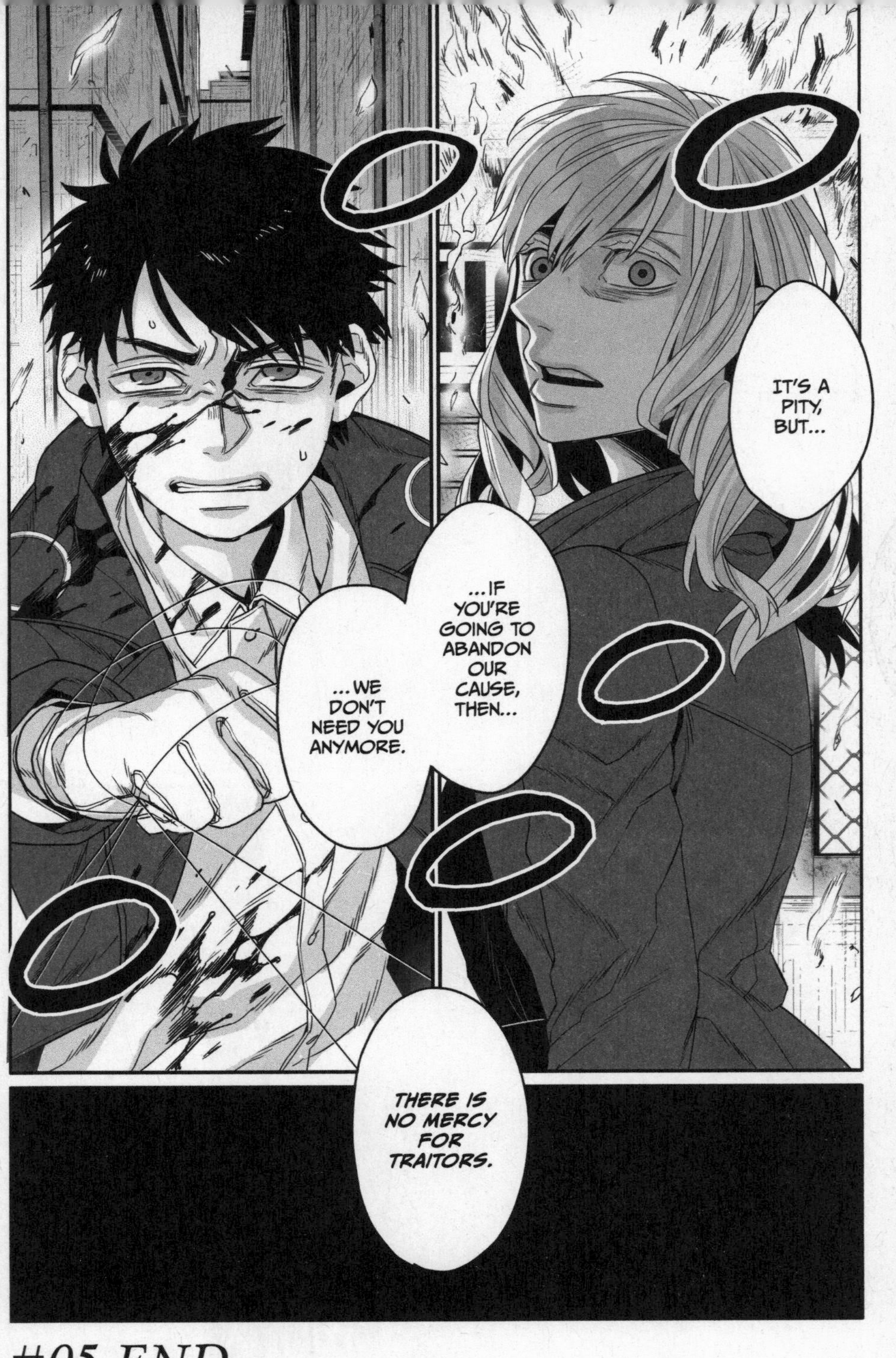
IT'S A PITY, BUT...
...IF YOU'RE GOING TO ABANDON OUR CAUSE, THEN...
...WE DON'T NEED YOU ANYMORE.
THERE IS NO MERCY FOR TRAITORS.

#05 END

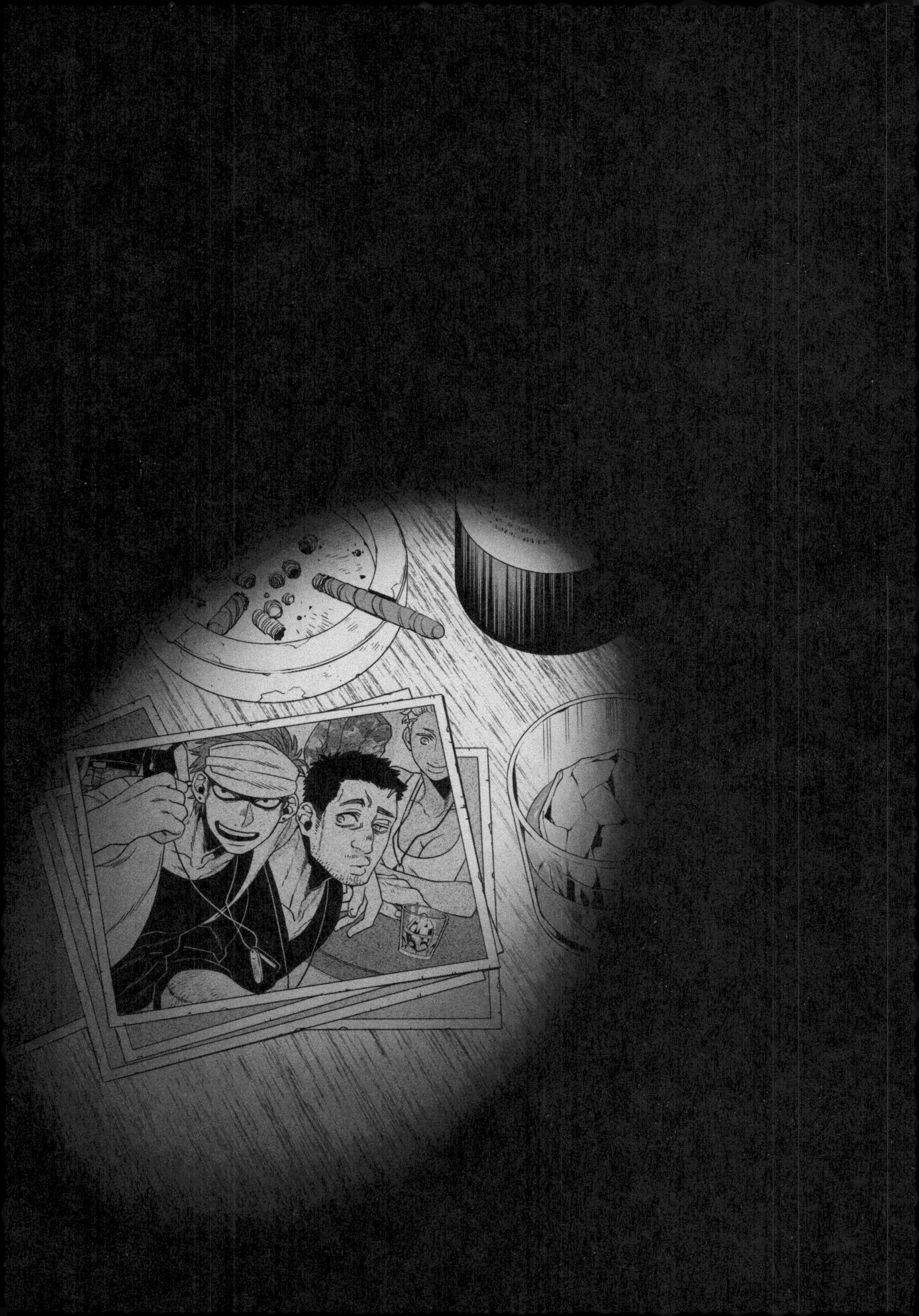

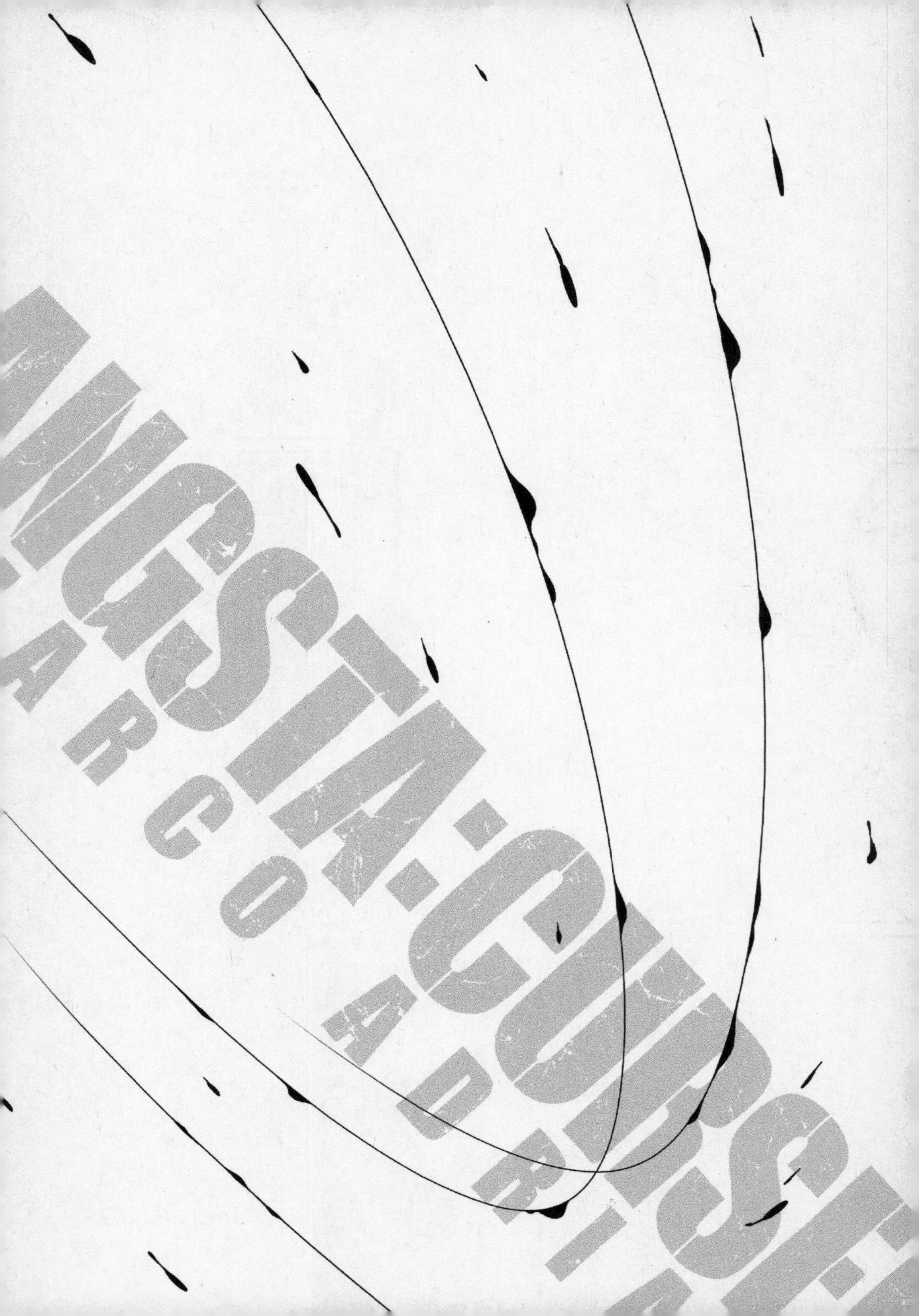

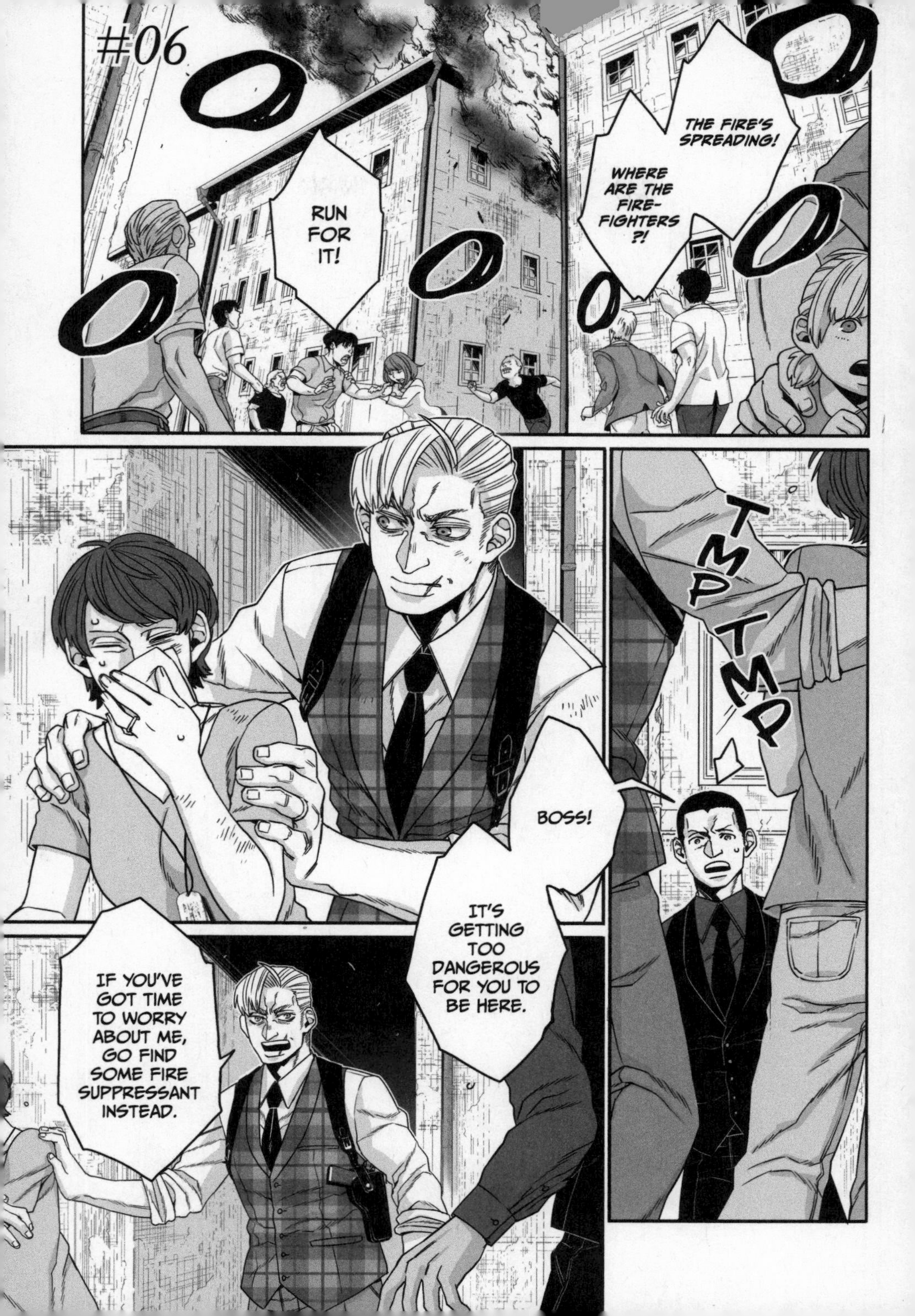
#06
THE FIRE'S SPREADING!
WHERE ARE THE FIRE-FIGHTERS?!
RUN FOR IT!
TMP TMP TMP
BOSS!
IT'S GETTING TOO DANGEROUS FOR YOU TO BE HERE.
IF YOU'VE GOT TIME TO WORRY ABOUT ME, GO FIND SOME FIRE SUPPRESSANT INSTEAD.

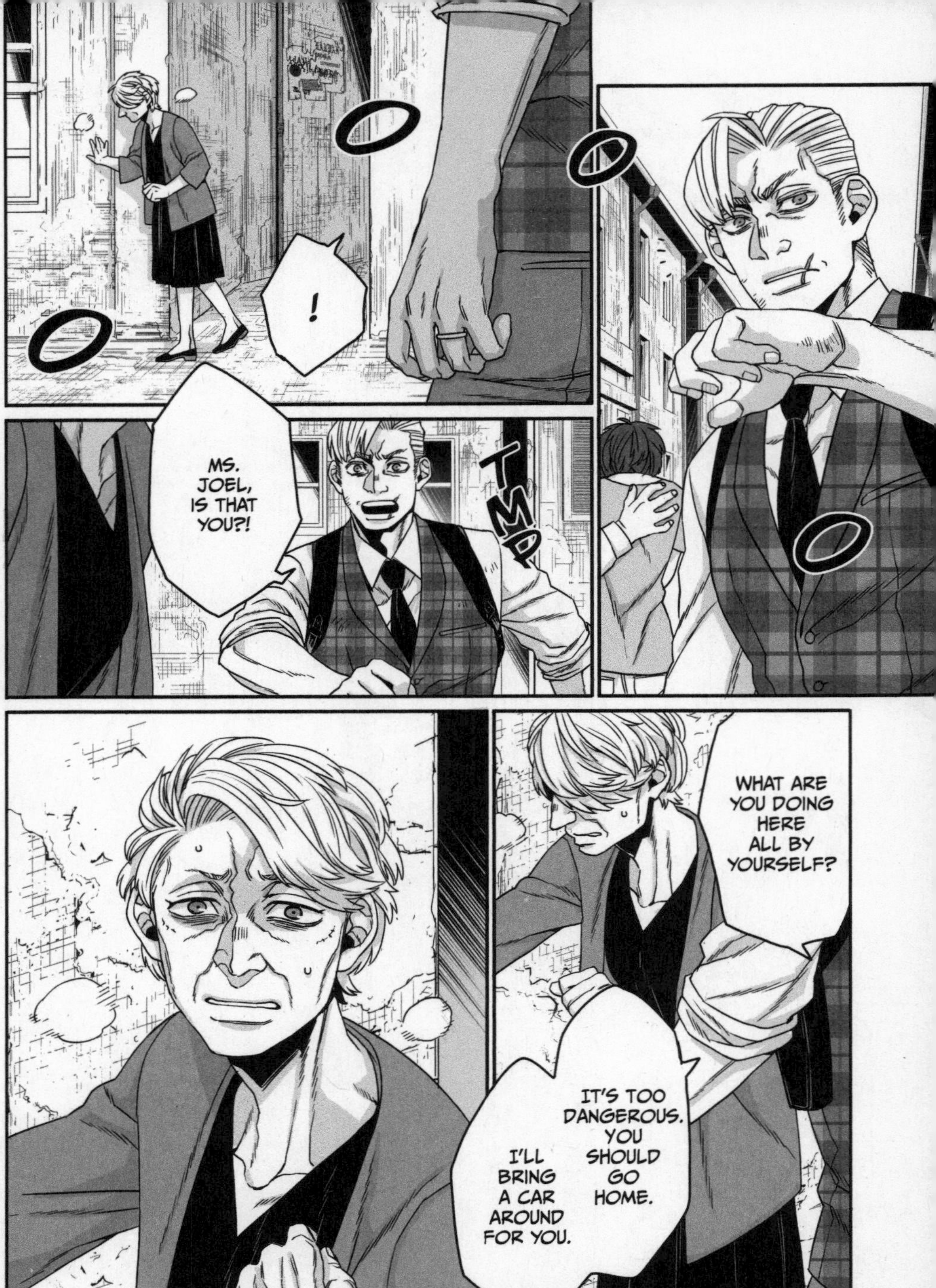
!
MS. JOEL, IS THAT YOU?!
TMP
WHAT ARE YOU DOING HERE ALL BY YOURSELF?
IT'S TOO DANGEROUS. YOU SHOULD GO HOME.
I'LL BRING A CAR AROUND FOR YOU.

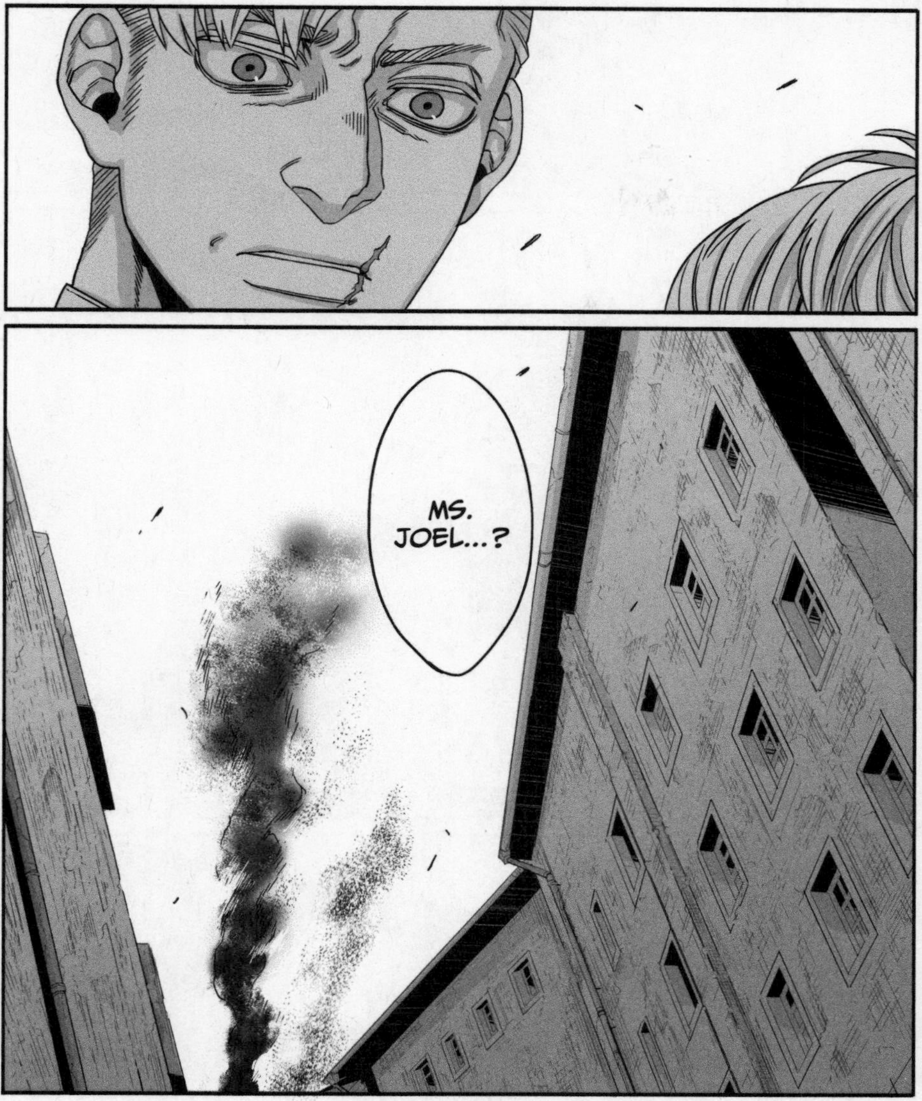
MS. JOEL...?

#06

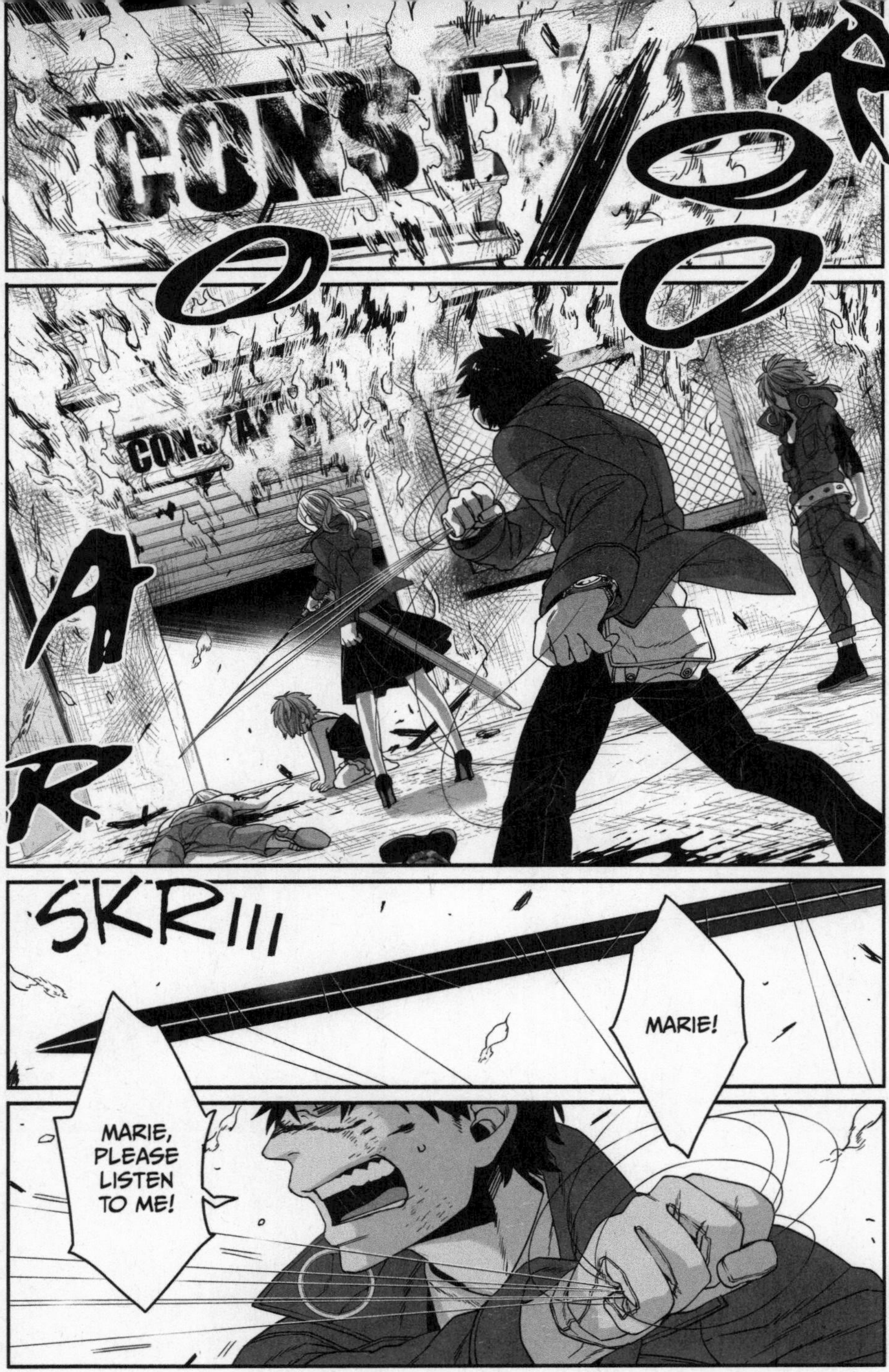
ROOOAR
SKRIII
MARIE!
MARIE, PLEASE LISTEN TO ME!

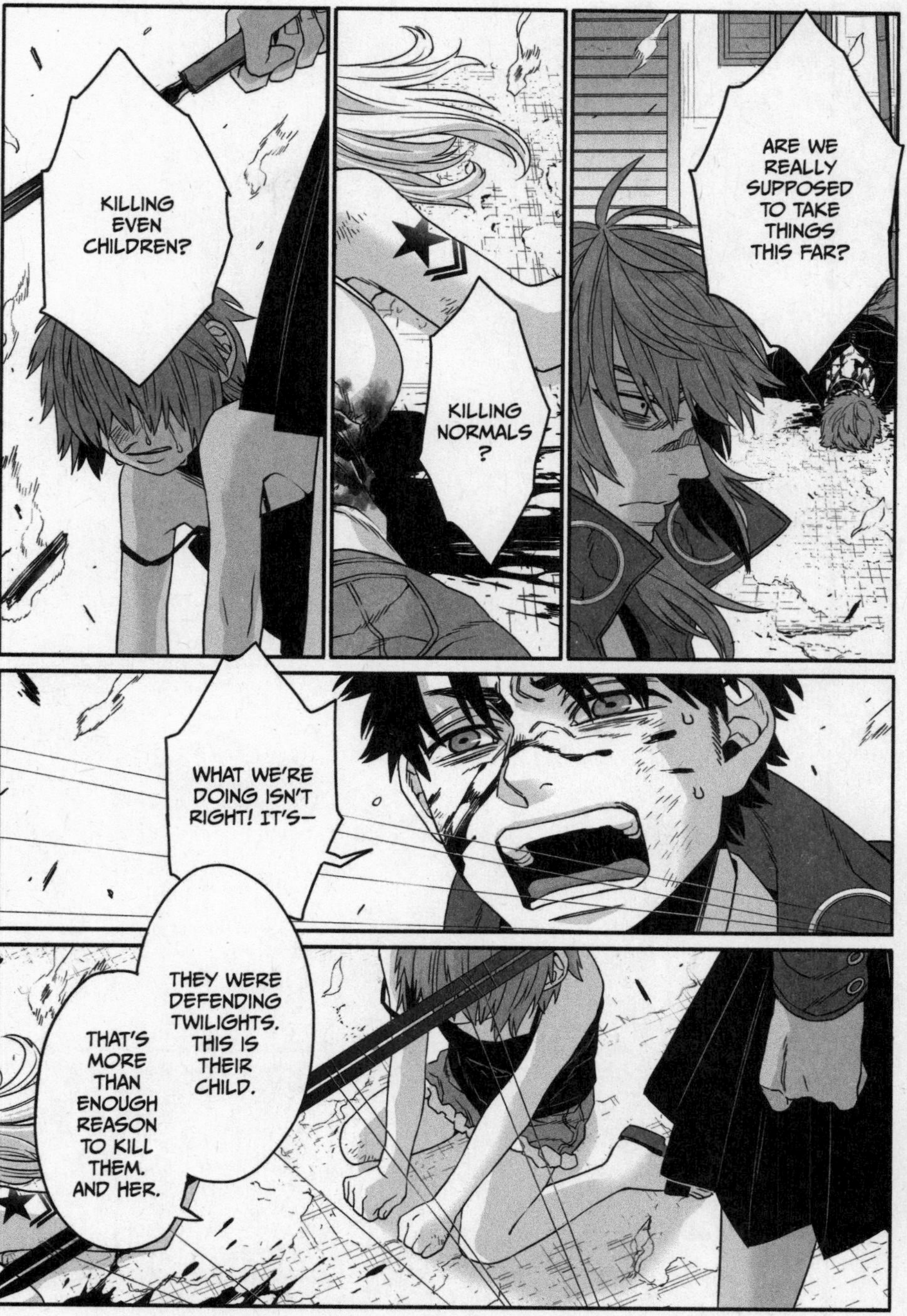
ARE WE REALLY SUPPOSED TO TAKE THINGS THIS FAR?
KILLING NORMALS?
KILLING EVEN CHILDREN?
WHAT WE'RE DOING ISN'T RIGHT! IT'S—
THEY WERE DEFENDING TWILIGHTS. THIS IS THEIR CHILD.
THAT'S MORE THAN ENOUGH REASON TO KILL THEM. AND HER.

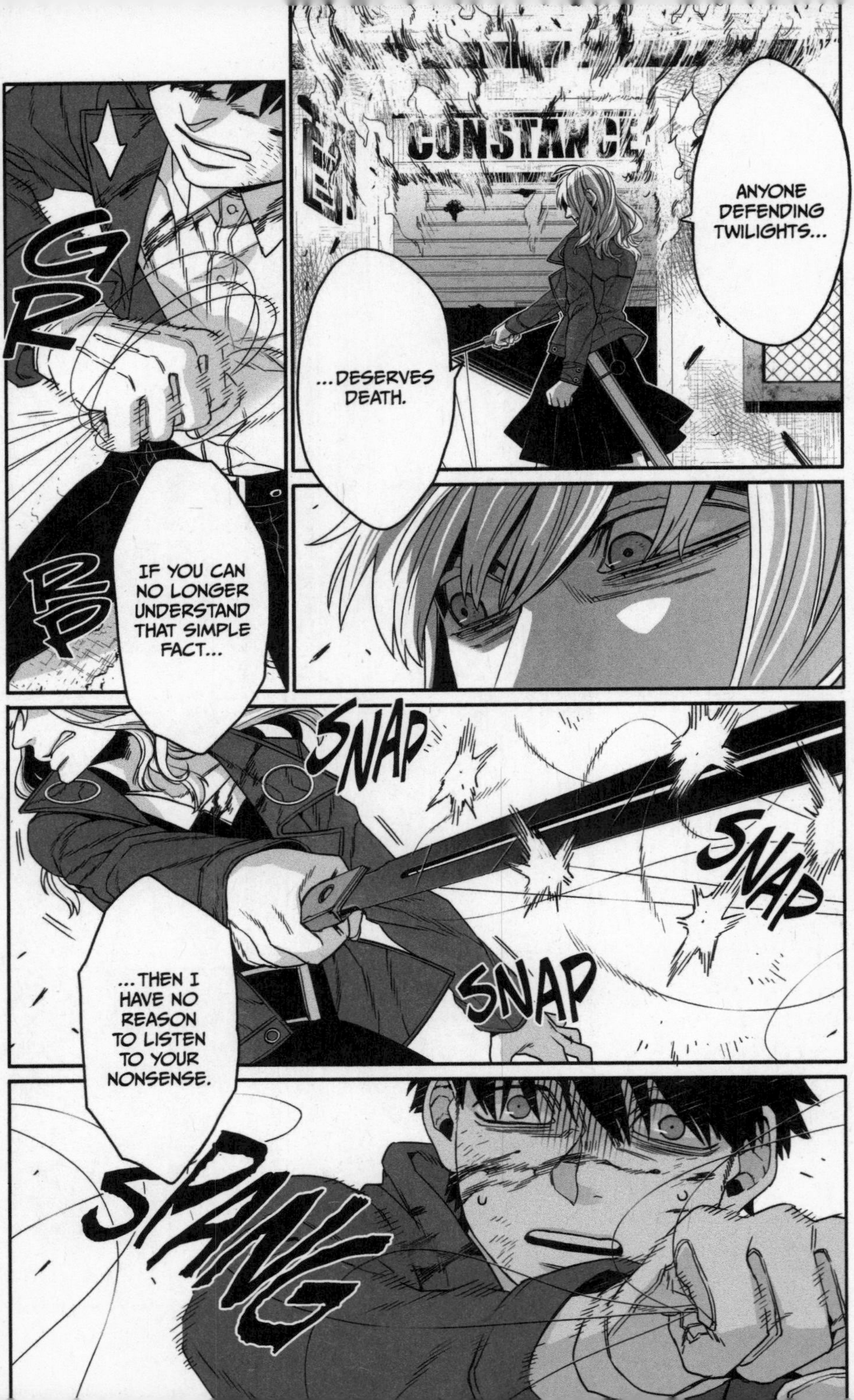
CONSTANCE
ANYONE DEFENDING TWILIGHTS...
...DESERVES DEATH.
IF YOU CAN NO LONGER UNDERSTAND THAT SIMPLE FACT...
GR
RP
SNAP
SNAP
SNAP
...THEN I HAVE NO REASON TO LISTEN TO YOUR NONSENSE.
SPANG

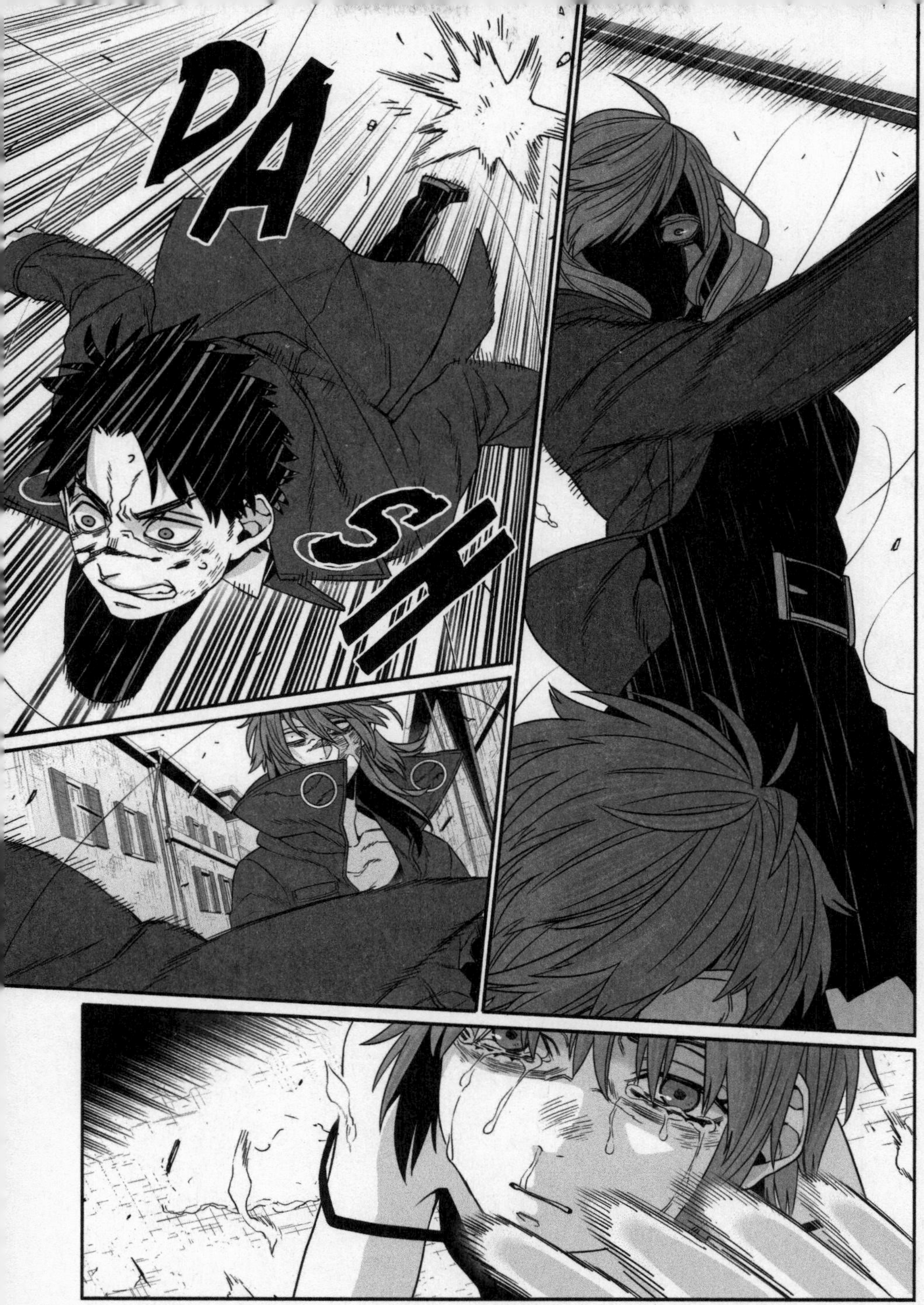
DA
SH

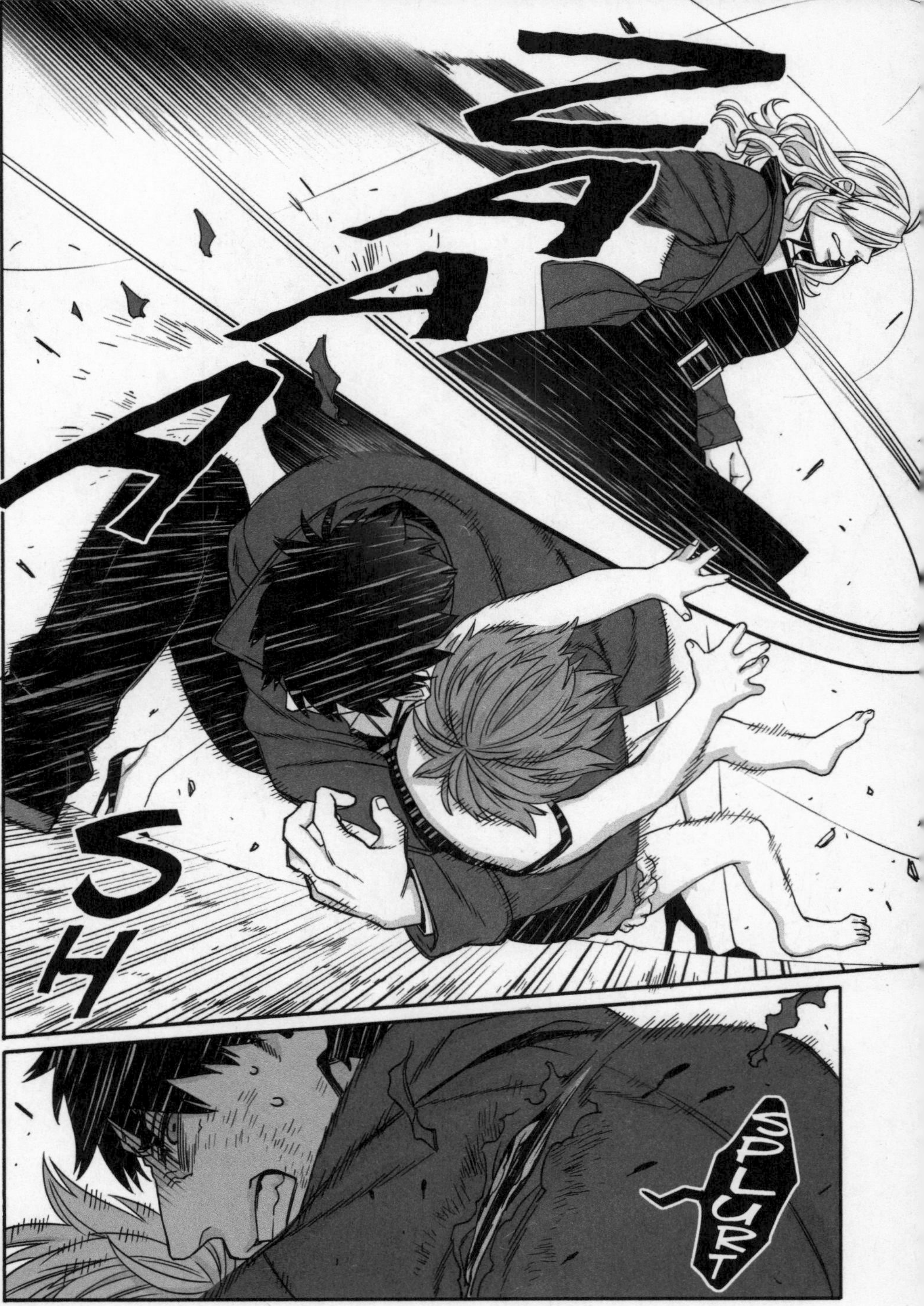
SPLURT

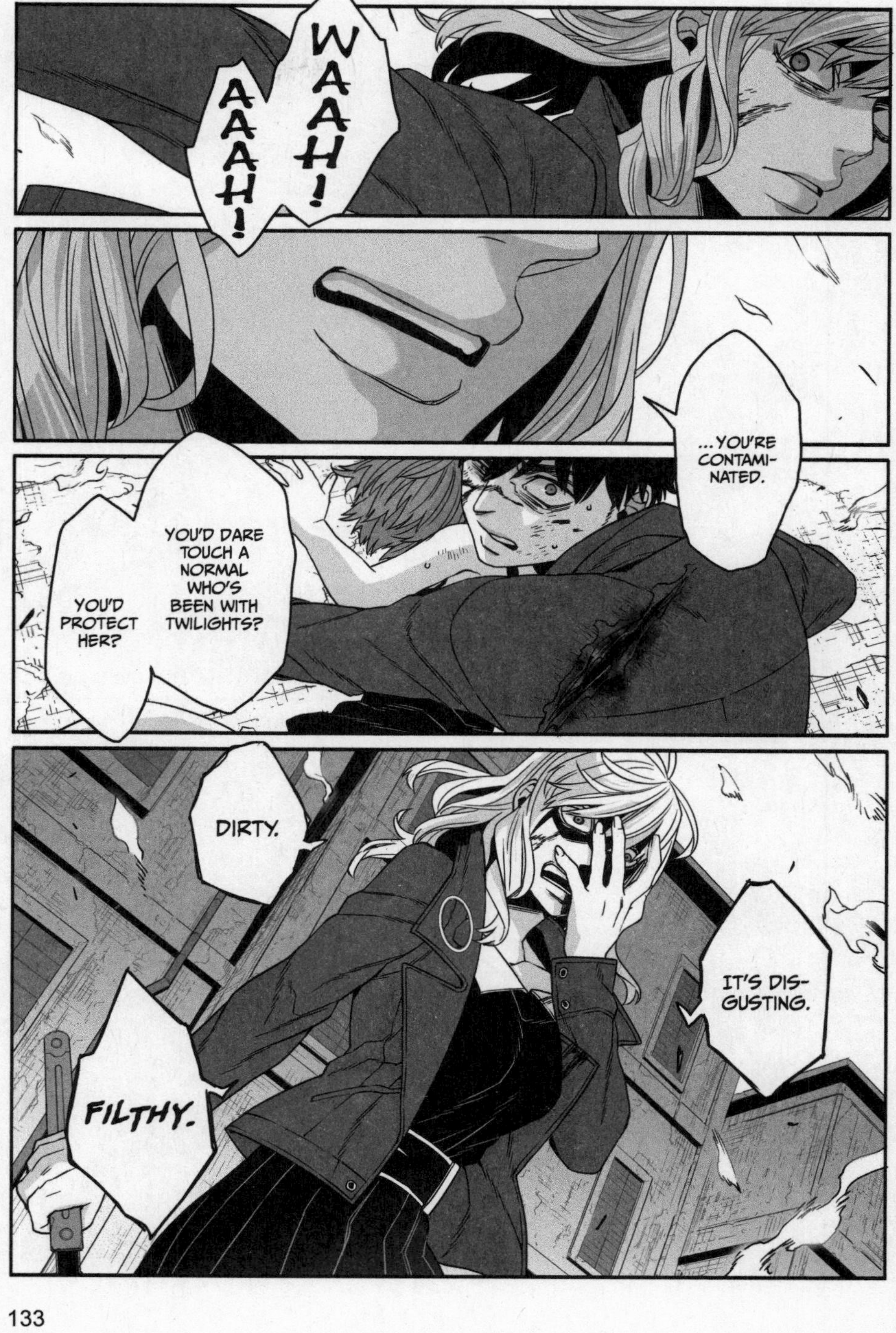
WAAH!
AAAH!
...YOU'RE CONTAMI-NATED.
YOU'D DARE TOUCH A NORMAL WHO'S BEEN WITH TWILIGHTS?
YOU'D PROTECT HER?
DIRTY.
IT'S DIS-GUSTING.
FILTHY.

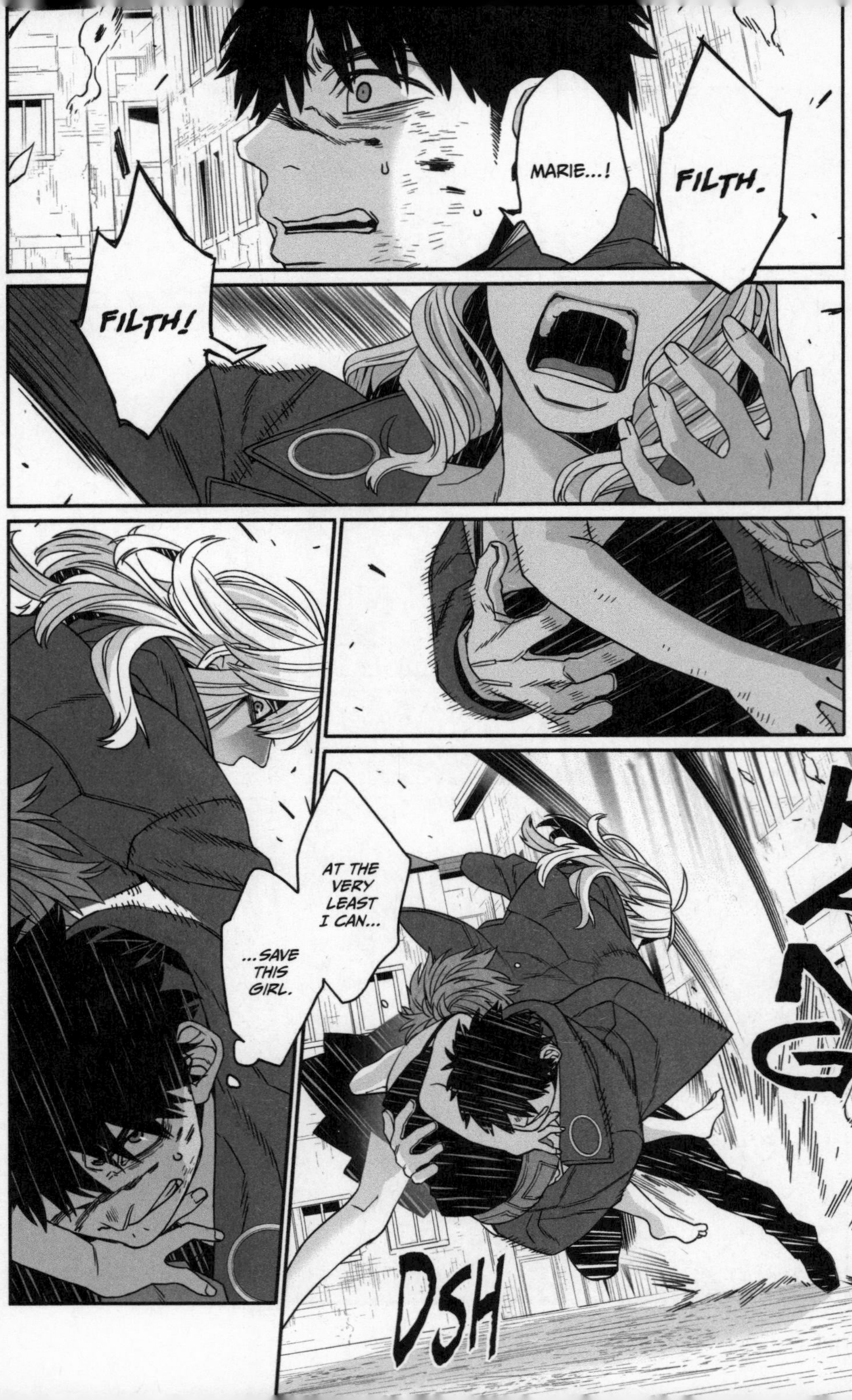
FILTH.
MARIE...!
FILTH!
KANG
AT THE VERY LEAST I CAN...
...SAVE THIS GIRL.
DSH

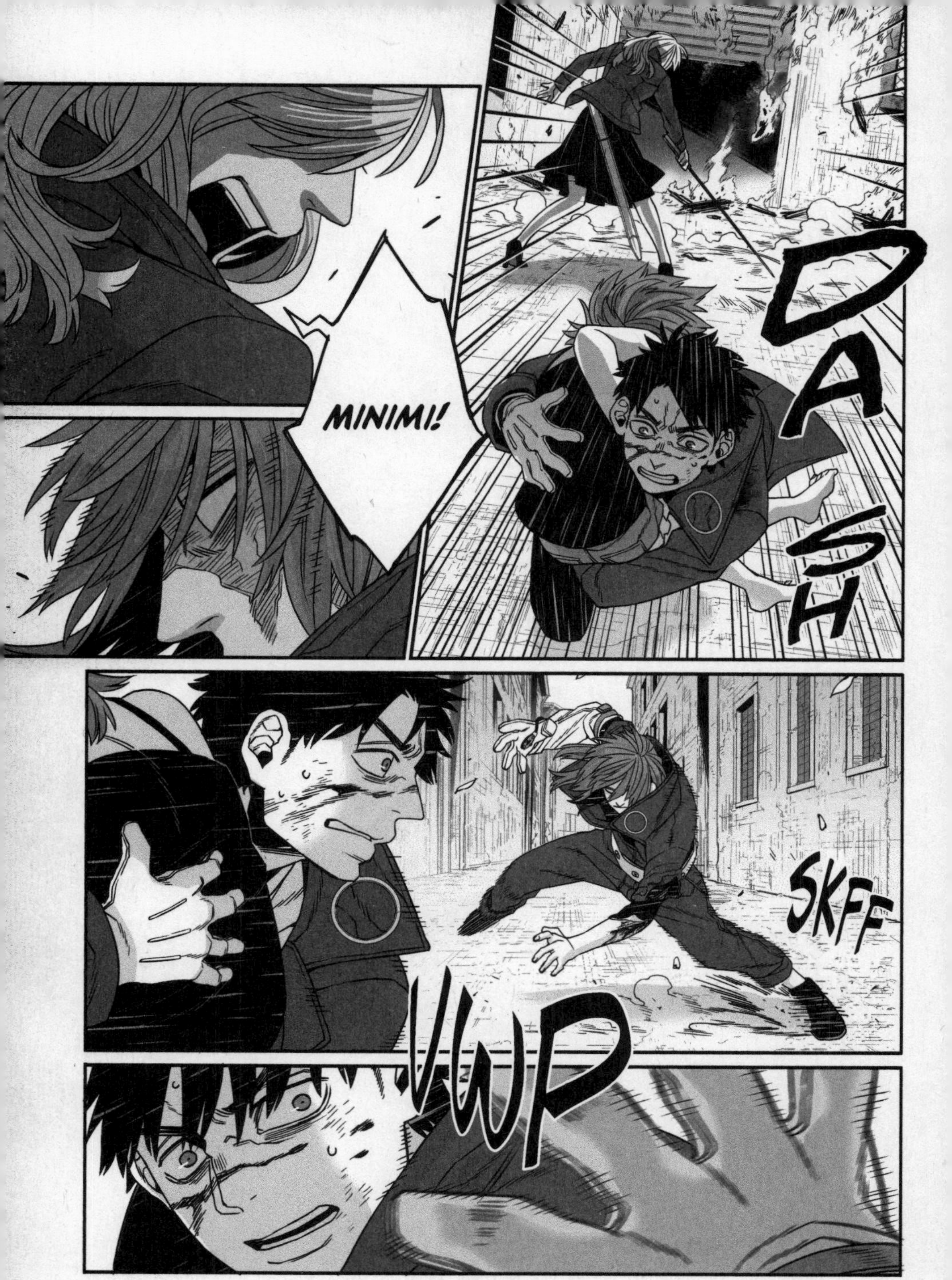
DASH
MINIMI!
SKFF
VWP

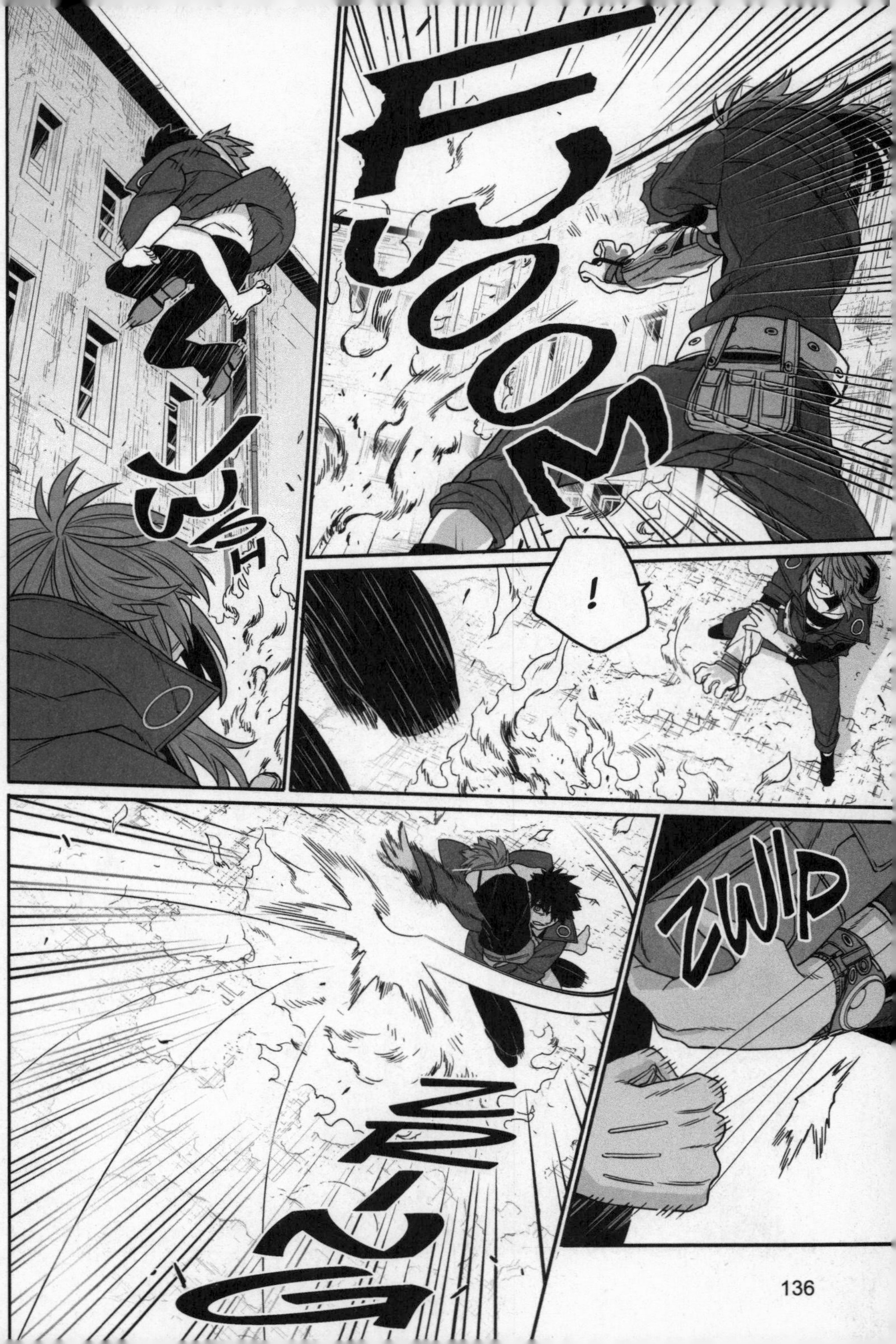
FWOOM
!
WHSH
ZWIP
ZRING

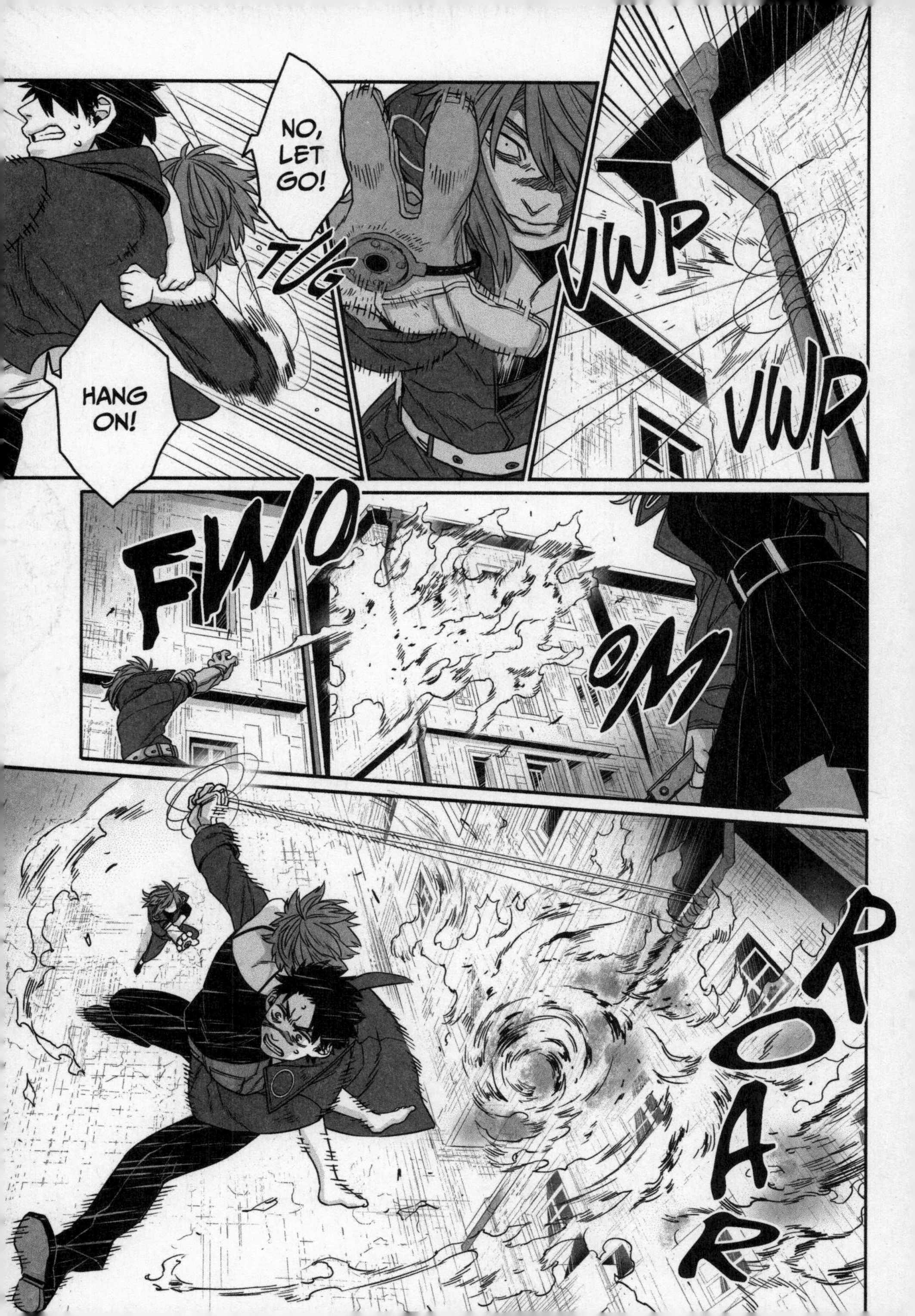
VWP
VWP
NO, LET GO!
TUG
HANG ON!
FWOOM
ROAR

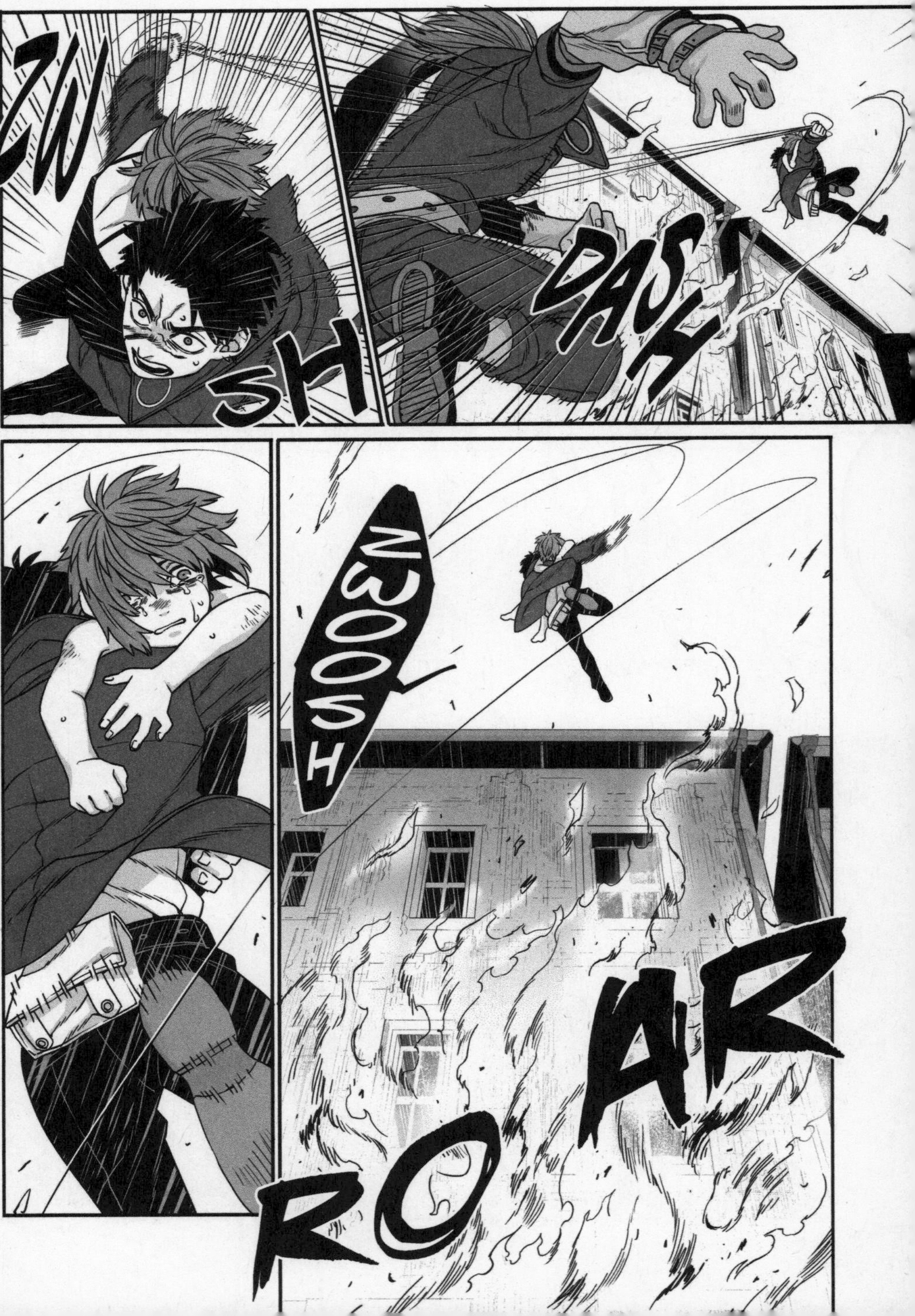
DASH
ZW
SH
ZWOOSH
ROAR

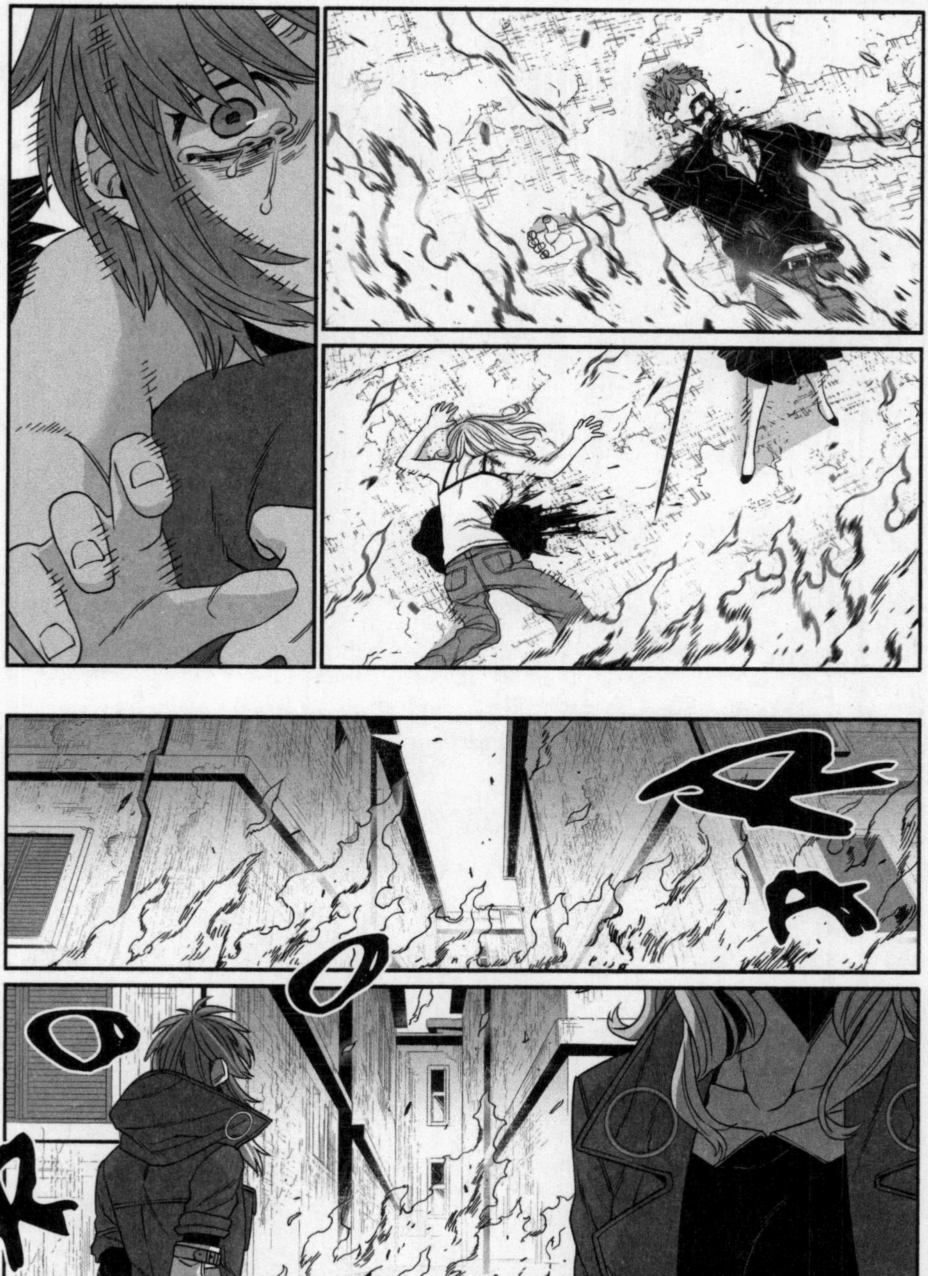
ROOAR

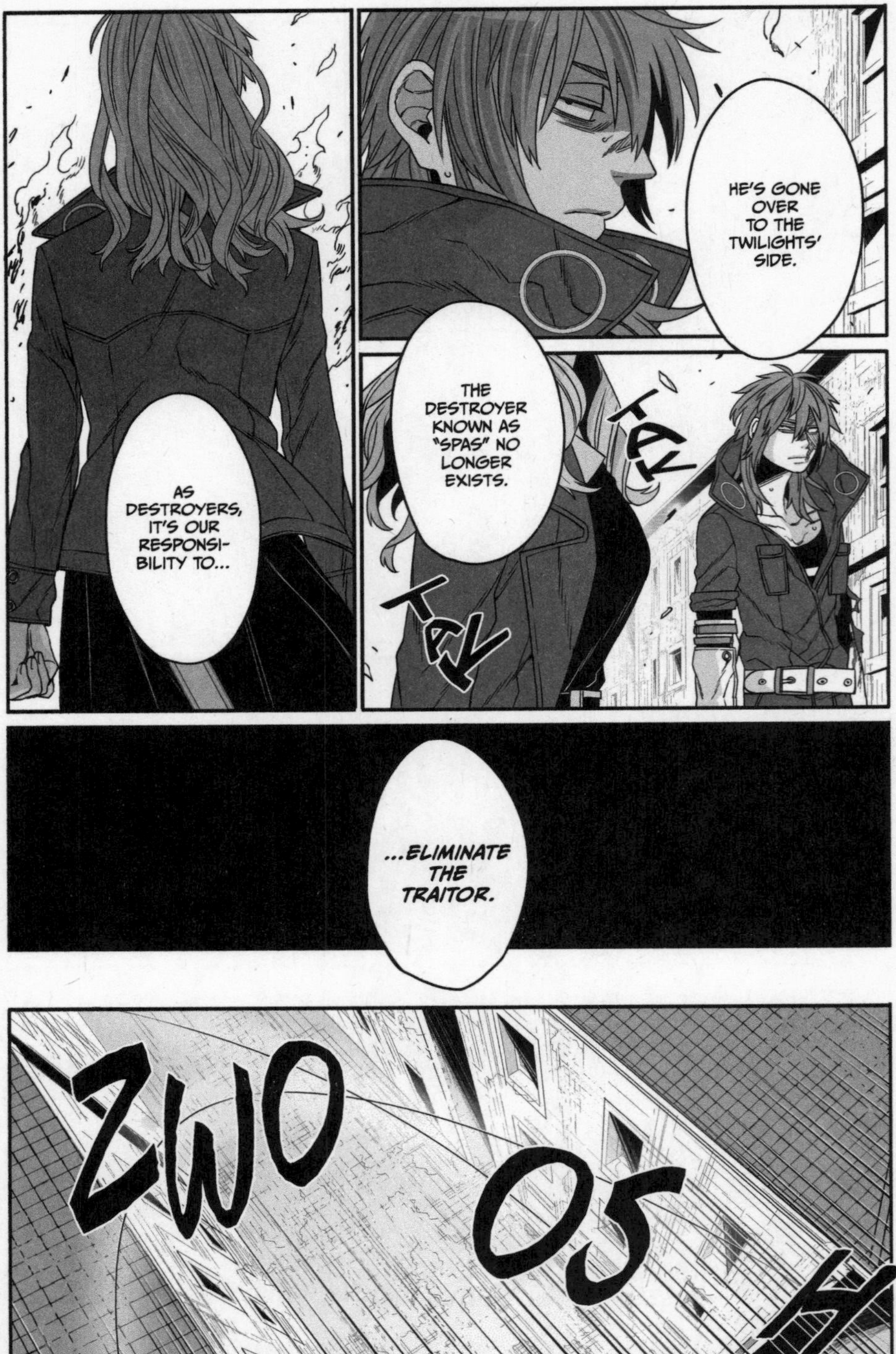
HE'S GONE OVER TO THE TWILIGHTS' SIDE.
TAK
TAK
THE DESTROYER KNOWN AS "SPAS" NO LONGER EXISTS.
AS DESTROYERS, IT'S OUR RESPONSI-BILITY TO...
...ELIMINATE THE TRAITOR.
ZWOOSH

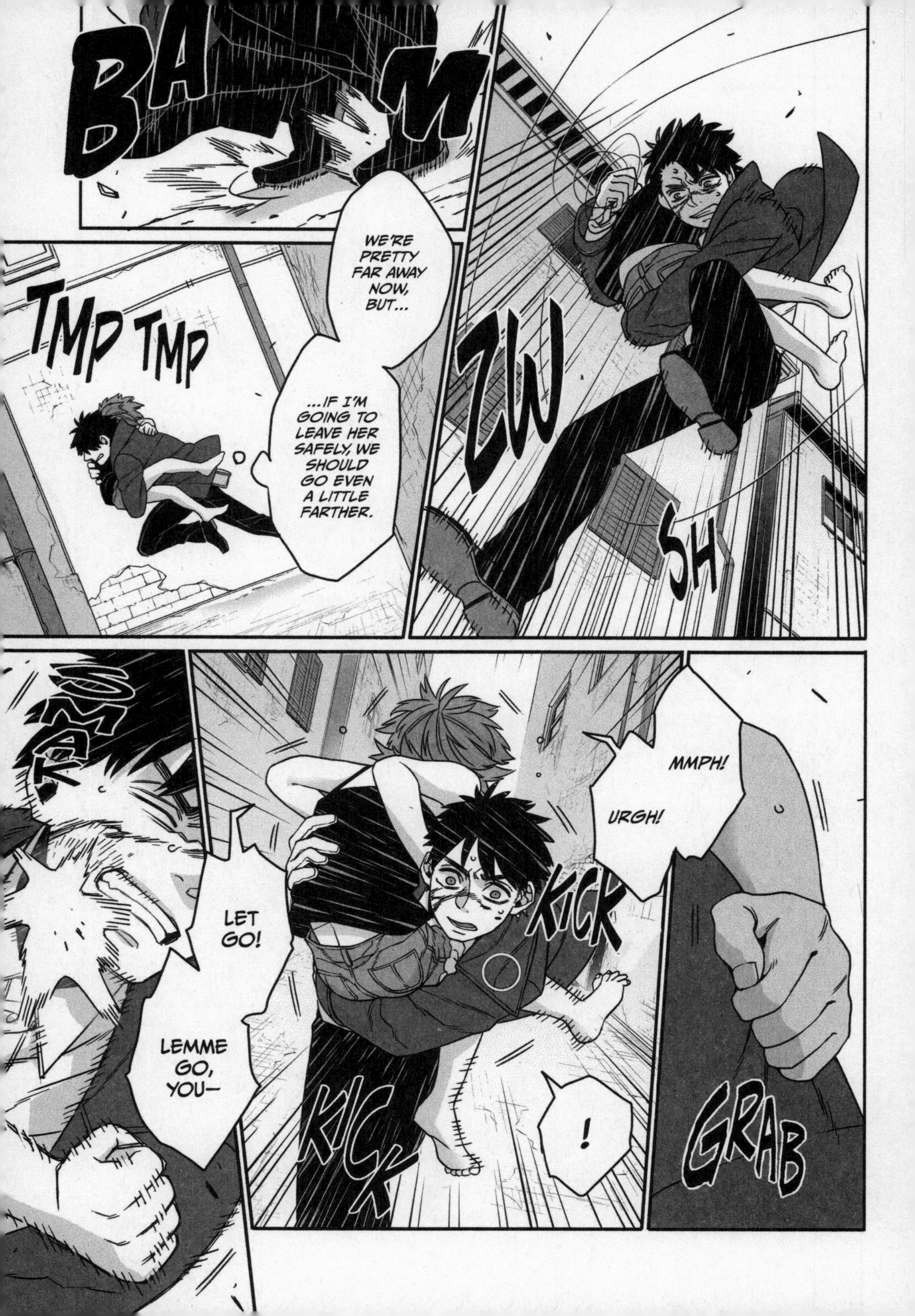
ZW
SH
BAM
TMP TMP
WE'RE PRETTY FAR AWAY NOW, BUT...
...IF I'M GOING TO LEAVE HER SAFELY, WE SHOULD GO EVEN A LITTLE FARTHER.
MMPH!
URGH!
KICK
GRAB
!
KICK
LET GO!
LEMME GO, YOU–

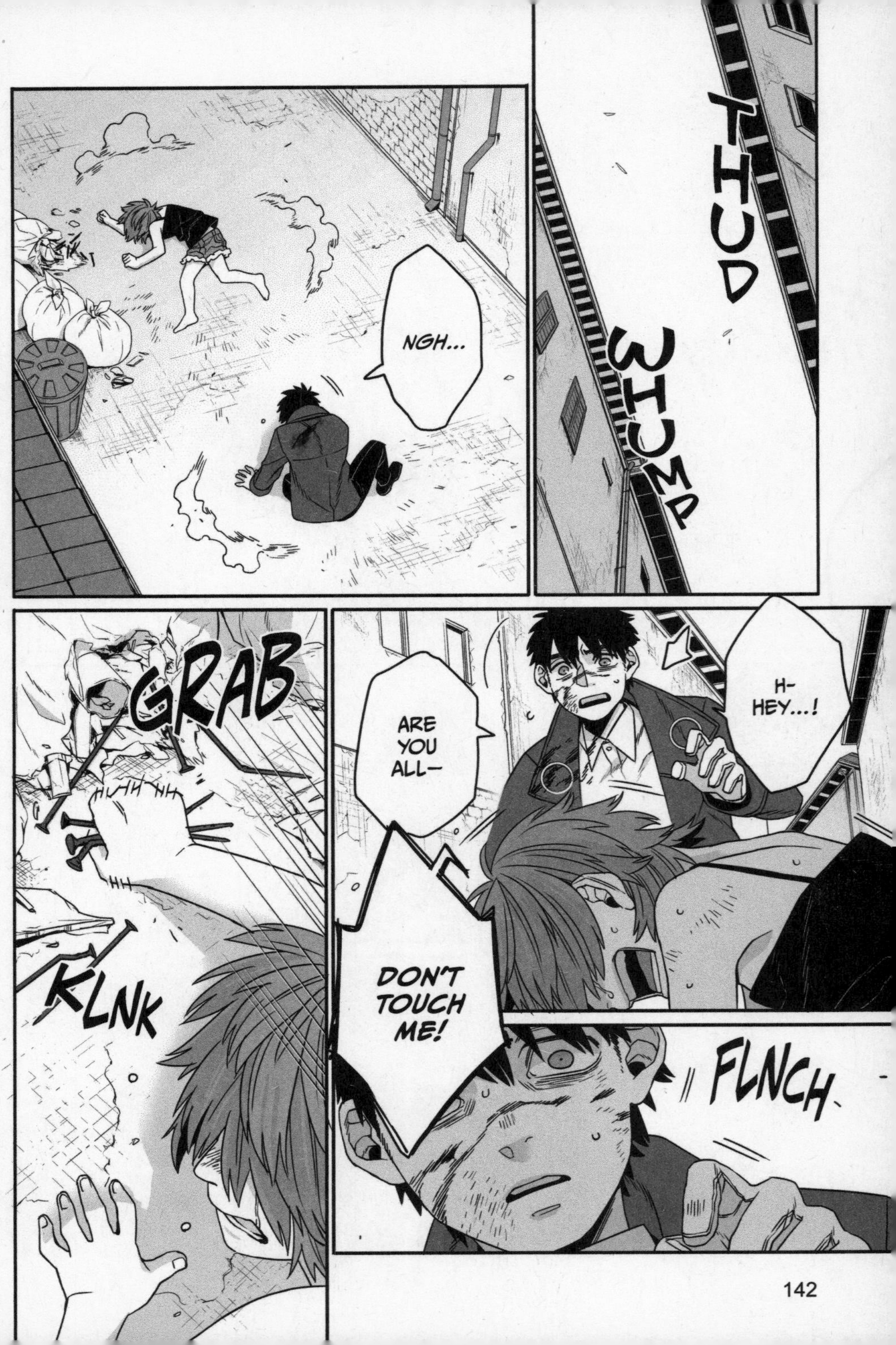
THUD
WHUMP
NGH...
H-HEY...!
ARE YOU ALL—
DON'T TOUCH ME!
FLNCH
GRAB
KLNK

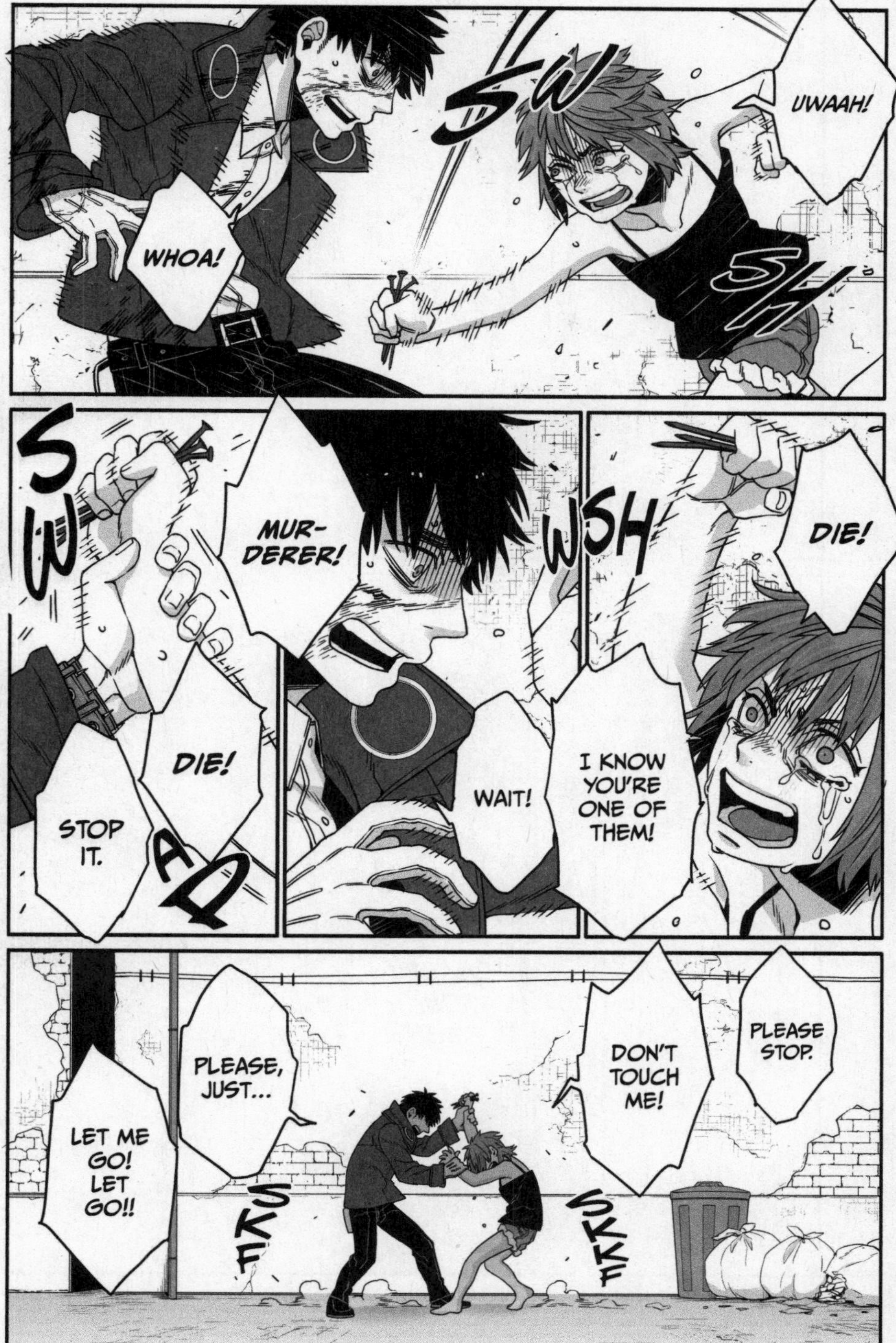
UWAAH!
SW
SH
WHOA!
DIE!
WSH
I KNOW YOU'RE ONE OF THEM!
MUR-DERER!
WAIT!
SW
DIE!
STOP IT.
PLEASE STOP.
DON'T TOUCH ME!
SKKF
PLEASE, JUST...
SKF
LET ME GO! LET GO!!

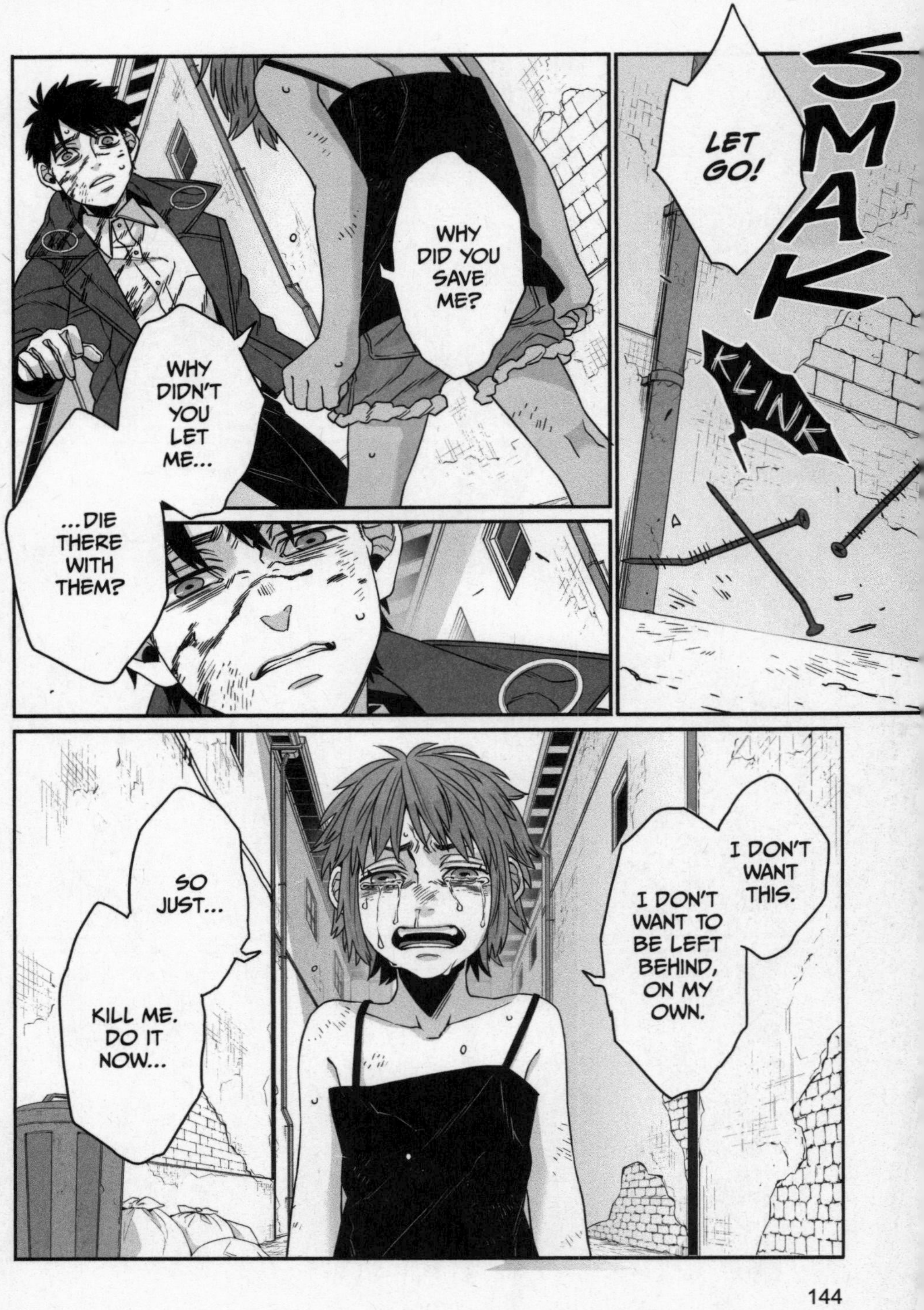
SMAK
LET GO!
KLINK
WHY DID YOU SAVE ME?
WHY DIDN'T YOU LET ME...
...DIE THERE WITH THEM?
I DON'T WANT THIS.
I DON'T WANT TO BE LEFT BEHIND, ON MY OWN.
SO JUST...
KILL ME. DO IT NOW...

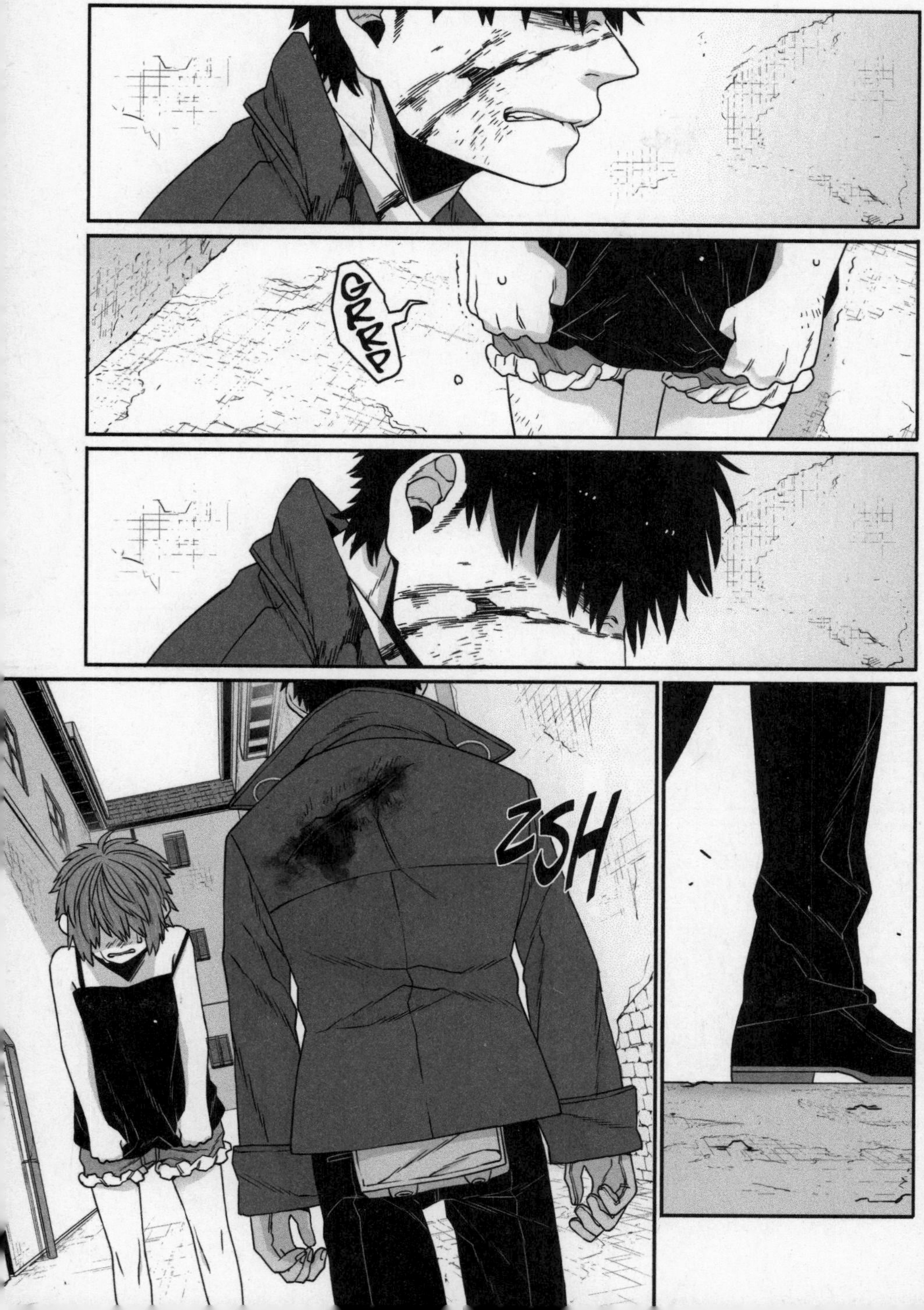
GRRP
ZSH

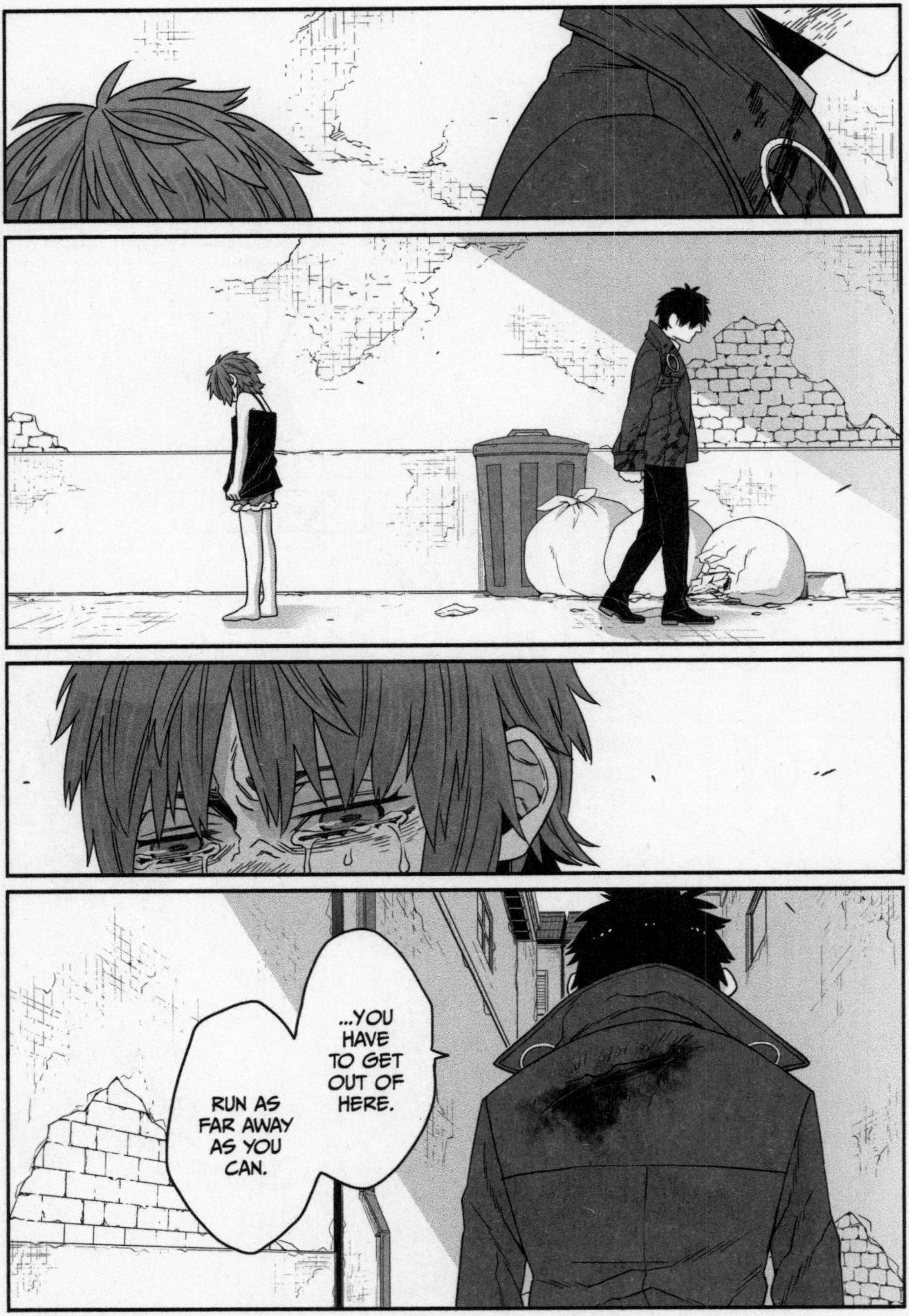
...YOU HAVE TO GET OUT OF HERE.
RUN AS FAR AWAY AS YOU CAN.

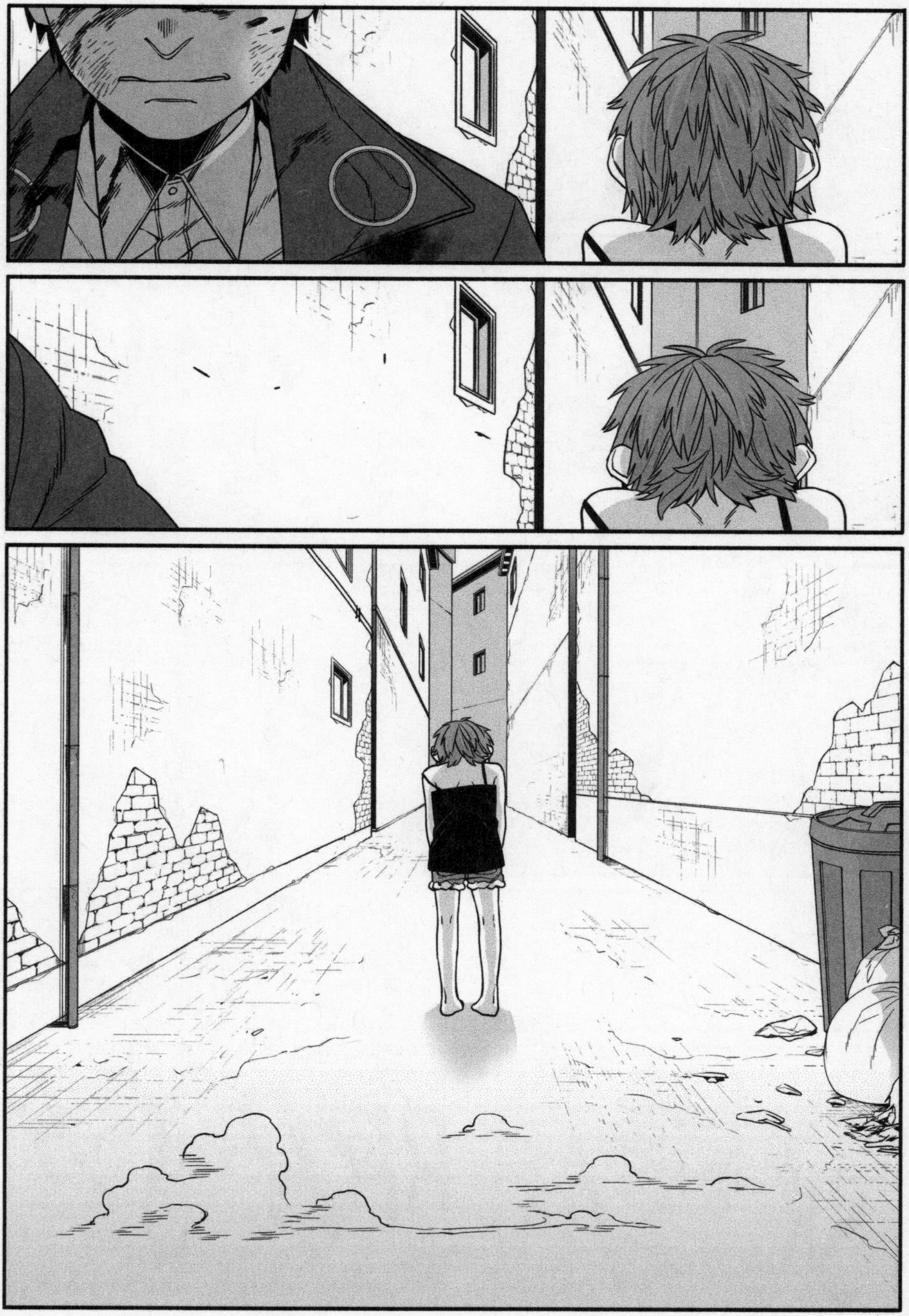

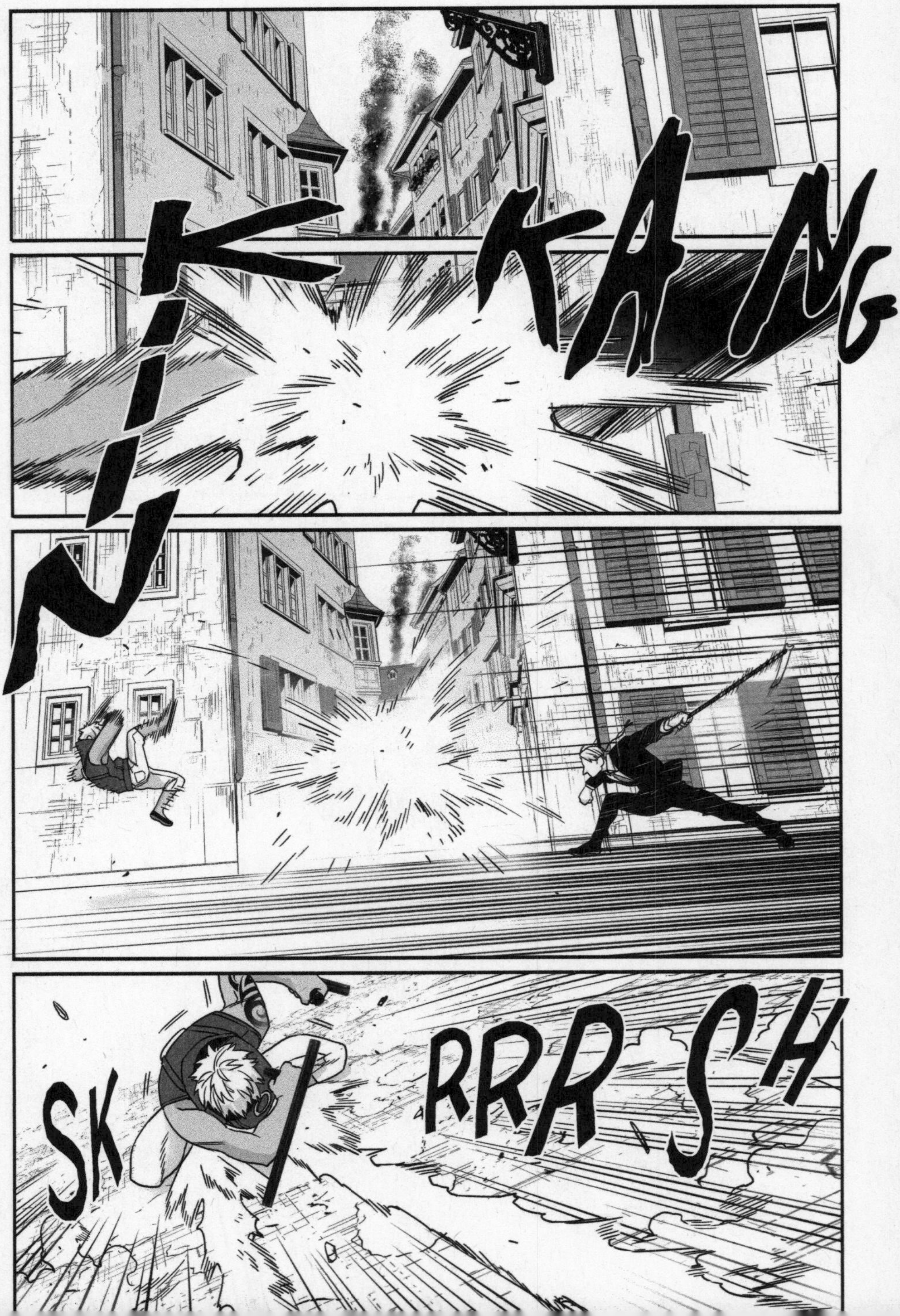
KANG
SKRRRSH

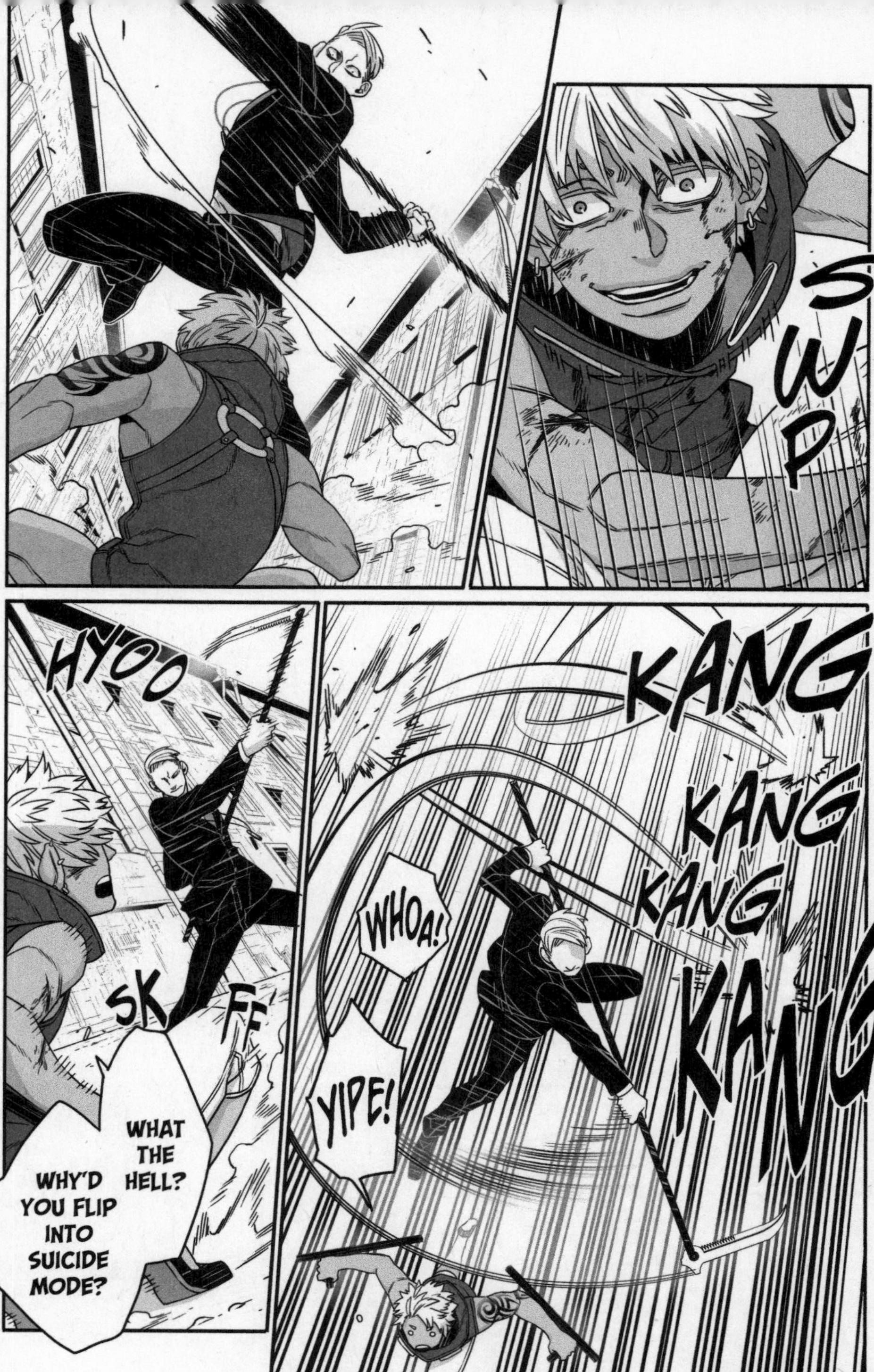
SWP
KANG
KANG
KANG
KANG
WHOA!
YIPE!
HYOO
SK FF
WHAT THE HELL?
WHY'D YOU FLIP INTO SUICIDE MODE?

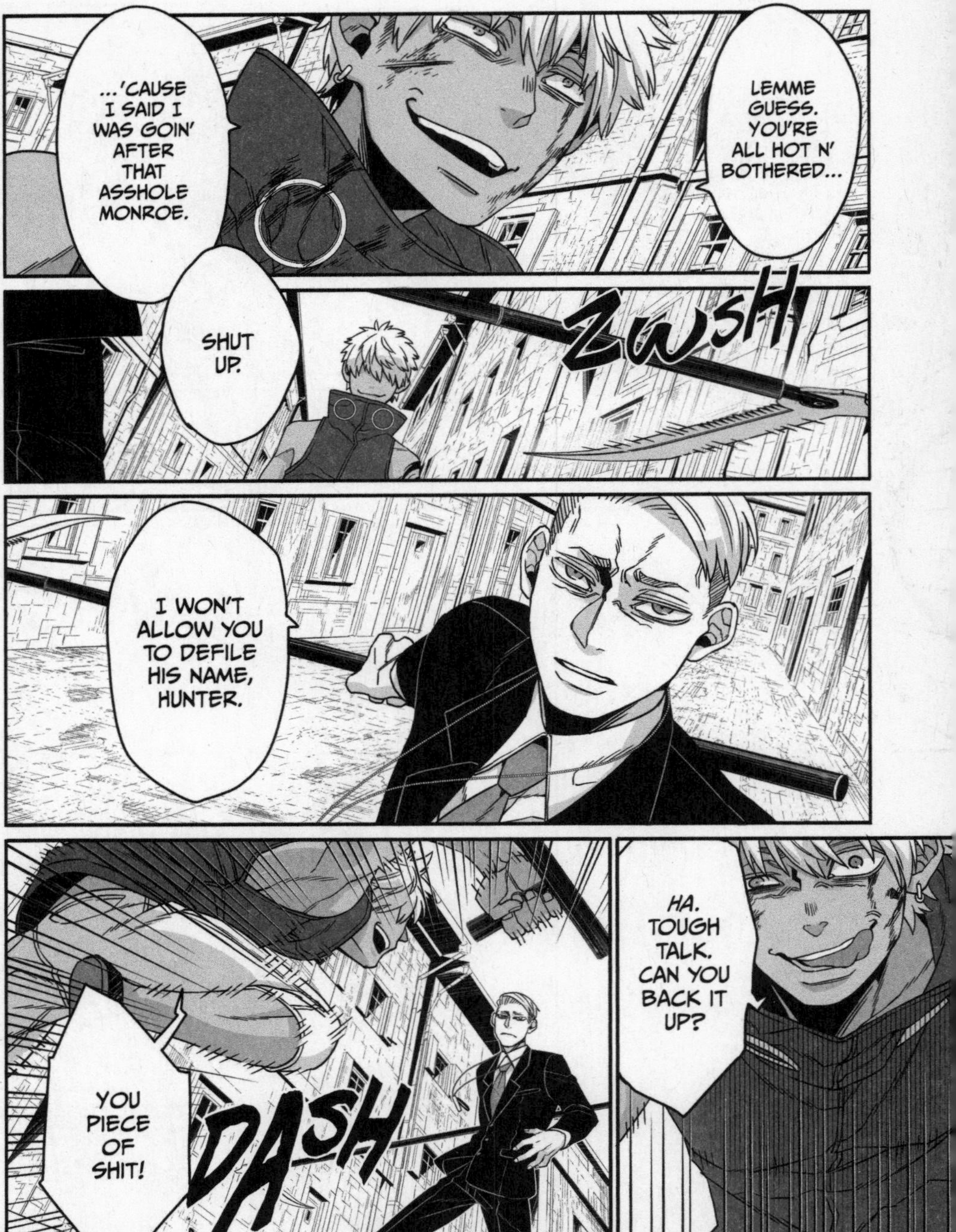
LEMME GUESS. YOU'RE ALL HOT N' BOTHERED...
...'CAUSE I SAID I WAS GOIN' AFTER THAT ASSHOLE MONROE.
SHUT UP.
ZWSH
I WON'T ALLOW YOU TO DEFILE HIS NAME, HUNTER.
HA. TOUGH TALK. CAN YOU BACK IT UP?
YOU PIECE OF SHIT!
DASH

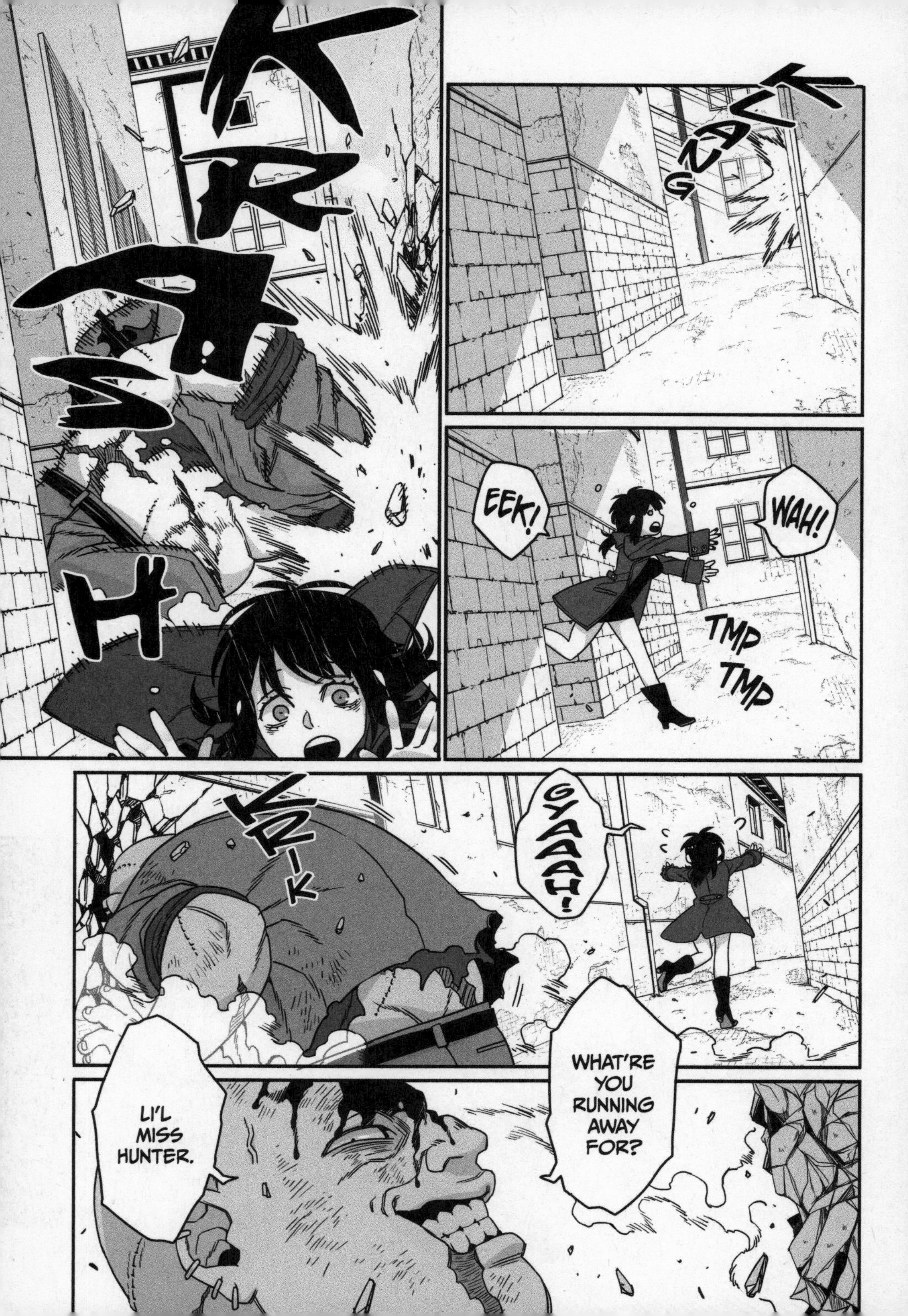
KLANG
WAH!
EEK!
TMP
TMP
KRASH
GYAAAAH!
KRIK
WHAT'RE YOU RUNNING AWAY FOR?
LI'L MISS HUNTER.

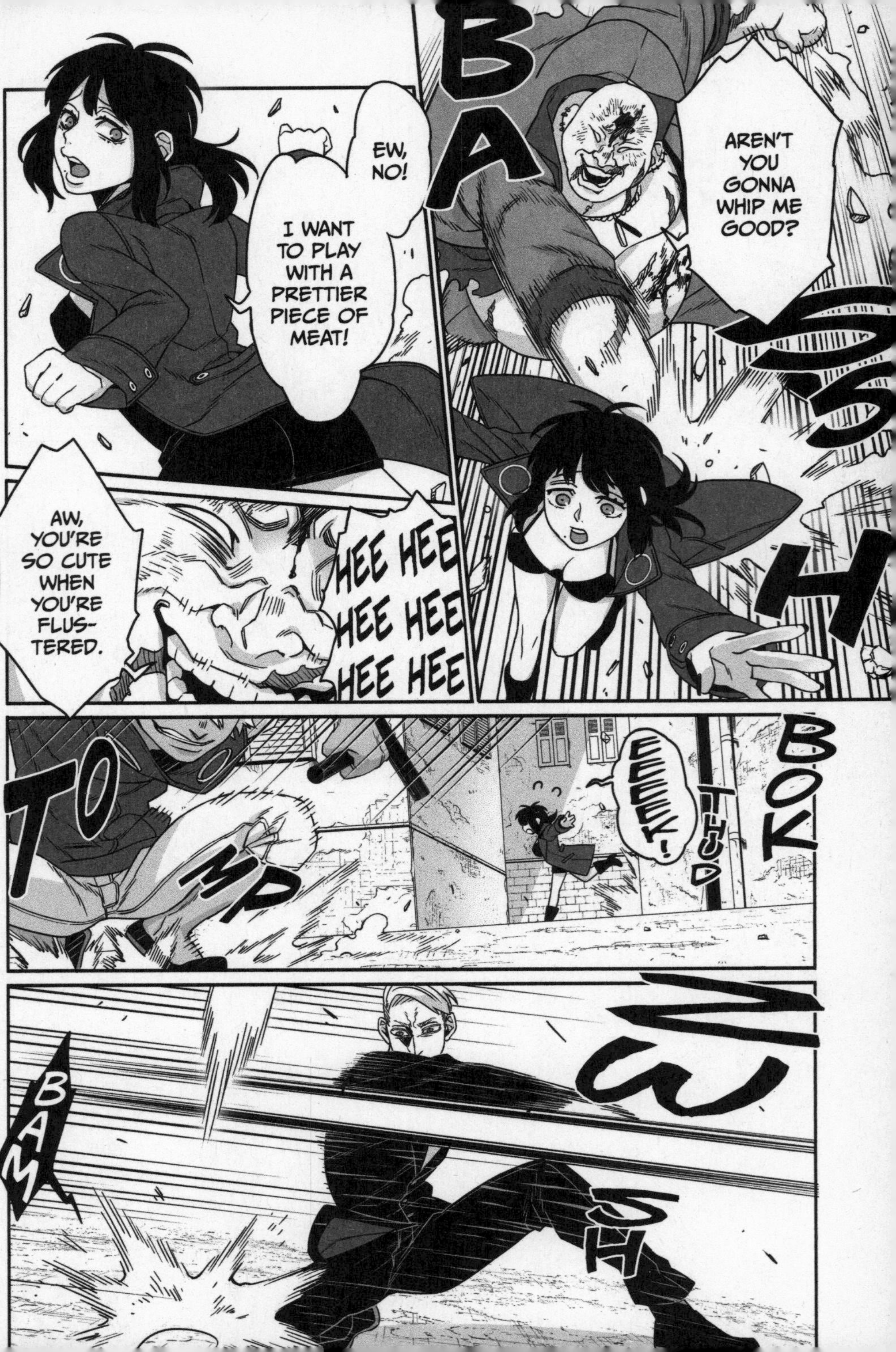
BA
AREN'T YOU GONNA WHIP ME GOOD?
SWISH
EW, NO!
I WANT TO PLAY WITH A PRETTIER PIECE OF MEAT!
AW, YOU'RE SO CUTE WHEN YOU'RE FLUS-TERED.
HEE HEE HEE HEE HEE HEE
BOK
THUD
EEEEK!
TOMP
BAM

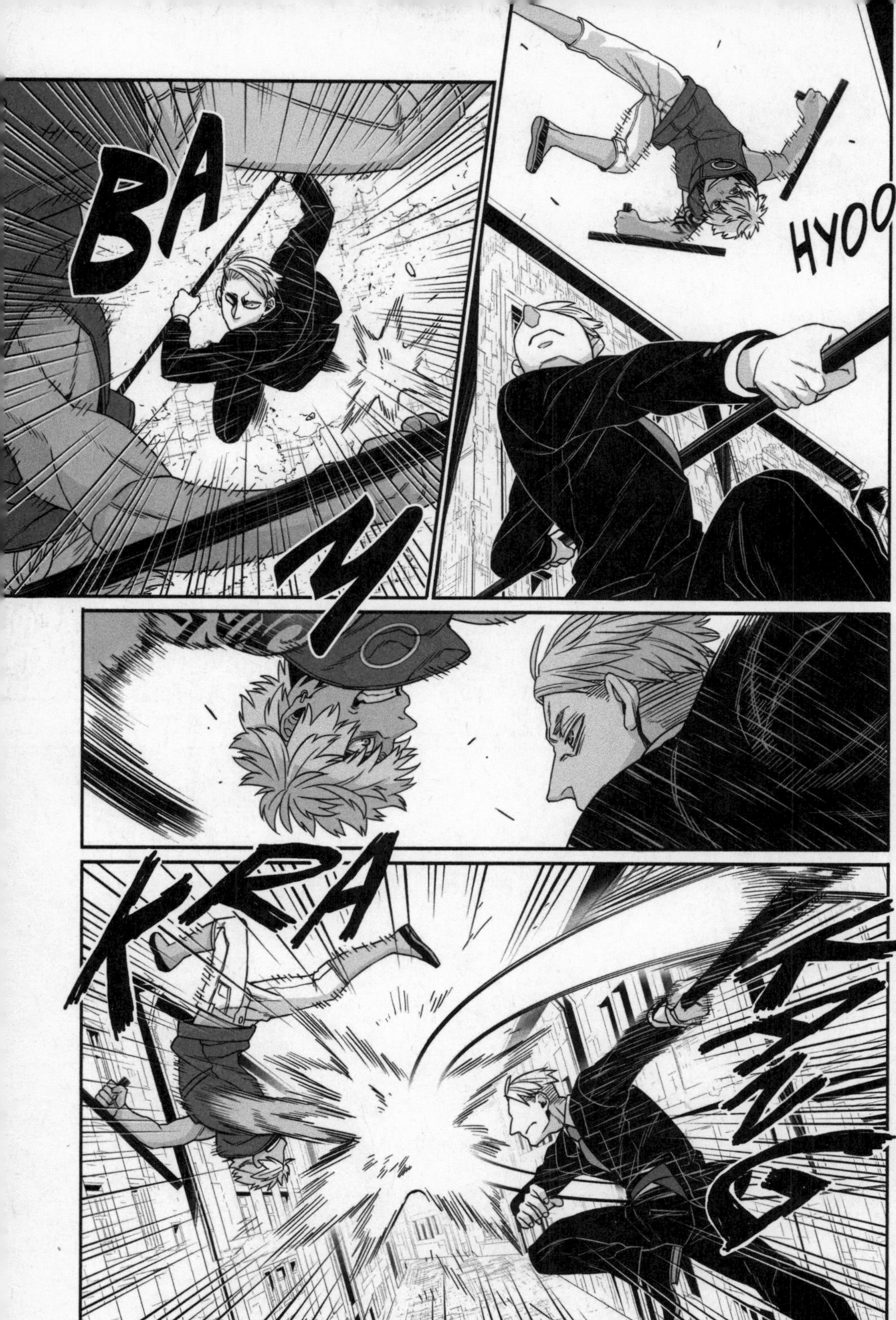
HYOO
BAM
KANG
KRA

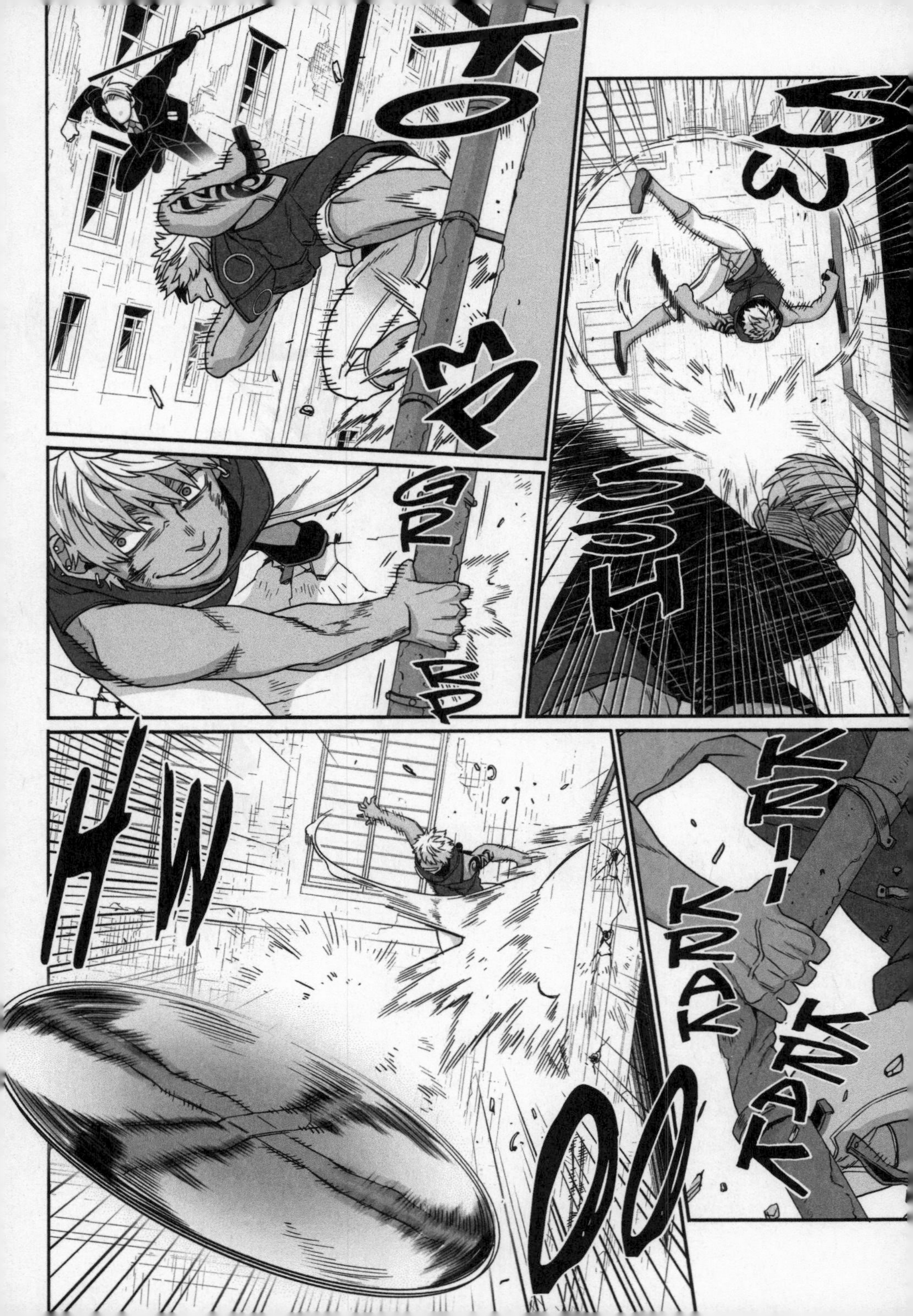
FO
MP
SW
SSH
GRRP
KRI-KRAK
KRAK
HW
OO

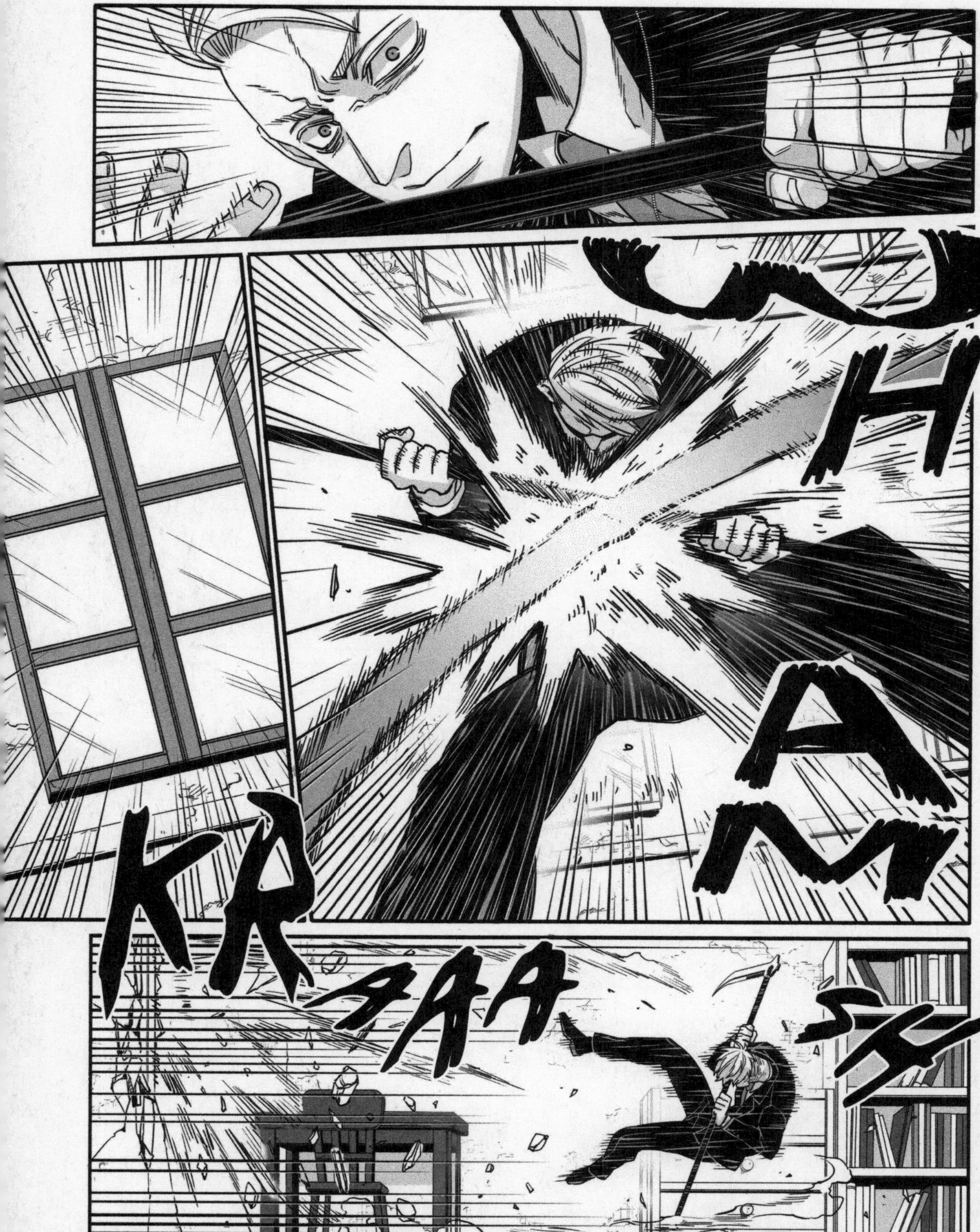
WHAM
KRAAASH

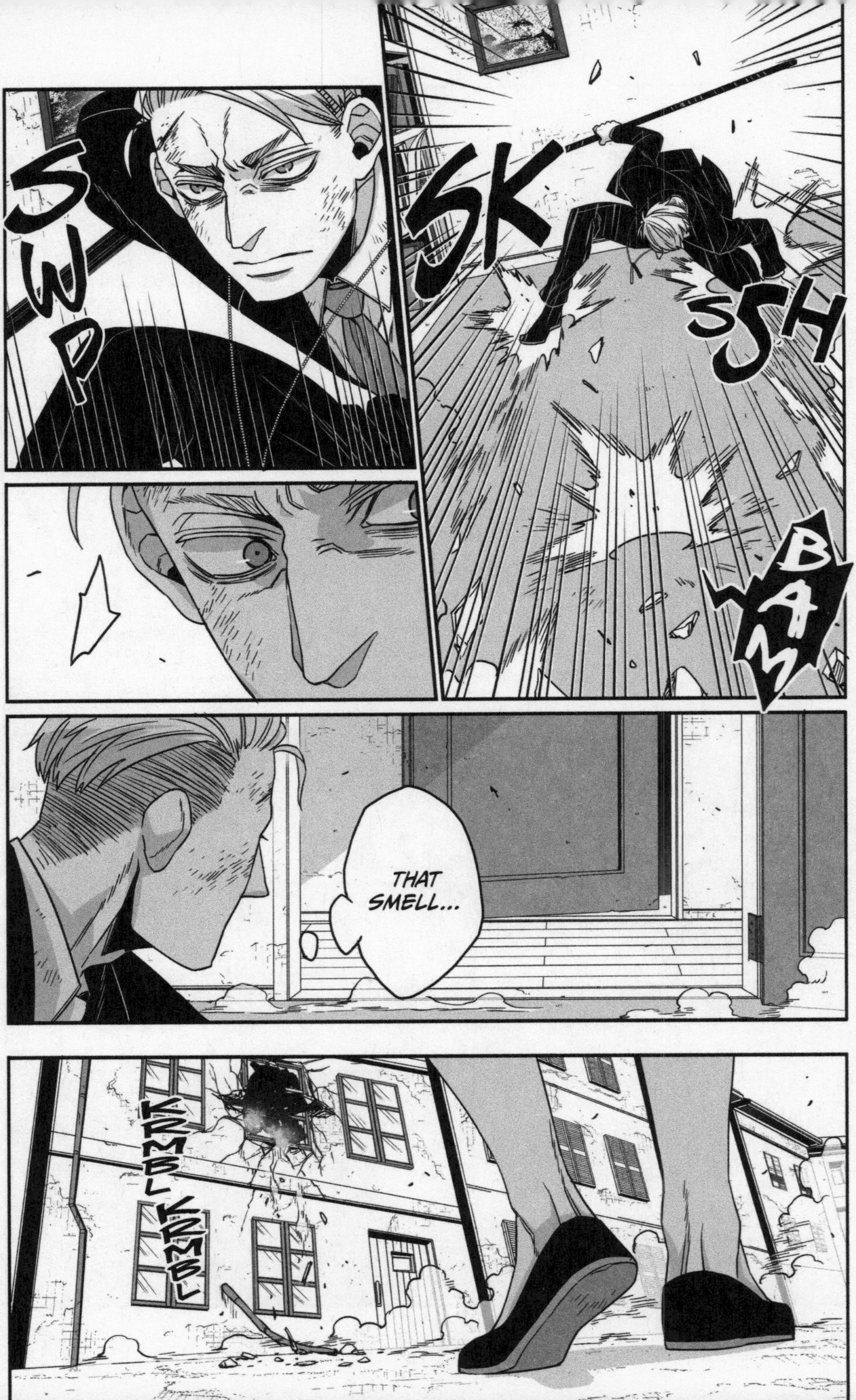
SK
SSH
BAM
SWP
THAT SMELL...
KRMBL KRMBL

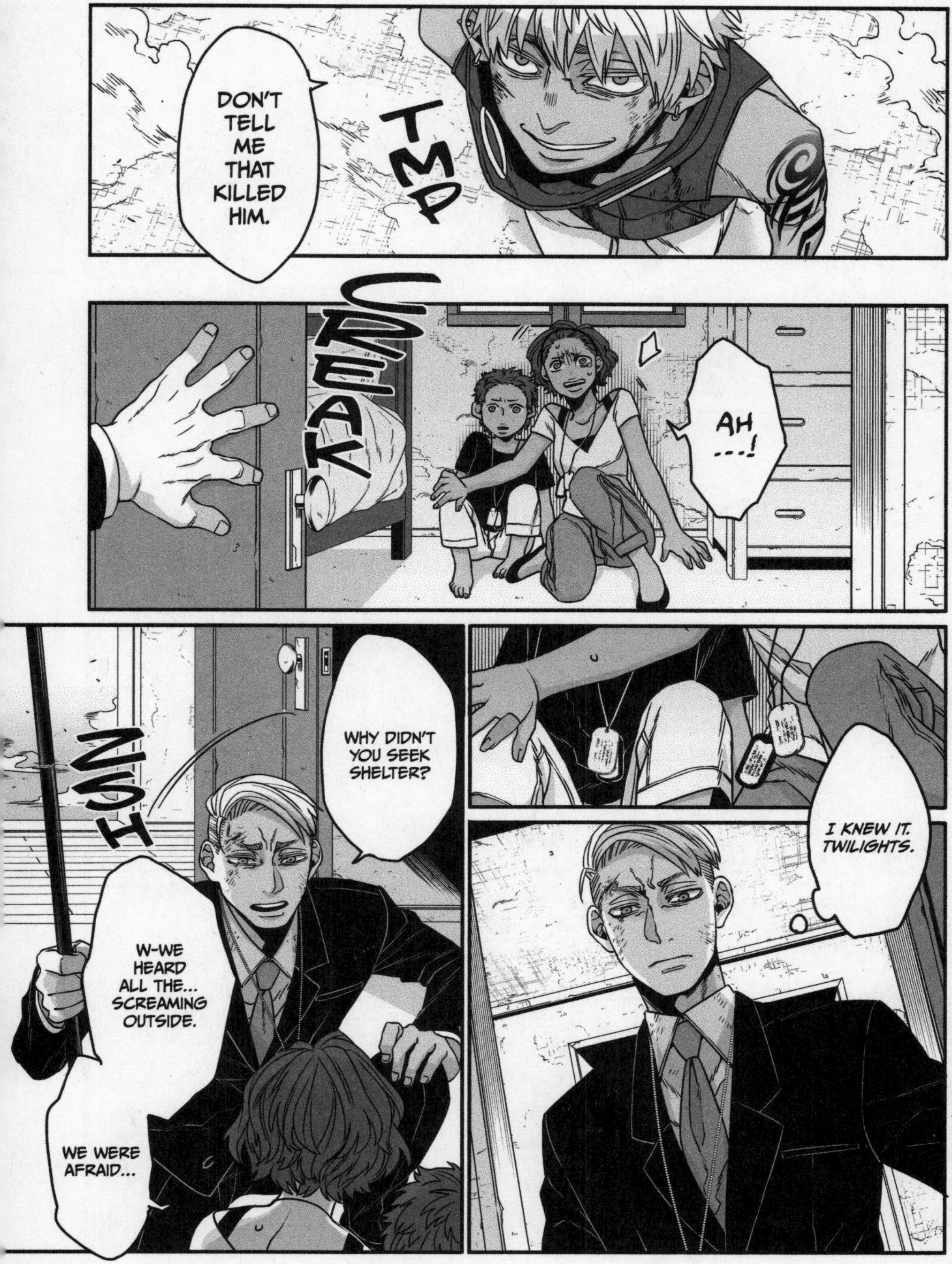
DON'T TELL ME THAT KILLED HIM.
TMP
AH...!
CREAK
I KNEW IT. TWILIGHTS.
WHY DIDN'T YOU SEEK SHELTER?
SHH
W-WE HEARD ALL THE... SCREAMING OUTSIDE.
WE WERE AFRAID...

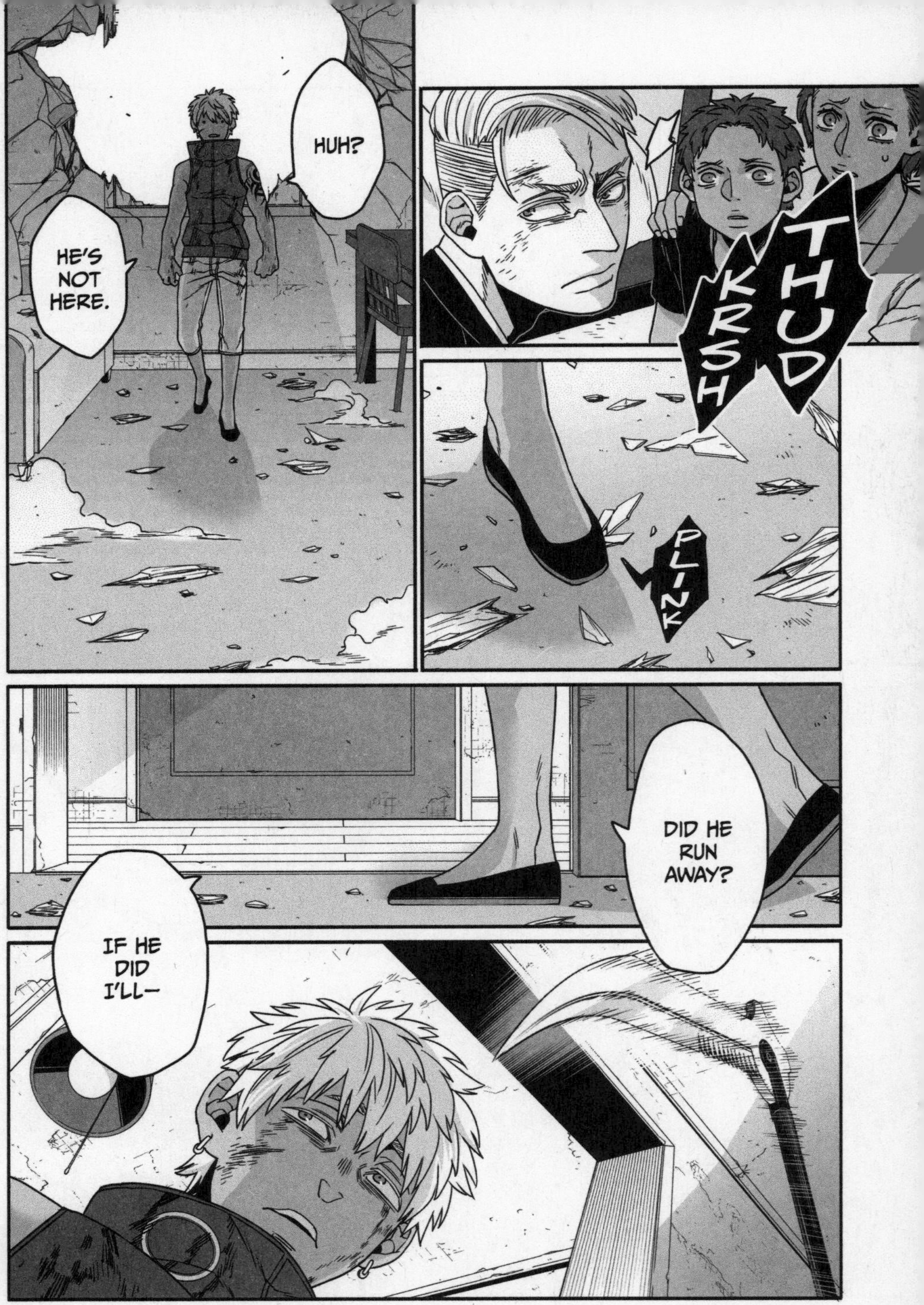
THUD
KRSH
PLINK
HUH?
HE'S NOT HERE.
DID HE RUN AWAY?
IF HE DID I'LL—

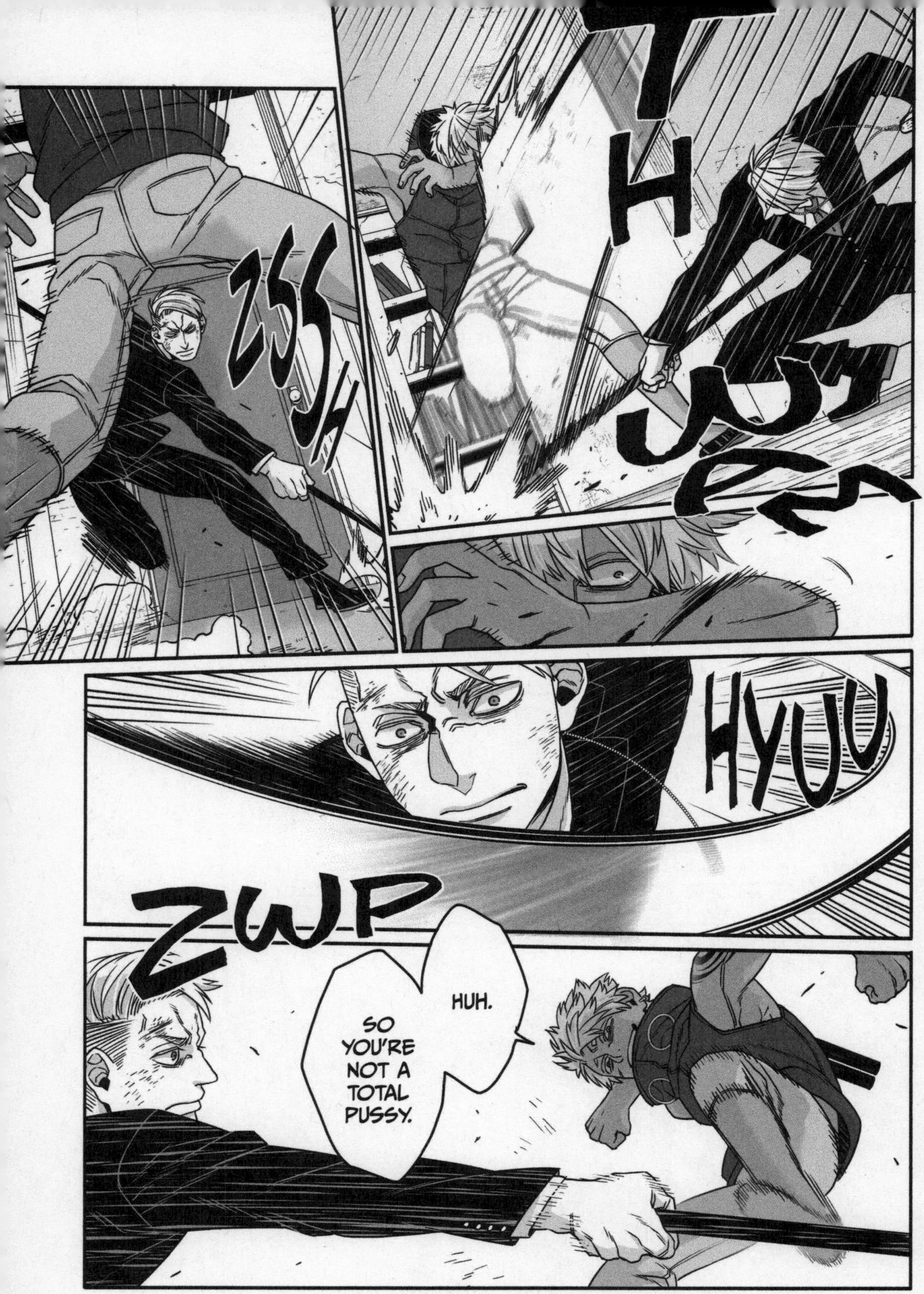
ZSSH
HYUU
ZWP
HUH.
SO YOU'RE NOT A TOTAL PUSSY.

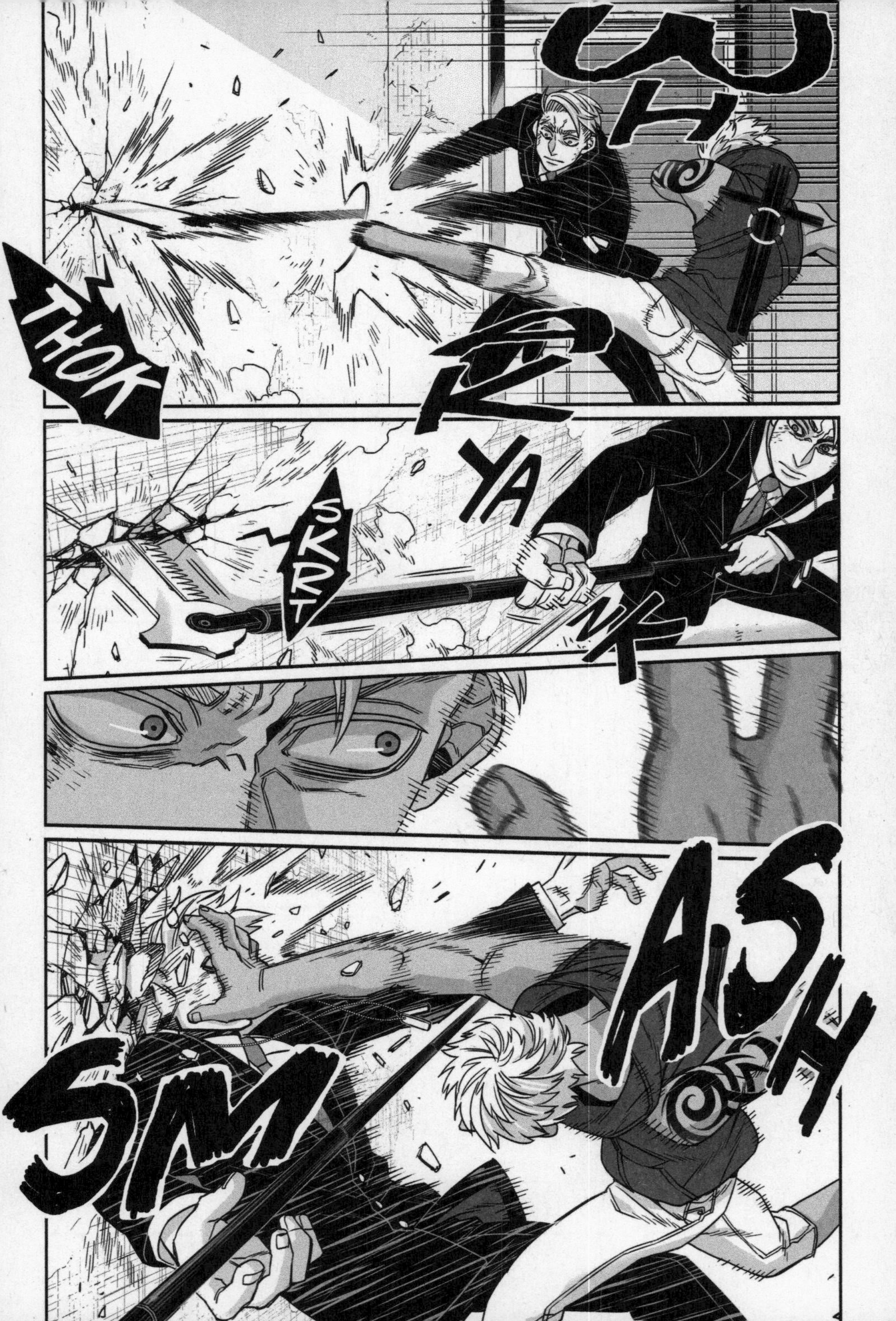
THOK
YANK
SKRT
SMASH

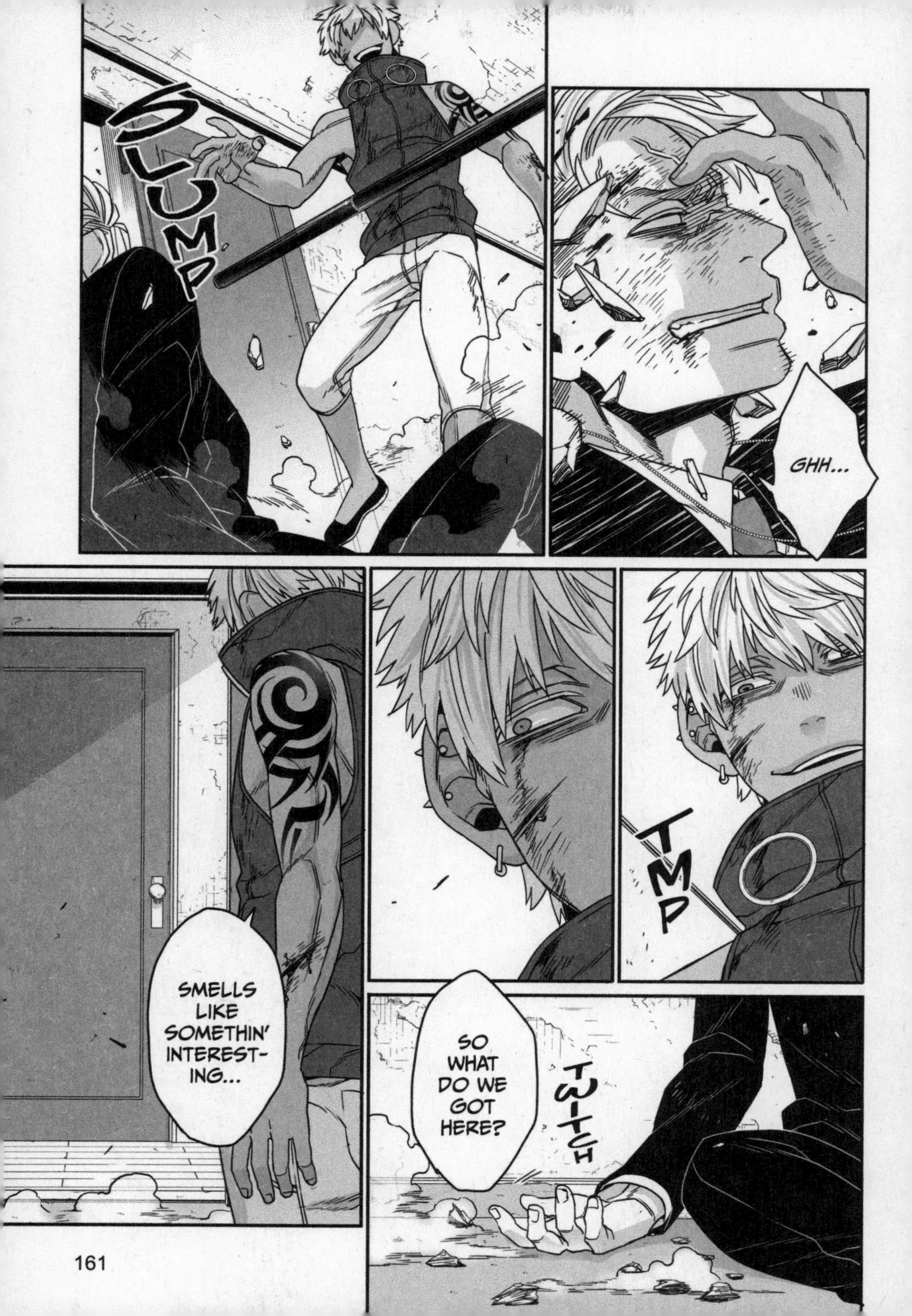
GHH...
SLUMP
TMP
SO WHAT DO WE GOT HERE?
TWITCH
SMELLS LIKE SOMETHIN' INTEREST-ING...

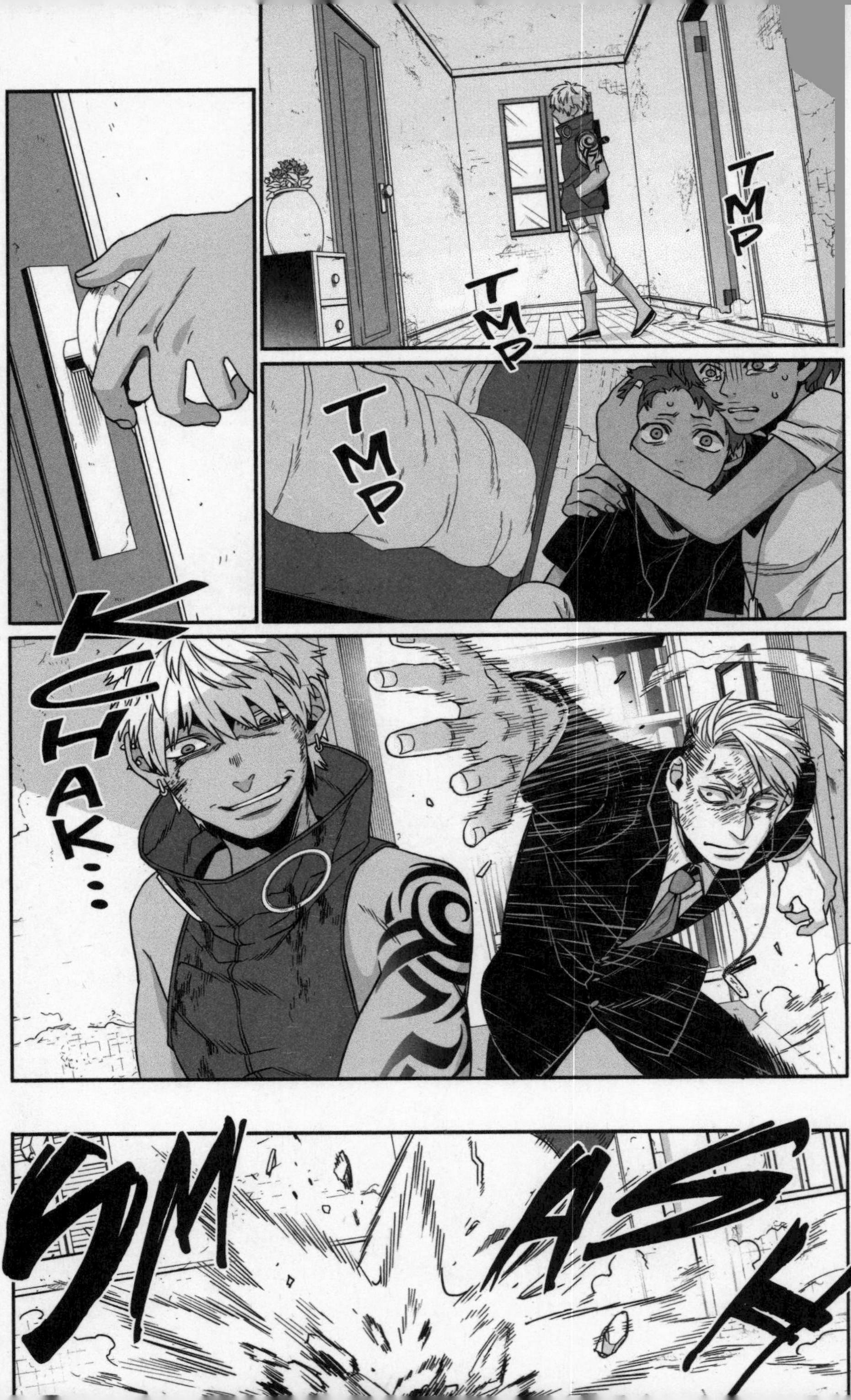
TMP
TMP
TMP
KCHAK...
SMASH

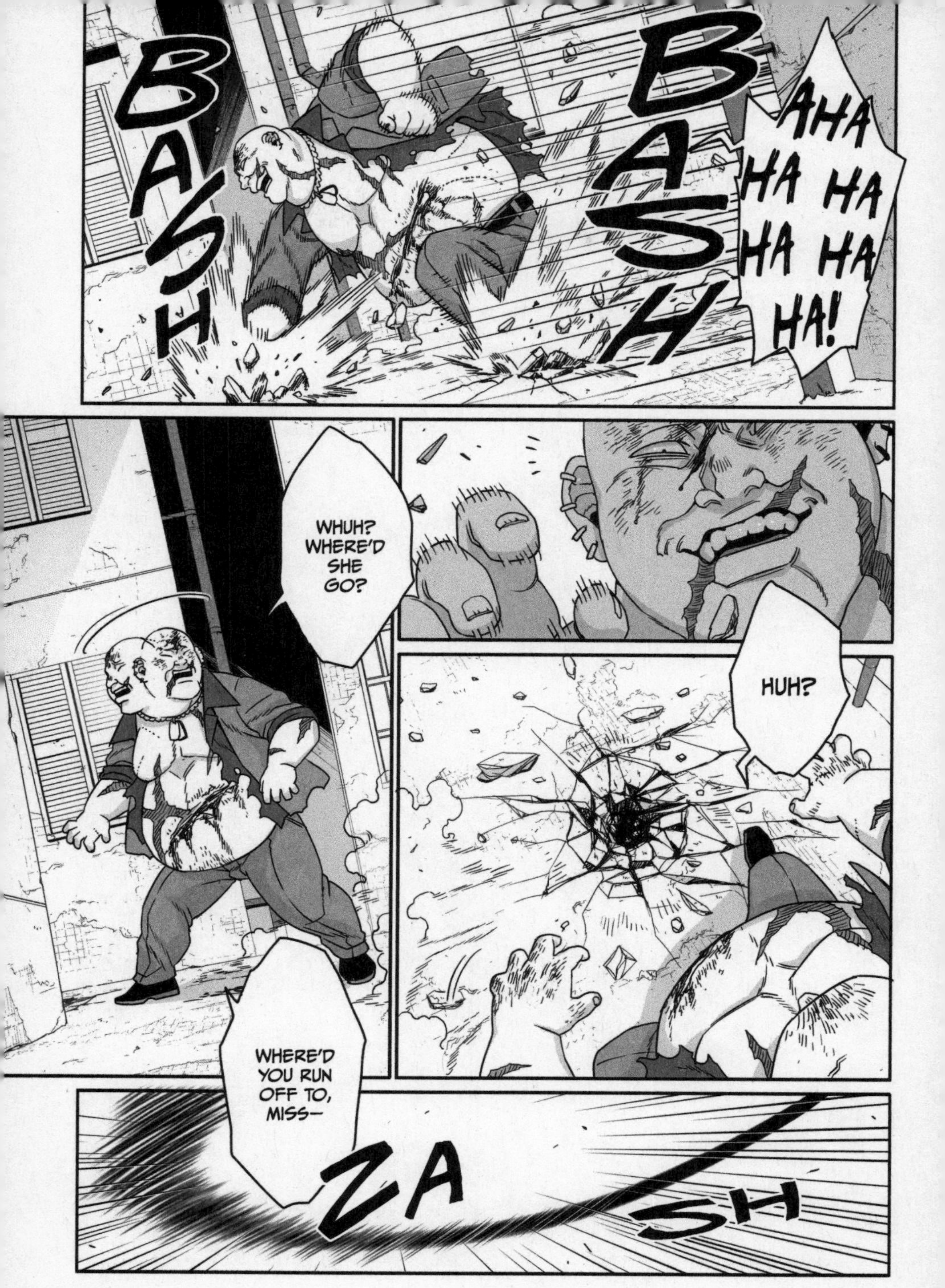
AHA HA HA HA HA HA HA HA!
BASH
BASH
HUH?
WHUH? WHERE'D SHE GO?
WHERE'D YOU RUN OFF TO, MISS—
ZASH

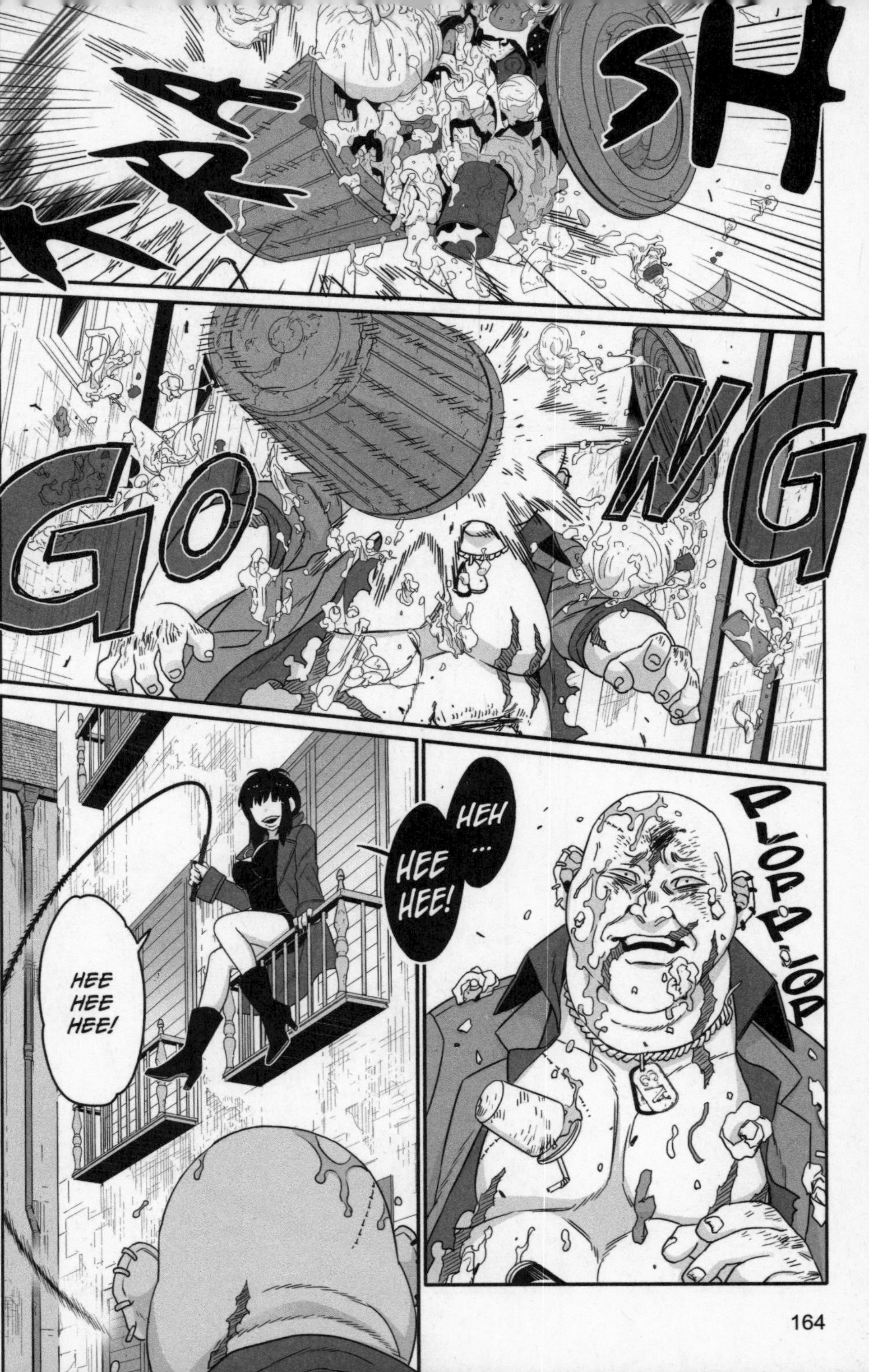
KRASH
GONG
PLOP PLOP
HEH ... HEE HEE!
HEE HEE HEE!

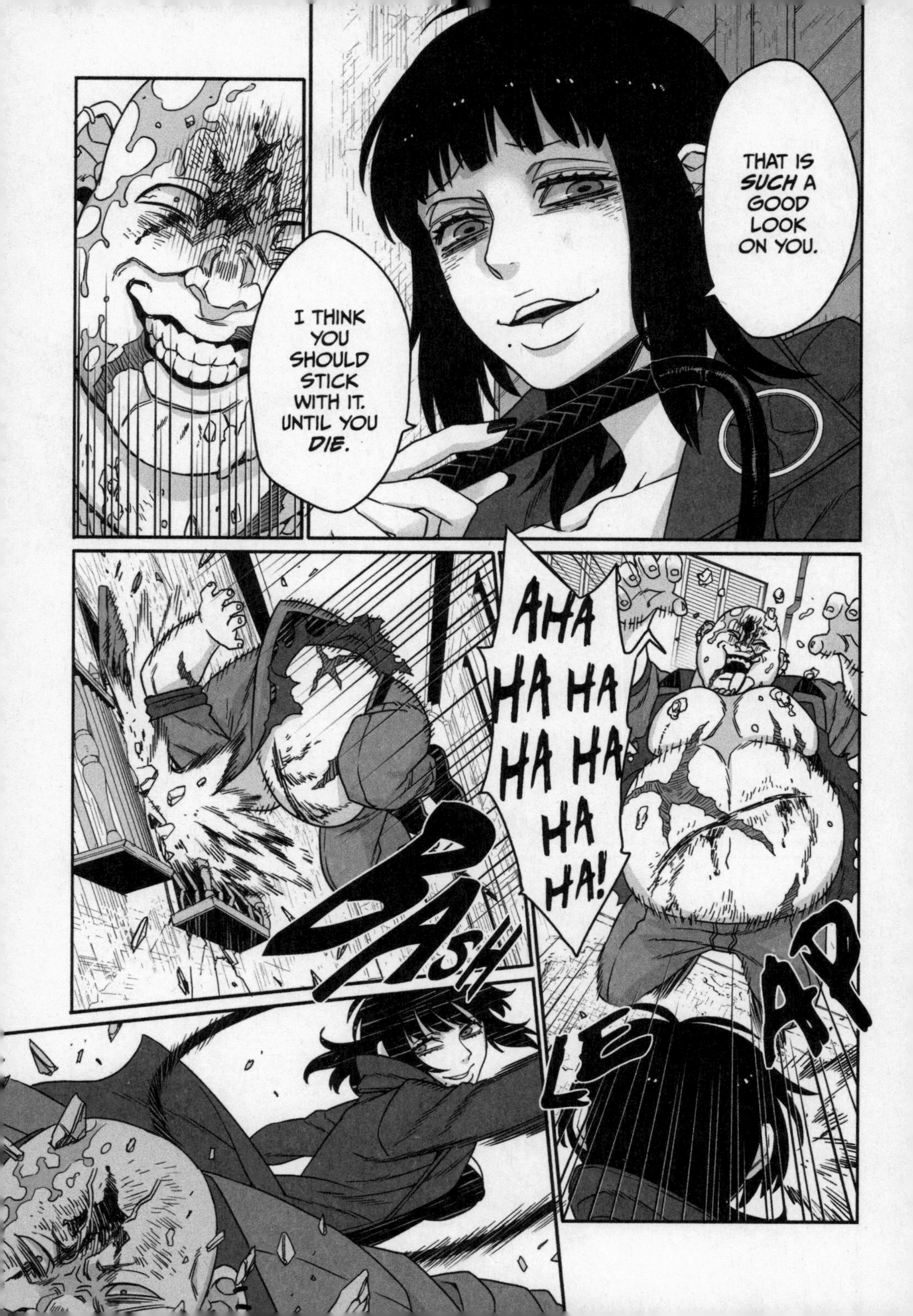
THAT IS SUCH A GOOD LOOK ON YOU.
I THINK YOU SHOULD STICK WITH IT. UNTIL YOU DIE.
AHA HA HA HA HA HA HA!
BASH
LEAP

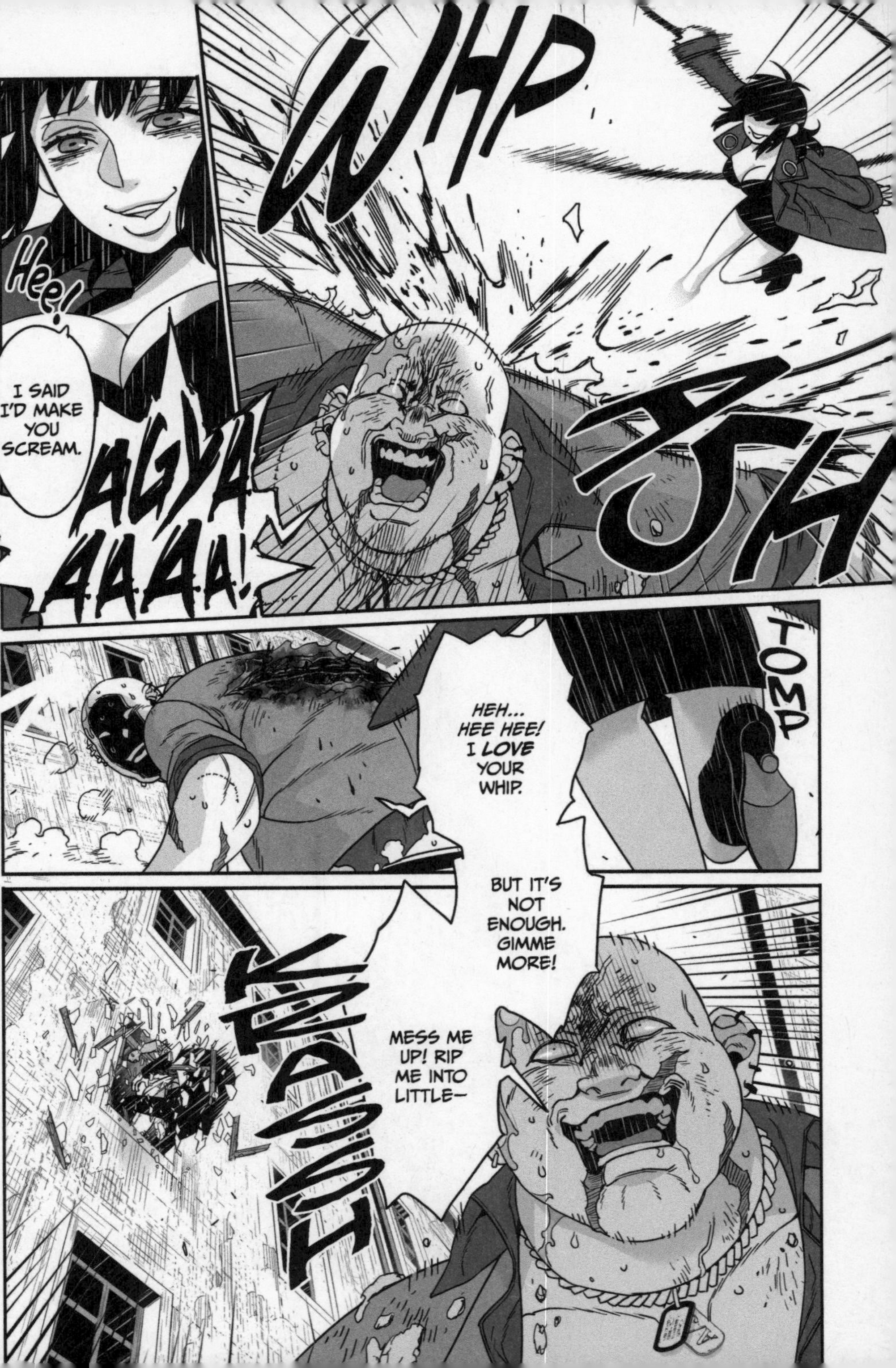
WHP
ASH
AGYA AAAA!
Hee!
I SAID I'D MAKE YOU SCREAM.
TOMP
HEH... HEE HEE! I LOVE YOUR WHIP.
BUT IT'S NOT ENOUGH. GIMME MORE!
MESS ME UP! RIP ME INTO LITTLE—
KRASH

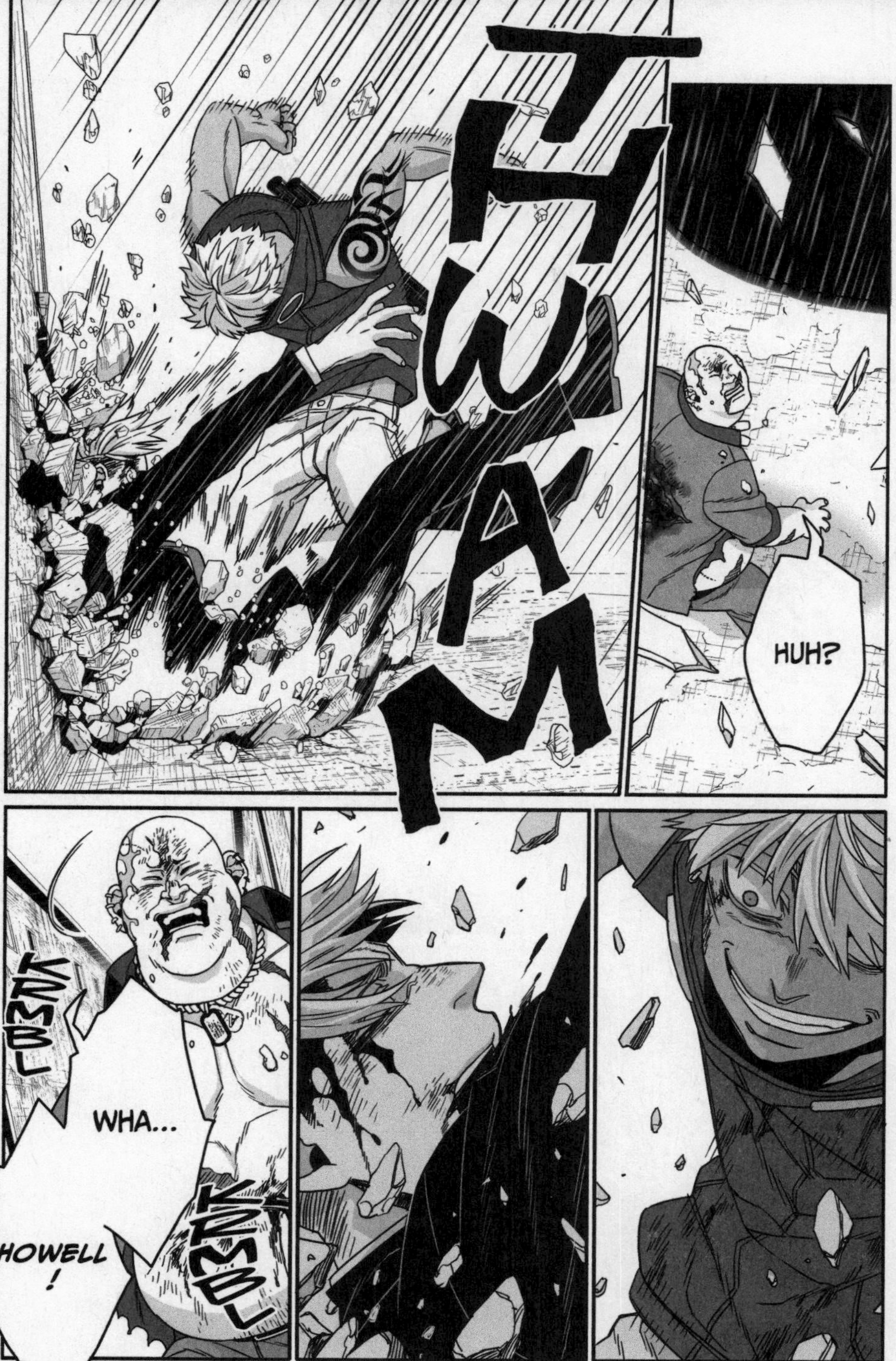
HUH?
THWAM
KRMBL
WHA...
KRMBL
HOWELL!

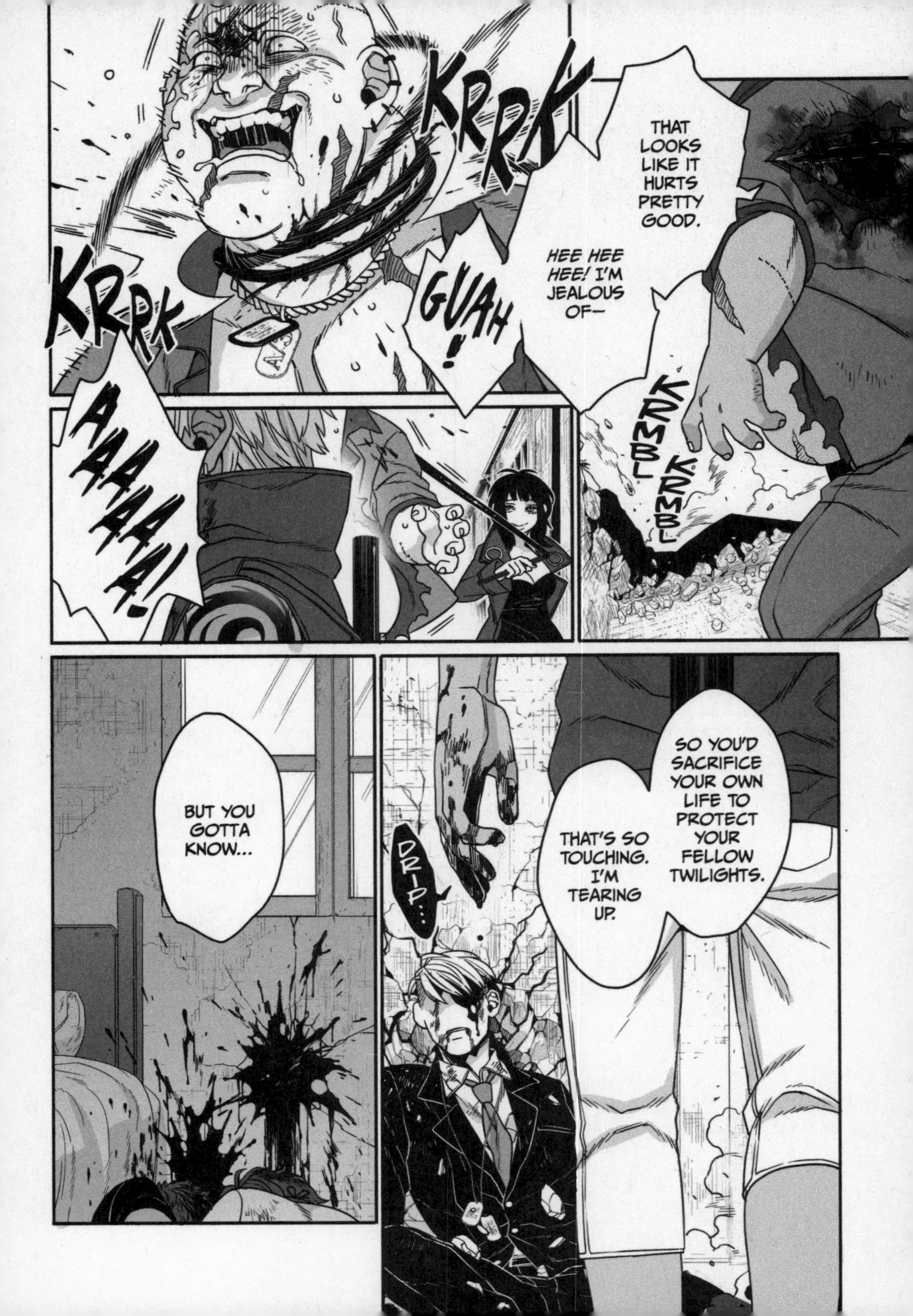
KRRK
KRRK
GUAH!
THAT LOOKS LIKE IT HURTS PRETTY GOOD.
HEE HEE HEE! I'M JEALOUS OF—
KRMBL KRMBL
AAAAAAAA!
SO YOU'D SACRIFICE YOUR OWN LIFE TO PROTECT YOUR FELLOW TWILIGHTS.
THAT'S SO TOUCHING. I'M TEARING UP.
DRIP...
BUT YOU GOTTA KNOW...

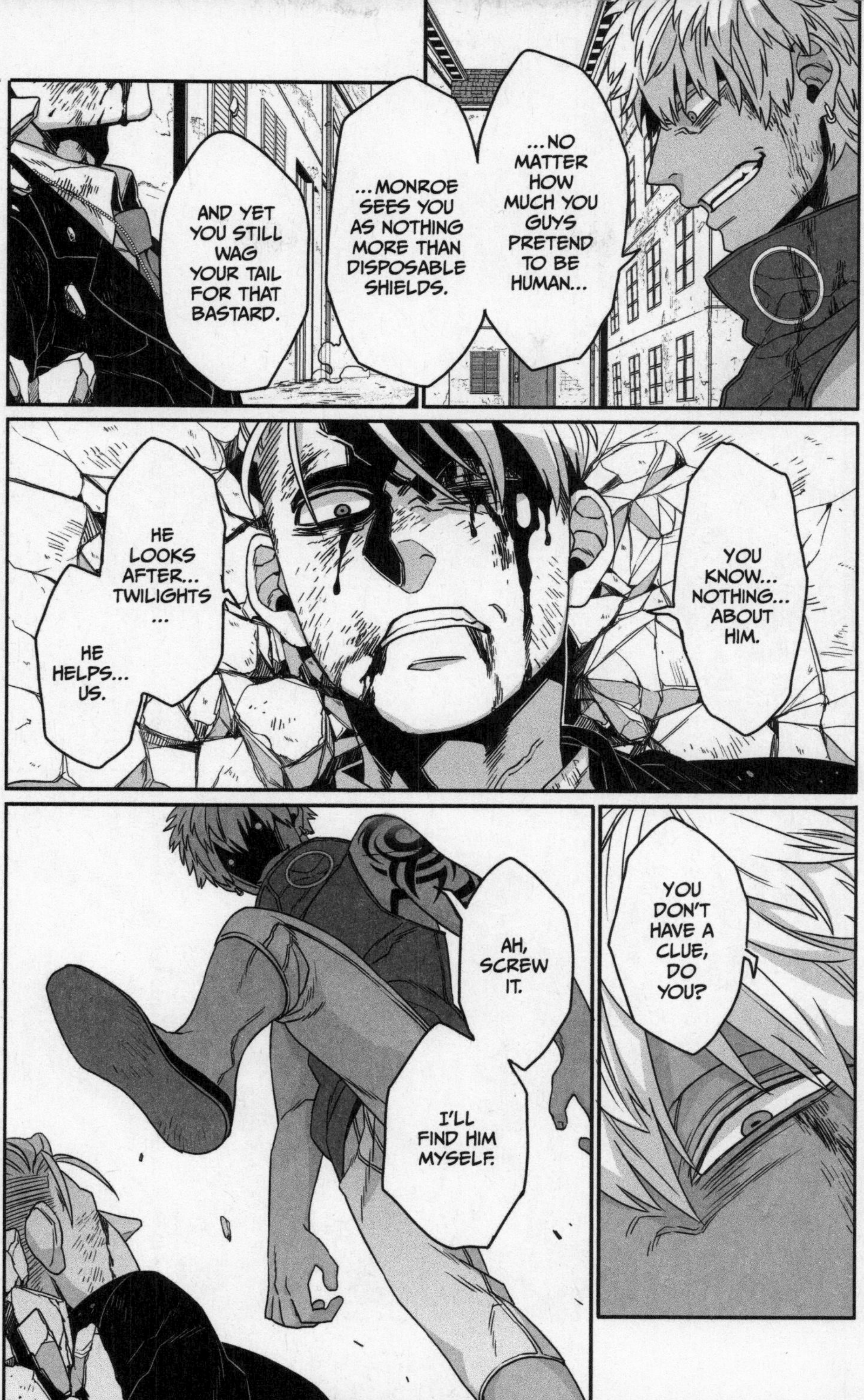
...NO MATTER HOW MUCH YOU GUYS PRETEND TO BE HUMAN...
...MONROE SEES YOU AS NOTHING MORE THAN DISPOSABLE SHIELDS.
AND YET YOU STILL WAG YOUR TAIL FOR THAT BASTARD.
YOU KNOW... NOTHING... ABOUT HIM.
HE LOOKS AFTER... TWILIGHTS...
HE HELPS... US.
YOU DON'T HAVE A CLUE, DO YOU?
AH, SCREW IT.
I'LL FIND HIM MYSELF.

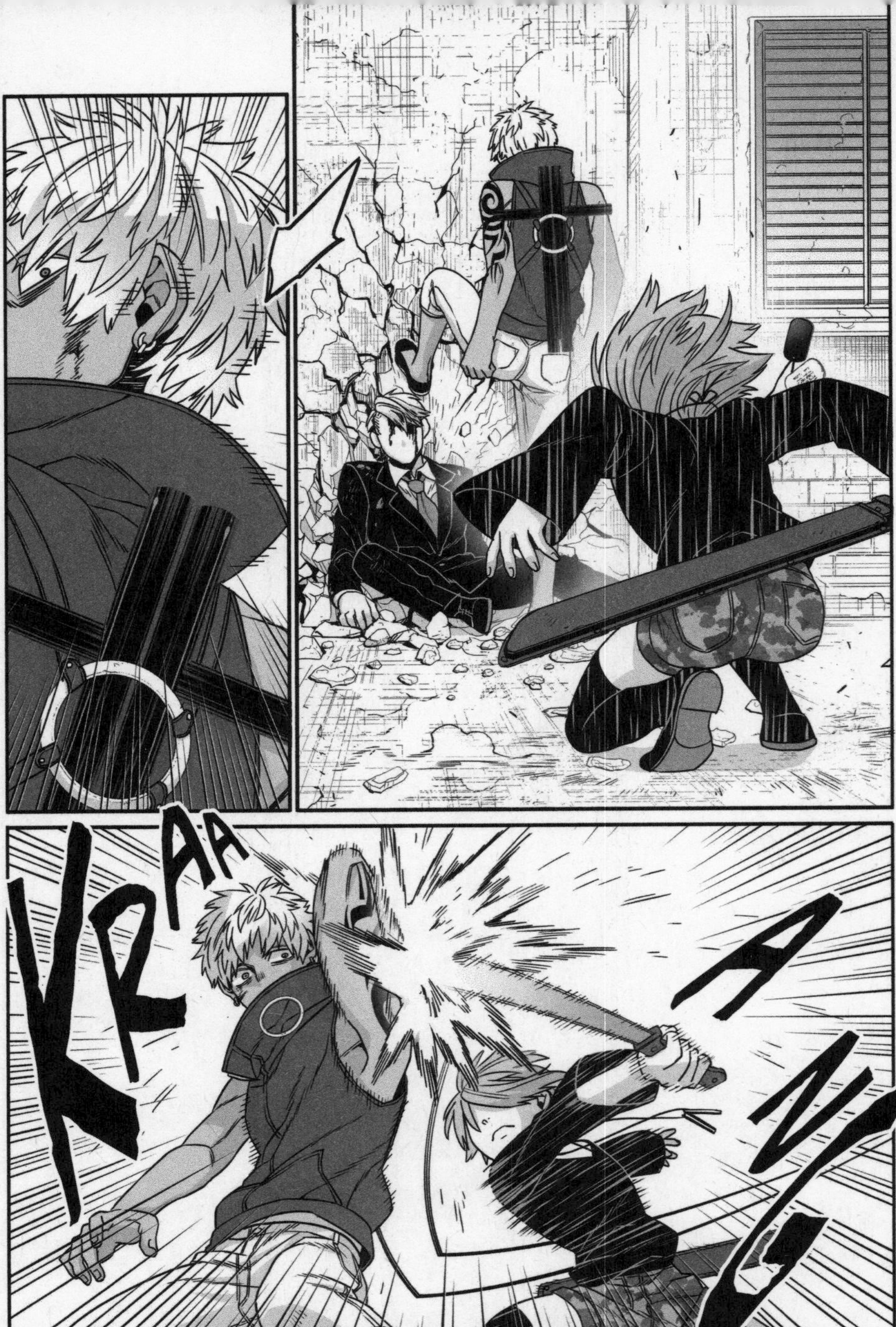
KRAAAANG

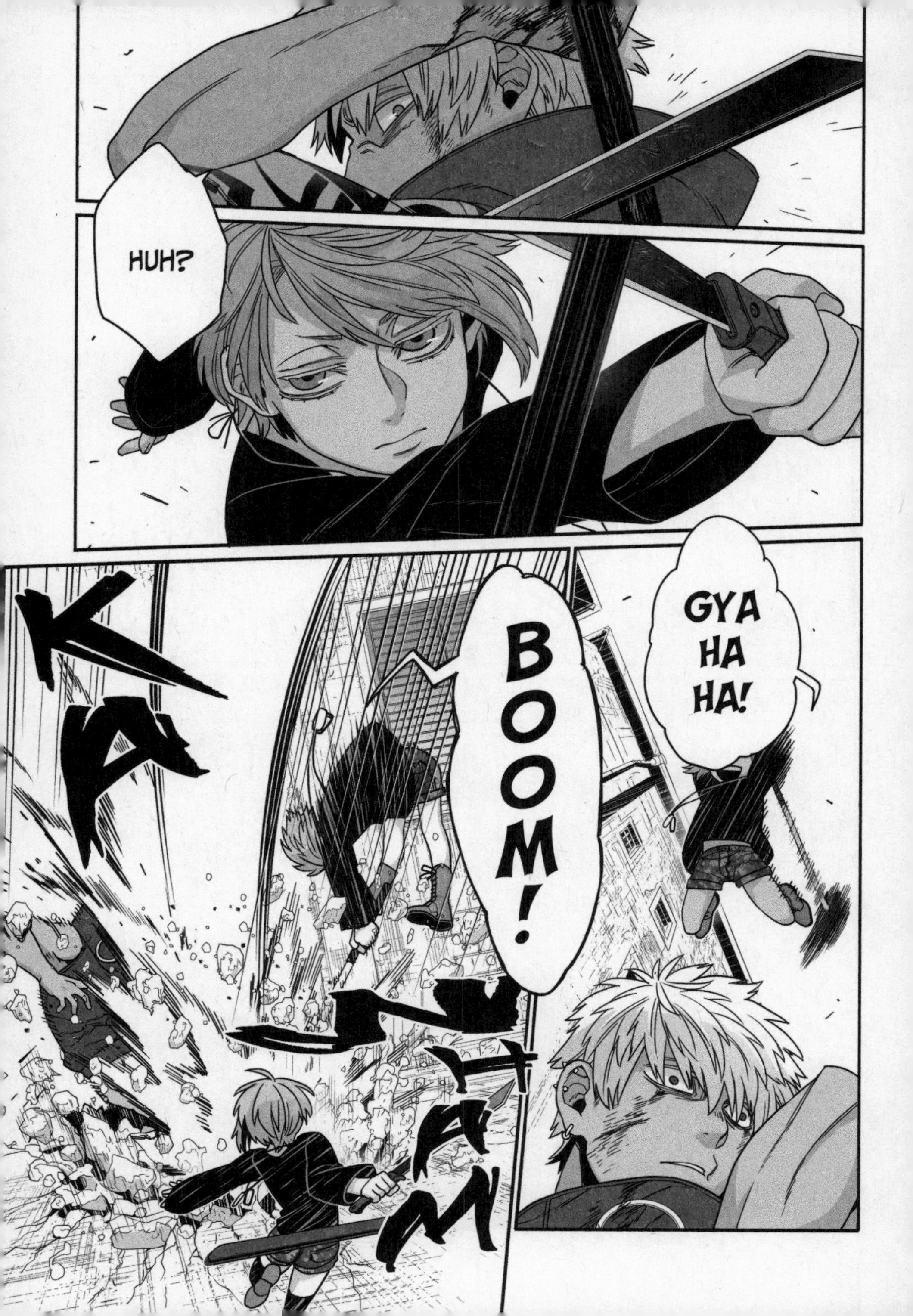
HUH?
GYA HA HA!
BOOM!

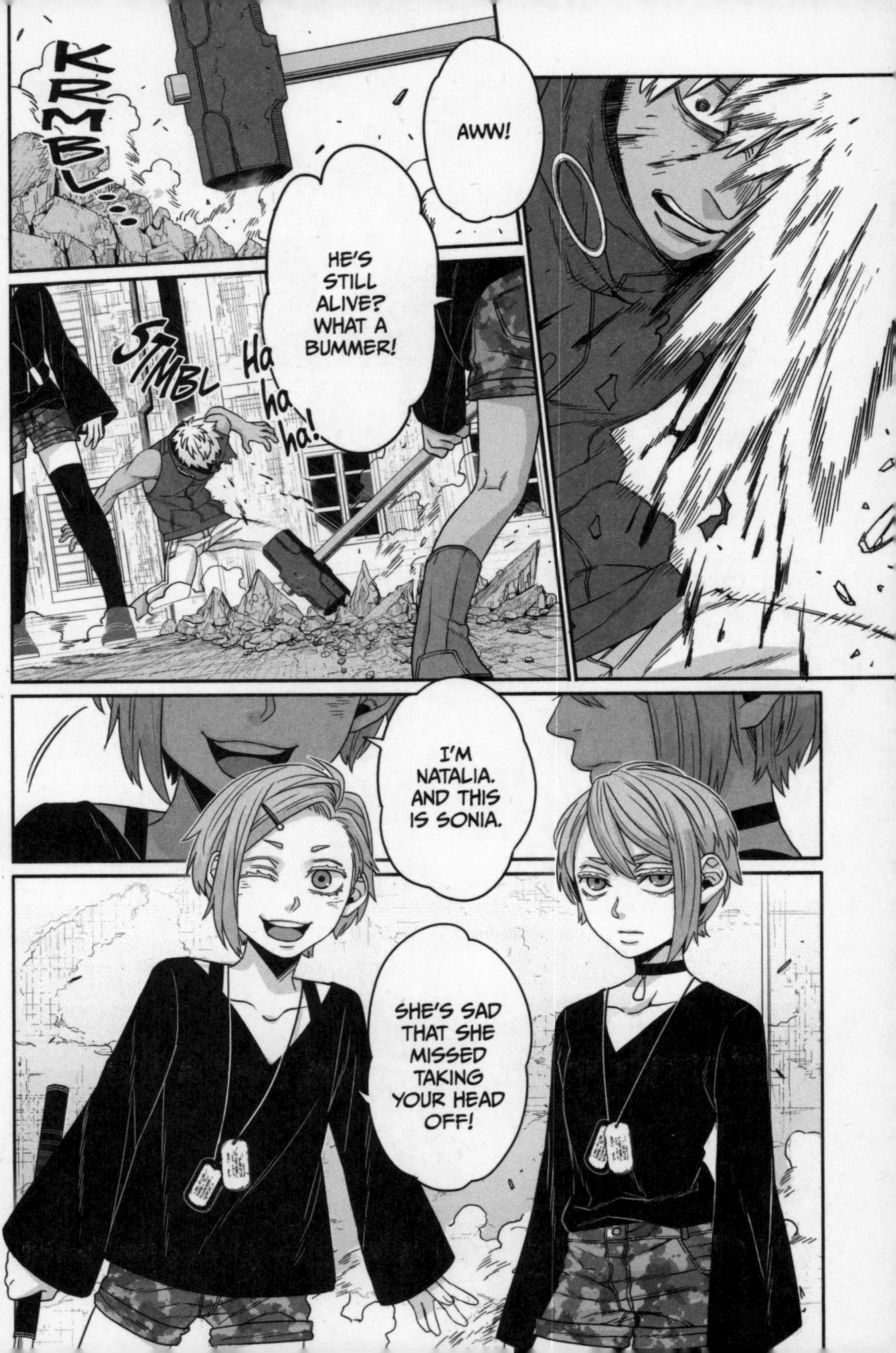
AWW!
KRMBL...
HE'S STILL ALIVE? WHAT A BUMMER!
Ha ha ha!
STMBL
I'M NATALIA. AND THIS IS SONIA.
SHE'S SAD THAT SHE MISSED TAKING YOUR HEAD OFF!

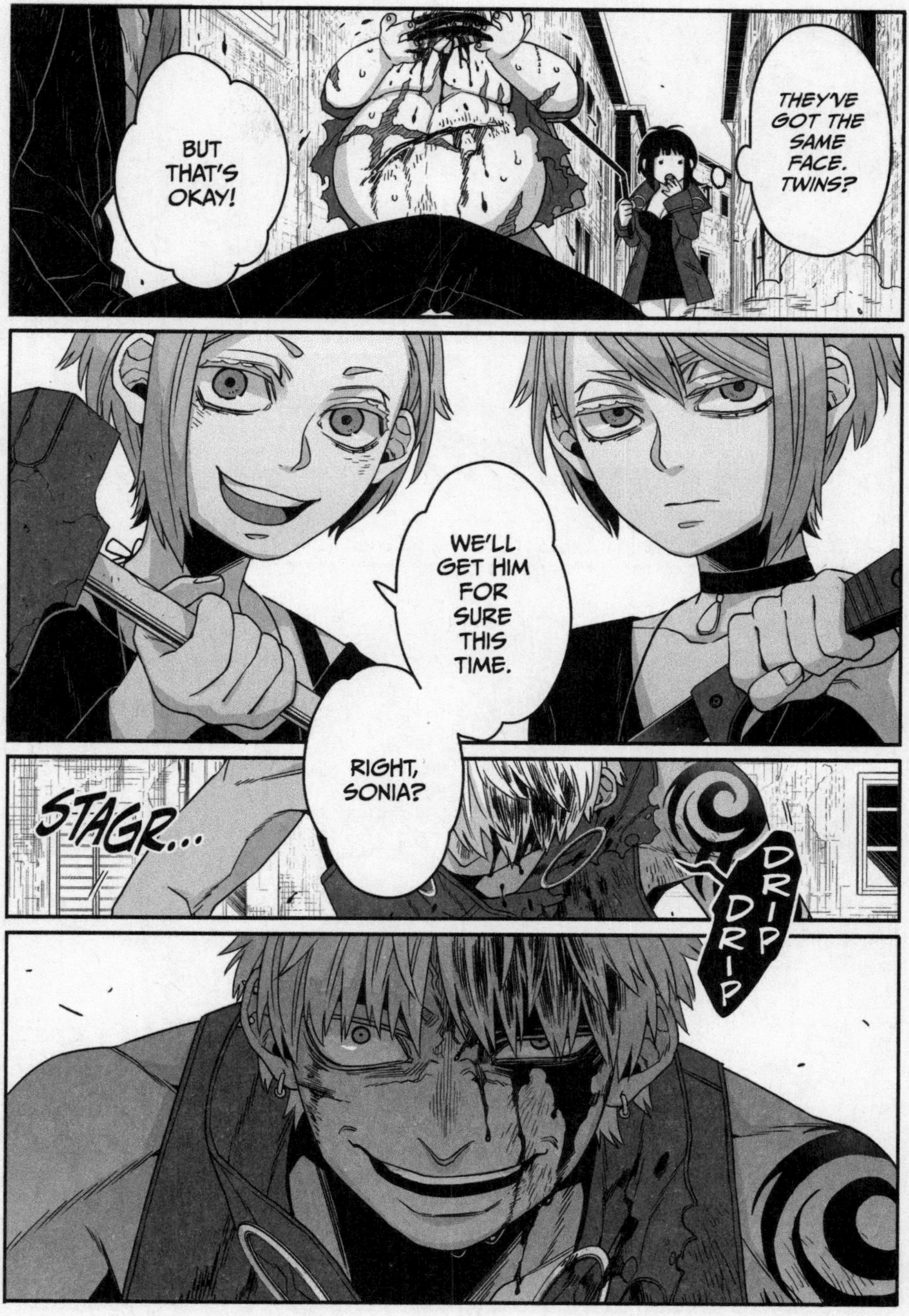
THEY'VE GOT THE SAME FACE. TWINS?
BUT THAT'S OKAY!
WE'LL GET HIM FOR SURE THIS TIME.
RIGHT, SONIA?
DRIP DRIP DRIP
STAGR...

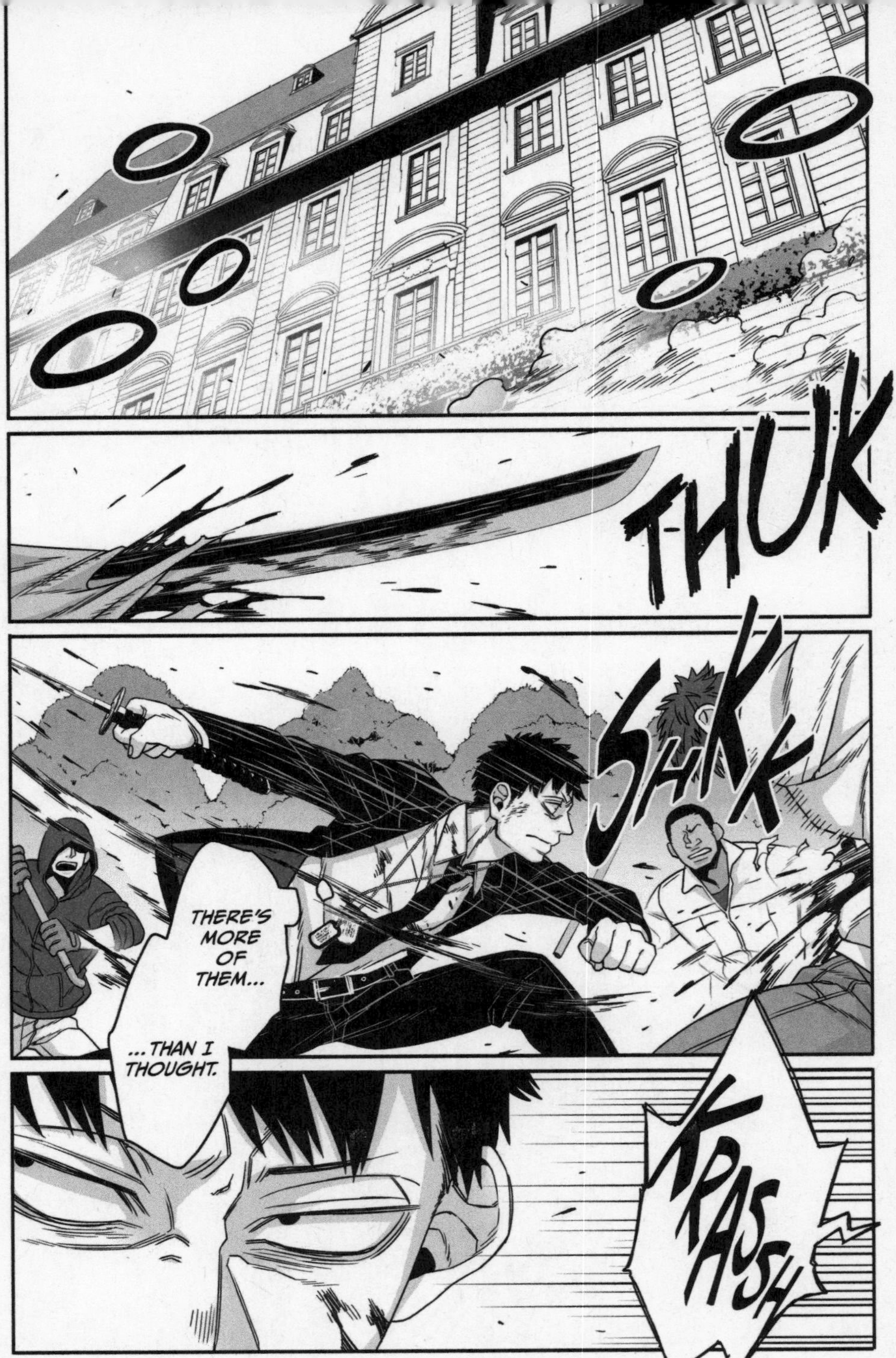
THUK
SHKK
THERE'S MORE OF THEM...
...THAN I THOUGHT.
KRASH

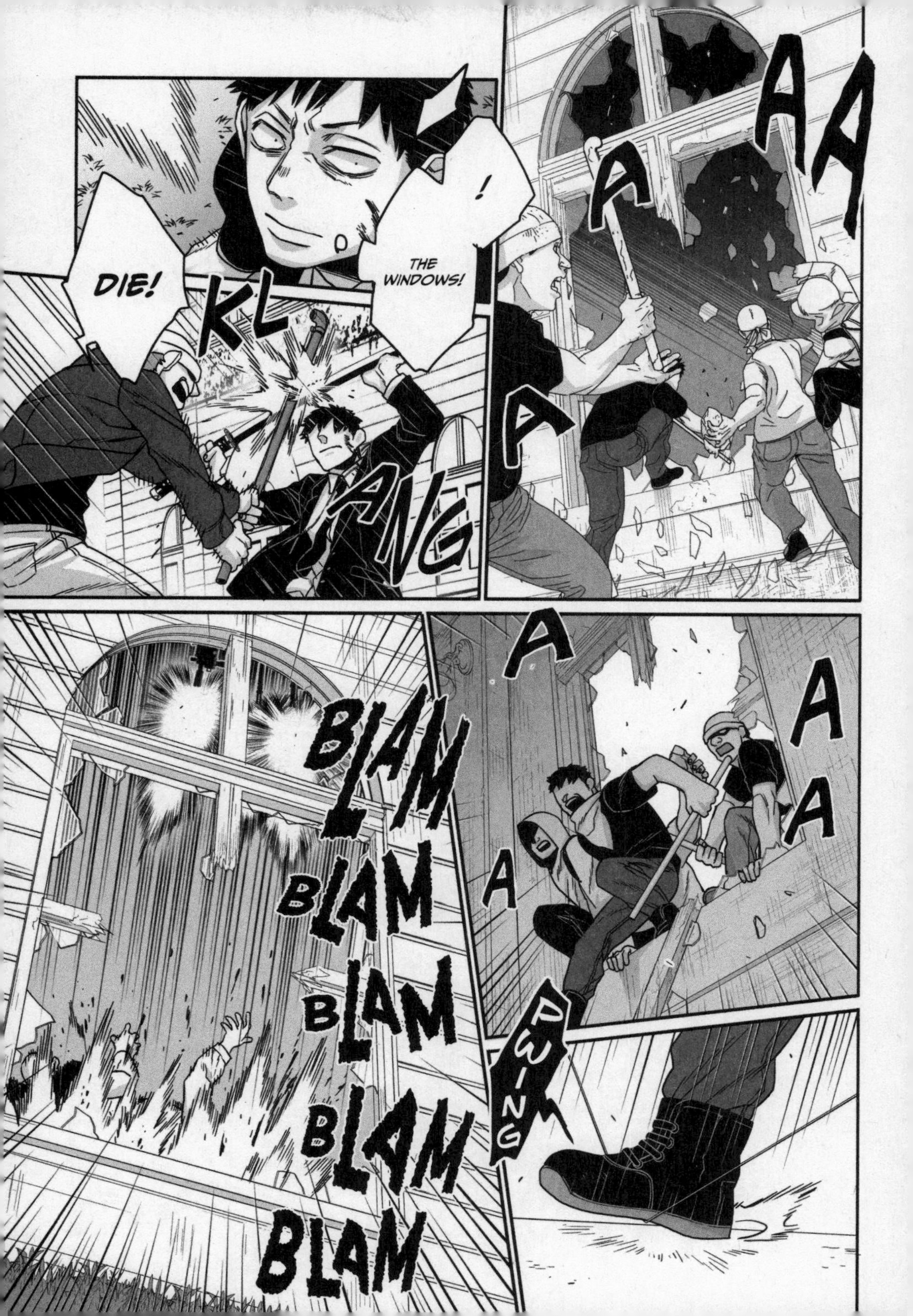
AAAA
A
A
!
THE WINDOWS!
DIE!
KL
ANG
A
A
A
A
A
PWING
BLAM
BLAM
BLAM
BLAM
BLAM
BLAM

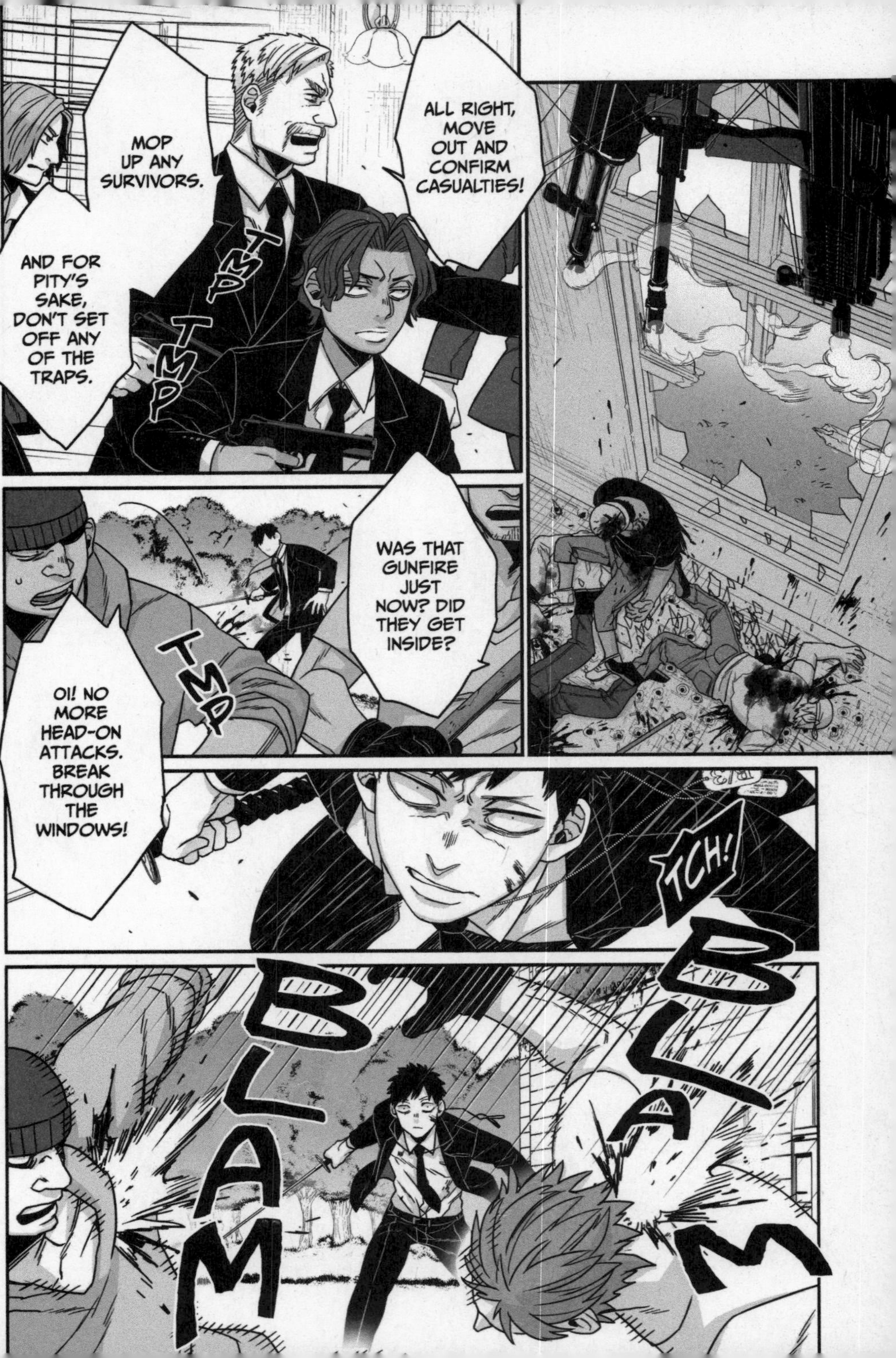
ALL RIGHT, MOVE OUT AND CONFIRM CASUALTIES!
MOP UP ANY SURVIVORS.
TMP TMP TMP
AND FOR PITY'S SAKE, DON'T SET OFF ANY OF THE TRAPS.
WAS THAT GUNFIRE JUST NOW? DID THEY GET INSIDE?
TMP
OI! NO MORE HEAD-ON ATTACKS. BREAK THROUGH THE WINDOWS!
TCH!
BLAM
BLAM

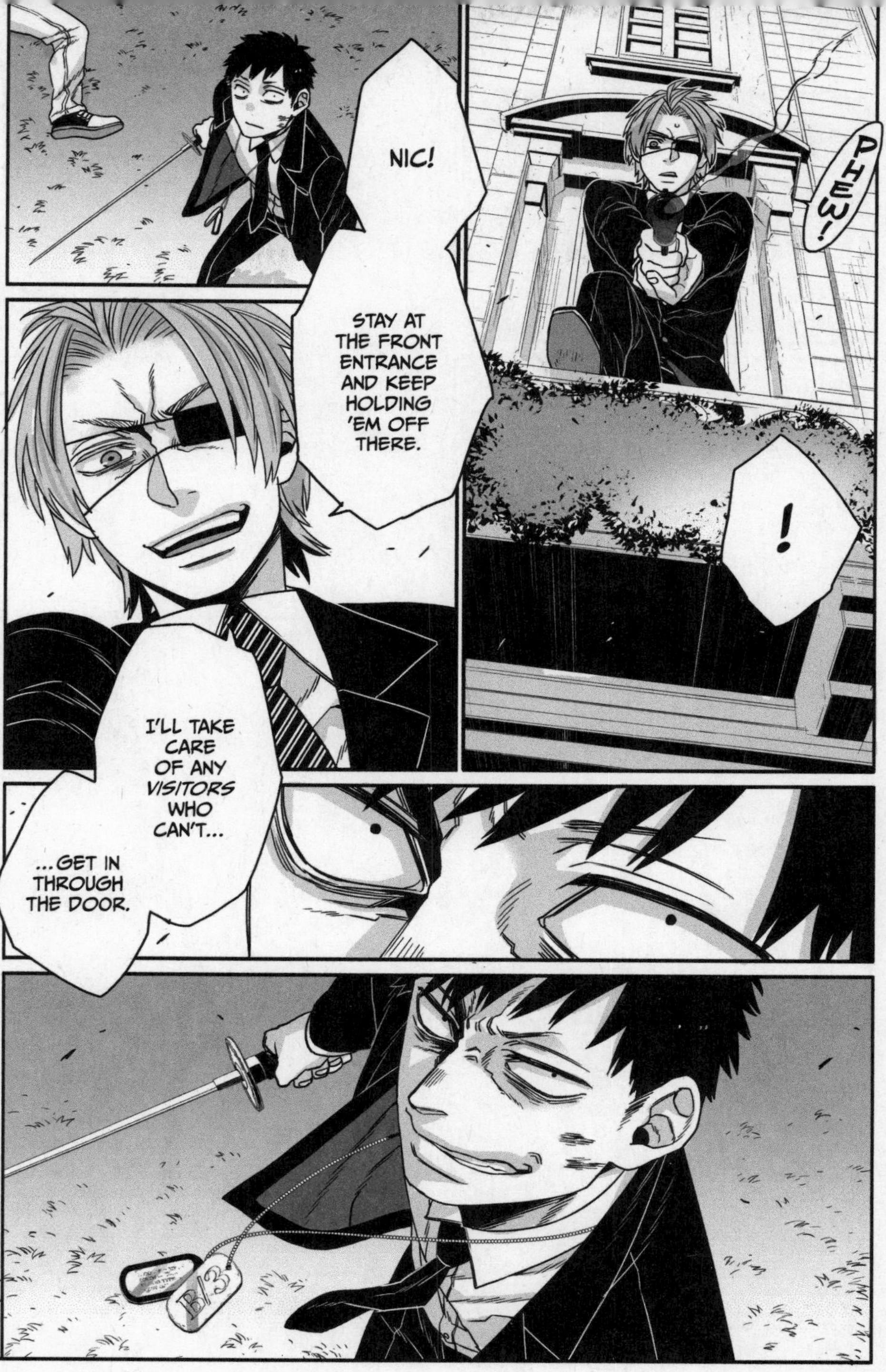
PHEW!
NIC!
STAY AT THE FRONT ENTRANCE AND KEEP HOLDING 'EM OFF THERE.
!
I'LL TAKE CARE OF ANY VISITORS WHO CAN'T...
...GET IN THROUGH THE DOOR.
B/3

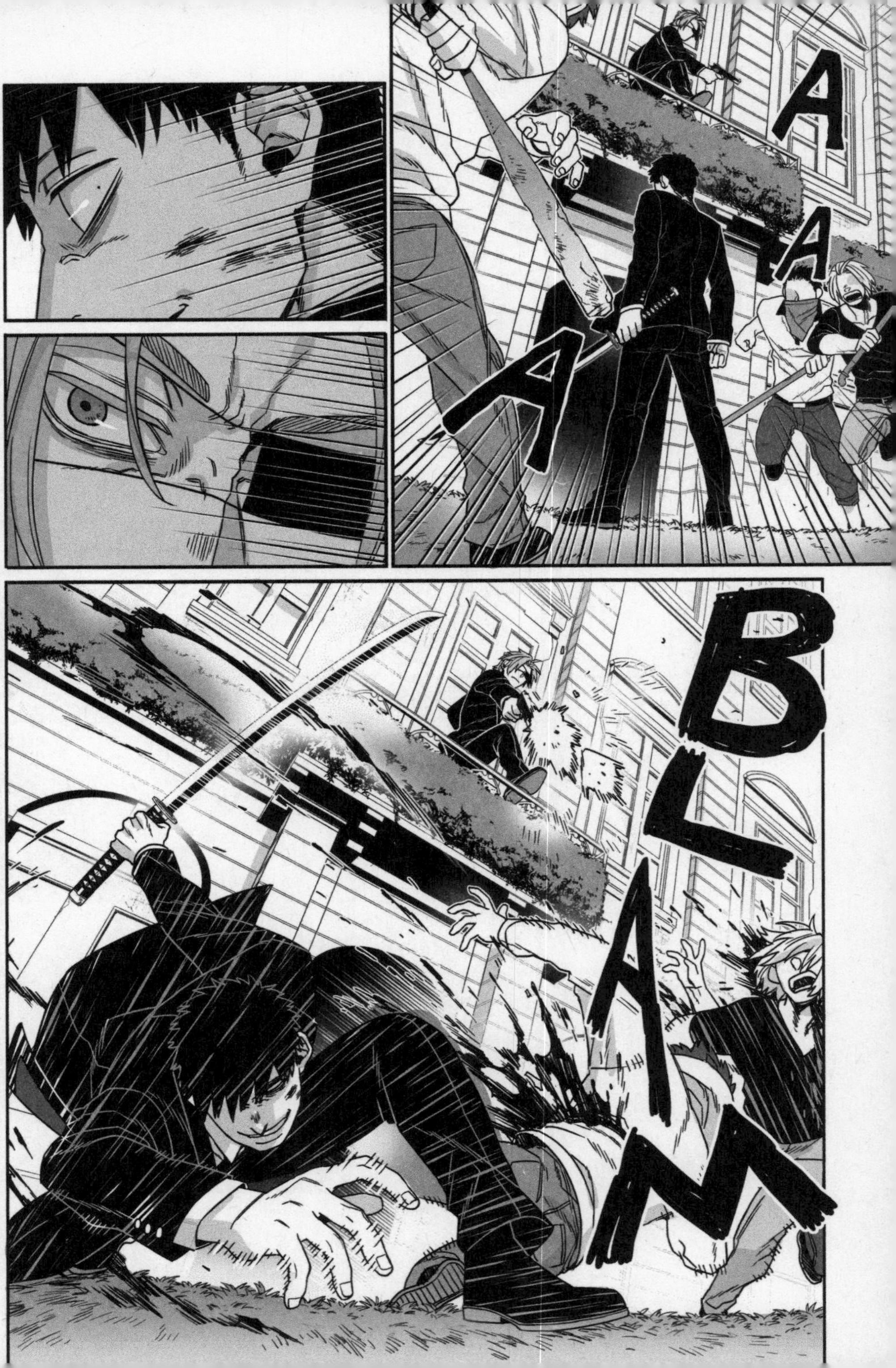
AAA
BLAM

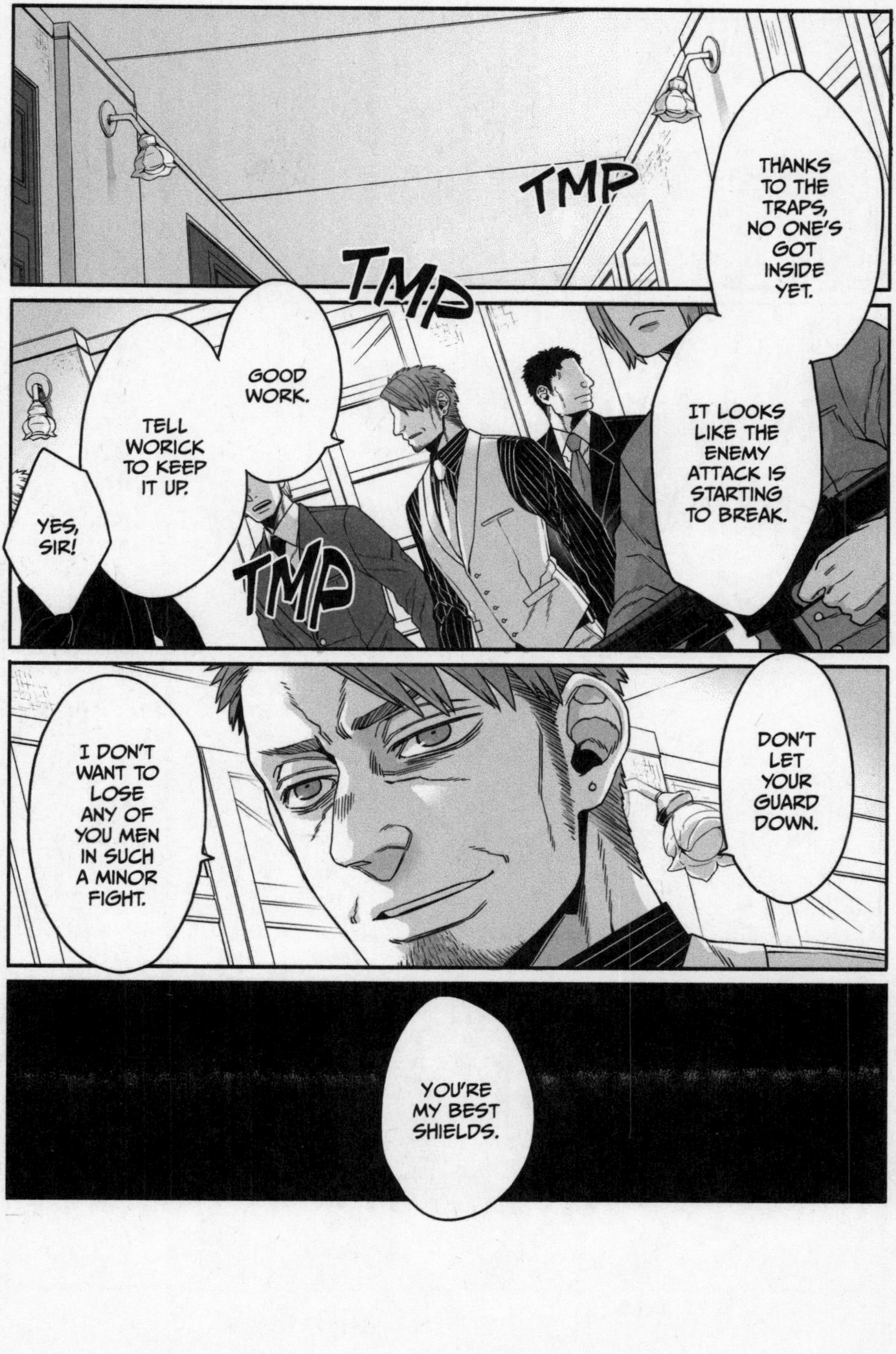
THANKS TO THE TRAPS, NO ONE'S GOT INSIDE YET.
TMP
TMP
IT LOOKS LIKE THE ENEMY ATTACK IS STARTING TO BREAK.
GOOD WORK.
TELL WORICK TO KEEP IT UP.
TMP
YES, SIR!
DON'T LET YOUR GUARD DOWN.
I DON'T WANT TO LOSE ANY OF YOU MEN IN SUCH A MINOR FIGHT.
YOU'RE MY BEST SHIELDS.

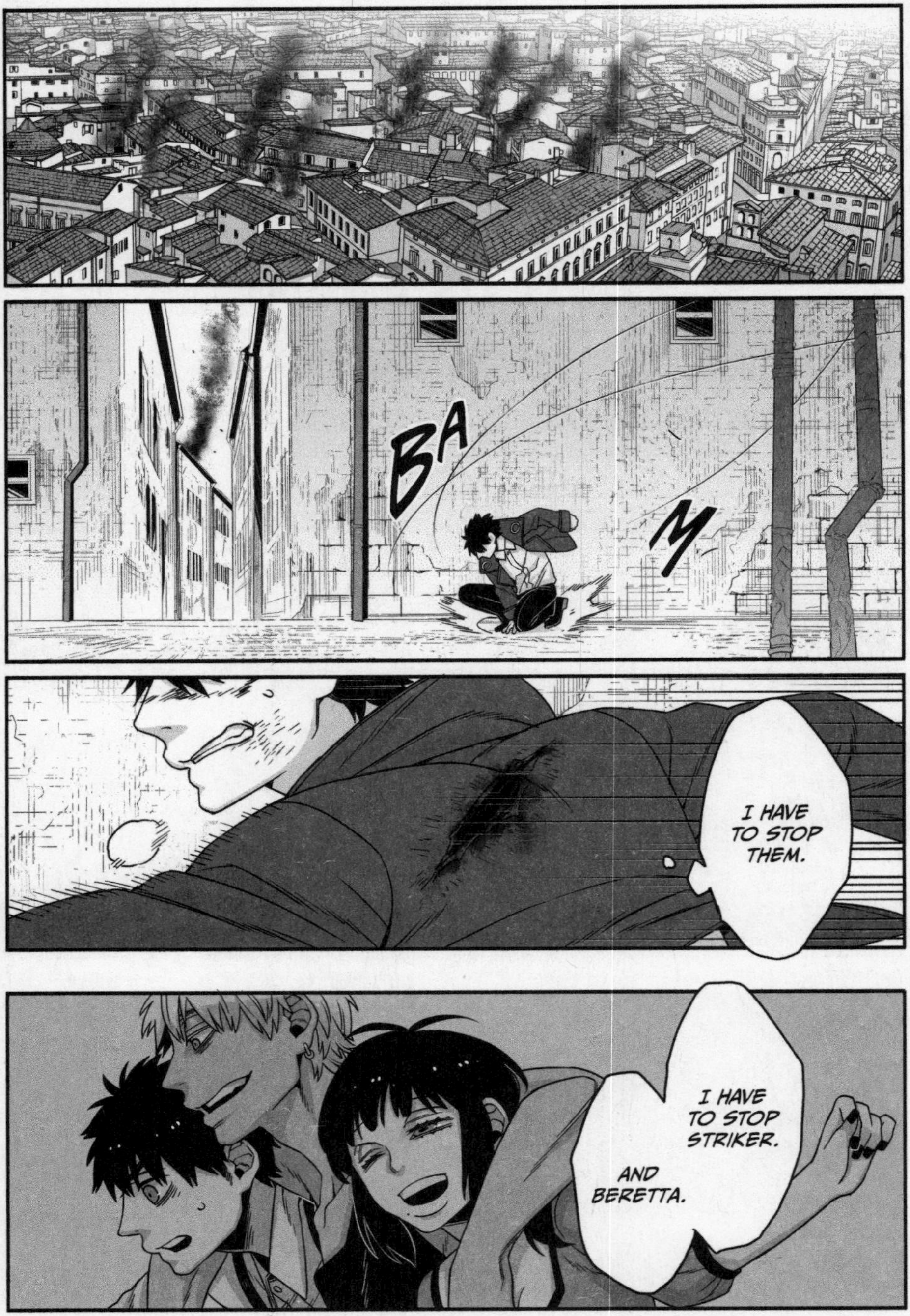
BA
M
I HAVE TO STOP THEM.
I HAVE TO STOP STRIKER.
AND BERETTA.

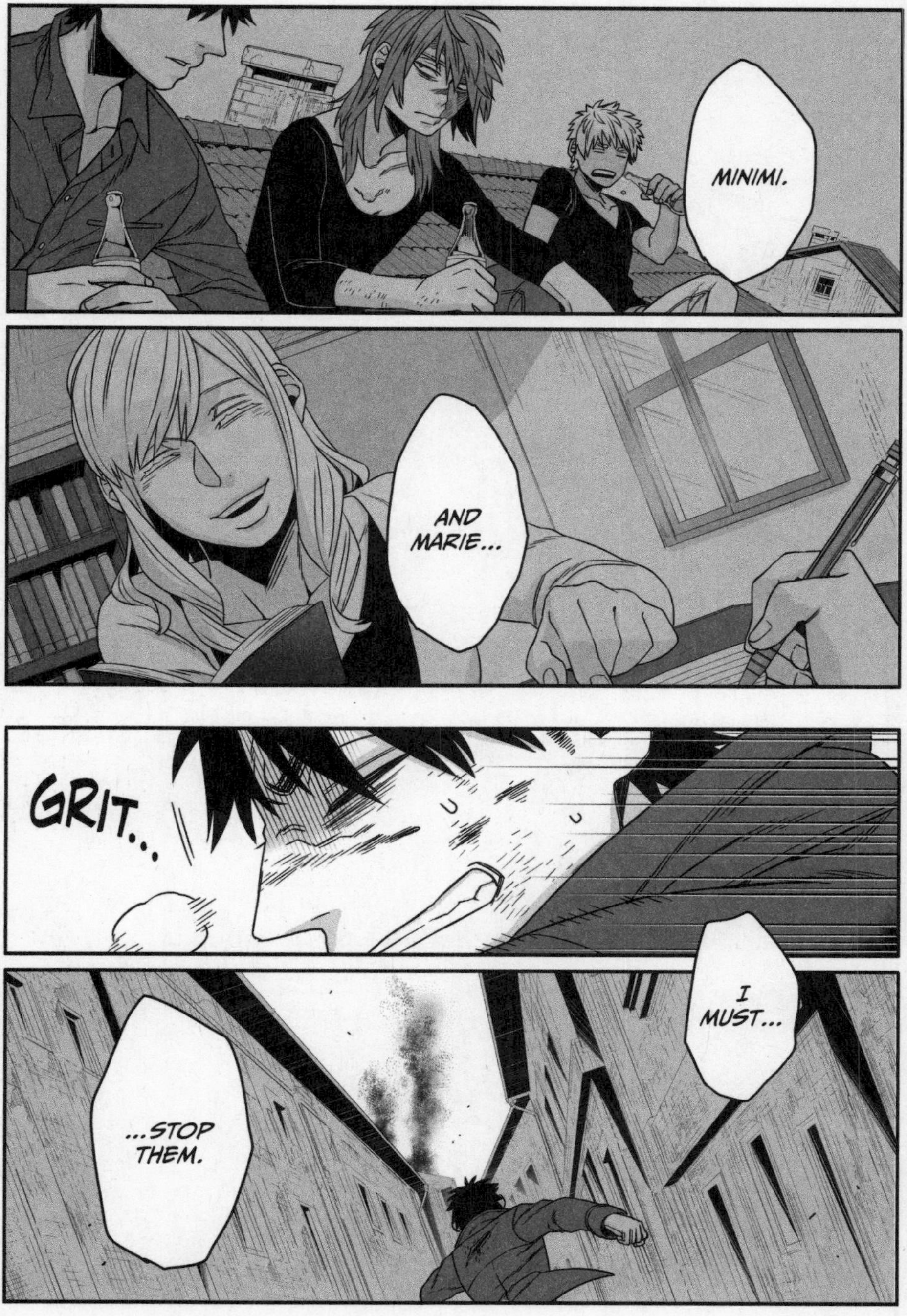
MINIMI.
AND MARIE...
GRIT...
I MUST...
...STOP THEM.

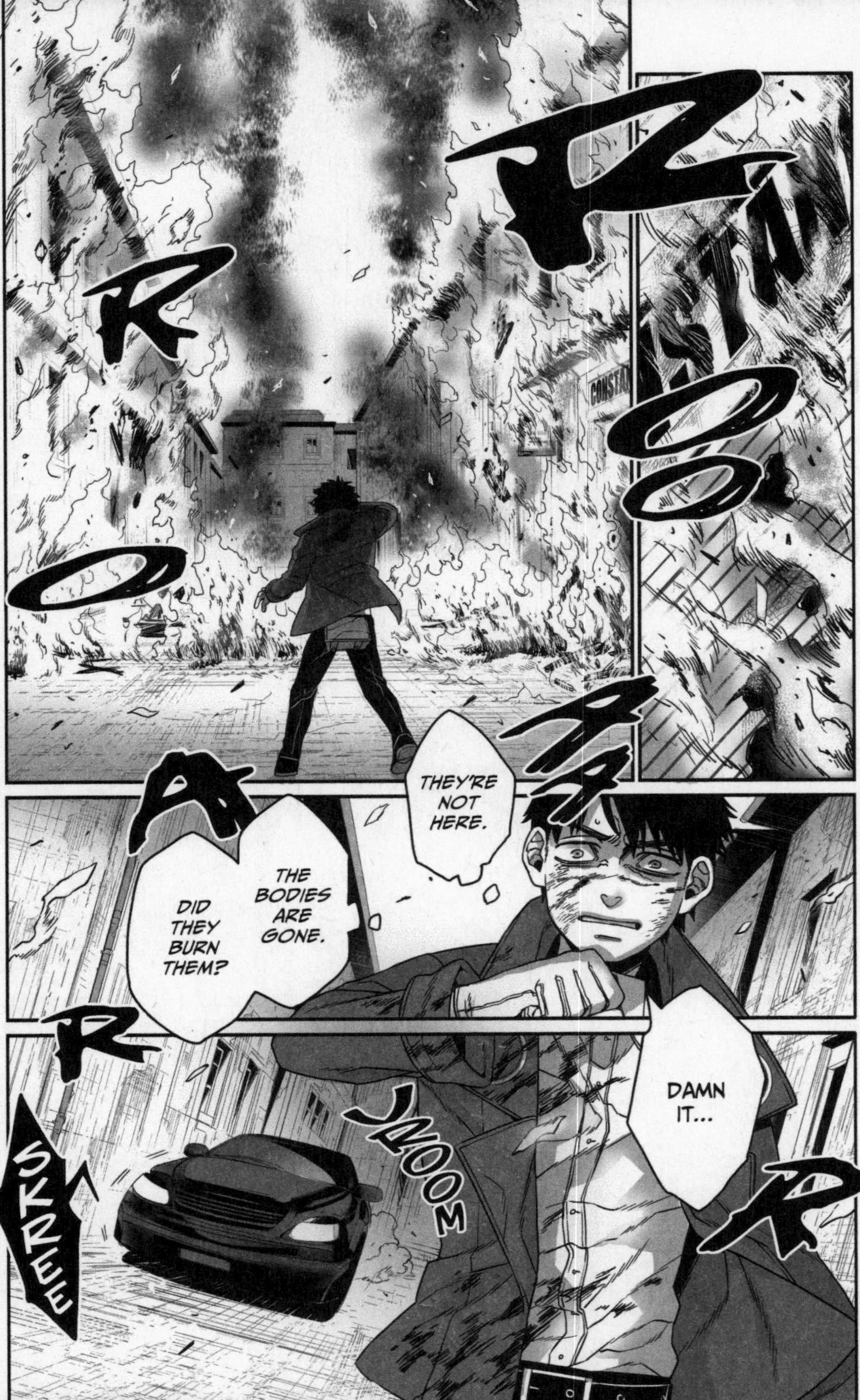
THEY'RE NOT HERE.
THE BODIES ARE GONE.
DID THEY BURN THEM?
DAMN IT...
SKREE

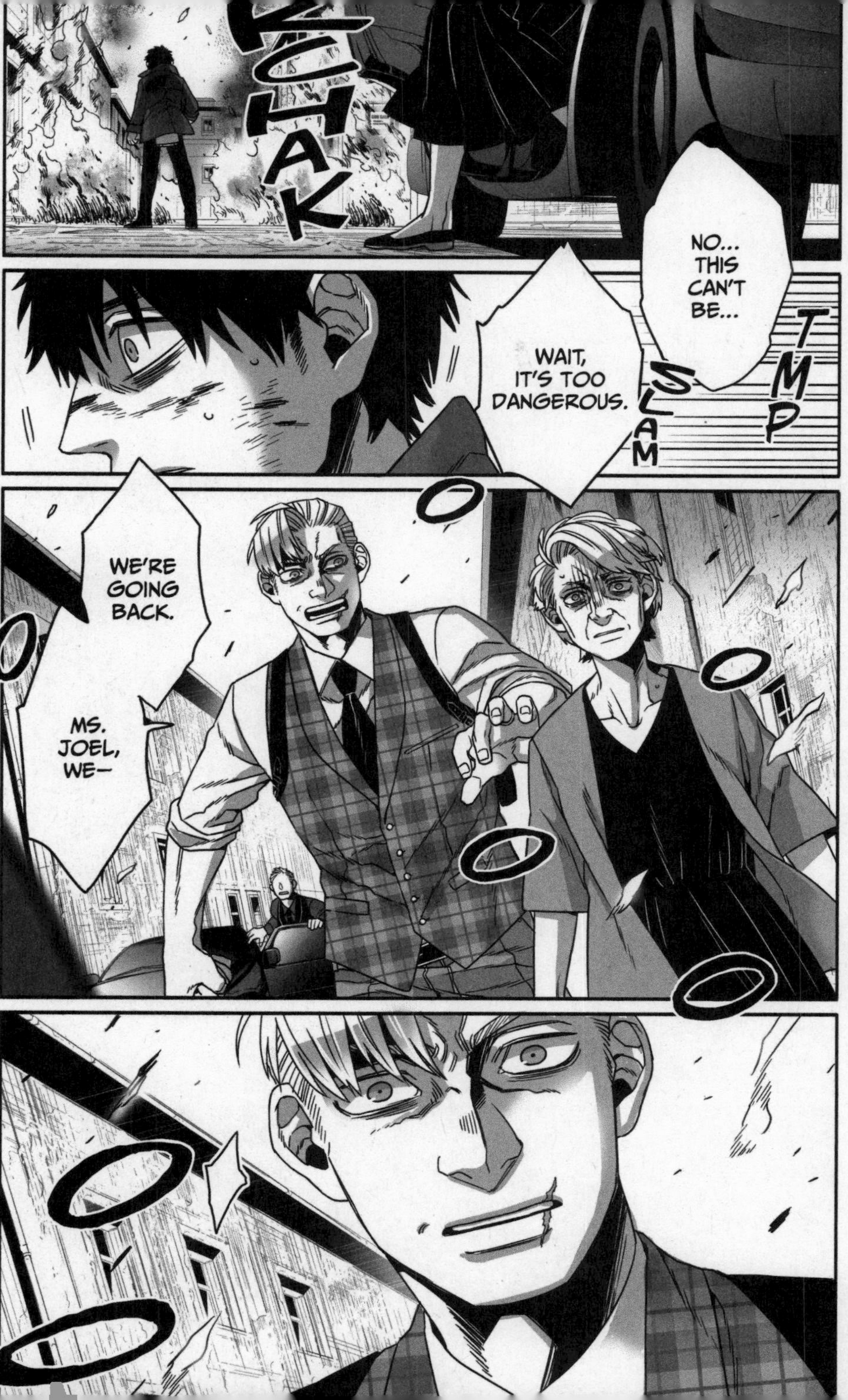
KCHAK
NO... THIS CAN'T BE...
TMP
SLAM
WAIT, IT'S TOO DANGEROUS.
WE'RE GOING BACK.
MS. JOEL, WE—

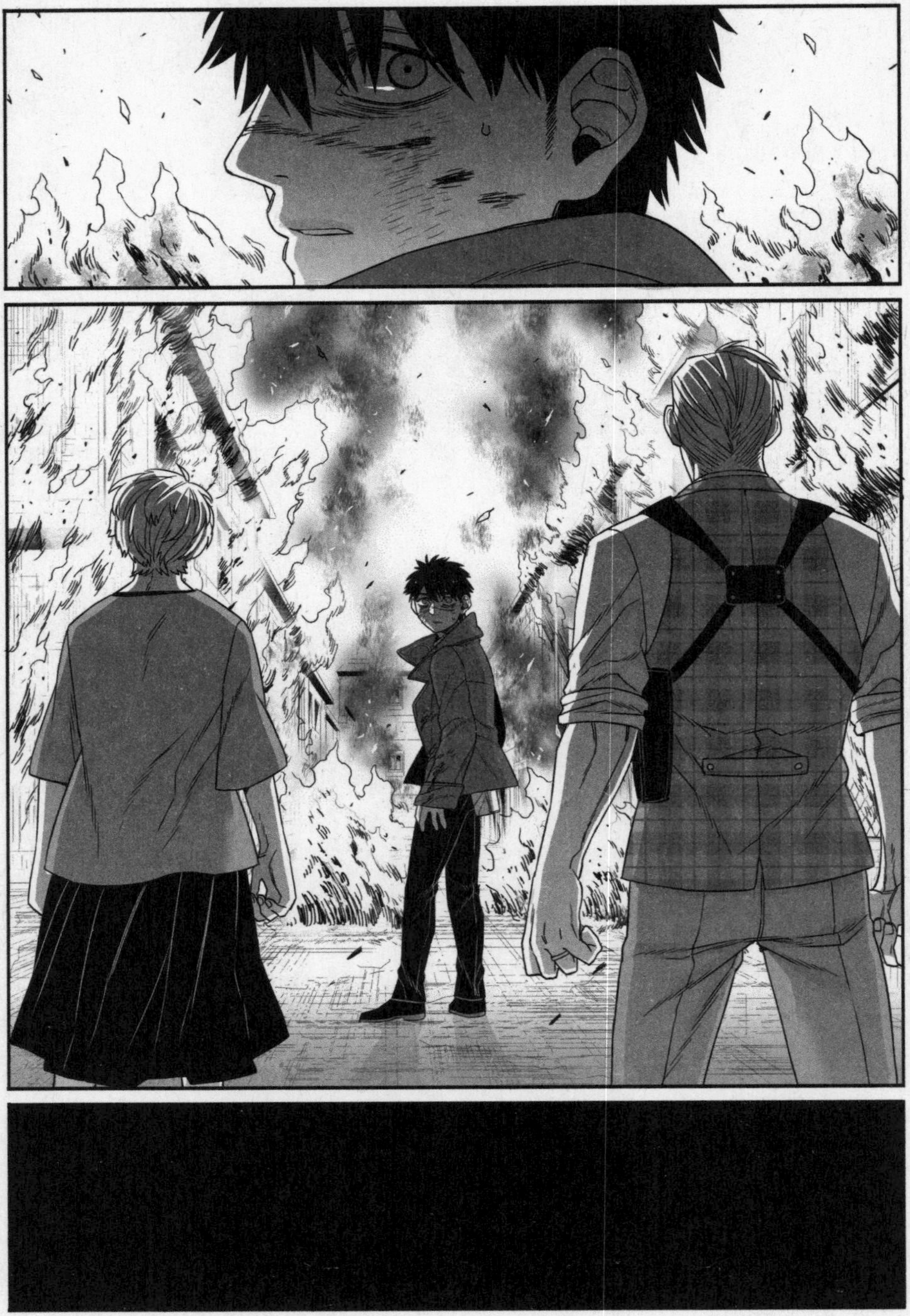

#06 END

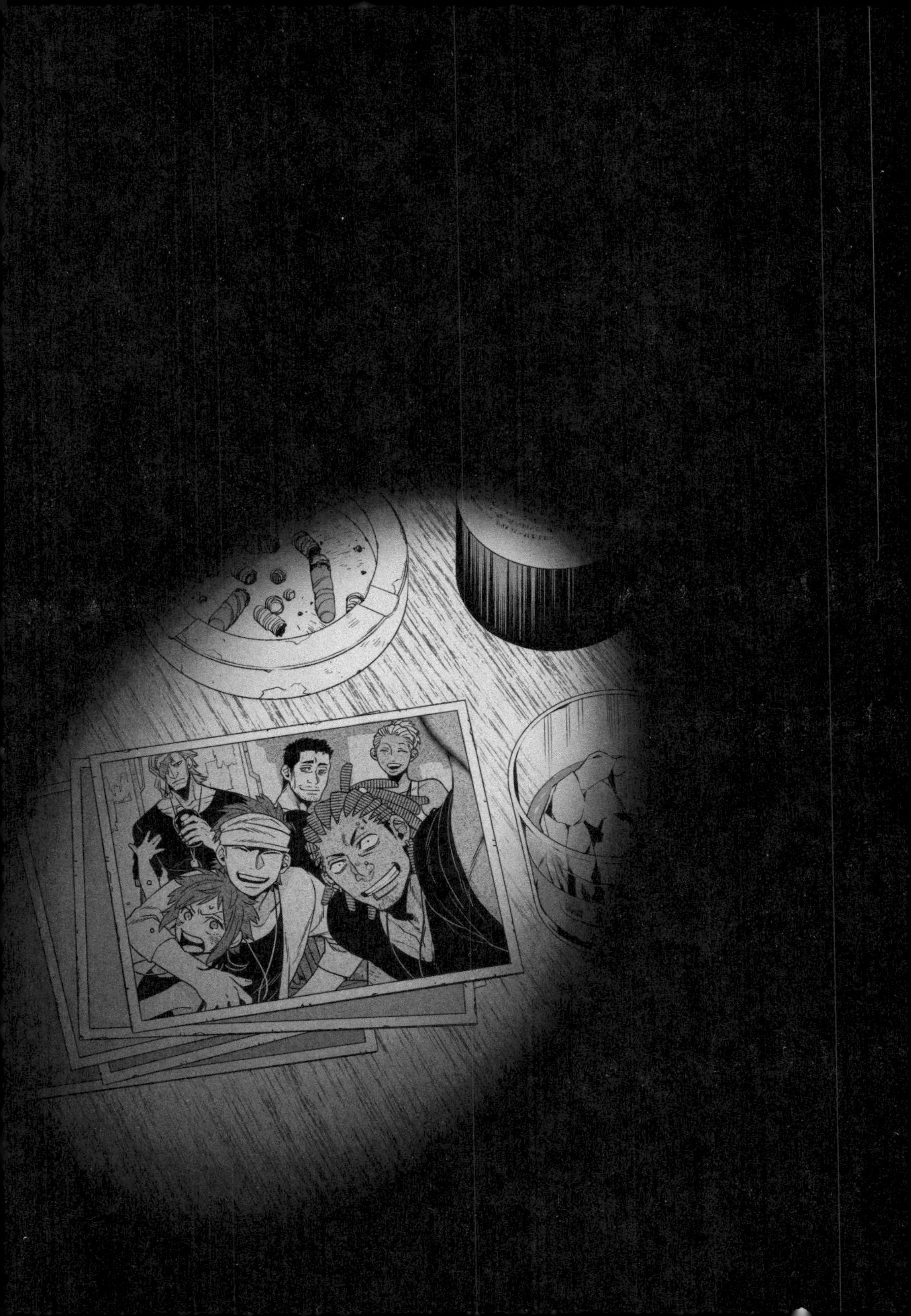

C

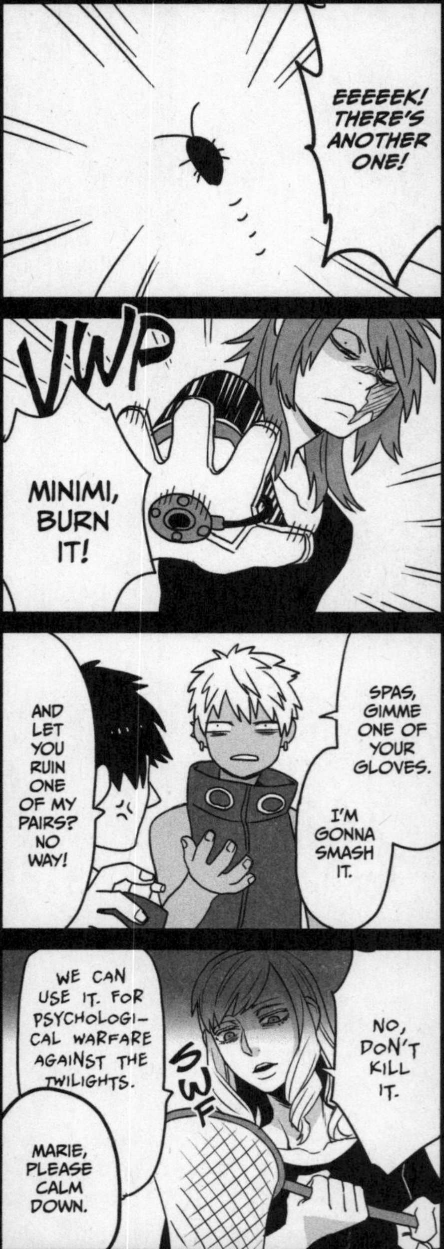
EEEEEK! THERE'S ANOTHER ONE!
VWP
MINIMI, BURN IT!
SPAS, GIMME ONE OF YOUR GLOVES.
I'M GONNA SMASH IT.
AND LET YOU RUIN ONE OF MY PAIRS? NO WAY!
NO, DON'T KILL IT.
SWF
WE CAN USE IT FOR PSYCHOLOGICAL WARFARE AGAINST THE TWILIGHTS.
MARIE, PLEASE CALM DOWN.

Sleep

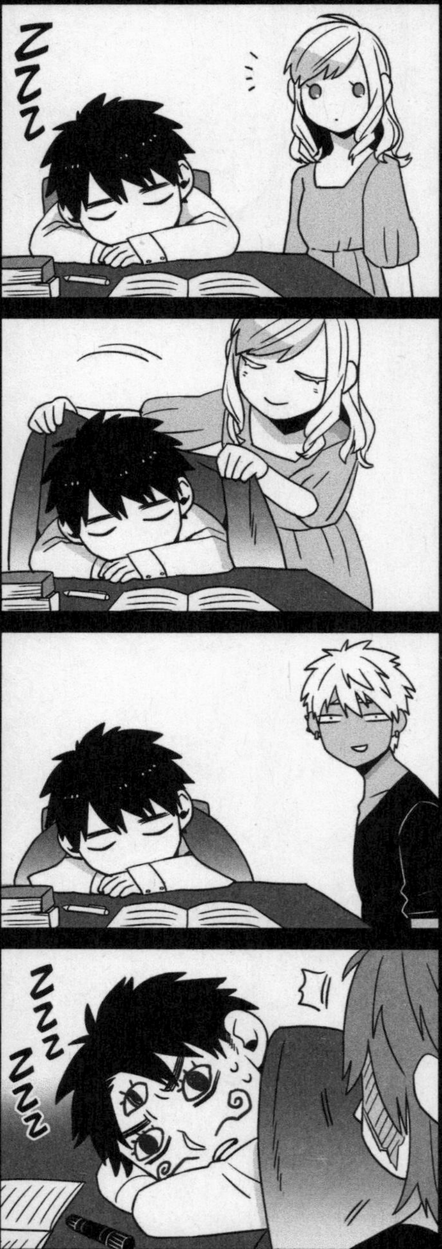
ZZZ
ZZZ
ZZZ

Hair

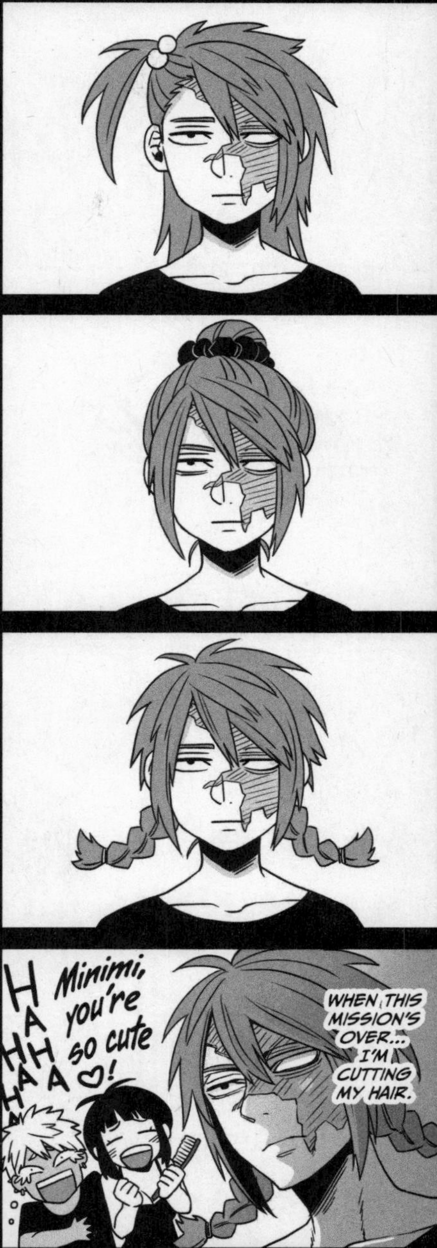
HAHAHAHA
Minimi, you're so cute ♡!
WHEN THIS MISSION'S OVER... I'M CUTTING MY HAIR.

Spikes

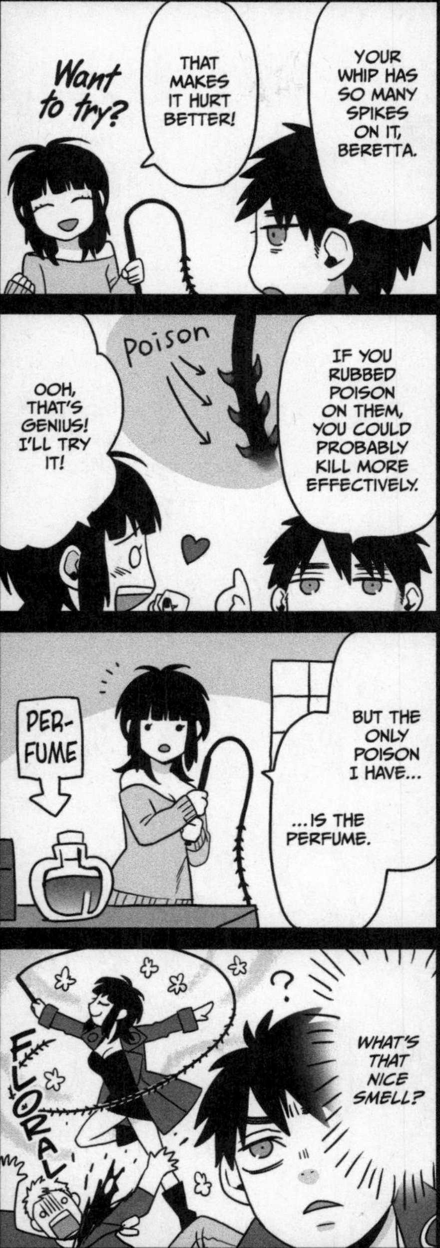
YOUR WHIP HAS SO MANY SPIKES ON IT, BERETTA.
THAT MAKES IT HURT BETTER!
Want to try?
IF YOU RUBBED POISON ON THEM, YOU COULD PROBABLY KILL MORE EFFECTIVELY.
Poison
OOH, THAT'S GENIUS! I'LL TRY IT!
BUT THE ONLY POISON I HAVE...
...IS THE PERFUME.
PER-FUME
WHAT'S THAT NICE SMELL?
?
FLORAL

Afterword

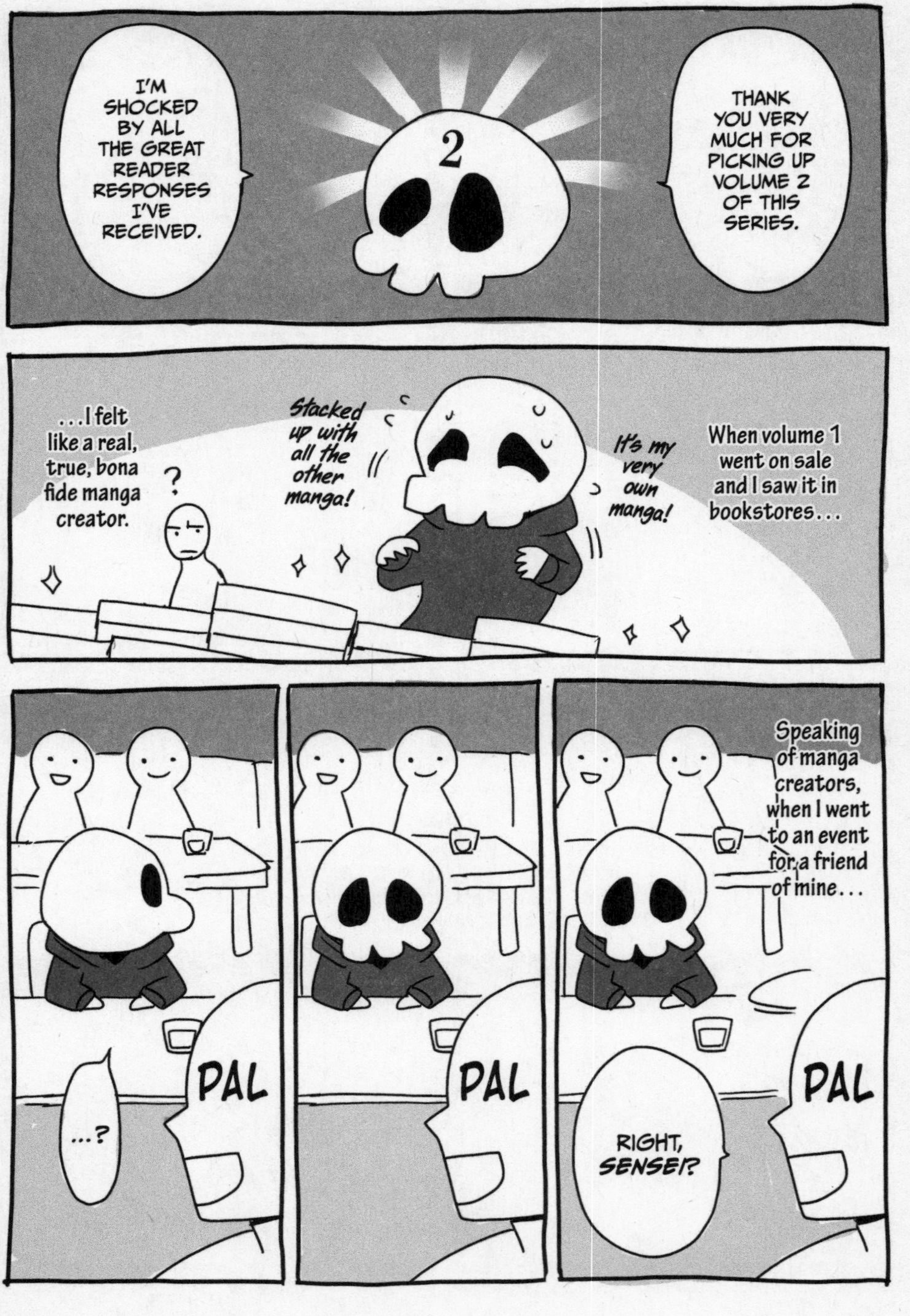
THANK YOU VERY MUCH FOR PICKING UP VOLUME 2 OF THIS SERIES.
2
I'M SHOCKED BY ALL THE GREAT READER RESPONSES I'VE RECEIVED.
When volume 1 went on sale and I saw it in bookstores...
It's my very own manga!
Stacked up with all the other manga!
?
...I felt like a real, true, bona fide manga creator.
Speaking of manga creators, when I went to an event for a friend of mine...
PAL
RIGHT, SENSEI!?
PAL
PAL
...?

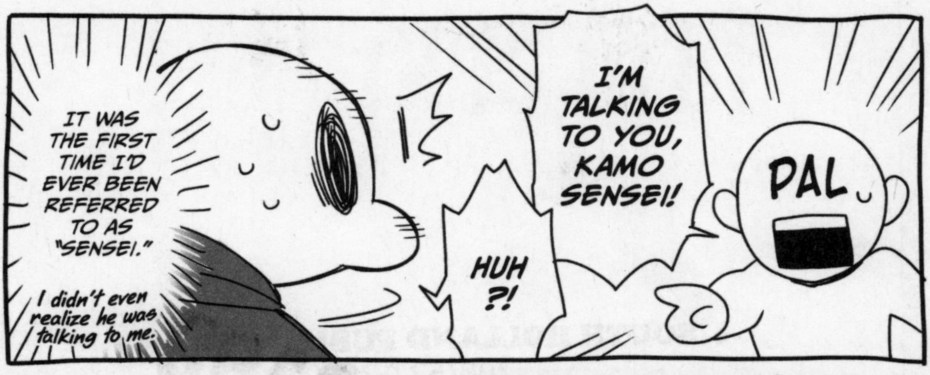
I'M TALKING TO YOU, KAMO SENSEI!
HUH ?!
IT WAS THE FIRST TIME I'D EVER BEEN REFERRED TO AS "SENSEI."
I didn't even realize he was talking to me.
PAL

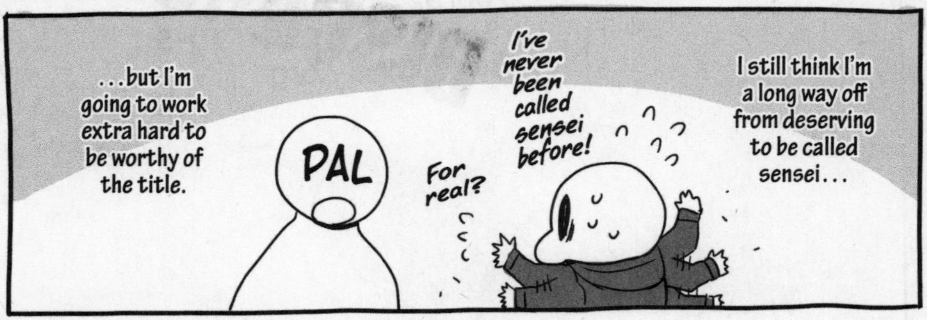
I still think I'm a long way off from deserving to be called sensei...
I've never been called sensei before!
For real?
...but I'm going to work extra hard to be worthy of the title.
PAL

SEE YOU IN THE
NEXT VOLUME!

KOHSKE
ASSISTANT K / ASSISTANT M / ASSISTANT H
EDITOR H / DESIGNER ISHIKAWA
MOM / DAD / LITTLE BRO / MY DOG
AND TO EVERYONE WHO'S HELPED ME.

THANK YOU ALWAYS!

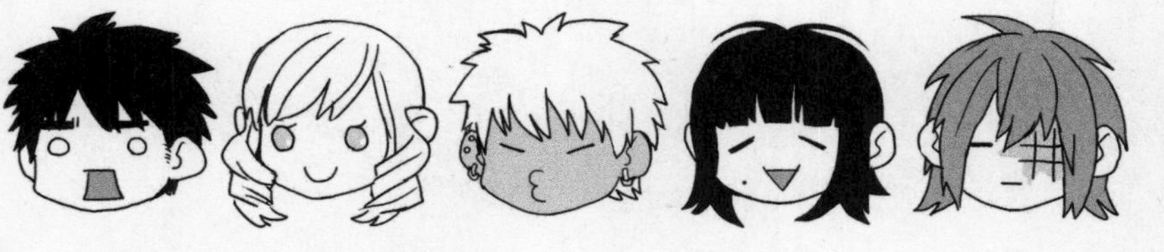

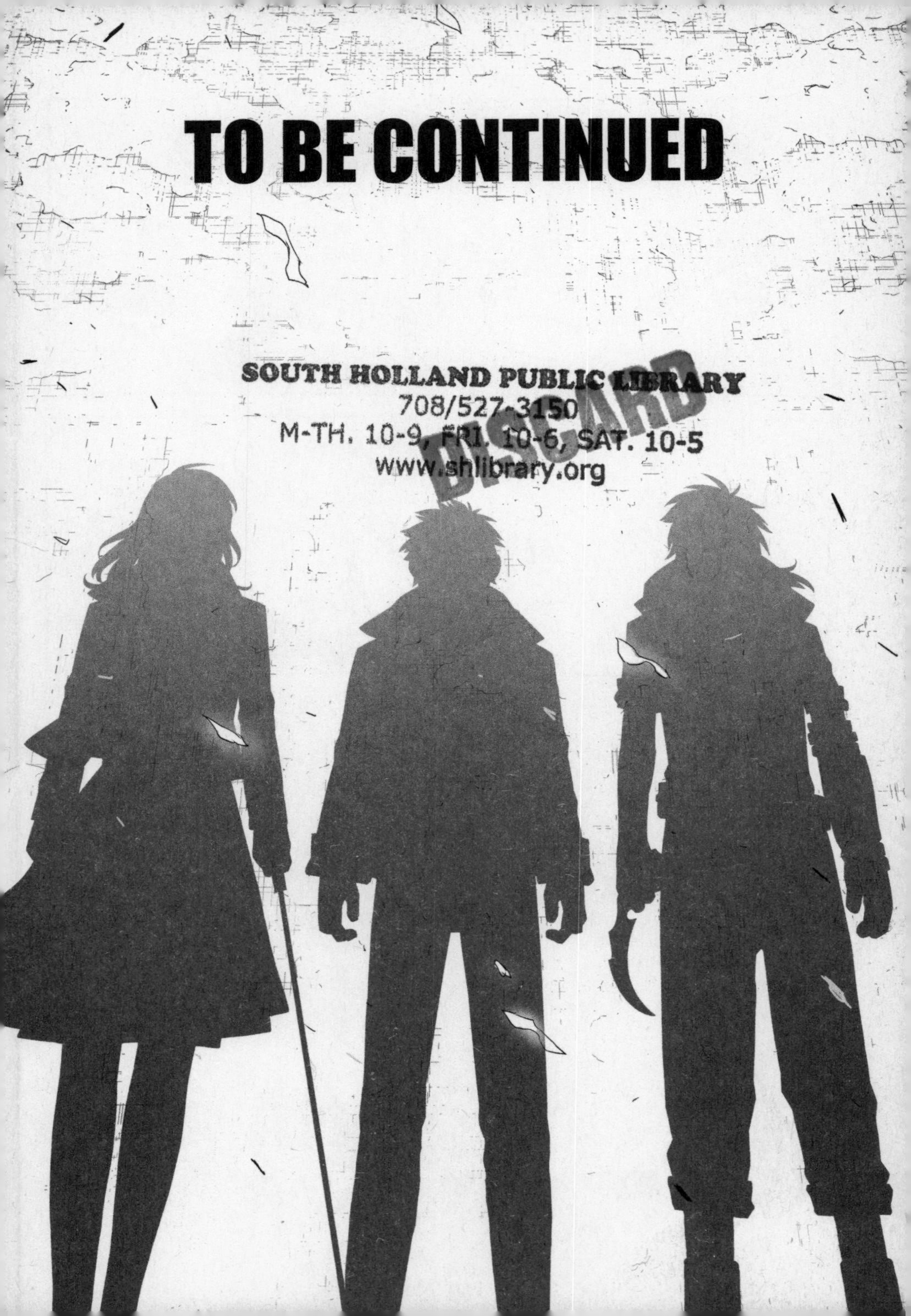
TO BE CONTINUED